Quicken 3 for Windows:

A Practical Approach

by Steve Cummings

MIS:
PRESS

A Subsidiary of
Henry Holt and Co., Inc.

First Edition—1993

ISBN 1-55828-337-4

Printed in the United States of America.

10 9 8 7 6 5 4 3 2 1

MIS:Press books are available at special discounts for bulk purchases for sales promotions, premiums, fund-raising, or educational use. Special editions or book excerpts can also be created to specification.

For details contact: Special Sales Director
MIS:Press
a subsidiary of Henry Holt and Company, Inc.
115 West 18th Street
New York, New York 10011

Trademarks

Throughout this book, trademarked names are used. Rather than put a trademark symbol after every occurrence of a trademarked name, we used the names in an editorial fashion only, and to the benefit of the trademark owner, with no intention of infringement of the trademark. Where such designations appear in this book, they have been printed with initial caps.

Acknowledgements

Steve Berkowitz, *Publisher*
Laura Lewin, *Development Editor*
Laura Specht, *Production Editor*
Amy Carley, *Associate Production Editor*

Table of Contents

Chapter 11: Customizing Financial Reports ..317

Chapter 12: Financial Overviews at a Glance: Quicken Graphics 349

Introduction

elcome to *Quicken 3 for Windows: A Practical Approach*. This book teaches you everything you need to know to get the most from the newest Windows version of Quicken, the all-time best-selling program for managing personal and small business finances. Whether you're just getting started with Quicken for Windows or you're ready to tap the program's advanced features for financial planning, budgeting, and record-keeping, this book will show you just how to put Quicken for Windows to work on your financial needs.

This book also covers Quicken 3's immediate predecessor, Quicken 2. Although Quicken 3 offers some important capabilities not found in Quicken 2—see *What's New in Quicken 3*—the core features of the two versions look and work almost identically. The main text assumes you're working with Quicken 3; differences in Quicken 2 are covered in special notes.

What's Quicken Good For?

If you're like most people, you enjoy earning money, saving money, spending money, even giving it away—but you hate keeping track of your finances. You'll forget your distaste for financial record-keeping when you learn how easy it can be with Quicken for Windows. Quicken for Windows starts with all the strengths of the DOS version of Quicken and adds the convenience, the easy information sharing, and the great looks of Windows.

With Quicken for Windows, you can write checks, record deposits, monitor your savings and investments, and produce highly informative reports in much less time and with far less hassle than you ever could by hand. Quicken takes care of all the calculations for you, reminds you when to pay your bills, helps you organize your records logically, and even cuts your typing to a minimum.

Quicken for Windows is unsurpassed as a tool for personal financial management. Besides making fast work of all your day-to-day record-keeping, it offers plenty of help with your long-range plans for financial success. For example, Quicken can help you create and adhere to a budget, a vital step in achieving financial success. When it's time to fill out your income tax returns, Quicken can distill the information you need from a year's worth of records within moments. And to help you assess your long- or short-term progress toward your goals, Quicken can present you with numeric or graphical overviews of your financial profile whenever you like with a few quick clicks of the mouse.

Quicken in Small Business

While Quicken's blend of efficiency and financial expertise has made it tremendously popular for personal financial management, these strengths are equally prized by small-business owners. Quicken is an excellent choice as a financial record-keeping tool for small service ventures, whether you're in business as a janitor, a beautician, a plumber, a consultant, or a legal or medical professional. The program is equally appropriate for managing rental real estate, and it can serve efficiently the needs of a low-volume retail shop or mail-order business. Larger businesses can use Quicken for specific purposes, such as writing checks or keeping track of departmental expense accounts or petty cash, and then transfer the records to a more sophisticated accounting system as necessary.

Before you commit yourself to keeping your business records with Quicken, however, you should be aware that the program does have some important limitations in this role. Some of these are related to features not available in Quicken. For example, although the program will help you keep track of the amounts your customers owe you, it doesn't figure finance charges for you, prepare invoices, or automatically flag the customers' unpaid bills. While you can keep track of the overall value of your inventory in Quicken, you can't monitor the items in the inventory themselves. And if you have employees, you should know that Quicken can't automatically calculate wages and payroll withholding amounts for you as many accounting programs do. However, Quicken's publisher sells a companion program, QuickPay, that supplements Quicken for payroll activities.

A limitation of a different kind involves the way that Quicken keeps your records. Unfortunately, some of the very characteristics that make the program so accessible to the nonaccountant also make it potentially less reliable than more complicated bookkeeping systems. Although you don't have to deal with the complexities of conventional double-entry accounting, Quicken lacks the inherent safeguards that the double-entry method provides, so it's easier for errors to slip through. Similarly, Quicken's unorthodox design sometimes makes it difficult to extract information in a form your accountant would normally expect.

But Quicken is what you make it. If you're willing to take the time to plan your accounts carefully, and if, above all, you enlist your accountant's cooperation during the planning process, you'll be rewarded with a fast bookkeeping system that's both easy to use and dependably accurate.

What's New in Quicken 3 for Windows

Compared to the Quicken 2 for Windows, Quicken 3 offers a number of refinements that you'll find immediately useful. For starters, Quicken 3 includes a new financial planning calendar that makes it easier than ever to streamline the bill-paying process, and that helps you catch trends in your income and spending patterns. Features for tracking loans and investments have been beefed up, giving you a clearer picture of these vital components of your net worth.

There are many new conveniences; for instance, a pop-up mini-calculator appears right where you need it as you write checks and record other transactions, and the options for customizing reports have been consolidated on a single, well-organized window. There are new specialized calculators for planning investment savings, and for deciding whether it pays to refinance. And Quicken 3 looks better, with better use of color and many more icons to help you find your way visually.

Although Quicken 2 is a very capable product that will serve many people adequately, I can't say the same for the original version of Quicken for Windows. It lacks several critical features, including the ability to automatically compute the totals you need for your tax forms on a line-by-line basis and the advanced reporting and graphing features introduced with Quicken 2. If you're still using the first version of Quicken for Windows, by all means, upgrade immediately to Quicken 3.

How to Use This Book

In this book, you'll find complete coverage of all of the important financial record-keeping and management tasks you can accomplish with Quicken. Along with basic skills such as writing and printing checks, recording cash and credit card transactions, and printing summary reports, you'll learn how to use Quicken—and how to use it appropriately—for more sophisticated budgeting and bookkeeping chores.

Just in case you're new to Microsoft Windows or have gotten a bit rusty, the first few chapters cover some of the basic skills you need to operate Windows itself and most Windows programs. We'll review how to use the mouse, how to pick choices from menus, and how to work with the "windows" themselves.

Most of the instructions in the book are presented in tutorial style, to help you gain the skills you need through hands-on, learn-by-doing exercises. You'll be led step by step through both basic and more complex procedures, and you'll study lots of practical examples of Quicken in action, including entering personal financial records, managing rental properties, running a consulting practice, and preparing tax forms. While you can work through the book sequentially, you might prefer to use it as a reference and dip into it anywhere you like for information once you have a handle on Quicken's basic features.

Learning Quicken by practicing with the examples makes sense, because you won't have to tinker with your own records until you're sure you've got the hang of the program. Yes, some of the examples are a bit fanciful, but you'll be able to relate them easily to your own situation. Once you've completed all the practice sessions, you'll find that you can delete the example transactions easily and start fresh accounts for your own real-life records.

If you're anxious to get started entering your own data, however, you can still use the exercises to learn Quicken by adjusting the sample transactions to fit yours. Just be sure to review all your entries for accuracy after you're fully acquainted with the program.

Preview of Contents

This book is divided into 17 chapters, each covering a distinct practical financial management task or Quicken skill. After its main text comes an Appendix with helpful miscellaneous information about installing and customizing Quicken.

Here's a summary of what you'll find in each chapter.

- **Chapter 1**, *Getting Started with Quicken for Windows*, serves as an introduction to the program. In this chapter, you'll learn how to start Quicken, you'll open your first Quicken checking account, and you'll learn your way around the Quicken menus and help system.

- In **Chapter 2**, *Writing Your First Check*, you'll actually "write" several checks on the checking account you set up in Chapter 1. You'll practice Quicken's system for organizing your records by assigning your checks to categories and classes. You'll also learn how to record checks in your account, how to browse through a stack of unprinted checks, and how to edit checks you wrote earlier.

- **Chapter 3**, *Printing Your Checks*, walks you through the process of printing your first checks with Quicken. You'll be given detailed instructions on how to position checks properly in your printer, and you'll see how to select the specific checks you want to print. This chapter closes with a section on troubleshooting printing problems.

- **Chapter 4**, *Recording Other Payments and Deposits*, covers the Quicken register, in which you record transactions other than your Quicken checks, in detail. You'll practice entering and recording several transactions, browsing through the transactions you've entered, assigning categories and classes, and printing a register list.

- In **Chapter 5**, *Organizing Your Accounts*, you'll gain in-depth experience with Quicken's categories and classes, which are the key to informative financial reports and graphs. You'll learn the theory and practice of using these two classification systems as you design and set up category and class lists of your own. You'll also practice "splitting" a single transaction so that the items it covers are distributed among two or more categories or classes.

- **Chapter 6**, *Balancing Your Checking Account*, covers the ins and outs of the monthly task of *balancing* your checkbook, that is, reconciling it with your bank statement. After you've completed this chapter, you'll see how Quicken can help you finish quickly what is now a simple chore.

- **Chapter 7**, *Taking Care of Regular Bills and Deposits Efficiently*, shows you how to make short work of regularly occurring transactions. You'll learn to use the new financial planning calendar to schedule payments visually. This chapter also covers memorized transactions and transaction groups, alternative methods for storing copies of your checks so you can recall them the next time these bills fall due.

- **Chapter 8**, *Keeping Track of Cash, Credit Cards, and Loans*, shows you how to account for other major elements in your financial profile. Whether you want to manage your cash, your credit cards, or your mortgage, this chapter will show you how a series of custom-tailored Quicken accounts can fill the bill. You'll also practice transferring funds between two accounts, and see how to manage your account files on disk.

- **Chapter 9**, *Managing Your Investments with Quicken*, goes into depth on Quicken's investment-tracking features. You'll learn how to record purchases and sales of stocks, bonds, and commodities, and how to account for broker fees and dividend income. Quicken's investment analysis features are also covered in full, including graphs, reports, and the new Portfolio View window.

- **Chapter 10**, *Fast Financial Reports*, begins your work with Quicken's powerful reporting features. In this chapter, you'll practice creating reports using the program's report settings for personal, business, and investment needs. You'll learn how to view reports on the screen, and also how to print them out.

- In **Chapter 11**, *Customizing Financial Reports*, you'll expand your reporting expertise to include customized reports. This chapter shows you when and how to choose various reporting options and how to restrict reports to the particular items you're interested in.

- **Chapter 12**, *Financial Overviews at a Glance: Quicken Graphics*, shows you how to prepare quick and easy graphs and charts that summarize various aspects of your financial situation in a visual way that's easily understood.

- **Chapter 13**, *Financial Planning and Budgeting,* is the first of four chapters covering solutions for real-world financial management problems. In this chapter, you'll learn to use Quicken's financial calendar and graphs to get an overview of your income and expense patterns. Based on this information, you can develop a realistic financial plan, and then set up a comprehensive budget in Quicken to implement it.

- **Chapter 14**, *Managing Your Personal Finances,* goes over other ways Quicken can help with personal financial management. Using Quicken's special calculators, you'll be able to plan a savings program for retirement or your kids' college educations. You'll see how to use the program for income tax record-keeping, how to track the value of your home and other personal assets, and how to monitor your investments.

- **Chapter 15**, *Handling Basic Business Records and Reports,* shows you how to set up your Quicken accounts for effective business record-keeping, and how to put together useful business reports over time. You'll get tips on business budgeting, as well as special coverage of investment real estate topics.

- In **Chapter 16**, *Business Bookkeeping and Payroll,* you'll learn how to use Quicken to monitor accounts payable and receivable, how to manage your payroll with the program, and how to forecast your cash flow and cash needs. You'll also learn to produce a business balance sheet.

- **Chapter 17**, *Paying Your Bills Electronically with CheckFree,* shows you how to use Quicken to make payments by transferring check data over the telephone lines to the CheckFree service. You'll also learn how to send and receive messages to and from the CheckFree service electronically.

- **The Appendix** includes instructions for installing Quicken for Windows on your computer system, for setting up the program to work with your printer, and for controlling the program itself so that it works as you want it to. Techniques for sharing information between Quicken and other programs are also covered. The appendix concludes with brief coverage of the Quicken companions, a trio of little programs for keeping track of your personal property for insurance purposes, estimating your income taxes, and obtaining stock quotes electronically.

Conventions Used in This Book

A few simple conventions are used in all of the instructions in this book to make it easier to differentiate between the things you're to do, the messages

Quicken displays, and the instructions and explanations. Before you actually start working with Quicken, please review this section briefly.

Characters that you are to type at the keyboard are printed in boldface, like this:

Now type **1000**.

Special keys that do not enter characters on the screen, but rather perform other functions, are printed as symbols or as standard abbreviations, as in these examples:

Now press **Enter**.
Press **F2**, then press **UpArrow**.

Messages displayed by Quicken in dialog boxes are printed in italics, like this:

Quicken displays the message Set the date.

To highlight important aspects of Quicken operations, you'll occasionally see short Notes, Shortcuts, and Warnings. Here is the kind of information you can expect in each of these messages:

NOTE	This signifies a note that supplements the text or that refers you to another section for more information.

SHORTCUT	This indicates a technique for getting something done more quickly and efficiently.

WARNING	This is a warning that alerts you to problems you may encounter in carrying out the function discussed in the text. Be sure to read these warnings.

NEW IN 3   This signifies that the features or functions mentioned are new in the new version 3 of Quicken.

Hardware and Software Requirements

To use Quicken 3 for Windows, you need the following:

- A 100% IBM-compatible microcomputer with an 80286, 80386, or 80486 microprocessor

- A high-resolution graphics display adapter and monitor (Hercules Graphics, EGA, or better).
- Microsoft Windows 3.0 or later.
- Approximately 5 megabytes of free hard disk space.
- A Windows-compatible dot matrix, inkjet, or laser printer (required for printing checks and reports).
- Two megabytes of memory.

Chapter One
Getting Started with Quicken for Windows

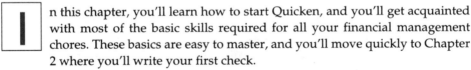n this chapter, you'll learn how to start Quicken, and you'll get acquainted with most of the basic skills required for all your financial management chores. These basics are easy to master, and you'll move quickly to Chapter 2 where you'll write your first check.

Before you can run Quicken, you must first install the program. If you haven't done so already, you'll find the necessary instructions in Appendix A.

Starting Quicken for Windows

To get Quicken up and running, begin by starting Windows:

1. Turn on your computer if it isn't already on.
2. Start Windows. At the DOS prompt, type **win** and then press **Enter**. When the hard disk stops chattering, Windows is ready.

From this point, start Quicken using the same method you would use to start any other Windows program.

11

Starting Quicken Using the Icon

If you run your Windows programs from Program Manager—as most people do—you must know which Program Manager group contains the **Quicken** icon. The icon is should be located in the group called "Quicken." If the window for that group isn't visible, you can display it by choosing Quicken from the Program Manager's Window menu (you'll find a review of basic Windows skills such as choosing menu items later in this chapter; see your Windows manual for details).

Once the **Quicken** icon appears in Program Manager, double-click on the icon to start Quicken. As Quicken readies itself for business, you'll see a logo screen. Once this screen clears, you're ready for work.

Other Methods for Starting Quicken

If you can't find the **Quicken** icon, you can still run Quicken using Program Manager or File Manager. In this case, however, you'll need to know where the Quicken is stored—in which directory on which hard disk. If someone else installed Quicken, ask them for the disk and directory information and have it handy in case you need it.

Now you're ready to start Quicken. In Program Manager, choose **Run** from the Edit menu from the Program Manager menu bar. In the Run dialog box, type in the disk drive and directory where Quicken is stored, followed by the program name, like this:

```
c:\quickenw\qw
```

In File Manager, switch to the hard disk and directory where Quicken is located. In the list of files, find the entry QW.EXE and double-click on it.

Using the Windows and Quicken Tutorials

The very first time Quicken for Windows runs, the program gives you a chance to get some on-screen education about Windows and about Quicken itself. You'll first see a small box asking whether you want to run the Windows tutorial. This tutorial comes with Windows, so you may have tried it before. If you're new to Windows or if you're out of practice, it might pay to review quickly through the tutorial, which covers topics such as working with menus and using the mouse. To start the Windows tutorial, press **Enter**.

If you're comfortable with basic Windows skills, or just want to get right to work with Quicken, press **Esc**. The next message you'll see asks if you want to run a tutorial about Quicken. Feel free to try the Quicken tutorial if you like by pressing **Enter**. But it's not a absolutely necessary—you'll get plenty of practice with all of Quicken's features by working through this book. Again, you press **Enter** to start the tutorial and **Esc** to bypass it.

Starting Your First Account

Whether or not you work through the tutorials, and assuming this is the first time you've worked with Quicken, you'll next arrive at the First Time Setup window. The very first time Quicken runs, the program knows that you haven't entered any information as yet. It asks you to start a new file for the accounts you'll be using for your records, and then to create your first account.

As the first step in this process, Quicken displays the First Time Setup window, shown in Figure 1.1 on the next page. This window is a *dialog box*, a window in which you make choices from various options that determine how the program works. You've probably used plenty of Windows dialog boxes before, but we'll review the necessary techniques briefly as we go through the first ones you'll see in Quicken for Windows. If you're already expert with Windows, just skim past any unnecessary material.

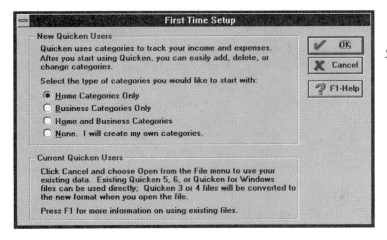

FIGURE 1.1

The First Time Setup window.

Throughout this book, I make a point of telling you how to use both the mouse and the keyboard to get things done in Quicken. The mouse is easier at first because you don't have to learn and remember any commands. Once you've had some practice with the keyboard, however, you'll find that it is much faster for most Quicken chores than using the mouse. If you're going to be working with Quicken regularly, I recommend that you familiarize yourself gradually with the keyboard commands. These are summarized inside the cover of this book.

In the First Time Setup dialog box, you select the *categories* you'll be using in your new account file. The categories you choose here apply to all the accounts in a file, so you won't see this window if someone has previously set up a file. Once you complete this window, if it does appear at this point, you won't see it again until you start a new file. (Account files are discussed in detail in Chapter 8.)

Assuming you're new to Quicken, your task here is to tell the program which of its built-in collections of categories you want to use. Whenever you record an income or expense item in your account, you assign it to one of these categories, just as you would if you were keeping track of your income and expenses in a ledger. If you are writing a rent check, for example, you might put it in the *Rent* category. That way, you can total what you earn and what you spend on a category-by-category basis, making it much faster and easier to track your income and spending patterns (details on using categories effectively are covered in Chapter 5).

NOTE	If you plan to use an existing Quicken file—probably one you created with a previous version of Quicken—you don't need to select categories because your file already has them. Instead, press **Esc**, then press **Alt**, then **F**, then **O** to open a window from which you can load the existing file.

Quicken's standard categories—the first three choices in the window—are divided into two groups: One is for home use and the other is for businesses. The built-in categories cover just about any conceivable type of transaction (see Tables 1.1 and 1.2 for details). But even if a particular category you need isn't in the built-in category lists, don't worry—you can add, rename, or remove categories whenever the need arises.

TABLE 1.1   *Category and Transfer List for Home Use*

Category	Description	Tax Rel	Tax Schedule and Line
Income			
Bonus	Bonus Income	*	W-2: Salary
Canada Pen	Canadian Pension	*	
Div Income	Dividend Income	*	Schedule B: Dividend income
Gift Received	Gift Received	*	
Int Inc	Interest Income	*	Schedule B: Interest income
Invest Inc	Investment Income	*	
Old Age Pension	Old Age Pension	*	
Other Inc	Other Income	*	
Salary	Salary Income	*	W-2: Salary
Expense			
Auto	Automobile Expenses		
Fuel	Auto Fuel		
Loan	Auto Loan Payment		
Service	Auto Service		
Bank Chrg	Bank charge		
Charity	Charitable donations	*	Schedule A: Cash charity contribution
Childcare	Childcare Expense		
Christmas	Christmas Expenses		
Clothing	Clothing		
Dining	Dining Out		
Dues	Dues		
Education	Education		
Entertain	Entertainment		
Gifts	Gift Expenses		
Groceries	Groceries		
Home Rpair	Home Repair & Maint.		
Household	Household Misc. Exp		
Housing	Housing		
Insurance	Insurance		

(continued)

Int Exp	Interest Expense	*	
Invest Exp	Investment Expense	*	Schedule A: Invest ment man. fees
Medical	Medical & Dental	*	Schedule A: Medicine and drugs
Misc	Miscellaneous		
Mort Int	Mortgage Interest Exp	*	Schedule A: Home mortgage interest
Other Exp	Other Expenses	*	
Recreation	Recreation Expense		
RRSP	Reg Retirement Sav Plan		
Subscriptions	Subscriptions		
Supplies	Supplies	*	
Tax	Taxes	*	Schedule C: Taxes and licenses
Fed	Federal Tax	*	W-2: Federal Withholding
FICA	Social Security Tax	*	W-2: Soc Sec Tax Withholding
Other	Misc. Taxes	*	
Prop	Property Tax	*	Schedule A: Real estate tax
State	State Tax	*	W-2: State Withholding
Telephone	Telephone Expense		
UIC	Unemploy. Ins. Commission	*	
Utilities	Water, Gas, Electric		
Gas & Electric	Gas and Electricity		
Water	Water		

TABLE 1.2 *Category and Transfer List for Business Use*

Category	Description	Tax Rel	Tax Schedule and Line
Income			
Gr Sales	Gross Sales	*	Schedule C: Gross receipts
Other Inc	Other Income	*	
Rent Income	Rent Income	*	Schedule E: rents received
Expense			
Ads	Advertising	*	Schedule C: Advertising
Car	Car & truck	*	Schedule C: Car and truck expenses

Commission	Commissions	*	Schedule C: Commissions and fees
Freight	Freight	*	Schedule C: Other business expense
Int Paid	Interest Paid	*	Schedule C: Interest expenses, other
L&P Fees	Legal & Prof. Fees	*	Schedule C: Legal and professional
Late Fees	Late Payment Fees	*	Schedule C: Other business expense
Office	Office Expenses	*	Schedule C: Office expense
Rent Paid	Rent Paid	*	Schedule C: Rent on other bus prop
Repairs	Repairs	*	Schedule C: Repairs and mainte-nance
Returns	Returns & Allowances	*	Schedule C: Returns and allowances
Tax	Taxes	*	Schedule C: Taxes and licenses
Travel	Travel Expenses	*	Schedule C: Travel
Wages	Wages & Job Credits	*	Schedule C: Wages

In the First Time Setup dialog box, you make your category choices using *radio buttons*, as indicated by the circular area to the left of each choice. You can select only one radio button from a group of them, just as you can only play a single station on your car radio. When you select one of the buttons, the circle next to it becomes filled with a smaller solid circle.

NOTE   The **Neither. I will create my own.** choice in the First Time Setup window is provided for special situations where very few of the standard categories apply, and you need to design your own category list from scratch.

For the sample accounts you'll create with this book, choose the **Home and Business** option, the third radio button choice. You can do this with the mouse or the keyboard.

Making Choices with the Mouse

If you're using the mouse, move it so that the mouse pointer, the little arrow on your screen, is over any part of the **Home and Business** choice. Then quickly press and release the left mouse button.

Now is a good time for a quick review of mouse skills and terminology. In Windows, *pointing* at something on the screen, such as a radio button, means to position the mouse pointer so that it's over the item. *Clicking* is the process of pressing down a mouse button just for a moment, then letting it up again. *Clicking on* something means to point to the item, then to click the mouse button. *Double-clicking* means to click twice in quick succession. *Dragging* means to hold the mouse button down while you move the mouse, letting up on the button when you're finished.

> **NOTE**   Unless I tell you otherwise, click and drag with the left mouse button. (Of course, if you've used the Windows control panel to reverse the way the buttons work, you should use the right button for most clicks and drags.)

Making Choices with the Keyboard

To select the **Home and Business** choice with the keyboard, press **Down Arrow** to move the dashed rectangular outline over the correct option. Alternatively, you can select it by pressing **Alt-O**. This technique works for any choice in any dialog box—you can activate it by holding down **Alt** while you press the underlined letter in the choice.

Using Buttons in Windows

Once you've selected the **Home and Business** option for categories, you can leave this dialog box. I'm sure you've already learned how to move through dialog boxes in Windows, but let's review the basics. The two gray rectangles at the right side of the window labeled **OK** and **Cancel** are *buttons*.

In Windows, a button on the screen is anything you can press to perform an action. Here, the **OK** button confirms your choice of categories, closes the dialog box, and tells Quicken you're ready for the next step. The **Cancel** button closes the dialog box, too, but leaves things as they were and takes you back to whatever you were doing before. (In this case, you weren't doing anything with Quicken prior to opening the Home and Business dialog box, so you would get a blank screen).

Usually, you can use either the keyboard or the mouse to activate buttons, and that's the case here. With the mouse, of course, you just click on the button.

Choosing Buttons with the Keyboard

With the keyboard, you can either press **Alt** and the underlined letter in the button name, or you can highlight the button and then press **Enter**. (If you look closely at the **OK** button, you should be able to see that it's already high-lighted: The outer border of the button is heavier than that of the **Cancel** button.)

Since all these techniques work for activating buttons, I'll use a generic term when it's time to do so: I'll ask you to *choose* the button by name. In this case, for example, you should choose **OK**.

| NOTE | I want to stop here to stress an important point about the way most dialog boxes and many other windows work in Quicken and other parts of Windows. Almost always, the button that you'll use most often on any given window is already highlighted when you open the window. In other words, all you have to do is press **Enter** to activate that button. |

In most dialog boxes, the **OK** button is highlighted automatically with the heavy outer border. Unless you move this highlight, pressing **Enter** always "okays" the box, even while you're making choices in other parts of a dialog box. (In other words, pressing **Enter** confirms your choices and closes the box).

To move the highlight to a different button, press **Tab** one or more times until the dark outline appears around the new button. Once the new button is highlighted, pressing **Enter** activates it. However, as soon as you go back to making entries in other parts of the window, Quicken automatically highlights the original button again.

| SHORTCUT | Keep this keyboard shortcut in mind, because I won't always remind you that you can press **Enter** when it's time to activate the main button on a window. |

So here's the bottom line: Pressing **Enter** OKs a dialog box, no matter what part of the dialog box you're working with (unless you just moved the border highlight to a different button). In the same way, other Quicken windows have a Main button that you can activate from any part of the window by pressing **Enter**, assuming you haven't just highlighted another button.

More on Navigating with the Keyboard

| NOTE | In Quicken for Windows, the way the **Enter** key works in some windows—to finalize entries—is different than in Quicken for DOS. If you prefer, you can have **Enter** function like **Tab** to move to the next field on these windows. This doesn't affect the function of **Enter** in dialog boxes. See the Appendix for information. |

> **NOTE**   One other point about working with dialog boxes with the keyboard: You've probably noticed that each time you press **Tab**, a dashed rectangle moves from one section or field of the dialog box to another. For example, if you move the heavy border to the **Cancel** button in the First Time Setup window, the dotted rectangle appears around the word **Cancel** (the button's label).

This dotted rectangle tells you which part of a window is currently active for keyboard entries. When the dotted rectangle is on a button, pressing the space bar activates the button just as if you pressed **Enter**. In other parts of a window, however, the dotted rectangle lets you select among options or type in entries yourself. For example, in the First Time Setup window, you can pick from the available categories by moving the dashed rectangle to that section of the window, and then pressing the **Up Arrow** or **Down Arrow** key.

Choosing the Account Type

If you haven't already done so, choose **OK** in the First Time Setup dialog box. The window closes. You'll next see the Select Account Type dialog box, shown in Figure 1.2.

Your job here is to pick the type of account you want to set up from Quicken's six different account types. The first choice, **Bank Account**, is already selected, since this is the most common type of Quicken account. It's the type you'll be setting up now.

There's something else on the screen you've probably already noticed. Just above the Select Account Type window, there's a smaller box with a message about choosing an account type. This message box is a *Qcard*. (If you don't see the Qcard, someone has shut off this feature—you'll see how to turn it on and off later).

Qcard reminds you of the essential steps for completing whatever Quicken task you're working on. The Qcard has two buttons at the lower-right corner of the box, one with a question mark, the other with a picture of a notebook. For now, ignore these buttons.

Since your first account will be a bank account to keep track of your checking, leave the Select Account Type window as it is. Click on **OK**, or press **Enter**. You'll begin learning about the other types of accounts in Chapter 2.

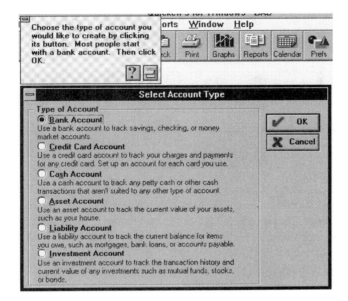

FIGURE 1.2

The Select Account Type dialog box with one of Quicken's Qcards.

| NOTE | You can cancel any dialog box, removing it from the screen, by clicking the **Cancel** button or pressing **Esc**. Quicken ignores any changes you made, and returns you to whatever part of the program you were using when you opened the dialog box. |

Editing Entries in Dialog Boxes

At this point, you'll see the New Account Information dialog box (see Figure 1.3 on the next page). The blinking cursor should be in the field labeled *Account Name*. In Quicken, a line or space where you type information is called a *field*.

To move to a particular field with the mouse, you just click anywhere on the field. Try this by clicking alternately on the *Balance, as of,* and *Account Name* fields. You'll see the cursor move to whichever field you clicked in.

With the keyboard, you have two alternatives for moving from field to field. Try the direct method first. Notice the field at the bottom, the window labeled *Description.* Since the D in Description is underlined, you can move to the field by pressing **Alt-D**. Try moving to the other fields by pressing **Alt** plus the underlined letter in the field name.

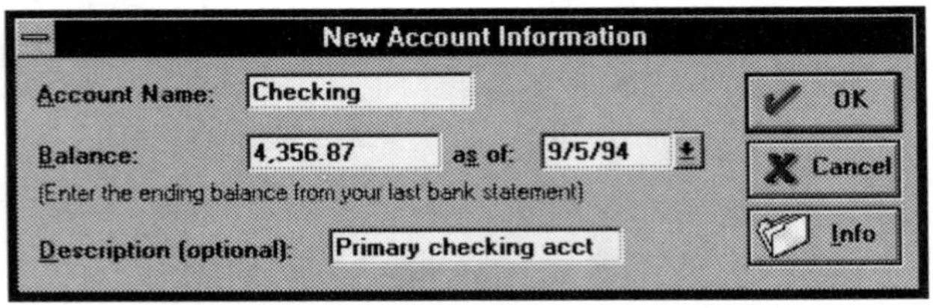

FIGURE 1.3

The New Account Information window.

```
┌─────────────────────────────────────────────────────────┐
│ ─              New Account Information                    │
│ Account Name:  [Checking          ]        ┌─────────┐   │
│                                            │ ✓   OK  │   │
│ Balance:       [4,356.87]  as of: [9/5/94 ±]└─────────┘   │
│ (Enter the ending balance from your last bank statement) ┌─────────┐ │
│                                            │ X Cancel│   │
│ Description (optional):  [Primary checking acct]└─────────┘ │
│                                            ┌─────────┐   │
│                                            │ 📁 Info │   │
│                                            └─────────┘   │
└─────────────────────────────────────────────────────────┘
```

You can also move from field to field in order by pressing **Tab**. But don't do that just now, since Quicken won't let you move out of certain fields in the Create New Account window until you fill them in. You'll see how the **Tab** key works in a moment.

Move the cursor back to the *Account Name* field. Now is a good time for you to learn the techniques you can use for making and changing typed entries in Quicken fields. For the most part, these techniques are the same as the ones you use for editing in your word processor.

SHORTCUT   In Quicken, your account names can be up to 15 characters long. They can include spaces, numbers, and punctuation marks except for [,], :, ^, and /.

Type in the words **My Checks** in the *Account Name* field. When you've completed the entry, the cursor will be one space to the right of the final **s**.

Now let's practice editing the name you've just typed. Start by simply moving the cursor around in the field. The **Left Arrow** and **Right Arrow** keys move the cursor one character at a time—try moving it back between the e and the c in the word *Checking* by pressing **Left Arrow** three times.

Next, move the cursor to the beginning of the entire entry by pressing the **Home** key. Then press **Ctrl-Right Arrow** once to move to the beginning of the word *Checks*. Finally, press **End** to move back to the end of the field. In any field, **Ctrl-Right Arrow** moves the cursor to the beginning of the next word, while **Ctrl-Left Arrow** moves to the beginning of the previous word. **Home** always moves the cursor to the beginning of the field, and **End** moves it to the end.

Now let's change the entry. The cursor should be at the end of the line. First, erase the final **s** in the word *Checks* by pressing the **Backspace** key once. Backspace deletes the character to the left of the cursor. Type **book** so that the field reads *My Checkbook*.

Now press **Home** to move to the beginning of the line again. This time press **Del** twice to remove the word *My* (**Del** deletes the character to the right of the cursor).

Without moving the cursor, type **New** in front of *Checkbook* and notice that the existing characters remain on the screen. The dialog boxes in Quicken for Windows operate in **Insert** mode, meaning that new characters you type push the remaining characters on the line to the right.

Quicken also lets you change typed entries by selecting a group of characters all at once. With the cursor between *New* and *Checkbook*, hold down the **Shift** key and press **Right Arrow**. As the cursor moves to the right, the characters it passes over become highlighted, or *selected*. When the entire word *Checkbook* is selected, let up on the keys. Now press the **Left Arrow** key to move the cursor back—since you didn't press the **Shift** key, too, this immediately deselects the selected text.

SHORTCUT	In dialog boxes only, you can use instead the standard Windows 3.1 shortcuts: **Ctrl-X**, **Ctrl-C**, and **Ctrl-V**. However, these shortcuts will not work in other parts of Quicken. The **Cut**, **Copy**, and **Paste** commands on the Edit menu are available when you work with Quicken data, but not in dialog boxes.
SHORTCUT	You can also move text around by cutting, copying, and pasting selected text as in most Windows programs. This is rarely useful in dialog boxes, but it can come in handy with your Quicken data. In Quicken, the keyboard shortcuts for the **Cut**, **Copy**, and **Paste** commands are **Shift-Del**, **Ctrl-Ins**, and **Shift-Ins**, respectively.

Now use the mouse to select text another way. The mouse pointer turns into an I-beam shape whenever you point to a text field. Point to the beginning of the word *New* and drag the mouse to the right. The text you drag over is selected. Now double-click over the word *Checkbook*. As you can see, when you double-click, the entire word under the pointer gets selected.

Ready for some editing? Select the word *Checkbook* with either method, then start typing the word **Day**. As soon as you press **D**, the entire selection disappears, replaced by the letter you typed. In other words, selecting text is an efficient way to make changes in an entry, since it lets you delete a whole group of letters at once as you start typing their replacements.

Continue experimenting with the **Editing** keys until you feel comfortable with them. Once you've had enough practice, enter the real account name you want—in the sample screens, the account is simply called *Checking*. Press **Tab** to confirm it, moving the cursor to the next field. As I said earlier, **Tab** moves the cursor from one field (or other dialog box item) to the next. You'll learn more about using the Tab key in the next chapter.

You're now at the *Balance* field. For our sample account, type in **$4,356.87**, since that's the starting balance you'll see in the examples. If you're setting up an account for your own real-life data, you would type in the balance listed on your most recent bank statement. When the number is correct, press **Tab**.

NOTE	To help prevent typing errors, Quicken won't accept letters or other nonnumeric characters in the *Balance* field or in any other field in which you're supposed to enter only numerals. If you enter invalid characters, Quicken simply displays a warning message when you move the cursor out of that field.

The next field, labeled *as of*, displays today's date. For the sample account, just leave the current date in the field. Later, when you enter the balance from your checking account statement, you'll enter the date of the statement in this field, using the month/day/year format. Press **Tab** to confirm the date entry and move to the next field.

The final field in the Create New Account window, labeled *Description (optional)*, is a place for you to type in anything you like that will help you differentiate this account from any others you may set up. Since your main bank account is so important and you'll use it so frequently, you don't really need a verbal description. If you have it handy, you may want to type in your real-life checking account number here. Whether or not you enter an account description, press **Enter** to finish the Create New Account window.

Based on the information you've entered in the Standard Categories and Create New Account windows, Quicken now sets up your new bank account. The account is added to the list of the accounts you can select to work with (at this point, of course, it's the only entry in the list).

Understanding the Account Register

As soon as you complete the Create New Account window, Quicken displays the *register* for the new account on your screen (Figure 1.4). You'll learn all about how the register works in Chapter 4. For now, just take a moment to look it over. As you can see, the place where you record your checks and deposits in your paper checkbook is similar to the register, although it includes spaces for entries the paper register doesn't have.

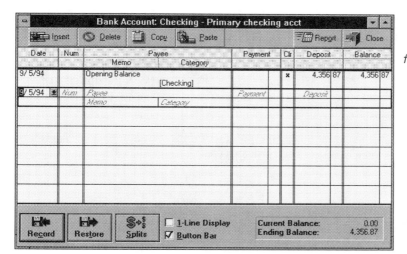

FIGURE 1.4

The register for your new checking account.

The Quicken Menu Bar

Shift your attention from the register to the top of the main Quicken window. Like almost all Windows programs, Quicken for Windows has a horizontal *menu bar* near the top of the main window (Figure 1.5). If you're at all familiar with Windows, you already know how the menu bar works, but let's briefly review this essential skill.

FIGURE 1.5

Quicken's menu bar.

Using Quicken's Menu System

Just as in a restaurant, a menu on your screen gives you a series of choices. In this case, you use the menu to tell Quicken what you want it to do.

The menu bar is the master menu—a sort of menu of menus. Each word on the menu bar (File, Edit, Activities, etc.) represents the name of a menu offering a set of related Quicken functions.

To use any of the menus listed on the menu bar, you have to *open* the menu first. You open a menu with either of these two methods:

1. Using the mouse, click on the menu's name on the menu bar.
2. Using the keyboard, press the **Alt** key, then press the underlined letter in the menu's name on the menu bar. To open the File menu, for example, you press **Alt**, then type **F**.

Try one of these methods now. Figure 1.6 shows how the File menu looks when you've opened it.

FIGURE 1.6

The File menu.

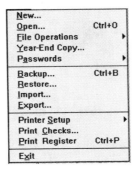

Each line of the menu, or *menu item*, stands for an action that Quicken will perform at your command. Notice that when you open the menu, Windows displays the first item in a highlighted color.

To activate a menu item, you *choose* it from the menu. Again, you can do this with the mouse or the keyboard:

-   With the mouse, click on the menu item.
-   With the keyboard, you can move the menu highlight to the item by pressing **Down Arrow** or **Up Arrow**, and then press **Enter**. Or just type the underlined letter for that item. In the File menu, for instance, you can choose the Open menu item by typing **O**.

Some menu items are commands that Quicken carries out immediately when you choose them. **Exit**, at the bottom of the File menu, is a good example (but don't choose **Exit** now). When you choose **Exit**, Quicken shuts down and returns you to the Program Manager.

But not all menu items are direct commands. On the File menu, notice that some items such as **New**, **Open**, and **Backup**, are listed with three periods after the item name. Choosing any of these items displays a dialog box, a window in which you can make a series of choices related to the menu item. Figure 1.7 shows the dialog box you see if you choose **New**—in this case, the dialog box lets you specify whether you want to create a new file or a new account.

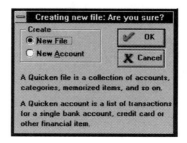

FIGURE 1.7

You'll see this dialog box when you choose New on the File menu.

Feel free to experiment with opening the dialog boxes available on the File menu. But for now, don't make any selections in the dialog boxes themselves. To remove or *close* a dialog box, click on **Cancel** or press **Esc**. Other items on the File menu, such as **File Operations**, **Passwords**, and **Printer Setup** include small black triangles at the right side of the menu.

Choosing any of these items opens a *cascading menu*. A cascading menu is a secondary menu that appears immediately to the right of the original menu, in this case the File menu.

You choose items on cascading menus just as you would on any other menu. Once you've displayed a cascading menu, you can remove it by pressing **Esc** or **Left Arrow**.

Using Keyboard Shortcuts

You can access many of the items on Quicken menus without ever opening the menu system by using *keyboard shortcuts*, special key combinations. For easy reference, the **Shortcut** keys are listed on the menus. On the File menu, for instance, several menu items have keyboard shortcuts. As the menu indicates, pressing **Ctrl-O** duplicates the function of choosing **Open** on the File menu. **Ctrl-B** does the same thing as choosing **Backup** from the File menu, and so on.

If you use Quicken frequently, you'll want to learn the most important keyboard shortcuts—they make your work with Quicken noticeably more efficient. I'll remind you of them at the appropriate times throughout this book.

Closing the File Menu

When you've finished exploring the File menu, close it by pressing **Alt** again or by clicking on the main part of the Quicken screen.

From now on, I'll assume you know how to open and close Quicken menus, and how to choose items on a menu. In fact, I'll be using a shorthand method for indicating which menu items you should choose. Instead of saying something like "Open the File menu, then open the File Operations cascading menu, and finally choose **Copy**," I'll simply say "Choose **Copy** File Operations in the File menu."

Using the Iconbar

Just below the menu bar is Quicken's iconbar, shown in Figure 1.8. The iconbar gives you a quick way to activate many of the Quicken commands you'll be using all the time. It consists of a series of icons, those little pictures you see so often in Windows. Underneath each icon is a label describing the icon's function.

FIGURE 1.8

Quicken's Iconbar.

All you have to do to use a command on the iconbar is click on its icon. It's a one-step way to take care of chores like printing, starting a new check, and so on—clicking on an icon is a bit quicker and more convenient than opening a menu and then choosing a menu item.

You can even customize the iconbar so that it displays your favorite commands. You'll learn how to do that in the Appendix.

Assuming you do have a mouse, let's give the iconbar a try now. Click on the question mark icon, the one labeled Help, toward the right side of the screen. The Quicken Help window will appear as shown in Figure 1.9.

One more thing about the iconbar: It only works if you have a mouse. If you're working without a mouse, you can get rid of the iconbar and thereby open up a little more space on your screen. Again, the instructions you need are in the Appendix.

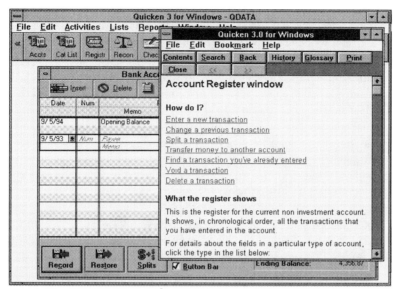

FIGURE 1.9

The Quicken Help window.

You'll learn how to use Help in the next section. The point right now is that you produced the Help window by one quick click on the question mark icon. Each icon in the iconbar activates a different feature, but they all give immediate results.

Getting Help

If you ever get stuck while working in Quicken, help is just a click of the mouse or a press of a key away. As you've already seen, you can display the Quicken Help window at any time by clicking on the question mark icon on the iconbar. Another equally easy way to get help is to press **F1**. Quicken takes advantage of Windows' Help system, so if you're familiar with the way Help works in other Windows programs, you already know how to use **Quicken Help**. As with most Windows programs, Quicken's help messages are *context sensitive*. This means that the message that appears in the Help window covers whatever Quicken feature or function you're currently using. If the Help window isn't already on your screen, use one of these methods to display it.

Many of Quicken's dialog boxes have Help buttons you can click to get information on completing the box you're working with. But even if you don't see a Help button, you can still press **F1** to get help on that box.

The size and position of the window on your screen depends on how it was set up when you last used the Windows Help system for any program. Figure 1.9 on the previous page shows how it looked on my screen.

The Help window contains a message telling you how to use the account register, since that's the Quicken window currently on the screen. In Windows, a Help message is called a *topic*. If an entire topic won't fit in the Help window, you can tell by the presence of a *scroll bar* at the right side of the window. The scroll bar is a vertical gray strip with small arrows at the top and bottom.

Whether or not you see a scroll bar at this point depends on how large your **Help** window is. In case your Help window is too small to display the whole register topic, I'll give you instructions here for seeing the rest of the topic using the scroll bar. If your window is big enough to show the entire topic, bear with me, because you'll need these skills soon, no matter what. Whenever you can't see the entire contents of a window, you can *scroll* through the window to see more. You can do this with either the mouse or the keyboard.

Using the mouse, you use the scroll bar. To bring later parts of the Help topic into the window, point to the arrow at the bottom of the scroll bar and press down the mouse button. Keep holding down the button until the text you want to see comes into view. The arrow at the top of the scroll bar displays earlier parts of the topic in the same way.

As you scroll, you can gauge how far into the topic you've gone by looking at the scroll box, that squarish box within the main part of the scroll bar. In fact, you can also scroll by dragging the scroll box up or down with the mouse.

With the keyboard, you scroll up or down a line at a time by pressing **Up Arrow** or **Down Arrow**. Press **PgUp** or **PgDn** to move up or down a window's worth of lines at a time. And press **Ctrl-End** to move to the end of the Help topic or **Ctrl-Home** to move to the beginning again.

Accessing Additional Help Information

Quicken's extensive Help system makes it easy to find information on related subjects. If necessary, scroll back to the top of the Account Register topic. Notice that several words and phrases in the text are displayed in a different shade (on color monitors, in green) and are underlined. These are *jumps*, links to other **Help** topics covering these subjects. To view the text for a jump, you choose the jump with the keyboard or the mouse. Here are the techniques:

- With the mouse, you just click on the jump you want to see.
- With the keyboard, pressing **Tab** repeatedly moves a highlight to the next jump in the Help window, while pressing **Shift-Tab** moves the highlight to the previous jump. Once you've selected the jump you want, press **Enter** to display it.

Look carefully at the jumps. In this window, all of them have a solid underline. When you choose a jump of this type, its text appears in the main Help window as a new topic.

Try it now. Choose the first jump in the window, "Enter a new transaction," with one of the methods described above. You'll be shown a new Help topic titled "Adding a transaction to the register." The new topic has jumps of its own, which you can choose if you like. Windows keeps track of the Help topics you've displayed. It's easy to retrace your steps by redisplaying the topics you've seen before in reverse order. The following section explains how you can also move directly to any particular previous topic.

Notice the button bar at the top of the Help window, just below the menu bar. These buttons are one-shot commands, much like those on Quicken's iconbar—when you choose a button, the Help system immediately carries out that command.

To move to the last Help topic you read, choose the **Back** button by clicking on it with the mouse or by pressing **Alt-B** (unlike choosing a menu from the menu bar, you have to press the two keys simultaneously). Once you've displayed a number of Help topics, you can read any of them again by choosing the **History** button. You'll see a small window listing the topics you've displayed; choose the topic you want, and it appears in the main Help window again.

As you explore the Help system, you'll undoubtedly come across jumps that work a little differently. When a jump is underlined with a dashed line, choosing it displays a brief Help message in a small pop-up window. Once you've read the message, close the window by clicking anywhere with the mouse or by pressing any key. You'll go back to the main Help window with its topic unchanged.

Getting Help on a Specific Topic

In addition to the Help entries for specific subjects, Quicken offers a table of contents for the entire Help system. Once you've opened the Help window for any topic, choosing the **Contents** button displays a separate window containing a directory of help topics, as shown in Figure 1.10. The Contents lists a series of entries covering the major tasks you can accomplish with Quicken.

FIGURE 1.10

Quicken's Help Contents window.

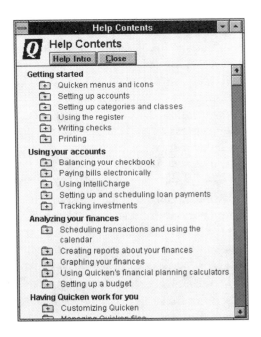

In Quicken for Windows 2, the directory of Help topics is called the *Index*, not the Contents, and appears in the main Help window.

NOTE

This list is organized in outline form. Under each major heading, you'll see a series of phrases, each beside a small picture of a closed file folder marked with a +. When you choose one of these entries, the folder "opens" (Figure

1.11), showing a series of subentries. The subentries are standard Help jumps—choose any of them to view the Help topic covering that subject.

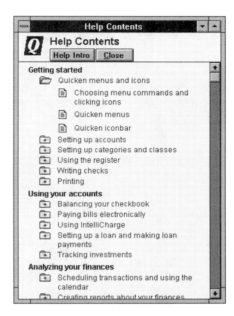

FIGURE 1.11

The Contents window when you open one of the main entries.

When you need to locate information on a very specific subject, use Help's **Search** feature. When you choose the **Search** button, you'll see the Search dialog box shown in Figure 1.12 on the next page. Type in the subject you're interested in. If there's a matching entry, Quicken highlights it in the list in the middle of the Search dialog box.

You then have to choose **Show Topics** (or just press **Enter**) to get a list of the individual Help topics available on that subject. To display a specific topic, double-click on it, or highlight the topic and press **Enter**. Spend some time experimenting with the Help system—once you're familiar with how it's organized, you'll be able to find the instructions you need for any Quicken procedure almost instantly. The Windows Help system has a few features we haven't covered here, but you'll find instructions in your Windows manual.

FIGURE 1.12

Use this dialog box to search Quicken's Help system for details on any subject.

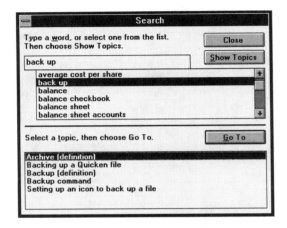

Using the Quicken Glossary

Quicken 3 offers a new glossary window, a sort of mini-dictionary of financial and computer terms. To see the list, choose the **Glossary** button at the top of the main Help window. The glossary pops up in a separate window. The terms are arranged alphabetically, of course. Since scrolling through the entire list would take a long time, there are three buttons at the top of the Glossary window, which divide it into thirds. Before you begin scrolling, click on the button for the section of the alphabet containing your term. Choose the term to pop up a small window containing its definition.

Leaving the Help System

When you're through working with the Help system, you can close its window just as you do any Windows program, by pressing **Alt-F4** or double-clicking in the Control Box at the top-left corner of the window. Alternatively, you can leave the Help window open and simply switch back to Quicken by pressing **Ctrl-Esc** and choosing Quicken from the Windows Task list.

Customizing Quicken to Your Taste: Basics

Quicken lets you control the way many aspects of the program work to suit your preferences. As you've already learned, for example, you can decide which icons should appear on the Iconbar and in what order—or you can shut off the Iconbar altogether. You can also choose colors for Quicken's windows, control the way your checks, reports, and graphs look, and determine whether or not to display, among many other options.

The Appendix provides complete instructions for changing all these settings. For now, it's enough to know that you have the controls, and where to find them. To set your preferences, click the **Prefs** icon on the Iconbar, or choose **Preferences** from the Edit menu. You'll see a small window packed with buttons, each governing one aspect of Quicken's operations. When you choose a button, a secondary dialog box appears with pertinent choices. For example, choosing the **Qcards** button displays the Qcards Preferences dialog box that lets you turn all Qcards on or off.

When you're through changing settings in a dialog box, choose **OK**. To close the Preferences window and return to Quicken proper, choose the **Done** button.

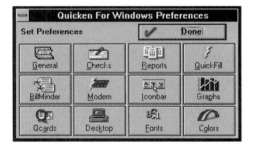

FIGURE 1.13

The Preferences window.

Summary

You've just learned most of the basic skills you need for working with Quicken: how to select choices on the menus, how to use the iconbar, and how to get help when you don't know what to do next. If you'd like to take a break at this point, you can exit Quicken by pressing **Alt-F4**, choosing **Exit** from the File menu, or by double-clicking on the control box at the top left of the main Quicken window. But if you're ready for more, leave everything as it is and go on to Chapter 2, where you'll learn to use Quicken windows and write your first Quicken checks.

Chapter Two
Writing Your First Check

ow that you've set up your first Quicken account, you're ready to get started on some real work with the program. In this chapter, you'll get step-by-step practice with writing Quicken checks. In the process, you'll also learn more about the Quicken screen and how to work with Quicken windows.

Understanding Quicken Accounts

Before you actually get down to the business of writing checks, let's take a few moments to discuss how Quicken organizes your financial information into accounts.

Quicken stores all your data into one or more *accounts*. You've already created your first bank account and the disk file for it when you started Quicken in Chapter 1. But there are a total of six different types (discussed on the next page) of Quicken accounts, each specially tailored to a specific purpose.

NOTE	See Chapter 8 for details on using all six types of Quicken accounts.

- *Bank accounts* record transactions in your "real-life" checking, savings, and money market accounts.
- *Cash accounts* monitor cash transactions.
- *Credit card accounts* track all your credit card purchases, charges, and payments.
- *Other asset accounts* are used to manage property, business equipment, or accounts receivable (the amounts owed to you by your customers).
- *Other liability accounts* are used to follow your mortgages, loans, and *accounts payable* (i.e., the amounts you owe for goods and supplies you've purchased).
- *Investment accounts* keep track of investments such as stocks, bonds, mutual funds, and so on.

Working with Bank Accounts

The account you set up in Chapter 1 is a Quicken bank account. Whatever other plans you may have for using Quicken, you'll want at least one bank account to serve as your computerized checking account.

A Quicken bank account looks and works on the screen much like your paper checkbook, except that Quicken makes all your calculations for you, automatically. The rest of this chapter leads you through the process of writing checks on your bank account. In Chapter 4, you'll learn how to use the bank account's register for entering transactions other than checks.

We'll start where we left off in Chapter 1—aside from the menu bar and iconbar, the register of your first bank account should be the only thing in the Quicken window. If you're not already running Quicken, start your computer, if necessary, get Windows going, and then run Quicken by double-clicking on its icon in the Program Manager.

You're now ready to display the Write Checks window where, of course, you'll actually write your checks. You can do this in several ways:

- Click on the **Check** icon on the iconbar (this is the quickest way).
- Choose **Write Checks** from the activities menu.
- Press **Ctrl-W**, the keyboard shortcut for switching to the Write Checks window.

In a moment, the Write Checks window appears, as shown in Figure 2.1. A quick look at the Write Checks window ought to convince you that it's a pretty fair imitation of a pad of real checks.

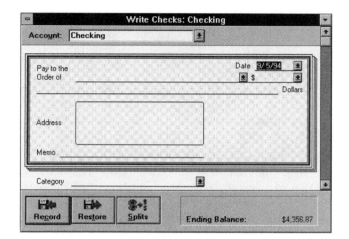

FIGURE 2.1

*The Write
Checks
window.*

Working with Quicken Windows

At this point, you should have two Quicken windows on your screen, the
Write Checks window you just opened, and the Register window you first
displayed in Chapter 1; Figure 2.2 shows you what I mean. I'm going to ask
you to postpone writing your first check just a little longer so you can see how
to use the Quicken window system.

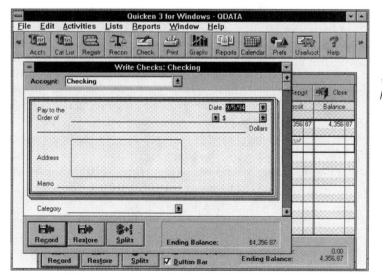

FIGURE 2.2

*The Quicken
screen with the
Write Checks
window and the
Register window
behind it.*

In Quicken for Windows, you can have an almost unlimited number of windows open at the same time, arranged on the screen as you see fit. This is great, because it means you can see what's going on in one window while you work with another.

At any one time, only one window is *active*, meaning that it's the only one you can actually do something with or to. If the active window overlaps any other window on the screen, the active one will always be "on top"—you'll be able to see the whole thing, and it will partially cover up the other window.

But when two windows don't overlap, the sure-fire way to tell which is the active window is the color of its *title bar*. (All windows have a bar stretching across the top that contains the title of the window.) Right now, the Write Checks window is active, and the color of its title bar is the color you'll see with any active window.

You can move from one window to another, activating the new window, any time you like. There are three main ways to activate a window, and you should try each of them now to go back and forth between the Write Checks and Register windows:

1. With the mouse, click on any visible part of the window you want to activate.
2. With the keyboard, press **Ctrl-Tab**. If more than two windows are open, you'll activate a new window in turn each time you press **Ctrl-Tab**.
3. With either the mouse or the keyboard, choose the window you want by name from Quicken's Window menu. Choose **Window**, then choose the name of the window on the menu. If you have more windows open than will fit on the list on the Window menu, a choice labelled **More Windows** appears at the bottom of the menu. Choosing this item displays a small list from which you can pick the window you want to activate.

You can change the size of any Quicken window or move it around on the screen with the standard Windows techniques for manipulating windows. To move a window with the mouse, drag the title bar wherever you want it.

To make the window exactly the size you'd like, point along any of the borders. When the pointer becomes a double-headed arrow, drag the border to your desired location (only that border moves). By dragging a corner, you can resize the window in both dimensions at the same time.

| NOTE | With the keyboard, it's more complicated, and slower, to move and resize windows, but you *can* do it. You can look up the instructions in your Windows manual if you're interested. |

You can *maximize* some Quicken windows, such as the register, so that they fill the entire workspace in the main Quicken window, letting you see more information. A window that can be maximized has a small button with an upward-pointing arrowhead in the top-right corner (but only when the window is active). Clicking on this button maximizes the window. The **Maximize** button turns into a little double-headed arrow. If you then click on the button, you *restore* the window to its former size.

NEW IN 3 In Quicken 3, the register window can be maximized. It cannot be maximized in Quicken 2.

SHORTCUT Actually, the easiest way to maximize a window (if it can be maximized) is to double-click anywhere on the title bar at the top of the window. This works throughout Windows.

Most active windows have **Minimize** buttons containing a downward-pointing arrowhead in the top-right corner. In windows that also have **Maximize/Restore** buttons, the **Minimize** button is just to the left. Minimizing a window by clicking this button removes it from view, turning the entire window into an icon at the bottom of the Quicken window. Try this now (assuming you have a mouse) with both the Write Checks and Register windows. The screen should look like Figure 2.3 when you're finished.

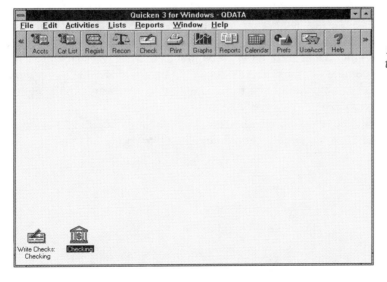

FIGURE 2.3

Your screen should look like this after you've minimized the Write Checks and Register windows.

To bring a minimized window back, just double-click on it. If you prefer, you can choose its name from the Window menu.

WARNING When you have only one account, there's no need to minimize the check or register windows, since you can call them up by clicking their icons on the iconbar. Once you have additional accounts, though, clicking the icons may bring up windows for the wrong accounts.

NOTE Why minimize a window? If you don't want the window to clutter up your screen, but you want to keep it really handy, just a mouse click away, minimizing it is the solution.

When you have multiple windows open, you can have Quicken arrange them neatly for you. Choose **Cascade** in the Window menu to display the windows in an offset "stack" on the screen. If you've minimized some windows and them moved their icons randomly, choose **Arrange Icons** in the Window menu to have Quicken space the icons evenly at the bottom of the screen.

Finally, you can *close* a window, removing it from the screen entirely. To do this, press **Ctrl-F4** (not **Alt-F4**—that shuts down Quicken itself) or double-click on the control box, the square containing a small rectangle at the top-left corner of the window. To close all open windows in one step, choose **Close All Windows** in the Window menu.

If you want to experiment with closing windows, go ahead, but bring them back to the screen by clicking on the **Register** and **Check** icons in the iconbar or by pressing **Ctrl-R** and **Ctrl-W**. Then move the windows so that they're at opposite corners: put the Write Checks window at the top left of the workspace and move the bottom-right corner of the Register window into the bottom-right corner of the workspace.

Activate the Write Checks window (if it's not already active, click on it or press **Ctrl-Tab**). The screen should now look like Figure 2.4.

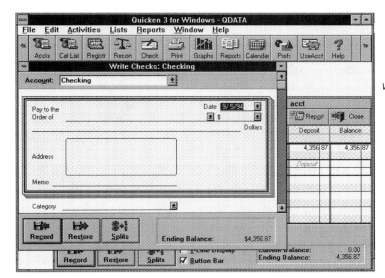

FIGURE 2.4

Arrange the Write Checks and Register windows like this on your screen.

Working with the Write Checks Window

All right, we're finally ready to tackle that first check. Take a close look at the Write Checks window. The screen check has fields that are just like a real check where you can fill in the date, the payee, the dollar amount, and a memo to remind you of your reason for spending the money.

Like many business checks, it even has a big space (a multiple-line field) for the payee's address. If you fill in this address field, Quicken prints the address on the check where it will show through the envelope window. (Windowed envelopes are available from Intuit along with Quicken checks.)

What's missing from the screen check? For one thing, there's no check number. That's because the check number is printed only on the real paper check. Quicken waits until you actually print the check to record the check number in your account, thus minimizing the possibility that you'll get the wrong number in your Quicken records. Missing, too, is your account number; but it's printed on your paper checks, and Quicken doesn't need it in order to work properly.

Of course, there's more to the Write Checks window than just the check. The window has a title bar across the top, which tells you you're in the Write Checks window and displays the name of the account this checkbook belongs to. Just under the check, the field labeled *Category* lets you assign the check to an expense category and/or class for more organized and informative record keeping.

At the right ends of four of the fields (*Date, Pay to the Order of, $,* and *Category*) notice the small downward-pointing arrows. As you'll see when you fill out the sample checks, these arrows provide shortcuts for making entries. For instance, the arrow in the *Date* field displays a tiny calendar from which you can select the date for the check. The arrow in the *$* field pops up a tiny calculator, with which you can enter dollar amounts using the mouse.

> **NOTE** In Quicken 2, only the *Pay to the Order of* and *Category* fields have arrows.

At the right side of the window, there's a scroll bar just like the one you've used in the Help window and probably in many other Windows programs. This is for moving through the "stack" of checks you've written—right now, of course, it doesn't do anything, since you haven't written any checks.

In the left half of the lower gray portion of the Write Checks window, notice the three buttons: The one on the left is labeled **Record**, the middle one says nothing at the moment, and the one on the right is labeled **Splits**. You'll learn what these are for shortly.

Over at the lower right there's space for three dollar amounts. At this point, you'll see only one of them, labeled **Ending Balance**. This is the balance of funds remaining in your account after the checks you've written have been recorded; at the moment, the amount is the same as the starting balance you entered when setting up the account.

Writing Your First Check

> **NOTE** Starting with this first check and continuing through Chapter 12, you'll be entering sample transactions into your Quicken accounts as you work through the tutorial exercises. You'll be reminded at the end of Chapter 12 to delete these practice transactions, but make a note to yourself to do so in case you don't complete all the exercises in order.

You're now ready to write your first check, but there's one more thing to clear up first. No matter how you plan to use Quicken, you should go ahead and fill in the check at this point in the tutorial. But be aware that the makers of Quicken recommend that you use the Write Checks window to enter checks only if you're planning to print them from within Quicken. If you plan instead to use Quicken simply to record the checks you've already written by hand, you're supposed to enter the check information in the register, rather than in the Write Checks window.

However, there are several good reasons for completing this part of the tutorial even if you plan to continue writing checks by hand. For one thing, when you see how easy it is to fill out checks in Quicken, it may convince you to give up your old ways. For another, you'll learn more about how the Quicken register works if you've written some checks before you use it. Finally, a little practice can't hurt, since you'll be deleting the sample checks you write during the tutorial anyway.

Now that you've gotten your bearings, it's time to write that first check. There's nothing to it. You just fill in the fields, exactly as you would on paper—except that Quicken fills in some of them for you.

NOTE	The procedure for writing checks varies slightly when you set up Quicken for electronic payment using the *CheckFree* service. See Chapter 17 for details.

Filling Out the *Date* Field

When you start on a new check, Quicken places the cursor in the *Date* field on the top line of the check to the right. As you can see, Quicken has already filled in the field with today's date, and has highlighted the entry in case you want to change it. In Quicken, as in most Windows programs, you can delete an entire set of highlighted characters simply by typing a new entry.

To see how this works, start typing a date prior to the one Quicken has entered using the month/day/year format. Don't type a later date, since Quicken makes special provisions for postdated checks—you'll learn all about postdating checks when you fill out your next practice check shortly. As you begin typing, Quicken erases the highlighted date in the field, making room for your new entry.

SHORTCUT	If you prefer, you can set Quicken to expect the day/month/year format for dates. See the Appendix for further details.

NOTE	Notice that as soon as you start making changes in a check the word *Restore* appears in the middle button at the bottom of the Write Checks window. Choosing this button restores the check's

contents to the way they were before you started making changes. By the way, Quicken won't let you type an incorrectly formatted date; if you do, you'll be asked to correct your entry before you continue.

Of course, to fill out a check you need a payee, an amount, and so on. At this point, since you'll be deleting the checks when you're through, it doesn't matter where these details come from. If you want to stick with the sample exercises I've prepared, copy the following fantasy information to the screen check:

Pay to the Order of:	**Mike's Music**
Amount:	**$545.19**
Address:	**Mike's Music**
	2993 Channing Way
	Hayfork, CA 96024
Memo:	**Saxophone purchase**
Category:	**Education**

Filling Out the *Pay to the Order of* and $ Fields

The cursor should now be blinking in the *Pay to the Order of* field (*payee* field, for short). Type in **Mike's Music** here, using the editing keys to correct any typing errors. Then press **Tab** (for this check, don't do anything with the little **Arrow** button at the far right of the field).

The cursor now jumps over to the $ field. Enter **545.19**, using either the numeric pad or the number keys along the top of your keyboard. When typing amounts in Quicken, don't bother adding the $, since it's there already, or any commas, since Quicken will put them in for you if there's room, and remove them if there isn't. When the amount is correct, your screen should look something like Figure 2.5.

SHORTCUT   If you're entering an even dollar amount with no cents in any Quicken money-related field, you don't need to type in the decimal point or the zeros past it; Quicken will add them for you.

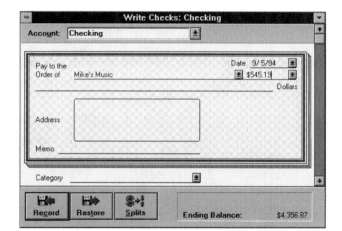

FIGURE 2.5

Your first check should look like this after you've filled in the $ field.

Now that the amount is filled in, you're about to experience one of Quicken's many remarkable timesaving features. Watch the screen while you press **Tab** to confirm your entry in the $ field. The results are shown in Figure 2.6. As you can see, Quicken writes out the amount of the check in words for you, using the same format most people use when filling out their checks by hand.

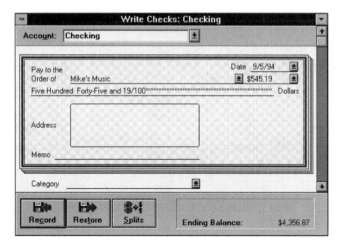

FIGURE 2.6

Quicken automatically writes out the amount of the check in words.

Filling Out the *Address* Field

The cursor should now be in the check's large *Address* field. When you're using a windowed envelope, you'll type the payee's address here. It will be printed so that it shows through the window when you put the check in the envelope.

NOTE

When you're writing checks that will be paid electronically via the CheckFree service, you can't type payee addresses into the *Address* field—in fact, the address field doesn't even appear on your screen. See Chapter 17 for information on writing checks for electronic payment.

If, as in the example, the first line of the address is the same as the payee name in the *Pay to the Order of* field, you don't need to retype the name. Make sure the cursor is still at the beginning of the top line of the *Address* field, and type ' (an apostrophe). Quicken will copy the name **Mike's Music** there and the cursor will move to the next line. Complete the remaining lines of the address, pressing **Tab** after each line.

NOTE

You can enter up to five lines in the *Address* field.

When you've entered the final line of the payee's address, press **Tab** until the cursor jumps down to the *Memo* field, which serves the same purpose as the memo blank on a paper check. Type in **Saxophone purchase** from the example, or anything you like—perhaps an account number, so your payee won't mix up your check, or something to jog your memory about why you wrote the check. If you're using Quicken window envelopes to mail your checks, whatever you've entered into the *Memo* field will show through the window.

SHORTCUT

If you need space for more memo-type information, you can have Quicken add an additional message field to your checks to the right of the *Address* field. That way, you'll be able to print both an account number and a reminder to yourself on the same check. To set up the extra *Message* field, use the **Checks** button in the Preferences window, as described in "Customizing Quicken" section of the Appendix.

Assigning the Check to a Category and Class

Press **Tab** to complete the memo entry. The check itself is finished. The cursor now jumps to the *Category* field below the check. Filling in the category field is optional, but you'll be sacrificing some of Quicken's most helpful capabilities if you leave the field empty. By assigning each check you write to an expense category, class, or both, you'll be able to examine your account to see where your money goes, or in other words, to see how much money you're spending on each kind of expense.

The format for an entry in the *Category* field is **category/class**. **Supplies/ Northeast** would be a valid entry, for example. You can enter a category only, such as **Supplies**, or a class only, such as **/Northeast**. As you can see, it's the / that indicates a class entry. You'll make your own entry in the *Category* field in a moment.

Understanding Categories and Classes

NOTE   Categories and classes are explained in detail in Chapter 5.

When applied to checks and other expense transactions in Quicken, a *category* is a general description of what type of goods or services you've spent your money on. In the realm of personal expenses, for example, typical categories in a personal bank account include food, housing, utilities, entertainment, taxes, and so on. If you're in business as a plumber, you might have categories for tools, travel, advertising, and taxes, and you might break down your expenses for supplies into separate categories such as pipes, fittings, toilets, and bathtubs.

Quicken's *classes* give you an alternative classification system for your expenses and other transactions that lets you see the same items from a different perspective. Often, a class name tells you who the check is made out to or who it's written by, or what project or property the check pertains to. Applied in this way, classes are very useful if you're in business. For example, your plumbing company might buy supplies from two or three different warehouses. To keep track of who's getting more of your business, and who has better prices over the long run, you might create a class for each of your two main suppliers: "Burgess & Round, Inc." and "Pete's Plumbing Palace."

Another good example is the situation where you use the same bank account for both business and personal expenses. You might have two classes, **Home** and **Business**, each of which would hold transactions that you've also assigned to the **Rent**, **Utilities**, and **Repairs** categories. This is the approach we'll take in the following examples.

Assigning Categories from the Category List

NOTE   When you write a single check to cover items that fall into two or more categories, you can split the transaction and enter separate amounts for each category in your records. You'll learn how to do this in Chapter 5.

You can type out your complete entries in the *Category* field if you like, but Quicken gives you several easier ways to assign categories and classes. Two of them let you do it by picking them from a list, which is how we'll do it this time; when you fill out the third sample transaction, you'll see how the QuickFill feature works to cut your typing.

With the cursor in the *Category* field, click the **Arrow** button at the right side of the field. As shown in Figure 2.7, this displays a list containing all the available categories in your account. Scroll through the list to any category you like and click on it to place it in the field (with the keyboard, you highlight the category name and then press **Enter**).

FIGURE 2.7

Selecting a category from the pop-up Category list.

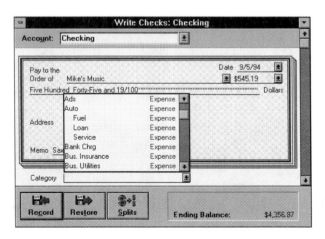

The pop-up Category list is convenient, but it only shows category names and whether they are income or expense categories. If you want more information to help you choose, you can pick your category from the Category List window. Do it that way for this check.

With the mouse, click on the **Cat List** icon on the iconbar; with the keyboard, press **Ctrl-C** (you can also choose **Category & Transfer**) from the List menu. Figure 2.8 shows the results.

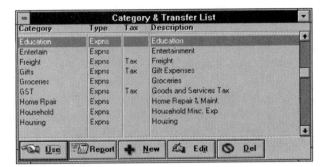

FIGURE 2.8

*The Category
and Transfer List
window.*

Using the Category List

As you can see, the Category and Transfer List window is devoted to a generous list of the categories already built into this account. You chose this group of categories back when you created the account file in the Standard Categories window.

NOTE | You'll learn what transfers are in Chapter 8.

The list is arranged in table format. The first column shows the category name. In this column, indented items are *subcategories*, which you can use to break down the main categories for more detailed record-keeping.

Then comes the type of category (expense, income, or subcategory, abbreviated **Expns, Inc**, and **Sub**, respectively). In the third column, Quicken displays the word *Tax* if the category is tax related; tax-related income categories are used for taxable income, while tax-related expense categories are used for tax deductible expenses. The final column shows a description of the category.

You'll learn how to add new items to the Category list, and how to enter their type, description, and tax information, when you fill out your second check in this tutorial. Later, in Chapter 5, you'll also learn how to edit and remove categories.

SHORTCUT   The quickest way to move to a particular category in the Category list is to press the key for the first letter of its name until that category is highlighted.

The Category list works much like a Quicken menu, but it gives you some additional ways to select items in the list. When the window first pops up, one of the items on the list is highlighted. To move the highlight to another choice on the list, use the **Up Arrow**, **Down Arrow**, **PgUp**, and **PgDn** keys.

You can also move directly to a particular section of the list alphabetically: When you press a **Letter** key, the highlight moves to the first item that starts with that letter. For example, try pressing **h**. If you chose the home categories when you set up your account, the highlight moves to **Home Rpair** immediately (another *h* category may be highlighted if you chose a different category group when you set up your account). Each time you press **h** again, the highlight moves to the next item that starts with an *H*—**Household**, then **Housing**, then back to **Home Rpair** again.

After you've experimented with these methods of moving around in the Category list, you'll be ready to select a category for the check you're filling out. If you're using our sample information, note that the saxophone purchase is being dignified as an educational expense item, so you should choose **Education**. If you opt for another category, be sure the one you choose is listed **Expns** in the **Type** column; you're paying this check, not cashing it.

Once you've highlighted the category, press Ent**er**. The Category and Transfer List window will disappear, and you'll see the category name appear in the *Category* field on the Write Checks window.

Making Corrections to Your Check

You've just completed all the fields for this check. But let's say you look at the screen and notice that you've made a mistake in one of the fields—in the payee's address, perhaps. To correct the error, start by moving to the *Payee* field. For practice, change the payee from **Mike's Music** to **Sound Tools**. Begin by moving the cursor to the *Pay to the Order of* field.

With the mouse, position the mouse pointer just to the left of the first M in Mike's, then drag to the right across the entire entry until it's completely highlighted. Then just type **Sound Tools**—the previous entry gets deleted automatically as soon as you start typing. (If you want to change only a single word in an existing entry, you can double-click the word to highlight it.)

<table>
<tr><td>SHORTCUT</td><td>You can move the cursor (and the highlight) from line to line of the Address field by pressing Up Arrow or Down Arrow.</td></tr>
</table>

Even if you have a mouse, you may find the keyboard is easier and quicker when you're typing in numerous checks. Start by pressing **Tab** repeatedly to move the cursor from field to field. Since you're beginning from the *Category* field, you'll first highlight each of the three buttons below the check in turn. Then the cursor jumps to the *Date* field. Press **Tab** again to move to the *Payee* field. Note that Quicken highlights the entire existing entry in each field when the cursor arrives.

Now try moving the cursor in the reverse direction by pressing **Shift-Tab.** When you reach the *Date* field, pressing **Shift-Tab** another time highlights the **Splits** button at the bottom of the window. If you keep going, you'll eventually reach the *Payee* field again where you can make the change. Again, since the entire existing entry is highlighted, you can replace it without deleting individual characters simply by typing **Sound Tools**.

If you want to update the address as well, highlight the first line of the *Address* field, then type ' to copy **Sound Tools** there. The check is complete, so record it by pressing Enter or choosing **Record**.

Recording the Check

Now that you've finished your first check, it's time to record it in your account. The quickest way to do this is simply to press **Enter**. If you prefer, you can choose the **Record** button at the lower left of the window, or you can click on it with the mouse, or press Tab again to move the highlight to the button and then pressing **Enter**.

The only reason to use the latter, more complicated keyboard method is if you've changed Quicken's settings on the Preferences menu so that pressing Enter moves the cursor from field to field, as the Tab key does.

Quicken beeps as it saves the new check in your account file on your data disk. As soon as the check is recorded on your data disk—the process is almost instantaneous—the finished check moves up and off your screen, revealing the next blank check in your electronic checkbook. Figure 2.9 shows what your screen will look like (the numbers in the lower-right corner will be different if you entered a different starting balance or check amount than the ones shown in the samples).

FIGURE 2.9

Your second blank check.

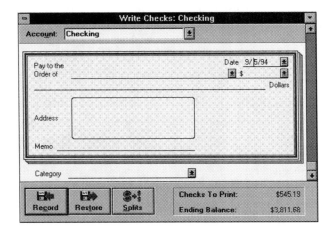

Since Quicken saves each check in your account file as soon as you record it, you never have to worry about losing large amounts of data if the power goes off suddenly while you're working. In addition, you don't need to bother remembering to save your work from time to time as you do in most programs. You do need to make backup disks, however; see the instructions in Chapter 4.

Everything looks pretty much like your first blank check, but notice that there are some changes in the window. For one thing, the ending balance at the lower-right corner has been reduced by the amount of the check you've just written. Above the ending balance, the *Checks to Print* notation keeps a running total of the amounts of all the checks you write until you print them, and at this point, it is simply the amount of the check you've just written. When you write other checks, their amounts get added in as you go.

Browsing Your Checks

If you have a number of unprinted checks and you want to view a specific one, you can use Quicken's **Find** or **Go to Date** features to locate checks that contain entries matching the information you're looking for. You'll learn how to use these features when you work with the register in Chapter 4.

NEW IN 3   Another change: The scroll box has moved to the bottom of the scroll bar. This means that the new blank check is the "bottom" check in your screen check pad, indicating that you've entered other checks before this one. In the Write Checks window you can move whenever you like from the check currently on the window to any other check you've written before or since. This lets you browse through the checks and, if necessary, make corrections before you print.

Try going back to the previous check, the one you just completed. Press **PgUp**, and you'll see the check you just completed appear. Figure 2.10 shows what the screen should look like when it comes to rest.

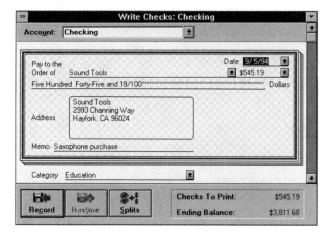

FIGURE 2.10

The Write Checks window after you've displayed the first check again.

| NOTE | The scroll box is now at the top of the scroll bar. This indicates that you've started or completed other checks (in this case, just one) after the one that's now on the screen. Notice that the numbers in the lower right of the screen haven't changed; they reflect the totals for all the checks you've written and not yet printed, no matter which check you're looking at. |

Whenever a check you've previously entered is on the screen, you can make changes or corrections in any of the fields as necessary. You'll practice this a little later. For now, press **PgDn** to move back to the new blank check. Again, the scroll box moves to the bottom of the scroll bar.

Writing Your Second Check

NOTE In Chapter 7 you'll learn how to get Quicken to *memorize* checks you write regularly, so that you don't have to retype them each time you want to print them.

Once you've filled out your first check, you should have no trouble with the next one. But to keep things interesting, you'll learn some additional skills this time. You'll see how to enter dates and dollar amounts with the mouse, how and why to postdate a check, and you'll learn how to create new categories and classes and assign them to your transactions.

The cursor should be in the *Date* field of the new check; Quicken has automatically selected the entire date. You should postdate this sample check: that is, enter a date a few day's *later* than today's date.

With the mouse, you can use Quicken's pop-up mini-calendar to do the job. Click on the downward-pointing **Arrow** button at the right of the *Date* field. The pop-up calendar appears, as shown in Figure 2.11. Notice that today's date is displayed in bold type, and it should be outlined as well. Click on another date a few days from now; if necessary, you can switch months by clicking on the **Arrow** buttons at the top of the calendar. When you choose the new date, the outline moves to that date. The calendar then closes automatically, and the new date appears in the check's *Date* field.

FIGURE 2.11

Use the pop-up calendar to date your check.

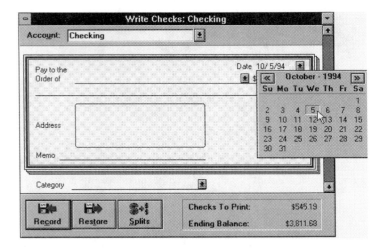

NOTE	Quicken 2 lacks the calendar, so you have to type in the date yourself or use the date shortcut keys: + to increase the date one day, - to decrease it.

Understanding Postdated Checks

As most of us know, postdating a check can be a crude but effective way to keep creditors at bay. In Quicken, though, postdating is usually used for more honorable purposes. If you like to pay all your bills in a single session, but want to hold onto your money as long as you can, you can fill out each check with a date a few days before the payment is actually due. Then when it's time to send in the check, you only need to print it and mail it. In fact, you can have Quicken remind you when it's time.

Postdating can also be a quick budgeting tool. Just fill out the checks you expect to pay, postdated to when the payments are due. Quicken will automatically total the amounts of all your postdated checks, so you can see how much money you're going to have to come up with to cover them. Finally, postdating is useful when you're working with the Checkfree system to pay your bills electronically (see Chapter 15).

You'll learn more about how postdating works in a moment. When you've entered a valid future date in the *Date* field, press **Tab** to advance to the *Pay to the Order of* field.

Entering the Payee

Before you start typing the payee for the new check, click on the little **Arrow** button at the right of the field. This button opens a drop-down list with all the payees to whom you've previously written checks—in this case, just Sound Tools. If you wanted to use the same payee, and even to copy all the check details from the check you wrote to that payee, you'd select the payee from the list.

But don't do that now. Instead, type in the payee's name for the second sample check as shown in Figure 2.12 on the next page. (The drop-down list remains visible until you press **Tab**, but it won't interfere with your typing).

After you press **Tab**, copy the dollar amount and address into the appropriate fields.

FIGURE 2.12

*The second
sample check.*

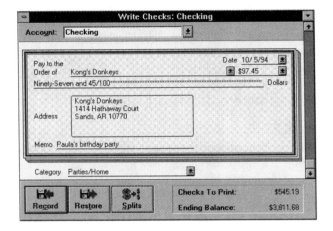

Creating a New Category

The cursor should now be in the *Category* field. This time, instead of using one
of Quicken's built-in categories, you'll create a new one and designate a class
as well.

Working from the sample check shown in Figure 2.11 on page 56, type in
the entry **Parties/Home**. If you want to make an entry of your own in the
Category field, feel free, but be sure to enter both a category and a class. You're
limited to 15 characters for each item. Remember to separate them with a /.

Press **Tab** to confirm your entry in the *Category* field. When you do,
Quicken scans the entry, comparing it to the categories already used in the
account. If it finds that your entry doesn't yet exist, Quicken assumes you
want to add the category and displays the Set Up Category window (Figure
2.13). (At this point, if you don't want to set up a new category, click on the
Cancel button or press **Esc** to return to the check.)

NOTE

If you are working with Quicken 2, you'll first see a small window
asking whether you want to set up a new category, select one from
the category list, or cancel the process, going back to the check to
type a new category entry.

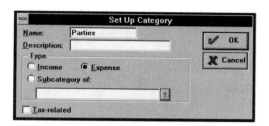

FIGURE 2.13

The Set Up Category window.

As you can see, Quicken has automatically copied the category name you entered on the check into the *Name* field in the Set Up Category window. The cursor is now in the field labeled *Description*. Since you're limited to only 15 characters in the category name, you may want to enter a more complete description of the category here. As you can see, however, filling in the *Description* field is optional. After you've made your entry, press **Tab**.

The next field, *Type*, consists of a set of three radio buttons: **Income**, **Expense**, and **Subcategory**. Since you're writing a check, Quicken assumes your new category is the expense type, and selects the **Expense** radio button for you. (If you needed to, however, you could specify another type by choosing the appropriate radio button here.) The **Expense** type is correct for our sample check.

| NOTE | As you'll learn in Chapter 5, you can assign each category to a specific line item on a particular IRS tax form. |

Use the field labeled *Tax-Related*, to tell Quicken whether to count entries in this category for tax purposes. This field is a checkbox, meaning that it can be either on or off. When a checkbox field is turned on, an X fills the box next to the field description. In this case, Quicken assumes that the new category is not tax related, so the checkbox remains blank. This assumption is valid for the sample check.

If you were creating a tax-related category—one for expenses that are tax deductible or can be used as tax credits—you would turn on this field. Here's how: With the mouse, click on anywhere in the field; with the keyboard, press Tab until the field is highlighted with the dashed rectangle, then press the space bar. Once a checkbox is checked, you use the same techniques to uncheck it, turning off the field.

Once all the fields are complete, press **Enter** or choose **OK** to finalize your new category and have Quicken store the category information.

Assigning Your Check to a Class

At this point, since you've also entered a class that doesn't yet exist in the *Category* field, you will see the Set Up Class window, as shown in Figure 2.14.

FIGURE 2.14

The Set Up Class window.

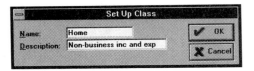

| SHORTCUT | Instead of typing the name of an existing class into the *Category* field you can enter it there by choosing it from a list, just as you can with categories. The details are covered in Chapter 5. |

As you can see, the Set Up Class window is a bit simpler than the Set Up Category window. All you have to do is enter a description for your new class, if you want one, and then press **Enter**. Quicken saves the class information and returns you to the Write Checks window, where the cursor should still be in the *Category* field.

To confirm that Quicken has really added your new category and class to the account, press **Ctrl-C**, the keyboard shortcut for popping up the Category and Transfer List window. The category you've just entered will be highlighted in the list. Press **Esc** to close the window, then press **Ctrl-L** to pop up the Class List window. Again, your new class will be highlighted in the list. Press **Esc** to close the Class List window.

Completing your Second Check

You've just finished filling out your second check. Record the new check in your checking account by pressing **Enter** or choosing **Record**. Quicken removes your check and displays another new blank check in its place (Figure 2.15). Remember that this was a postdated check; that's why there's now a new notation, **Current Balance**, in the lower-right corner.

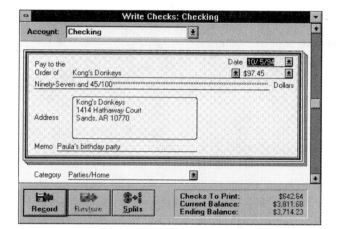

FIGURE 2.15

The Write Checks window after you've completed your second check.

The **Current Balance** line tells you how much you'll have in your account after you print the checks dated today or earlier. In other words, the **Current Balance** does not reflect the amounts of any postdated checks you write, since Quicken assumes those checks won't be paid until the dates on the checks. On the other hand, the **Ending Balance** shows how much you'd have if all the checks you've written were cashed today. The **Ending Balance** comes in handy because, if you want to know the total amount of all the postdated checks you've written, all you need to do is subtract it from the **Current Balance**.

Finally, the **Checks to Print** item totals all the checks you've written and not yet printed, postdated or not. After you print the checks dated today or earlier, **Checks to Print** will also give you the total amount of your postdated checks.

Completing a Third Check

You can take advantage of another shortcut for selecting category and class entries. To practice this technique, fill out a third sample check. Begin by changing the check date back to the current date, since you don't want this check to be postdated.

This time, use one of Quicken's date shortcut keys to change the date: Press repeatedly the **Dash** or **Minus** key to decrease the date by one day each time. Keep going until the field shows today's or an earlier date.

You'll fill in the remaining fields as follows:

Payee: **Lincoln, Blincoln, & Knodd**
Amount: **$545.25**
Memo: **Tax audit, monthly retainer**
Category: **L&P Fees/Business**

Using the Quicken Calculators

After completing the *Payee* field, press **Tab** to move to the $ field. Let's say you're writing this check to cover two separate bills from your lawyers, one covering the monthly retainer you pay them, and one for a special consultation about an upcoming tax audit. They sent the two bills separately and didn't total them for you.

Of course, Quicken automatically handles the calculations for you on data that you actually enter into your accounts. But whenever you need to do some scratch-pad arithmetic, you can pop up a Quicken calculator to handle the computations.

This is especially easy when you're filling out a check. In fact, you may prefer to enter the dollar amounts of your checks using the pop-up calculator, even if you don't have any calculations to make. Just click on the **Arrow** button at the right of the $ field to display a small calculator. It works like any hand-held calculator, except that you can enter numbers and select math operations by clicking on the "keys" with the mouse. Use the button marked with an arrow pointing to the left to erase the last numeral you typed.

The numbers that you type or that Quicken calculates appear directly in the $ field on the check. As soon as you click the = button, the calculator closes.

| NOTE |

Actually, Quicken can account for a series of separate items that you pay with one check, adding their amounts without requiring you to use the calculator. This feature, called **splitting a transaction**, is covered in Chapter 5.

NEW IN 3   Quicken also provides a larger, slightly more capable calculator in a separate window for use at other times. To activate the calculator, click on the **Calculator** icon on the iconbar, or choose **Use Calculator** in the Activities menu. As you can see in Figure 2.16, this Quicken calculator has buttons for storing a number in memory, recalling a stored value, and clearing the calculator's memory (labeled **MS, MR**, and **MC**, respectively). When a value has been stored, an *M* appears in the small square toward the upper right of the calculator.

The calculator is new in Quicken 3. Quicken 2 lacks its own calculator, but it does allow you to call up the standard Windows calculator automatically with the same commands.

FIGURE 2.16

The Quicken calculator.

Unfortunately, you can't transfer results from the Quicken calculator to other parts of Quicken. Another drawback of the Quicken calculator is that you can't use it in combination with some dialog boxes, including those for planning retirement and evaluation mortgages. To overcome these problems, use Windows' standard calculator instead.

NOTE   If you need to transfer the results of a calculation into a *Memo* field or into a field in a dialog box, use the Windows calculator instead of Quicken's. Run the calculator by double-clicking on its icon in Program Manager, usually located in the Accessories group. Once the calculator is running, you can switch back and forth between it and Quicken by pressing **Alt-Tab**—even when a Quicken dialog box is active. When you've completed a calculation, transfer it to Quicken as follows: Choose **Copy** from the Edit menu on the calculator's menu, or press **Ctrl-C**. Switch back to Quicken (by pressing **Alt-Tab** or by clicking anywhere on the Quicken window). With the cursor in the field where you want to enter your calculation result, press **Ctrl-V** or **Shift-Ins**.

Making Category Entries with QuickFill

When you reach the *Category* field, you're ready to use QuickFill. QuickFill "watches" as you type, searching the category list to find a matching category. It automatically fills out the rest of your entry based on the first match it finds. The characters QuickFill types for you are displayed in another color or shade to distinguish them from your entry.

The category entry for this check will be **L&P Fees/Business**. With QuickFill, all you have to do is type **L** and Quicken finishes the **L&P Fees** entry for you. You're then ready to type in the class entry.

Press **End** to move to the end of the **L&P Fees** entry and then type **/Business** and press **Enter**. Since this is a new class, you'll be given the opportunity to create it through the Set Up Class window just as when you defined the **Home** class for the previous check. After the class entry is complete, record the check by pressing **Enter**.

QuickFill works when you're making nearly automatic class entries just as it does for categories. You can find more details on using QuickFill for category and class entries in "Assigning Transactions to Categories and Classes" in Chapter 5.

You can use a modified version of this shortcut if your category list contains several categories that begin with the same first few letters. Type the first letter of the category you want, and then press **Ctrl-C**. The Category list will appear, showing the first category beginning with that letter. The correct item will be nearby on the list, so scroll to it with the **UpArrow** or **DownArrow** key and press **Enter** to enter it in your check.

Changing an Earlier Check

Now that you've written some checks, let's review how to browse through them and try changing one in the process. Again, since the scroll box is at the bottom of the scroll bar, this is the most recent check you've started, and you've written other checks before it.

Press **Home** three times to move to the first check you filled out, the one made out to Sound Tools if you've been copying the samples provided here. Again, notice that the scroll box is at the top of its bar, showing that this is the first check in the stack. Now press **PgDn** to move to the second check in the stack (no longer the second check you wrote, since Quicken has reordered them by date). You'll see both upward and downward arrows, indicating you're in the middle of the stack. This is the check we'll change.

When you move to another check in the stack, Quicken always places the cursor at the beginning of the *Date* field. Feel free to make any change you like in the check. Move from field to field by pressing **Tab** or **Shift-Tab**, then delete characters and type in new ones. Use the editing techniques you learned in "Editing Entries" earlier in this chapter.

No matter how radical your changes, you can restore the original check data at any time by choosing the **Restore** button; try it now.

Feel free to make permanent changes in the check. When you're happy with the new entries, record the new version of the check in one of the ways you've learned.

Quicken makes the changes in the permanent data file, completely replacing the previous information. As usual, you will be advanced to the next check in your stack automatically. Press **PgDn** to move to the fourth check, which should be blank.

Filling Out Additional Checks

In the next chapter, you'll be shown how to print out your first Quicken check. Before you do, though, take the time to enter a few more checks, so you'll have several to work with when you practice with the Check Register and Reports activities (four or five more checks will be enough).

By now, you're in a position to fill out some real checks and pay some real bills, if you know the payees and amounts for them. But if you're not ready for this, you can use the following sample checks to get you started. Fill out each check with the techniques you've just learned. If you want your screens to look like the illustrations in this book, date the first two checks with today's date, but postdate the third check to a later date.

Date:	(today's date)
Payee:	**Mid-States Gas and Electric**
Amount:	**$74.87**
Memo:	**Utilities bill**
Category:	**Utilities/Business**

Date:	(today's date)
Payee:	**Professor Horace Quickmire**
Amount:	**$350.00**

Memo: **Microscope purchase**
Category: **Education/Home**

Date: (postdated)
Payee: **Kelly's BellyDancers**
Amount: **$40**
Memo: **Paula's birthday party**
Category: **Parties/Home**

Once you've filled out six or more checks, you'll be ready to part with some of the play money when you print out practice checks in the next chapter. Of course, if you want to keep working now, you can go directly to Chapter 3. Remember, Quicken saves each check as you go, so you don't need to worry about saving your work from time to time. But if you'd rather take a break at this point, press **Alt-F4** to leave Quicken and to return to the Program Manager.

Summary

Now that you've completed this chapter, you've already mastered some of the most critical Quicken skills: how to fill out and correct fields, how to assign transactions to categories and classes, and, of course, how to write and record checks. You've also learned how to browse through a stack of completed checks. With these basics under your belt, you're ready to print the checks you've written, a task you'll complete in Chapter 3.

Chapter Three
Printing Your Checks

s easy as Quicken makes it to fill out checks on the screen, your creditors won't be happy until they have those all-important paper checks in their hands. Obviously, if you want to keep the collection agency at bay, you're going to have to print the checks you fill out.

If you've been following the tutorial, you've just written approximately half a dozen checks. In this chapter, you'll move on to print two of them for practice. If you left Quicken at the end of the last chapter, restart the program now. The Write Checks window should be active. If not, activate it by pressing **Ctrl-W** or clicking on any part of the window you can see.

NOTE	You can also use Quicken's **CheckFree** feature to pay your bills electronically, without checks—an option you'll learn about in Chapter 17.

Getting Ready to Print

To make learning to print checks really easy, Quicken comes with about 20 sample checks you can use for your practice check-printing session. They're just like the checks you can order from Intuit, Quicken's manufacturer, except that they have a generic address and account number where your own would be printed.

NOTE   Even if you've lost the sample checks, you can still practice printing checks using ordinary paper. Of course, with this stop-gap, Quicken will only print the entries you've typed in the fields on your screen checks, not information, such as your address and account number, that is supposed to be preprinted on the paper check. You'll have to imagine the missing details, but you'll still get an excellent idea of the steps involved in check printing.

I recommend that you try the printing part of the tutorial even if you don't plan to use Quicken for check printing. You'll see how easy and convenient the process is, and you'll understand more about the way the checking account register works when we get to the next chapter. Besides, once you see how easy Quicken makes check writing, you'll probably want to print as many checks as possible with it.

Unless you're absolutely sure you'll never use Quicken to print your real checks, your first task should be to order personalized checks for use with the program if you haven't already done so. There are three check styles for each of the two main types of printers (continuous feed and page oriented, meaning laser printers and similar models). The three check-style choices are standard, voucher, and wallet.

- *Standard checks* are the large business-type checks. They are 3" tall and come three to a letter-size page.
- *Voucher checks* print one to a page and include a separate tear-off voucher on which Quicken prints a summary of the check information.
- *Wallet checks*, of course, are small enough to fit in your wallet—they're the same size as the typical check for a personal checking account.

The sample checks included with Quicken are the standard variety. If you plan to use voucher or wallet checks, you should wait until your check order arrives and print your samples on them.

Setting Up Your Printer

Like almost all Windows programs, Quicken communicates with your printer through Windows. So, before you begin printing Quicken checks, you must be sure that you've set up Windows properly for your printer.

Most likely, you've already configured Windows to work with your printer, probably at the time you installed Windows itself. If you've been printing successfully from other Windows programs, Quicken should print properly as well. You may need to fine-tune some printer settings for best results, but you can make these minor adjustments from within Quicken (see "Printer Setup in Quicken").

However, there are two situations in which you'll need to leave Quicken to make changes to your printer setup:

- To set up a new printer for use with Windows, you must use the Windows control panel to install the correct printer driver, the software module needed for your printer model.

- If you connect the printer to a different *port* (*serial*, *parallel*, or *direct*) on your computer, you must use the Connect dialog box in the control panel to tell Windows about the change.

Using Windows' task-switching capabilities, you can switch to the control panel and make the necessary changes while Quicken is still running. You'll find instructions for using the control panel to install printer drivers and select printer ports in your Windows manual. When you're finished, close the control panel and switch back to Quicken; any changes you've made take effect immediately.

Printer Setup in Quicken

Once you've set up Windows for your printer and the correct printer port, you can focus your attention on the details of printer setup with Quicken. Most of these adjustments pertain only to Quicken, but in some cases, you'll need to modify Windows' settings for your printer. In particular, if you're using a continuous-feed printer, you must change the Windows' paper size setting for your printer to match the type of checks you're printing. You can make such changes without leaving Quicken (see the following section "Changing Windows' Printer Settings").

Quicken for Windows lets you specify two separate printer setups, one for printing reports, and one for printing checks. If you have two physically separate printers, you can assign one machine to check-printing duties and the other to reports, if you prefer. More commonly, you'll be using the same printer for both jobs. Still, having two setups to work with lets you use, say, one font for checks, and different fonts for reports.

Since you'll be printing checks in this chapter, I'll walk you through the steps for setting up your check printer here. The basics are the same for setting up the report printer, but I'll cover the details in Chapter 10.

To begin the setup process, choose **Printer Setup** and **Check Printing Setup** in the File menu. You'll see the Check Printer Setup dialog box, shown in Figure 3.1. This dialog box looks pretty simple, but there's more to it than first meets the eye.

FIGURE 3.1

The Check Printer Setup dialog box.

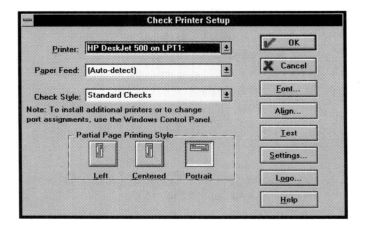

The first field, *Printer*, lets you choose which printer you want to print checks with, of those you've installed into Windows. Pick the name of the printer you want from the drop-down list. To see the list, click on the **Downward-Pointing** arrow to the right of the field. With the keyboard alone, you can't see the entire list, but you can move through the various options by pressing the **Down Arrow** or **Up Arrow** keys.

The next field, *Paper Feed*, tells Quicken whether your printer feeds paper as continuous, fan-folded sheets (as most dot-matrix printers do) or as individual pages, one at a time (like all laser printers and many inkjet machines). In most cases, you can leave this field set to **Auto-detect**, meaning that Quicken will figure out which type of paper feeding your printer uses. If there's a problem, you can explicitly set the field to **Continuous** or **Page Oriented**, as appropriate.

The next field is labeled *Check Style*. From this list, choose the type of check you're using: **standard, wallet,** or **voucher.**

At the bottom of the window is a set of three buttons labeled **Partial Page Printing Style**. You can only make a choice here if you're setting up a page-oriented printer. This setting provides for a common check-printing situation. Inevitably, you will sometimes print only one or two of the three checks on a laser check page. In order to avoid wasting the remaining blank checks, Quicken will print on a partial page of one or two checks at your command. However, Quicken needs to know how these partial pages will be positioned (oriented) in your printer.

With some page-oriented printers, it's best to feed a partial page rotated "sideways," with the long edge of the check parallel to the paper path. Choose either the **Left** or **Centered** button for this type of printer, depending on whether you're supposed to feed the page flush with the left side of the input tray or down the center of the tray. Other printers accept partial pages the "regular" way, with the long edge of the check toward the printer. If you have this type of printer, choose **Portrait**.

NOTE	Some page-oriented printers (e.g., HP DeskJet) require special "forms leaders" you can purchase from Intuit in order to print partial pages of checks. When you order, be sure to specify that you have a page-oriented printer.

How do you know which of these settings is best for your printer? The answer is simple: Use the instructions given in your printer manual for printing envelopes. Here are the settings for some popular printers:

Centered   HP LaserJet Series II and LaserJet III, Apple LaserWriter II, Canon LBP-8

Left   HP LaserJet IIp and IIIp, Apple Personal LaserWriter, Canon LBP-4

Portrait   HP DeskJet series

Changing the Font for Check Printing

You've always wanted to make an impression with your checks, right? How about a big, bold, gaudy font that makes the payee name and the amount jump out at the innocent reader? Or, for a more subtle effect, how about reinforcing your small business's public identity by printing your checks with the same font you use on your distinguished-looking letterhead?

In Quicken for Windows, you can print your check data in any Windows font available for your printer. Quicken prints all the information in the same font, but at least you're not restricted to dull, typewriter-like Courier anymore.

To select a new font for check printing, choose the **Font** button in the Check Printer Setup window. The Check Printer Font window appears (Figure 3.2). In the appropriate fields, select the name of the font, the font style (regular, italic, bold, or bold-italic), and the size. You can choose any whole-number size from 8 to 13 points. Quicken won't accept larger or smaller entries or fractional point sizes.

NOTE For high-quality printing, the safest course is to select a TrueType font (or, if you're using another font manager such as Adobe Type Manager, any other scalable font). That way, you don't have to worry whether you have a copy of the font in the particular size you want to use.

FIGURE 3.2

The Check Printer Font window.

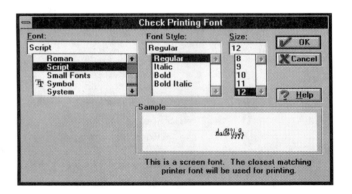

As you make selections in the Font dialog box, Quicken displays a sample of how your font choice will look on the check in the lower-right corner of the window. When you're happy with the font, click **OK**.

NOTE One caveat: The font you choose does not appear on the screen check in the Write Checks window.

Printing a Logo on Your Checks

NEW IN 3 Quicken 3 lets you print a custom logo on your checks. You'll need a "bitmap" graphic image no larger than 1" square, which is stored in the standard Windows format (the BMP format—the file's name should end with the extension **.BMP**).

To designate this file as your logo, choose the **Logo** button in the Check Printer Setup window. The Check Logo Artwork dialog box that appears (Figure 3.3) shows the current logo graphic (or if there is none, a blank area). To select a new logo file, choose the **File** button, then navigate to the disk drive and directory where the file is stored. Select the file from the File Name list, then choose **OK** to return to the Logo dialog box. The graphic should appear there. If all looks well, choose **OK** again to go back to the Setup Check Printer window.

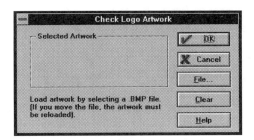

FIGURE 3.3

Add a logo to your checks with the Logo dialog box.

Changing Windows' Printer Settings

In some cases, you'll have to make adjustments to Windows' basic settings for your printer. For example, if you've previously set up your printer using the control panel for sideways or landscape-orientation printing, you must switch it to portrait orientation to print checks with Quicken. And it's especially vital in the case of continuous-feed printers that the paper size, another control panel setting, match the size of your checks.

To simplify this process, Quicken lets you access the control panel's Setup window for the current printer. To do this, start from the Check Printer Setup dialog box. After selecting the printer you want to work with in the *Printer* field, choose the **Settings** button. In the new dialog box that appears, what you'll see depends on the particular printer you're working with. Typically, you get options for specifying paper size, available memory, paper-feeding method, and fonts. You can now make any necessary changes in the printer settings using the same techniques you would in the control panel to select from the available options. Figure 3.4 on the next page shows the Setup window for the Hewlett-Packard DeskJet 500.

FIGURE 3.4

*This is the first
setup window if
your printer
is an HP Desk-
Jet 500.*

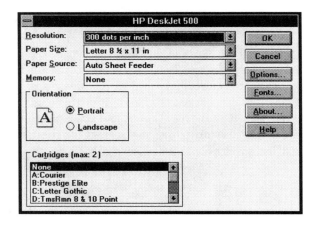

If you have a continuous-feed printer, you must make Windows' paper-size
setting match the height of a single check. The correct height varies depending
on the type of check you'll be using (standard, voucher, or wallet).

In Windows 3.1, use the *Paper Size* field. Begin by opening the drop-down
list by clicking on the arrow to the right of the field. Select the choice labeled
User Defined Size at the bottom of the drop-down list (you may have to scroll
the list to see it). If you don't have a mouse, press the **~DA** key until *User
Defined Size* appears in the field.

At this point, a secondary dialog box appears as shown in Figure 3.5. Select
the **Units** radio button labeled 0.01 inch, then type one of the following values
into the *Length* field:

Check Type	Length
Standard	350
Wallet	284
Voucher	700

FIGURE 3.5

*Enter the
correct length
in this dialog box.*

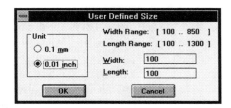

When you're through making changes to the Windows printer settings, choose **OK** to return to Quicken's Check Printer Setup window.

Printing a Test Check

To make sure that your checks are positioned properly in the printer, and that the printing process itself is working, it's best to start by printing a test check. Quicken has a built-in feature for this very purpose.

After you've printed your first test check, you'll examine it, adjust Quicken's check positioning as necessary, and repeat the process until the check looks right (you shouldn't have to print more than three test checks to get satisfactory results). Again, if there's a problem with printing the test check (other than positioning) you'll find the solution in the section on printer troubleshooting at the end of this chapter. Once you've printed a test check correctly, you can go on to printing some real checks.

Let's review in detail the process of printing test checks. Begin from the Check Printer Setup window.

NOTE	In Quicken 2 for Windows, test checks are referred to as "sample" checks, and the button for printing samples appears on the Print Checks window, not the Check Printer Setup window. To open the proper window, choose **Print Checks** in the File menu or press **Ctrl-P**. Other parts of the procedure are the same as described here.

From this point on, the method you use to print test checks varies a bit depending on the type of printer you have:

- If you have a laser printer, a Hewlett-Packard DeskJet, or any other printer that prints only single sheets and pulls the paper in automatically, refer to the following section.

- If your printer uses continuous paper, use the instructions in the subsection "Printing Test Checks with a Continuous-Feed Printer."

- If you have a daisy-wheel or other printer that accepts only single sheets of paper, but that lets you control paper position, read "Printing Test Checks with a Single-Sheet Printer."

Printing Test Checks on a Laser or Other Page-Oriented Printer

If your printer feeds single sheets of paper automatically, so that it alone controls how they are positioned, you obviously can't change the way your test check is positioned. All you need to do is make sure that Quicken knows exactly where on the check to print the check information.

Prepare for check printing by placing the separate-sheet pages of sample checks into the printer's input paper tray. If you have any model of Hewlett-Packard LaserJet Series II, III, or 4, you should place the checks in the tray printed side up, with their tops toward the printer. With the original LaserJet, LaserJet Plus, or the DeskJet, place the checks face down in the tray. If you have another make of printer, consult your owner's manual for advice on how to load the checks properly.

The Check Printer Setup window should already be on your screen. If not, choose **Printer Setup** and **Check Printer Setup** in the File menu to display it. Be sure the correct check style, **standard**, **voucher**, or **wallet**, is selected in the *Check Style* field.

Be aware that the adjustments you make in the process of printing the test checks are specific for the selected check style. If you change check styles, you'll have to repeat the adjustments for the new style.

Printing the Test Checks

Be sure the printer is on and ready to print, then choose **Test** to print the test check.

| NOTE | Quicken only prints one test check even on a three-check page.

After the check emerges, look it over closely. Quicken has printed example entries where it thinks the date, amount, and payee are supposed to be and a saccharine message in the *Memo* field. Satisfy yourself that the text is printed in the proper fields and with the proper spacing.

If everything looks right, proceed to the section "Printing Your Practice Checks," which follows. If you need to adjust the print position, choose **Align** in the Check Printer Setup window to display an alignment window, which you'll work with in the next section.

Adjusting the Check Printing Position

The Check Printer Alignment window shown in Figure 3.6 lets you change the position on your checks where Quicken prints the check data (the date, the amount, and so on). You can only adjust the relative position for the entire check, not the positions of the individual fields.

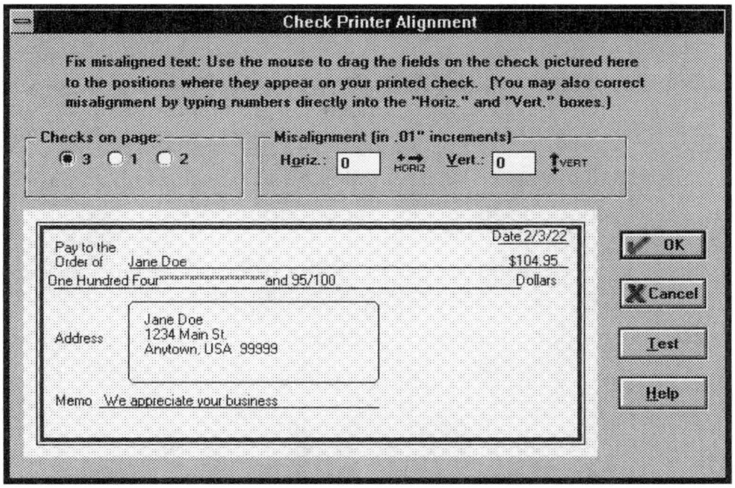

FIGURE 3.6

The Check Printer Alignment window.

As you can see, the window lets you type in horizontal and vertical adjustments to the printing position in 0.01" (1/100") increments. You can also use the mouse to move the print position "by hand."

After you print each test check, you use this window to make the necessary adjustments if the text printed on the sample doesn't fall where it should. You can also use the mouse to do this. The idea is to drag the example check information so that the check in the window looks just like your printed test check, with the same misalignment. But although that method is easy, it's inexact. I recommend doing it the hard way, by measuring with a ruler how far off the sample printout was. Here's how:

1. Measure the distance horizontally between the left edge of the word Quicken printed in the text check's field *Pay to the Order of* and the point where it should have been printed. If the sample payee is too far to the right, consider this distance a negative number; if it's too far to the left, the adjustment should be positive.

2. Measure the vertical distance between the bottom edge of the payee entry and the place where the bottom edge should have fallen. If the test entry is too high on the check, consider the distance to be negative; if it's too low, the distance is positive.

3. Convert your measurement into hundredths of an inch.

4. Add your measured adjustments to the values already in the *Horiz* and *Vert* fields in the Check Printer Alignment window.

SHORTCUT If you like, you can use the Windows calculator to convert a fraction such as 3/16" into hundredths. (In this example, you'd divide 3 by 16 and take the first two digits to the right of the decimal point). Switch to Program Manager by pressing **Alt-Tab** and start the calculator. After your calculation is complete, press **Alt-Tab** again to move back to the Check Printer Alignment window.

When you've completed the entries, **OK** the box and go back to the Print Checks window. There, print a new test check page. Repeat this cycle until the print is aligned properly on your test checks (it should take a maximum of three checks).

Printing Test Checks with a Continuous-Feed Printer

Use these instructions if your printer can feed continuous, *fan-fold* sheets of checks (the kind with the strips of sprocket holes along either edge). Most of the printers in this category are of the dot-matrix type, but some daisy-wheel printers also have the necessary pin-feed mechanism.

SHORTCUT Some continuous-feed printers can't print on the first check that you feed into the printer. If this problem occurs, order special "forms leaders" from Intuit; be sure to specify that you have a continuous-feed printer when you order.

Load your continuous-feed checks into your printer just as you would ordinary fan-fold paper. Take careful note of the position of the top of the first check, using as a landmark part of the printer that's easy to see and immobile. This might be a mark or corner on the printhead or the plastic housing.

Next, make sure your printer is on, connected properly to your PC, and on-line (ready to print). In the Check Printer Setup window, verify that the entry in the *Check Style* field corresponds to the type of check you're printing (**standard**, **wallet**, or **voucher**).

Now choose **Test** to print a test check. When the check emerges from your printer, don't move the check, but do look at it. Quicken will have printed sample information where it thinks the various fields are supposed to be. If you're lucky, everything is aligned properly; these entries will actually be in the proper fields, with the text printed just above the lines, and with each entry beginning just after its label.

If you luck out and the check is printed properly, you're set. Just make a mental or (preferably at this stage) written note of two important items. First, record the side-to-side position of the paper-feeding mechanism, if the mechanism can be moved on your printer. This determines horizontal alignment, and you should be sure that the mechanism is in this position each time you print checks. Second, to ensure proper future vertical alignment, record the position of the top of the checks relative to the printer landmark you used when you first fed them into the printer. You may want to place a small piece of tape on the printer as a reminder. Again, before you print, you should be sure that the first check is in that same position. You can now go on to the section "Printing Your Practice Checks," which follows.

If the horizontal alignment is off, fixing it is simply a matter of adjusting the side-to-side position of the paper-feeding mechanism as needed. Vertical alignment problems take more work, but Quicken simplifies the chore.

To fix an improper vertical position, choose **Align** in the Check Printer Setup window. To use the Check Printer Alignment window, refer to the instructions in "Adjusting the Check Printing Position," earlier in this chapter.

Once you've printed a test check with proper alignment, make a mental or written note of the current position of the top check in the printer, once again using as your landmark some stationary part of the printer. Alternatively, mark a reference spot by placing a small piece of tape on the printer. Each time you start a printing session, the first check should be in that same position for proper alignment. You can now go on to the section "Printing Your Practice Checks," which follows.

Printing Test Checks with a Single-Sheet Printer

If, like many daisy-wheel printers, your printer prints only a single sheet of paper at a time, but allows you to control the paper-feeding position (unlike a laser printer or the DeskJet), use the hints on paper and paper positioning that follow.

You should use sample laser checks, the ones that come on single sheets, to print your test checks. Otherwise, follow the instructions in the section on printing test checks with a continuous-feed printer. Since your printer allows you to adjust the vertical and horizontal position of your checks, be sure to note the physical alignment of your checks in your printer once you have successfully printed a test check.

Printing Your Practice Checks

Once you've successfully printed a test check or two, it's time to try printing a couple of the practice checks you filled out in Chapter 2. (If you haven't been following the tutorial, you can use these instructions for printing any check you'd like. Just skip over the steps with which you're already familiar.)

To print the checks you've written, place fresh blank checks in your printer. Be sure your printer is on, connected to your PC, and ready to print. Then pop up the Select Checks to Print window (see Figure 3.7) with one of these three techniques:

- Click on the **Print** icon on the Iconbar.
- Press **Ctrl-P**.
- Choose **Print Checks** in the Edit menu.

FIGURE 3.7

The Select Checks to Print window.

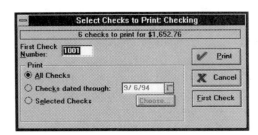

The line under the window title tells you how many checks you have written but not yet printed and the total of their amounts.

These are the choices you can make each time you print checks with Quicken:

- What check number you're starting with.
- Which checks you'd like to print.
- For laser checks, how many checks on the page there are and how many extra copies of each check you'd like to print.

- What type of paper checks you're using.

The first field at the top left of the Print Checks window is **First Check Number**. Here, type the number of the paper check that's next up to be printed. There's enough room for five digits. Quicken will keep track of the numbers for you from this point on, incrementing the check number each time you print a new check, and assigning the correct number to each check's entry in your Quicken account. If you happen to load a check into the printer out of sequence, just enter a new number the next time you print.

Then comes a set of three radio buttons labeled **All Checks**, **Checks Dated Through**, and **Selected Checks**. The **All Checks** button does exactly what its name implies: It prints all your checks, including the postdated ones.

SHORTCUT	Being able to print postdated checks ahead of time can be handy. You might want to print all your checks at one sitting, and just put aside the postdated ones until it's time to send them in. Or maybe you just want to use postdating for its traditional value in stalling your creditors. You can print postdated checks ahead of time by selecting either the **Checks Dated Through** or **Selected Checks** buttons. If you choose **Selected Checks**, you then pick out the individual postdated checks you want to print in the Select Checks to Print window.

The next button, **Checks Dated Through**, lets you pick a date limit for the checks Quicken will print. You can only select this button if there are postdated checks to be printed. Say you've written three postdated checks, one dated two days from today, the other two dated a full week later. To print the first postdated check plus all your nonpostdated checks, you'd select the **Checks Dated Through** button. You'd then enter the date of the first post-dated check, increasing or decreasing the date by one day at a time.

NEW IN 3   The pop-up calendar is new in Quicken 3.

If you're following the tutorial, don't select this button. If you do select it for your own checks, you can type the new date into the field, or press + or - to adjust the date. Another option is to click on the **Arrow** button to the right of the field to display the mini-calendar and pick the date from it.

The final button, **Selected Checks**, lets you decide exactly which checks to print among all those you've written. That's the method we'll use for printing the practice checks.

When you choose this button, the button labeled **Choose** at the right becomes available. Choose this button. A list of all the checks you've written and not yet printed pops up (Figure 3.8).

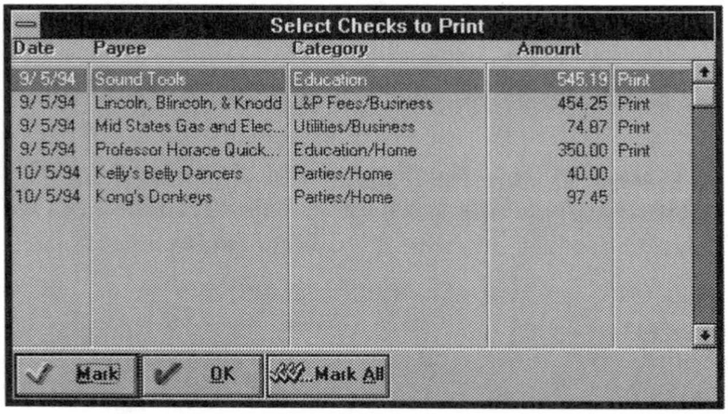

FIGURE 3.8

This window lists your unprinted checks.

Select Checks to Print

Date	Payee	Category	Amount	
9/ 5/94	Sound Tools	Education	545.19	Print
9/ 5/94	Lincoln, Blincoln, & Knodd	L&P Fees/Business	454.25	Print
9/ 5/94	Mid States Gas and Elec...	Utilities/Business	74.87	Print
9/ 5/94	Professor Horace Quick...	Education/Home	350.00	Print
10/ 5/94	Kelly's Belly Dancers	Parties/Home	40.00	
10/ 5/94	Kong's Donkeys	Parties/Home	97.45	

Mark   OK   Mark All

Each check has its own line in the list. For each one, Quicken shows you the date of the check, the payee, the *Memo* field, and the amount. In the far-right column, the word *Print* appears if the check is selected for printing.

At this point, all the nonpostdated checks are selected for printing. To practice how this window works, change the current selections so that only two of the checks will print. As in other Quicken lists, the item you're currently working with—in this case, the top check—is highlighted. To select a check that's not currently selected, move the pointer to the desired check using the **Up Arrow** and **Down Arrow** keys. (If you have more checks than will fit in one window, use the **PgUp** or **PgDn** keys to see the other checks.)

Once you've highlighted a check you want to select, press the space bar or choose the **Mark** button. You'll see the word *Print* appear in the far-right column for that check. To deselect the check so that it won't print, press the space bar or choose **Mark** again; the *Print* notation will disappear. Another way to alternately select and deselect a check is to double-click on it in the list. Selecting **Mark All** alternately selects and deselects all the checks in the list.

After you've finished your experiments, select three checks and then choose **OK** to return to the Select Checks to Print window. Now choose the **Print** button to display still another window, titled Print Checks (see Figure 3.9).

NOTE   If you have a continuous-feed printer (not a laser printer or a DeskJet), and if you're printing more than one check, you can choose to print only the first check. Just choose **First Check** and it begins to print. Otherwise, to print all the checks you've selected, choose **Print**, displaying the Print Checks window.

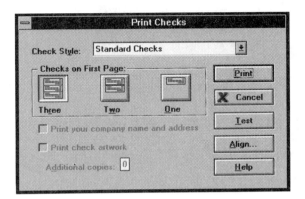

FIGURE 3.9

The Print Checks window.

Here, the check type listed in the *Check Style* field at the top should already agree with the checks you're using. If it doesn't, that probably means you've changed check styles since you last printed. If you haven't previously set up Quicken for this check style, you should go back and follow the directions in the section "Printing a Test Check" to print another test with the new checks.

If you're printing with a laser or other page-oriented printer, check the selection in the **Checks on First Page** setting (**Three**, **Two**, or **One**). It should match the number of checks on the first check page you'll be printing (Quicken assumes that you'll be printing on full pages after the first page). Now load the partial sheet of checks into the manual feed tray of your printer, aligned as you specified in the Check Printer Setup window (see *Setting Up Your Printer* earlier in this chapter).

If you're printing on standard or voucher checks, check the **Print Check Artwork** box if you want to print your logo on the checks. This only works if you designated a graphic logo in the Check Printer Setup window.

Finally, if you're printing voucher checks, you may want to print more than one copy of each check. This option is intended to let you print on special multipart laser checks. Since a laser printer doesn't strike the paper like a conventional dot-matrix or daisy-wheel printer, it can't make carbon copies. Instead, you must order special laser checks that come with two or more copies of the same check number, and print each copy in turn.

Type in the number of additional copies in the *Additional Copies* field at the bottom (not the total number of copies). So, if you want to print a total of two copies of each check, you'll type **1** in the field.

NOTE   Like the Check Printer Setup window, the Print Checks window has **Test** and **Align** buttons. These simply give you an alternate way of performing the same functions described earlier in this chapter.

You're finally ready to print, so choose **Print**. You'll see a window with a message that Quicken is printing. This window has a **Cancel** button, and theoretically, you can interrupt the printing process at any point by choosing **Cancel**.

However, printing may continue even if you try to cancel it, if your printer has a buffer that allows it to accept more data than it can print right away. If your printer has a buffer—and most recent models do—the printer may keep on printing until its buffer is empty. In this case, the only way to stop the printer is to turn it off.

If Quicken can't communicate with your printer, you'll see a message to that effect. Recheck to make sure the printer is on, that it's ready to print, and that it's connected properly to your PC. Then press **Enter** to try again.

Completing a Print Job

Once Quicken has sent all the check information to your printer, it will ask you to verify that the checks have printed properly. If you printed more than one check, you'll see a message telling you which check numbers were printed. Look over the checks as they emerge from your printer. Choose **OK** in the message window if all went well. If not, type in the number of the first incorrectly printed check in the space provided, and then choose **OK**. (If you printed only one check, the message simply asks, *Did check #x print correctly?* In this case, choose **Yes** if it did and choose **No** if it did not.

If the checks printed correctly, Quicken lists them by number in your account. (You'll see how this works in Chapter 4.) If not, what happens next depends on the type of printer you have. For continuous-feed printers, you're returned directly to the Print Checks window where you can try again. If you have a page-oriented printer, Quicken first asks, *Does your printed check need alignment?* If the problem was improper positioning of the printed text, choose **Yes** to bring up the Check Printer Alignment window, covered earlier in this chapter. For other problems such as paper jams, choose **No** to go back to the Print Checks window instead.

Reprinting Checks

Once you've printed a check successfully, Quicken records that fact in your account file and takes the check out of the list of checks to be printed. If the need arises, however, you can easily print any check again. Quicken indicates unprinted checks in your account register by placing the word *Print* in the *Num* field (see Chapter 4 for details on using the register). Once a check is printed, on the other hand, Quicken fills the *Num* field with the check number.

Therefore, to reprint a check, all you have to do is locate it in the register and enter **Print** in place of the number listed in the *Num* field. After you press **Enter** to record the modified transaction, switch back to the Write Checks window. The check will be available for normal printing.

Similarly, you can avoid printing a check you've written but haven't printed by switching to the register and deleting the *Print* entry in the *Num* field. You'll probably want to type in a check number in its place, but you don't have to. Quicken will no longer include the check in the list of checks to be printed.

Knowing When to Print Checks

One of Quicken's key convenience features is that it not only keeps track of the checks you've written and not yet printed, but also lets you know when it's time to print them.

| NOTE | Train yourself to look for the Quicken Reminder window every time you start Quicken, to see if you have any checks waiting to be printed. |

Every time you run Quicken, the program examines all your accounts in all your account files to see whether you have checks that you've written but not yet printed. If so, you'll see a small window with a reminder similar to the one in Figure 3.10 on the next page.

FIGURE 3.10

This message reminds you of unprinted checks.

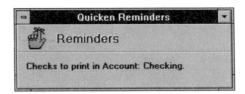

The Billminder program, described in the Appendix, will also tell you when it's time to print checks as soon as you turn on your computer, or every time you start Windows, even if you're not running Quicken and don't plan to do so.

Summary

In this chapter, you learned how to align checks in your printer, and you then produced your first printed checks. From now on, the twin benefits of neat, professional-looking checks and automatic record-keeping are yours whenever you want them. The tips on setting up your printer and on dealing with printing problems discussed in this chapter will be helpful when you're ready to print reports and graphs as well. In Chapter 4, you'll learn how to record other transactions in your Quicken checking account.

Chapter Four
Recording Other
Payments and Deposits

I f you're like me, you're lucky if you can remember to write down the checks you fill out; as for keeping a running balance in your checkbook, it's a feat you've never managed. Of course, such laxity can get you into hot water when it's time to pay a big bill, and you're not quite sure how much money remains in your account.

With Quicken, you can forget forever about the hassle of figuring out your balance as you write down each transaction; Quicken's *register* will take care of the calculations for you. Then, when your statement comes in, balancing your account against the statement will take only a few minutes. Of course, you'll still need the discipline to record your deposits and checks by hand, but Quicken has ways to make even these minimal requirements easier.

Although you've only worked with one account so far, Quicken offers six types of accounts, and every Quicken account has a register. Some register details vary from one type of account to the next, but all the registers look much the same and work similarly. You'll learn all about the other types of Quicken accounts and how to use their registers in Chapter 8.

This chapter is a working introduction to the register in the checking account you've already set up. You'll learn to use the register to enter all transactions that affect your account balance other than the checks you write in the Write Checks window. Chapters 5 and 7 cover ways you can make all the entries in your account more informative, and the shortcuts Quicken provides for making repetitive entries quickly and easily. In Chapter 6, you'll use the register to practice balancing your checkbook.

Using the Quicken Check Register

As you already know, Quicken's check register looks almost exactly like the familiar paper register most people use to record the checks they write. It works in the same way, too—except that this register stays current automatically. Figure 4.1 shows the Register window containing the sample checks that you wrote in Chapter 2.

FIGURE 4.1

The Register window showing sample checks.

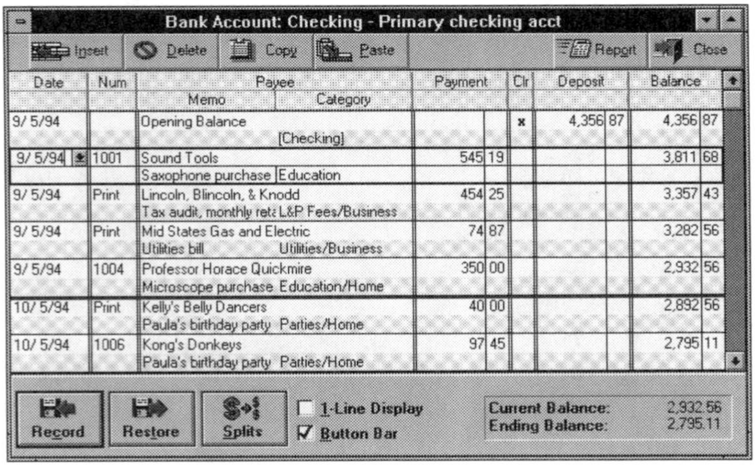
Bank Account: Checking - Primary checking acct
Insert
Delete
Copy
Paste
Report
Close
Date
Num
Payee
Memo
Category
Payment
Clr
Deposit
Balance
9/ 5/94 Opening Balance [Checking] x 4,356 87 4,356 87
9/ 5/94 1001 Sound Tools Saxophone purchase Education 545 19 3,811 68
9/ 5/94 Print Lincoln, Blincoln, & Knodd Tax audit, monthly ret: L&P Fees/Business 454 25 3,357 43
9/ 5/94 Print Mid States Gas and Electric Utilities bill Utilities/Business 74 87 3,282 56
9/ 5/94 1004 Professor Horace Quickmire Microscope purchase Education/Home 350 00 2,932 56
10/ 5/94 Print Kelly's Belly Dancers Paula's birthday party Parties/Home 40 00 2,892 56
10/ 5/94 1006 Kong's Donkeys Paula's birthday party Parties/Home 97 45 2,795 11
Record
Restore
Splits
1-Line Display
Button Bar
Current Balance: 2,932.56
Ending Balance: 2,795.11

The register is the part of Quicken you'll use for most of your day-to-day work with the program. Here's where you'll record and review the details of every individual transaction that changes your account balance.

Each check that you write in the Write Checks window is transferred automatically to your checking account register—one excellent reason to use Quicken's built-in check-writing feature. But many other types of transactions may be recorded in your account, including any checks you write by hand, deposits, direct withdrawals via a human or mechanical teller, checking fees, interest you earn, even wire transfers of funds. But you will have to enter these into the register yourself, as you will soon see.

You can view any part of your register any time you like, and even enlist Quicken's help in finding particular transactions by payee, date, or other information. If you'd like, you can print out the entire register for reference. As you'd expect, each bank (checking) account you establish in Quicken has its own register.

Using the Register Window

The Register window for your checking account should still be on your screen, but it's "behind" the Write Checks window. To bring the Register window to the foreground, just choose **Bank account** from the Window menu or click on the part of the register you can see. Another quick way to switch to the Register window is to press the keyboard shortcut **Ctrl-R**. Just to be complete, you can also choose **Use Register** from the Activities menu.

As shown in Figure 4.1, the register now holds the half dozen or so checks you've written. Following the format of an ordinary paper register, a Quicken bank account register sets aside a tall row for each transaction, with separate columns for *Date*, *Check number*, *Payee*, *Amount of payment*, *Cleared Transactions* (the column labeled *Clr*), *Amount of deposit*, and *Account balance*. Unlike a paper register, though, the Quicken register also has space for memos and for the categories and classes to which you assign your transactions. Notice that Quicken has entered the check numbers of the checks you printed in Chapter 3 in the *Num* column. The *Num* column contains the notation *Print* for the unprinted sample checks.

At the top of the Register window you'll probably see the button bar, a series of buttons for common register tasks. You'll learn how these buttons work as you work through this chapter. Here's a summary of their functions:

- The **Insert** button inserts a new transaction into the register.
- The **Delete** button removes the current transaction from the register.
- The **Copy** button makes a copy of all the information in the current transaction.
- The **Paste** button places the information into the current transaction.
- The **Report** button produces a report listing all the transactions in the register.
- The **Close** button closes the register window.

You'll also see three large buttons labeled **Record**, **Restore**, and **Splits**, at the bottom left of the Register window. These work just like those in the Write

Checks window (we haven't covered the **Splits** button yet, but we'll get to it in Chapter 5).

Just to the right of these buttons are two checkboxes labeled **1-Line Display** and **Button Bar**. When the **Button Bar** checkbox is checked, the button bar at the top of the window is visible. If you want to use that space to see more register transactions, you can turn off the button bar by choosing the checkbox and removing the checkmark. You'll see what the **1-Line** button is for in a moment.

The lower-right corner of the register contains the same information displayed in the Write Checks window—the balance in your account.

How Quicken Organizes the Register

Notice that one register transaction is always highlighted in a slightly different color than the others. The highlight indicates that you can make changes in the transaction. If you'll look closely, you'll see that Quicken adds lines to the highlighted transaction to better define the individual fields.

Notice also that the transactions are arranged in order of date, with the earlier ones toward the top of the list. Regardless of the order in which you enter your transactions, Quicken always reorders them by date. Remember those two postdated checks back in Chapter 2? Notice how Quicken has brought them to your attention by highlighting the date and by separating them from the other transactions with a heavy line.

Full Versus Compressed Register Display

When you first run Quicken, the program allots two lines per transaction in the register: one for the payee and the amount and another for the *Memo* and *Category* fields (the *Date* field extends over the first two lines).

If you prefer, Quicken lets you see more transactions at once by listing each on a single line. To change to this compressed view of the transactions, press **Alt-1** or click on **1-Line Display** at the bottom of the window, removing the checkmark from the box. As shown in Figure 4.2, Quicken shortens the *Payee* and *Category* fields so they'll fit on one line together and omits the *Memo* field altogether.

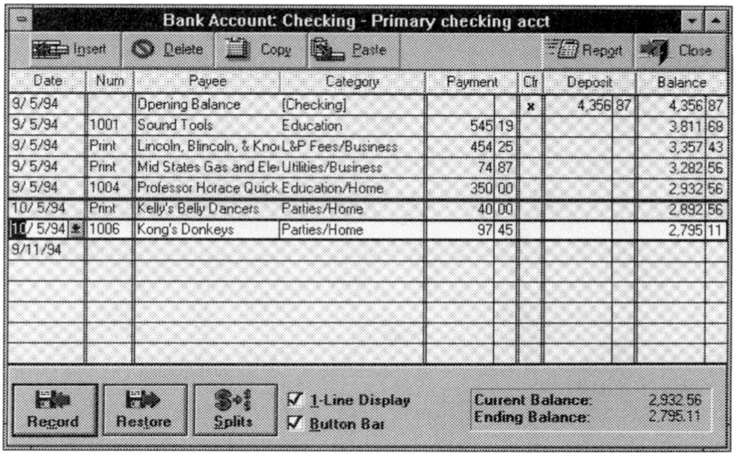

FIGURE 4.2

The condensed view of the register—one line per transaction.

To switch back to the full, multiple-line view of transactions, press **Alt-1** again or click **1-Line Display** so that a checkmark appears in the box.

Browsing the Register

Once you've recorded a large number of transactions, you will notice that they won't all fit in the Register window at one time. Therefore, to examine a register entry, you'll have to display that transaction first. Quicken provides a variety of different ways for moving around in the register to locate a particular transaction.

With the mouse, you can use the scroll bar to move to any part of the register you'd like. As you move the scroll box, Quicken displays the date of the transaction you've scrolled to in a tiny window near the mouse pointer. You can also use the keyboard to scroll through the register. This is the easiest method to do if the cursor is in the *Date* field at the left side of the window. In this case, pressing the **Up Arrow** or **Down Arrow** keys moves you to the previous or the next transaction.

Now experiment with the **PgUp** and **PgDn** keys, which move the register display up or down by an entire screen. Next, press **Home** four times to move to the first transaction in the register, then **End** four times to move the highlight to the first empty transaction slot at the bottom of the register.

NOTE **Ctrl-PgUp** and **Ctrl-PgDn** move to the first transaction in the previous or next month, respectively.

Finding a Specific Transaction

Once you've entered a month or two's worth of transactions, finding a specific transaction gets a lot more difficult. Quicken's **Find** feature will search through your register to locate a particular transaction by any of the information you've recorded: *Date, Check number, Payee, Memo, Category, Amount,* or *Cleared status.*

SHORTCUT   You can also use the **Find** feature to locate unprinted checks in the Write Checks window.

Let's use **Find** to track down the first check you wrote in the tutorial, the one made out to "Sound Tools." If you aren't following the tutorial, or if you didn't enter the tutorial checks exactly as shown, change what you type to match one of your own checks.

To make this an instructive exercise, make sure you're not already on the check you're looking for by pressing **End** four times to move the highlight to the first blank transaction at the end of the register. Choose the **Find** option in the Edit menu. You'll see the Find window, as shown in Figure 4.3.

FIGURE 4.3

The Find window.

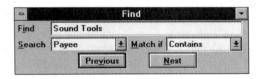

NOTE   **QuickFill**, the feature that automatically completes entries in the register and on checks, does not work in the Find window.

In the *Find* field, type **Sound Tools**. The next field, *Search*, is a list box you use to tell which fields Quicken should check when looking for a match. At this point, this field is set to **All Fields**, meaning that the search would pick up transactions that show "Sound Tools" in the *Memo* field, if any mentions existed. If you'd like, you can further refine the search by selecting the **Payee** option from the drop-down list in this field.

Leave the *Match if* field set to **Contains** for now; we'll discuss the other choices there in a moment. You're ready to start the search, so press **Alt-P** or choose **Previous** to search backward in the register, that is, toward the beginning of the list. Quicken displays and highlights the first matching check. To search forward, press **Alt-N** or choose **Next**.

As long as you don't close it, the Find window remembers what you searched for last. To search for the next matching transaction, just press the same search key (**Alt-P** or **Alt-N**) you used before. With these two keys, you can move back and forth through the matching transactions to your heart's content. Of course, you can replace the existing entry with a new one at any time.

Finding Other Transactions

You can have Quicken hunt for transactions that match your entries in any of the register fields. There may be times, for instance, when you want to look up a specific check number in the register. You might want to see if Quicken's record of a particular check matches the entry for that check in your bank statement. To locate a check by number, just type in the number in the *Find* field, then choose **Check Number** in the *Search* field.

If you want to search for transactions in a certain category, class, or both, enter the category and class name in the *Find* field. If you like, you can have Quicken enter the category and class names into the field for you by choosing the names from the category list. With the cursor in the *Find* field, pop up the Category List window by pressing **Ctrl-C** or clicking on the **Cat List** icon. For the Class List window, use **Ctrl-L**. Then choose **Category/Class** in the *Search* field. In either list, use the techniques you've already learned to find the category or class you'd like, and then press **Enter** to have Quicken insert the name in the Find window.

SHORTCUT	Don't bother typing the /. If you use **Class List** to enter a class name for your search—Quicken enters the slash automatically.

You can have Quicken search for cleared transactions, or those that you've starred with an asterisk in the *Clr* field. To find cleared transactions, type **x** in the *Find* field. To find the starred transactions, type **b***. Then choose **Cleared Status** in the *Search* field.

NOTE	Transactions marked with * or x are used for checkbook balancing. See Chapter 7 for details.

Finding Transactions by Date

Quicken's **Find** command also makes it easy to find checks or other transactions from a particular date. Let's try it. Bring up the Find window again by pressing **Ctrl-F**. After typing the date of the transactions you want to locate in the *Find* field, change the setting of the *Search* field to **Date**. When you press **Alt-N**, the register display will shift so that the first transaction with your date is highlighted at the top of the window. If no transaction matches your date exactly, you'll be taken to one that is closest, but earlier.

Finding Transactions by Partial Entries

When the Find window's *Match if* field is set to the **Contains** option, Quicken's **Find** feature locates the first transaction that contains your search request anywhere within the *Payee* field. That means you only have to remember part of the entry for which you're searching (you must, however, spell that part correctly).

Let's see how this works. In Chapter 2, you made out a check to a Professor Quickmire for a microscope purchase. Let's say that all you can remember about the man who sold you the microscope is that his last name started with "Quick." That's all you'll need to find the check in your register.

This time, pop up the Find window directly from the register by pressing the keyboard shortcut **Ctrl-F**. Type **quick** into the *Find* field. Be sure the *Search* field is set to **Payee** or **All Fields**. Then press **Alt-N** to search forward from the currently highlighted transaction. If Quicken doesn't find the entry, press **Alt-P** to search in the reverse direction; that should turn up the transaction you seek.

Using Other Search Methods

The *Match if* field tells Quicken what kind of match to look for. If you leave the standard entry, **Contains** in the field, Quicken will locate any transaction that contains your entry anywhere within the field or fields you're searching. You can select other choices from the drop-down list, as follows:

- **Exact**: Matches transactions only if the field entry is identical to your search entry, with no more and no fewer characters.

- **Starts with**: Matches transactions if the field begins with your search request.
- **Ends with**: Matches transactions if the field ends with your search request.
- **Greater**: Matches transactions if the field entry is a larger number than the search request, or begins with a letter later in the alphabet.
- **Greater or Equal, Less, and Less or Equal**: Like the **Greater** choice, but with different comparisons.

Adding New Transactions to Your Register

Now that you know how to get around in your checking account register, it's time to add some new transactions. The process isn't really any different from writing a check, except that the fields are in different spots on your screen.

NEW IN 3 In Quicken 3, you can also add transactions to the register via the financial calendar, covered in Chapter 7.

What follows are several transactions for you to enter. If you prefer, make up your own examples, or enter them from your bank statement:

Num	Payee	Payment	Deposit	Memo	Category
1007	Sound Tools	143.43		Electric Sitar	Education/Home
1008	City Treasury	95		Business License	Fees/Business
	Deposit-dividends	125	Bonanza Oil	Dividends	
	Deposit-paycheck		1452.25	Salary	

Start with the register on your screen. (If Quicken is not still displaying the register, press **Ctrl-R**, click on Register in the Iconbar, or choose **Bank Account: Checking** from the Use Register or Window menu once you have selected **Activities**. There's already one empty transaction in the register: the very last one. So, if the blank transaction at the bottom of the register isn't already highlighted, move to it now. You can scroll there with the mouse, or you can press **End** four times, but the fastest way is to press **Ctrl-N** (for **New Transaction**).

SHORTCUT | You can insert a new transaction with the same date as any existing transaction in the register by clicking the **Insert** button on the button bar, or by pressing **Ctrl-I**. Quicken creates a new, empty transaction just below the transaction you started with, copying the date to the new transaction. You can then fill out the new transaction using the steps covered here.

When you arrive at the bottom of the register, the cursor should be in the new transaction's *Date* column at the far left of the screen, with today's date already entered. If you want to change the date, you can do so in one of several ways:

- You can type in the new date using the standard Quicken date format
- You can press the + or - keys to increase or decrease the date one day at a time.
- You can click on the **Arrow** button to display the mini-calendar and choose the date with the mouse (see Chapter 2 for details)
- You can press one of Quicken's date shortcut keys: **T** for today's date, **M** for the first day of the current month, **H** for the last day of the month, **Y** for the first day of the current year, or **R** for the last day of the year.

| SHORTCUT | Just as in the Write Checks window, you can enter a future date to create a postdated entry. Chapter 2 discusses how you can use postdating for more efficient financial management. Remember that Quicken separates postdated transactions from other register entries with a heavy line. |

When the date is correct, press **Tab** to advance the cursor to the next column, labeled *Num*. (In the remaining steps, I'll assume you know how to use **Tab** to complete one column and move to the next.) The *Num* column displays the check numbers of checks you've printed and contains the word *Print* for checks you wrote in Quicken but haven't printed yet. When entering transactions in the register, you can use this column to enter the numbers of the checks you write, and you can also use it to distinguish other types of transactions, such as deposits, ATM withdrawals, and electronic transfers of funds. An entry in the *Num* column is not required, however.

Using **QuickFill** to Automate Transaction Entries

The **QuickFill** feature you used to assign a category to your third check back in Chapter 2 also works for completing entries in the register. As soon as you move to the *Num* field, Quicken drops down a list of the most common entries in this field. If one of these options fits your transaction, you just pick it from the list. Alternatively, you can begin typing the entry you want to make and allow **QuickFill** to complete it for you.

NOTE Remember, you can use the Preferences menu to control the way **QuickFill** operates or even to shut it off altogether. See the Appendix for details.

When you're recording a series of consecutive checks, such as the first two sample transactions, typing **+** or **N** in the *Num* field causes Quicken to enter the next available check number (one higher than the number of the last check). You can accomplish the same thing by choosing **Next Chk #** in the drop-down list.

Once a number is entered—whether you type it yourself or use **+** to have Quicken enter it for you—typing **+** or **N**, or choosing **Next Chk #** again, increases the number by one, whereas typing **-** decreases it by one.

When the *Num* field is complete, tab to the *Payee* field. If you're recording a handwritten check, you'll copy the name of the payee from the check to this field. If you're recording another type of transaction, enter an appropriate description, such as **Deposit**, **Withdrawal**, or **Overdraft Charge**.

In the *Payee* field, **QuickFill** again automatically displays a drop-down list, this one containing all the payees of previous transactions over the past three months. If you've previously used the payee you want to enter, you can choose it from this list, or type the first few letters of the name until **QuickFill** correctly completes the entry for you.

Use the latter approach to begin entering the payee for the first sample register transaction, **Sound Tools**. Since you already wrote a check to this payee, **QuickFill** enters the full name as soon as you type **S** (assuming your account contains only the sample checks from Chapter 2).

As shown in Figure 4.4 on the next page, the characters **QuickFill** enters—those you didn't type yourself—appear in a different shade. If the match **QuickFill** finds isn't the transaction you'd like, just keep typing. As you enter new letters, **QuickFill** looks for a better match for your entry.

FIGURE 4.4

*QuickFill has
entered
characters in
the new Sound
Tools transaction.*

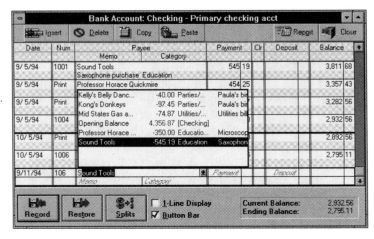

When you're happy with the **QuickFill** entry, you have two choices. If you're sure that the transaction **QuickFill** has found is identical to the one you're now working on, press En**ter** to copy the entire earlier transaction (except the date) to the new one, recording the new transaction in the process.

On the other hand, if you want to have a chance to inspect or edit the information in the new transaction, press **Tab**. Again, **QuickFill** copies all of the previous transaction's information to the new one, but this time the new transaction isn't recorded, and you can edit it as you like.

QuickFill works in this same way when the cursor is in the **Pay to the Order of** field in the Write Checks window.

Finishing the Register Entry

Whether or not you've recalled a previous entry via **QuickFill**, you can now go on to the other fields in the transaction. In the *Payment* field, enter the amount of any transaction that takes money out of your account, whether it's a check you wrote by hand, a face-to-face or ATM withdrawal, a fee or charge, or a payment made for you by one of those automatic payment plans.

Don't bother to type the dollar sign or commas. If the entry is an even dollar amount, you can also forego typing the decimal point or the zeros, and Quicken will fill in the cents column for you. Just as in check writing, you can click on the arrow button to pop up the mini-calculator and make your entries by clicking on numerals with the mouse.

You'll use the next field, labeled *Clr* for *Cleared*, when you balance your account against the account statement your bank sends you. Cleared transactions are indicated by **x** or *****. Skip over this column for now; you'll find instructions on using it in Chapter 6.

In the *Deposit* column, enter the amount of any transaction that adds to your account balance—deposits, interest payments, gifts, and so on. Again, don't type dollar signs or commas, and leave out the decimal point and cents if you're entering an even dollar amount. You can use the pop-up calculator here as well.

After you complete the *Payment* or *Deposit* field, press **Tab** to drop the cursor down a line to the *Memo* field in the second row. Here, you can type in anything you want to help you remember what the transaction was for.

NOTE   Quicken won't allow you to make entries in both the *Payment* and *Deposit* fields for the same transaction. If you've already typed in an amount in the *Payment* field, entering numbers in the *Deposit* field automatically erases the *Payment* field entry.

The *Category* field is the last one in the transaction. Just as when you write checks in the Write Checks window, the register lets you assign any transaction to a category, class, or both. As soon as you tab to this field, Quicken drops down a list of all the categories in your file. Although you can scroll through this list to choose the desired category, it's usually easier to start typing the category name and let **QuickFill** complete it for you.

NOTE   If you need full descriptions of the categories before making a selection, press **Ctrl-C** or click on the **Cat List** icon in the Iconbar to display the Category list. Make a selection from the list and press Enter to place it in the *Category* field.

To add a class entry, type / after the category name. Begin typing the class and let **QuickFill** complete it, or press **Ctrl-L** to pop up the Class list and select an entry there. See Chapter 5 for more detailed information on using categories and classes.

Filling in the *Category* field is optional, but categories are important. In fact, Quicken comes set to warn you if you try to record a transaction without a category. You'll see a message asking you to select a category or to explicitly skip assigning a category this time. You can turn this reminder on or off via the Preferences menu, as detailed in the Appendix.

When you complete the *Category* field it's time to record the transaction into your account. Just as with checks, you can either press **Enter** or choose the **Record** button. You'll hear a beep, and, if necessary, Quicken will move the transaction you just recorded to where it belongs in the register, according to date. The highlight will again be on the first empty transaction at the end of the register.

Making Changes in Existing Transactions

Quicken makes it extremely easy to make changes in any of the transactions in your register. All you have to do is highlight the transaction you'd like to change, move the cursor to the field that needs revision, and type in your changes. You can make revisions to entries in the register at any time, even in the middle of adding new transactions.

> **WARNING**

Be very careful about changing transactions that have already been reconciled, as indicated by an **X** in the **Clr** (cleared) column. Changing the amount of these transactions or deleting the **X** will change the reconciled balance, and you won't be able to balance your account accurately the next time you try (see Chapter 6).

Use any of the methods described in the above section *Browsing the Register* to move the register highlight to the transaction you want to alter. When you've reached the right transaction, move the cursor to the field that needs revision and press **Tab** to move forward field by field, or **Shift-Tab** to move backward. If you have a mouse, just click over the correct field to move the cursor there.

With the cursor in the field you want to change, use the **LeftArrow** or **RightArrow** key to position it beside the character or characters that need correction. With the methods you've learned in previous sessions, delete existing characters and type in new ones until the entry is correct. Then re-record the transaction in the register.

Copying Information from an Existing Transaction

The **Copy** and **Paste** buttons on the button bar (and the **Copy Transaction** and **Paste Transaction** commands on the Edit menu) let you duplicate an existing transaction elsewhere in the register. In fact, you can use these commands to copy transaction information to a different register altogether. You'll learn when to use these commands in Chapter 7 (see *Copying and Pasting Transactions*).

Voiding and Deleting Transactions

In most cases, when something goes wrong with a transaction, it's better to void it, retaining a record, rather than to delete it altogether from your records. Voiding is appropriate when a check you've printed or written by hand has errors or gets lost, or when you decide to stop payment on a check. On the other hand, if you discover that you accidentally entered the same transaction twice, you'll want to delete one of the duplicates.

Quicken allows you to take either action. Begin by moving the register highlight to the transaction you'd like to change; you can use any of the methods laid out in "Browsing the Register." Then, to void the transaction, choose **Void Transaction** from the Edit menu or press **Ctrl-V**. To delete it, click the **Delete** button on the button bar, or press **Ctrl-D**.

If you're voiding the transaction, Quicken inserts the notation *VOID:* at the beginning of the *Payee* field, removes the amount in the *Payment* or *Deposit* column, and places an **X** in the *Clr* field so that it won't appear the next time you balance the account. You may want to add a memo indicating why you voided the transaction and the original transaction amount. Then record the changes by one of the usual methods.

If you're deleting the transaction, you may first see a warning message, depending on whether you've set Quicken to require confirmation for transaction changes (see the Appendix for details). If the warning appears, choose **OK** to proceed deleting the transaction. It will disappear from your screen, and its data will be permanently erased from your account. At the same time, the remaining entries in the register will move up to close the gap.

WARNING	Deleted transactions are gone for good; there's no way to get the data back. Be absolutely sure you won't need the information before you go ahead and delete a transaction.

If the message appears and you decide not to proceed with voiding or deleting the transaction, choose **Cancel** in the window or press **Esc** and you'll be returned to the register with the original transaction intact.

Backing Up Your Account

Keeping extra copies of your financial records is always good practice, and it's doubly important when you use a computer. Although your PC is very reliable, the disks on which you store your data are its most vulnerable component. With time, they eventually wear out. Besides, there's always the possibility of human error (accidentally deleting the files from your disk) and of loss or damage to your computer from another source (theft, fire, or your two-year-old child pouring water onto the machine).

You must also resolve to make copies regularly of all your Quicken accounts onto backup disks. Plan to do this once a month at bare minimum. But depending on how often you use the program, and how detailed and crucial your records are, it wouldn't hurt to back them up weekly or even daily. As long as you make backups faithfully, if something ever does go wrong with your PC or your Quicken disks, you'll be able to retrieve most or all of your records from the backup copies. Without the copies, your records will be gone forever.

SHORTCUT	Get into the habit of using Quicken's shortcut backup commands. When you're finished with a session, but before closing Quicken, press **Ctrl-B** to back up your accounts.

Fortunately, Quicken makes it extremely easy to save backup copies of your accounts onto a set of floppy disks, and it takes only a few seconds. Without delay, then, to get you started on the habit of doing regular backups, let's back up the transactions you've recorded in your register so far.

Find a blank, formatted floppy disk and label it as your Quicken backup. Place the disk in the floppy drive you'll be using, and choose **Backup** from the File menu or press **Ctrl-B**. You'll see the Select Backup Drive dialog box shown in Figure 4.5.

FIGURE 4.5

The Select Backup Drive dialog box.

The radio buttons in the *File to Back Up* field let you specify whether to back up the file that's currently open or to choose a file for back up from a list of those available. Since you only have one file at this point, leave the **Current File** button selected (you'll learn to manage multiple files in Chapter 8).

In the *Backup Drive* field, choose the letter name of the drive on which you want the backup stored from the drop-down list. Then choose **OK** to start the backup process. Quicken will instruct you to change floppies as needed until the entire file is backed up. When the copy is complete, Quicken will return you to the register.

NOTE	Quicken lets you choose a hard disk as the destination for your

backup files, but you should not store backups on the same hard disk on which you keep the original copy. If you have a second hard disk, you can consider using it for backups, but remember that your files won't be protected against theft or major damage to your whole computer.

Printing Your Register

Sometimes it's nice to have a paper record of your checking account register. You might want to mark on it as you sketch out a new budget plan, carry it to another room where you can discuss it with your spouse, or take it with you to your bank to clarify a mixup. Fortunately, Quicken makes it easy to print out your register. In fact, you can print any portion of the register that particularly interests you, from a single day to as many years as you have records for.

To print the register, click on the **Print** icon in the Iconbar or press **Ctrl-P**, the keyboard shortcut. (You can also choose **Print Register** from the File menu; the *Print Register* item appears on the File menu only when the register is the active window.) You'll see the Print Register dialog box, as shown in Figure 4.6.

FIGURE 4.6

The Print Register dialog box.

Making Choices in the Print Register Window

By now, you should be comfortable with making choices and filling out fields in a Quicken window. As usual, Quicken provides pre-set choices for each field in the Print Register dialog box. For the entries you'd like to change, type in the appropriate information. Where Quicken's choices suit you, skip over the field without changing it by pressing **Tab**. To go back to a previous field, press **Shift-Tab**.

To Print Transactions within a Range of Dates

The first two fields at the top of the Print Register dialog box let you select a range of dates for the transactions Quicken will print. Each time you start a session, Quicken automatically assumes you want to print the entire register. If you want to narrow the range of dates, type in the correct dates in these fields.

NEW IN 3 In Quicken 3, you will find printing options in the Print Report dialog box.In the previous version of Quicken, the Print Register dialog box includes a *Print To* field that lets you decide how to print the register: on paper or "printed" as a standard text file on disk, so that you can read it into a word processor or desktop publishing program. Choose the Radio button for the printing destination you prefer.

NOTE | Quicken prints your register using the setup defined for printing reports. See Chapter 9 for information on report printer setup.

NOTE | To create a title for the register printout you must type in a title of your own in the *Title* field, Quicken will print the title "Check Register" at the top of your register printout.

To Choose Between a Full or Condensed Register Format

Ordinarily, Quicken prints a full three-line entry for each transaction in your register, as shown in Figure 4.7. If this is what you want, leave the **Print One Transaction Per Line** checkbox unchecked. If you'd prefer a condensed printout with three times as many transactions per page, check this field. In the printout, Quicken will abbreviate each transaction to fit on one line, as shown in Figure 4.8.

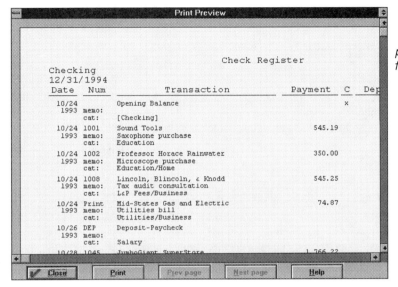

FIGURE 4.7

Register printout with full three-line entries.

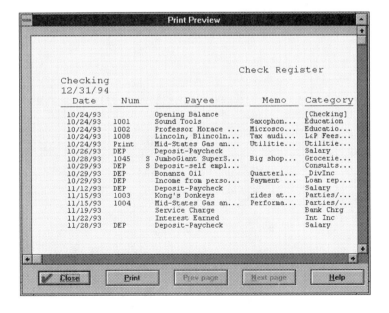

FIGURE 4.8

Register printout with abbreviated entries.

Printing Transaction Splits

We've mentioned Quicken's ability to record split transactions—ones in which a single transaction represents several items—but this topic isn't covered in full until Chapter 5. Suffice it to say at this point that Quicken doesn't automatically break out the split transactions as separate items in your register printouts; as you can see, **Print Transaction Splits** is unchecked. If you do want to see them itemized, check this checkbox.

Sorting the Printout by Check Number

Unless you tell it to do otherwise, Quicken will order the transactions primarily by date when it prints out the register. If you made more than one check transaction on a given day, it will order the transactions for that date by check number. If you'd prefer to have the check transactions printed out in check number order, ignoring dates, check the *Sort By Check Number* field. Quicken will still sort the transactions that don't have check numbers, such as deposits and fees, by date.

Starting the Printout

NEW IN 3   Once the choices in all the fields are correct, you can proceed to print the register. Choose **Print** to display the Print Report window. You'll see the Print Report dialog box, shown in Figure 4.9, every time you print a Quicken report.

FIGURE 4.9

The Print Report window.

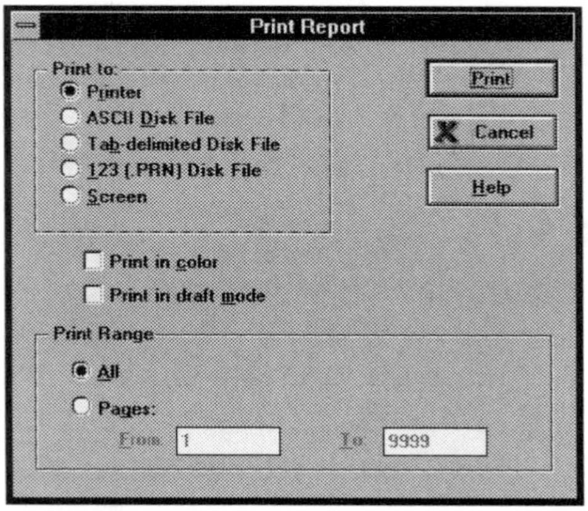

Chapter 10 has all the details on how the Print Report window works. For now, I'll assume that you're printing the register on paper (not as a disk file) using the standard settings.

Check to make sure your printer is turned on and ready to print, and that you've loaded it with paper. Choose the **Print** button. If everything is working properly, you'll soon see a message indicating the printout is in progress. The printout will then emerge, looking much like Figure 4.7 or 4.8.

| NOTE | If you have problems with the printout, see Chapters 3 and 10 for tips on printing successfully. For instructions on printing to a disk file, see Chapter 11. |

Reporting on a Specific Payee

From the register, you can also prepare a report summarizing all the transactions for a given payee. Let's say you're browsing through the register and you begin to notice that you've written more checks than you thought you have to your cousin Edna. At times like this, Quicken's ability to list all the transactions involving Edna becomes extremely convenient.

You'll learn all about Quicken reports in Chapters 10 and 11; for now, here is a quick rundown of how the register report works. Move to any transaction for the payee in question, then choose the **Report** button on the button bar. Within moments, a report appears on your screen showing all the relevant transactions as shown in the example in Figure 4.10. If you find a transaction of particular interest, you can view it in the register by pointing to it with the mouse pointer (which becomes a magnifying glass) and double-clicking.

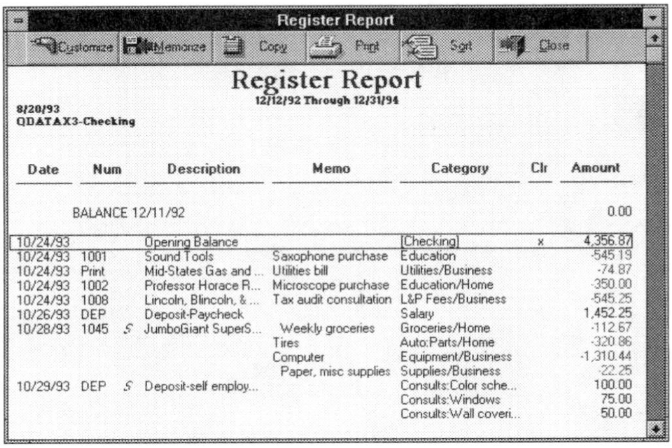

FIGURE 4.10

A Payee report prepared directly from the register as it looks on the screen.

Like any Quicken report, this can be customized, memorized so that you can use it again later, copied to the clipboard for export to other programs, or printed. Chapters 10 and 11 have the details.

Summary

This completes your introduction to the Quicken checking account register. You now know how to enter both payments and deposits in the register, how to move about in the register, how to find transactions that match specific criteria, and how to print the register on paper or disk. Now that you know these mechanics, you're ready to learn more in Chapter 5 about organizing your account with categories and classes to get the most from your financial records and reports. By the time your next bank statement arrives, you'll be ready for Chapter 6, in which you'll learn to balance your checking account. In Chapter 7, you'll learn how to have Quicken automatically fill out and record checks or register transactions that occur regularly.

Chapter Five
Organizing Your Accounts

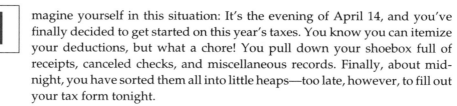 magine yourself in this situation: It's the evening of April 14, and you've finally decided to get started on this year's taxes. You know you can itemize your deductions, but what a chore! You pull down your shoebox full of receipts, canceled checks, and miscellaneous records. Finally, about midnight, you have sorted them all into little heaps—too late, however, to fill out your tax form tonight.

Let's rewind the tape back to January of the previous year. This time you have begun keeping financial records with Quicken instead of in that shoebox. Whether you prepare your tax return early or on deadline day, all you have to do is press a few Quicken keys, and you'll instantly have a complete breakdown of all your taxable income and deductible expenses.

Without question, one of Quicken's most useful talents lies in this ability to keep track of groups of related transactions for you. Of course, you must tell the program which group each transaction belongs in. That's where Quicken's *categories* and *classes* come in. You can assign every transaction in your Quicken account to a category, or a class, or both. When you need more detailed classifications, you can further divide your transactions by subcategories and subclasses.

Then, whenever you want to see a breakdown of your account according to these categories and/or classes, just press a few keys and you'll have it. At tax time, all you have left to do is transfer the totals to your tax forms. For budgeting, categorized reports of your income and spending patterns are invaluable. For small-business accounting, Quicken can prepare a wide variety of predesigned and custom reports, with your income and expenses broken down according to any classification scheme you require.

What if a single check or deposit happens to cover two or more different items that fall into different categories or classes, such as business and personal supplies? When this happens, Quicken lets you *split* the transaction to record each component in its own category or class.

This chapter explores the use of categories and classes in detail. As you develop a list of them for your own account, you'll learn the difference between categories and classes and how to use them together effectively. You'll also discover when and how to use subcategories and subclasses. Finally, you'll practice splitting individual transactions among separate categories.

Grouping Transactions into Categories and Classes

You've already learned how to assign transactions to categories and classes while writing checks and entering register transactions. At that time, though, you were concentrating on the basic skills. Now that you know them, let's review the process of using categories and classes in more detail.

Understanding Categories and Classes

As you'll recall from Chapters 2 and 4, a category identifies the source of an income transaction, or the type of goods or services paid for by an expense transaction. Typical income categories would cover your salary, interest income, income from a business, and dividend income. In most personal bank accounts, there will be categories for food, housing, utilities, entertainment, and so on. If you wish, you can further divide categories into subcategories, a topic also covered in this chapter.

| NOTE | Another use for the *Category* field is to indicate transfers of funds to or from another Quicken account. (See Chapter 8 for details.) |

Classes form a second and complementary classification scheme for your transactions. They are best used to group transactions according to the pertinent person, project, location, or time period.

Classes work hand in hand with categories to give you a cross-sectional view of your financial picture. If you're using Quicken for your family checking account, for example, you might establish separate classes for you and your spouse; that way, you'll know not only how much money is being spent in each category, but who's spending it. One of the classic business uses of Quicken is for managing rental properties. If you own more than one rental building, you can set up a separate class for each. Then, when you write a check for the utilities on (let's say) your Park Avenue apartment building, you'll record it in the **Park Avenue** class as well as the **Utilities** category—distinguishing this expense from the utilities payments you made on that rental cabin in the Adirondacks.

You can set up subclasses just as you can subcategories. If you run a mail-order business, you might have a separate class for your income from each region of the country, with subclasses for orders generated by the ads in different magazines as shown here.

Class	*Subclasses*
East	*Atlantic Crafts; Harper's*
North	*New England Times; Quilter's Bee; Harper's*
South	*Bayou Bugle; Harper's*
West	*Western Ways; Harper's*

In Quicken, you'd create classes called **East**, **North**, **South**, and **West**, and subclasses named *Atlantic Crafts, New England Times, Quilter's Bee, Bayou Bugle, Western Ways,* and *Harper's.* If you also created categories for each type of item you sold, you'd then be able to analyze your sales from various perspectives. For example, you could have Quicken show you the part of the country that tended to order which type of item, and to how many customers each magazine was delivered.

You don't need to use classes to break up your records according to common time periods; Quicken can do this for you automatically, as you'll see when you learn about reports in Chapter 10. If you want to break down your income and expenses by other time periods, such as three-week blocks or seasons, just assign each transaction to the appropriate class, such as **1/1–1/21** or **Fall**.

Planning Categories and Classes for your Accounts

Now that you understand in general terms how to use categories and classes, it's time to learn the mechanics of working with them. In Chapter 1 when you first set up your checking account, you chose one of Quicken's built-in lists of categories in the First Time Setup dialog box. As a result, your account is already equipped with an extensive list of categories, including most of those you'll probably need.

> **NOTE**   Each Quicken file, which may contain many separate accounts, has only one Category list and one Class list, shared by all the accounts in the file. Quicken files are discussed fully in Chapter 8. Unless you create and switch to a new account file, you'll use the same Category list in your checking account as in your cash, credit card, and other Quicken accounts.

Still, you'll probably find that you want to add categories that fit your own financial situation better. You may also want to remove or rename some of the categories you won't be using. In some cases, you may even want to design all your categories yourself from scratch. What's more, Quicken doesn't provide any built-in classes, so you will need to create any classes you plan to use yourself. Although you can make any of these changes as you work, it's better to plan an overall strategy for classifying the transactions in your account before you make many real entries. When you set up accounts in the future, you should add categories and classes for each account right away, before you enter any transactions into it.

The examples in the rest of this chapter will be based on sample lists of categories and classes that I'll describe in a moment. You can use these sample lists for practice now and develop your own categories and classes later. Alternatively, you can choose the categories and classes you actually want in your account now, and make the necessary mental adjustments as you work through the tutorial.

Whenever you do decide to set up your own lists of categories and classes, be prepared to spend a little time on the planning process. Think carefully about the kinds of information you'd like to obtain from your records, and about any other software you may want to exchange data with (see the Appendix for some of the possibilities). Chapters 13 through 16 offer lots of advice on selecting categories and classes for specific purposes, and you should feel free to read the relevant sections in one or more of those chapters before designing your lists.

> **NOTE**   If you plan to use Quicken to monitor your investments, be aware that the program automatically adds a set of investment-related categories to your account file as soon as you start any investment account. That means you probably won't have as much work to

do when setting up such an account. These automatically added categories are discussed further in Chapter 9.

For example, if one of your major reasons for buying Quicken is to improve your tax records, you'll want to set up categories and classes that correspond very closely to the various items on your tax returns (as you'll see, Quicken lets you assign each category to a specific IRS form and line number). If you're thinking about using CheckFree, the electronic bill-paying service, you may want your Quicken category names to be identical to the ones you use in CheckFree. Quicken lets you set up both subcategories and subclasses, allowing you to subdivide a group of related items so that you can analyze your income and expenses in whatever level of detail is appropriate at a given time. Used judiciously, subcategories and subclasses can add flexibility and precision to your record-keeping; you can even create second- and third-level subcategories, and so on, to a theoretical limit of 15 levels. But don't overdo it. Too many subcategories and, especially, too many levels will make your records so complicated that you'll have trouble seeing meaningful trends.

In any case, choose category and class names that are easy to remember and easy to type. To make related categories and classes appear near one another in the list and on reports, choose similar names, such as **Inc-int** for interest income and **Inc-sal** for salary income. Table 5.1 shows the Category and Class Lists as they should be modified for the example transactions in this book.

TABLE 5.1   *The Sample List of Categories and Classes*

Categories:

Category	Description	Tax Rel	Tax Schedule and Line
Income			
Bonus	Bonus Income	*	W-2: Salary
Consults	Consulting fees		Schedule C: Gross receipts
Bathroom	Bathroom design	*	Schedule C: Gross receipts
Color scheme	Color scheme consult	*	Schedule C: Gross receipts
Wall coverings	Wall covering consult	*	Schedule C: Gross receipts
Windows	Window consult		Schedule C: gross receipts
Div Income	Dividend Income	*	Schedule B: Dividend income

Gift Received	Gift Received	*	
Int Inc	Interest Income	*	Schedule B: Interest income
Other Inc	Other Income	*	
Salary	Salary Income	*	W-2: Salary

Expense

Ads	Advertising	*	Schedule C: Advertising
Auto	Automobile Expenses		
Fuel	Auto Fuel		
Loan	Auto Loan Payment		
Parts	Parts/supplies		
Service	Auto Service		
Bank Chrg	Bank Charge		
Charity	Charitable donations	*	Schedule A: Cash charity contribution
Childcare	Childcare Expense		
Christmas	Christmas Expenses		
Clothing	Clothing		
Dining	Dining Out	*	Schedule C: Meals and entertainment
Education	Education		
Entertain	Entertainment	*	Schedule C: Meals and entertainment
Equipment	Depreciable purchases	*	Schedule C: Depletion
Freight	Freight	*	Schedule C: Other business expenses
Gifts	Gift Expenses		
Groceries	Groceries		
Home Rpair	Home Repair & Maint.		
Household	Household Misc. Exp		
Insurance	Insurance		
Business	Business insurance	*	Schedule C: Insurance (not health)
Health	Health insurance	*	Schedule A: Medicine and drugs
Home	Homeowner's insurance		
Life	Life insurance		
Unemp	Unemployment ins premium		
Int Paid	Interest Paid	*	Schedule C: Interest expense, other
L & P Fees	Legal & Prof. Fees	*	Schedule C: Legal and professional

Late Fees	Late Payment Fees	*	Schedule C: Other business expenses
Medical	Medical & Dental	*	Schedule A: Medicine and drugs
Misc	Miscellaneous		
Mort Int	Mortgage payments		
Insurance	Mortgage insurance		
Interest	Mortgage interest		Schedule A: Home mortgage interest
Principal	Mortgage principal		
Office	Office Expenses	*	Schedule C: Office expense
Other Exp	Other Expenses	*	Schedule C: Other business expenses
Parties	Parties, picnics		
Recreation	Recreation Expense		
Rent Paid	Rent Paid prop	*	Schedule C: rent on other bus
Repairs	Repairs	*	Schedule C: Repairs and maintenance
Subscriptions	Subscriptions		
Supplies	Supplies	*	Schedule C: Supplies
Tax	Taxes	*	Schedule C: Taxes and licenses
Fed	Federal Tax	*	W-2: Federal Withholding
FICA	Social Security Tax	*	W-2: Soc Sec Tax Withholding
Other	Misc. Taxes	*	
Prop	Property Tax	*	Schedule A: Real estate tax
State	State Tax	*	W-2: State Withholding
Telephone	Telephone Expense		
Travel	Travel Expenses		Schedule C: Travel
Utilities	Water, Gas, Electric		
Garbage	Garbage pickup		
Gas & Electric	Gas and Electricity		
Water	Water		

Classes:

Class	Description
Business	Business expenses
Cabin	Subclass-vacation cabin
Home	Personal/home expenses
House	Subclass-main home

Creating Your Account Categories

The first task you'll tackle is to modify the categories currently in your account to match the list you've drawn up. When that's done, you'll go on to develop your list of classes.

Begin by examining the list of categories already in place in your Quicken account. To display the Category & Transfer List dialog box, start from the Write Checks window or the register. Press **Ctrl-C**, click the **Cat List** icon in the Iconbar, or choose **Category & Transfer** from the Lists menu. The Category & Transfer List dialog box will pop up on your screen, as shown in Figure 5.1.

FIGURE 5.1

The Category & Transfer List dialog box.

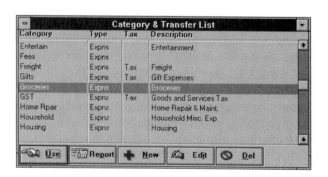

Let's pause a moment to take a closer look at the Category list. First of all, notice that the dialog box pops up with one of the categories already highlighted. The highlighted category is the one that most closely matches the category of the current check or register transaction you started from.

| NOTE |

There is only one Category list for all the transactions in your account, whether they are income items, expense items, or other types.

Now look at the various columns in the window. The first column, labeled *Category*, holds the category's official name in Quicken, that is, the name that Quicken uses when it finds and sorts your transactions by category. The next column, the *Type* column, indicates the type of transaction that will be stored in that category. Use the **Up Arrow** and **Down Arrow** keys to move randomly through the list. Notice that categories for income items are labeled "Inc" in the *Type* column, whereas those for expense items are labeled **Expns**. Subcategories of either income or expense categories are labeled **Sub**.

At the bottom of the list, Quicken has added categories for each of the accounts in the current account file to allow you to transfer funds among your accounts. For these items, Quicken uses the account's name in square brackets as the category name and the type of account (bank, investment, and so on) as the category type. If you're following the tutorial in this book, you only have one account so far, a bank account named *Checking*. You should see it at the bottom of the Category list. Chapter 8 tells all about creating other Quicken accounts and using all your accounts together.

In the *Tax* column, the entry **Tax** indicates that the category listed on that line is somehow tax related. An expense category for interest on mortgage payments would be tax related, but one for spending on food would not. Most income items will be tax related, of course—unfortunately.

The final column in the dialog box is labeled *Description*. This is simply a place for an optional longer description of the category than will fit in the space allotted to the category name.

Printing the Category List

Now it's time to start making changes to the current Category list. Although you can read the current list on the screen, it will be easier to work with if you print it out on paper first.

To print the account's current Category list, start by making sure your printer is connected and ready to print. Then, with the Category & Transfer list still active, click the **Print** icon or press **Ctrl-P**. You'll see the standard Print Report dialog box, the same one you used to print the register in Chapter 4.

For a standard paper printout, just choose **Print**. If all goes well, you'll receive a printout of the complete Category list that looks much the same as the list in the window, and you'll be returned to the Category & Transfer list.

> **NOTE**   Consult Chapter 10 for details on the options in the Print Report window. In Quicken 2, you print the Category list from a special Print Category & Transfer List window, not from the Print Report window.

Noting Changes to be Made

With your paper printout of the category list in hand, use pen or pencil to modify it to match your custom list. Cross out any categories you won't be using, and write in any changes you want over the categories you plan to keep. At the bottom of the printed list, write in the names of any new categories that you want to add. Again, if you want to follow the examples in this book, you should use Table 5.1 as a guide.

Creating New Categories

Before you actually begin creating categories, there's one critical preliminary step to take care of: setting up Quicken so that you can associate each category with a specific item on your federal tax forms. Unless you turn on the **Tax Form** feature, you won't be able to use Quicken for efficient tax accounting.

Here's what you must do: Display the Preferences window by clicking the **Prefs** icon on the Iconbar, or choosing **Preferences** in the Edit menu. Then choose the **General** button to display the General Preferences dialog box.

NOTE

Quicken 2 has a separate Preferences menu. To display the General Preferences dialog box, choose **General** from the Preferences menu.

Make sure that the checkbox at the very bottom of the window, the one labeled **Use Tax Schedules with Categories**, is checked. If not, check the box now, and then choose **OK** to close the General Preferences dialog box.

WARNING

Quicken comes set up so that the program warns you before recording a transaction without a category assignment. Although you can remove this warning as detailed in the Appendix, I recommend you leave it active.

Now it's time to add the missing categories from your list to the account. Find the first new category where you've written it, at the bottom of the printed list, and then proceed as follows.

1. Choose the **New** button at the bottom of the Category & Transfer List dialog box. The Set Up Category dialog box will appear, as shown in Figure 5.2.

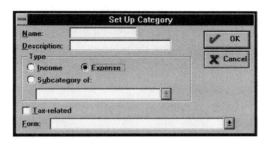

FIGURE 5.2

The Set Up Category dialog box.

2. Fill out the Set Up Category dialog box by transferring the entries from the columns on your marked-up printed list to the corresponding fields in the window. At the *Type* field, choose the radio button that corresponds to the type of category you're creating, an income or expense category or a subcategory of either main category type.

3. If you're entering a subcategory—there are a couple on the sample Category list—enter the category it belongs to in the text box below the **Subcategory of** radio button. You can select the category name from the drop-down list or start typing the name and let QuickFill complete it for you.

| NOTE | See the section *Assigning Transactions to Categories and Classes* later in this chapter for more on how subcategories work. |

4. To specify that a given category is tax related, check the *Tax-Related* field.

5. Indicating that a category is tax related in general can sometimes be useful, but the real key to getting help with your taxes from Quicken is this: You must assign each tax-related category to a particular line on a particular federal income tax form. To do this, fill in the *Form* field. Use the drop-down list to select the appropriate tax form or schedule along with a description of the specific line on that form to which the category corresponds. Figure 5.3 shows this process in progress.

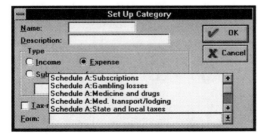

FIGURE 5.3

Assigning a category to a specific item on a particular tax form.

6. When all the fields are complete, choose **OK** to create the new category. Quicken returns you to the Category & Transfer List dialog box, with the new category in its proper alphabetical location. If you've added a subcategory, it appears indented below the main category to which you assigned it.

Repeat these six steps for all the new categories you need to add.

Changing Existing Categories

When you've added all your new categories to the Category list, you can go on to modify the existing categories that don't quite match the corresponding ones on your own list. Changing an existing category is very similar to adding a new category.

Start by searching in the Category & Transfer List dialog box for the category you wish to change. The easiest way is to press the letter key corresponding to the first letter in the category's name. When you do, Quicken moves the Arrow pointer to the first category that starts with that letter. If that's not the right category, press the same letter key repeatedly until the pointer is on the category you want to change. Alternatively, you can use the **Up Arrow**, **Down Arrow**, **PgUp**, and **PgDn** keys or the mouse to move the highlight until it's on that category.

Having found and marked the category, choose **Edit** or press **Ctrl-E** to pop up the Edit Category dialog box (other than the title, it's the same one shown in Figure 5.2). The existing entries for the various fields of the category definition—*Name*, *Description*, *Type*, *Tax Related*, and *Form*—will be visible. Make the necessary changes to the item in each field using the standard techniques (see the next section if you plan to change the category's type). To skip a field without changing it, press **Tab**.

When you've made all the changes, choose **OK** to finalize them. Quicken will return you to the Category & Transfer List dialog box, with the changes you've made recorded in the list. In addition, if you've changed the category name, that name will also be changed in all transactions assigned to it in your account. Repeat these steps for all the categories that need modification.

Restructuring the Category List

If the organizational scheme you originally choose for your categories and subcategories turns out not to reflect the realities of your financial situation,

Quicken is flexible enough to let you restructure the Category list. If you decide that a given subcategory would better serve you as a full-fledged category, or vice versa, you're free to make the switch. You can move a subcategory from one main category to another just as easily.

After displaying the Category list, highlight the category or subcategory whose location you want to change, and choose **Edit**. You'll use the *Type* field for the task at hand. If you're turning an existing subcategory into a main category, select the appropriate radio button, income or expense, for the category. To convert a main category to a subcategory, select the **Subcategory** button and then fill in the Text box below it with the name of the category it should belong to. Finally, to move a subcategory from one main category to another, just change the entry in the Text box below the **Subcategory** button.

| WARNING | Since Quicken allows you to move a subcategory that originally belonged to an income category to an expense category, be sure to check that the final category type is correct after you make the move. |

Once you've placed the category where you want it, choose **OK** to finalize the changes. Any subcategories that belonged to the category you moved will move with it. Quicken automatically changes the category assignments in all transactions affected by the move.

Deleting Categories

The last step in customizing your Category list for your own needs is to delete categories that you don't need. It's no disaster to have the extra ones in your Category list, but they are extra baggage that will make it a little harder to find the categories you do use.

Refer to the printed Category list you modified for your own situation earlier in this chapter. Categories you planned to delete have been crossed out. To delete these unnecessary categories, track each one down in the list, and then, when you have it highlighted, choose the **Del** button or press **Ctrl-D**.

Quicken will warn you that you're about to permanently delete a category. Choose **OK** to go ahead with the deletion, or **Esc** or **Cancel** if you've changed your mind.

As soon as Quicken deletes the category, you'll be returned to the Category & Transfer List dialog box. In the process, the category name will also be removed from all the transactions that had been assigned to it in your account.

Merging Categories

If you decide that two categories in your list overlap so much that they are redundant, Quicken lets you merge them into a single category while maintaining all your existing transaction assignments. However, this works only if neither of the categories has subcategories.

Here's how to proceed: Pop up the Category list and select the category that you no longer plan to use. Using the steps laid out in the section *Restructuring the Category List*, change the type of this soon-to-be-discarded category so that it is a subcategory of the category you plan to keep.

Once that's done, delete the new subcategory. Quicken asks you if you want to go ahead with the deletion, merging the transactions currently assigned to the subcategory with those of the "parent" category. At this point you have three options:

- If you choose **Yes**, Quicken sees to it that all of the transactions originally assigned to the deleted subcategory remain assigned to the category you kept.

- Choose **No** if you want to delete the subcategory without reassigning its transactions—in this case, Quicken empties the *Category* field for these transactions.

- You can change your mind and not delete the subcategory at all by choosing **Cancel**.

Creating Your Own Class List

Since Quicken does not offer a built-in list of classes as it does of categories, you must create your own list of classes. The process is almost identical to the one for creating new categories, except that there are only two parts to the definition of each class, its name and its description.

With your list of classes in hand, follow these steps to add the classes to your Quicken checking account. Open the Class List dialog box by pressing **Ctrl-L** or choosing **Class** in the List menu. The Class List dialog box, shown in Figure 5.4, is a simple list with only two columns for each class.

The *Class* column displays whatever name you give the class, while the *Description* column is for a longer optional description of the class's function.

At this point, the window displays only **Business** and **Home**, the two classes that you set up while entering sample transactions in Chapters 2 and 4.

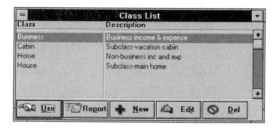

The Class List dialog box works exactly like the Category & Transfer List dialog box. You move the pointer to the desired class with any suitable combination of the **Up Arrow**, **Down Arrow**, **PgUp**, **PgDn**, **Home**, or **End** keys. Alternatively, you can jump to the desired class by typing the first letter in the class name.

To create a new class, choose the **New** button. This displays the Set Up Class dialog box (Figure 5.5). In the window, transfer the new class's name and description from your written list into the corresponding fields. Use the standard Quicken typing and editing techniques to make your entries. When fields are complete, choose **OK** to finalize the entry for the new class.

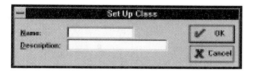

Quicken then returns you to the Class List dialog box, with the new class entered into the list (it may not be visible, however, since Quicken will have placed it in proper alphabetical order). Repeat the steps above for all the classes you'd like to add.

Quicken permits you to have subclasses, but they work a little differently from subcategories. To create a subclass, you set it up just as you would an ordinary class. Then, to use the new class as a subclass in a transaction, you assign it to the transaction in the *Category* field by typing **:** (colon) after the main class, then entering the subclass. See the section "Assigning Transactions to Categories and Classes," later in this chapter.

Changing and Deleting Classes

If you realize you've made a mistake in entering a class, or if you find later that you need to modify the Class list to reflect changes in your financial situation, Quicken makes the necessary adjustments easy for you.

To delete a class you no longer need, highlight it in the Class list and choose **Del** or press **Ctrl-D**. Quicken deletes the class and removes its name from all the transactions that had been assigned to it in your account.

To change a class, highlight it in the Class list and choose **Edit** or press **Ctrl-E**. The Edit Class dialog box—identical except for its title to the one shown in Figure 5.5—will appear, allowing you to change the class name or description as you'd like. When you've completed the changes, choose **OK**. They'll be recorded in the Class list; and if you've changed the class name, it will also be changed in any transactions assigned to that class.

Adding Category and Class Lists from Another File

Quicken lets you transfer Category and Class lists you develop in one account file to any other file. You can also add Quicken's standard home or business categories—the ones you could have chosen when you first set up an account file—to the file at a later time. For details on the procedure involved, see *Transferring Data between Accounts* in the Appendix.

Assigning Transactions to Categories and Classes

You already learned in Chapters 2 and 4 how to assign checks and register transactions to categories and classes. As a refresher, though, let's review the steps involved here, and learn how to use subcategories and subclasses.

WARNING When you want a breakdown of your account according to its categories and classes, you need Quicken's reporting and graphing features, outlined in Chapters 10 through 12. Chapters 13 through 16 show you how to put your categories to work in common financial situations.

Let's say you want to enter a handwritten check covering the electric bill on your mountain cabin (this example assumes you've set up your Category and

Class lists exactly as shown in Figure 5.1). Move to an empty transaction by pressing **Ctrl-N**. Skip over the *Date* and *Num* fields, type **Seabright Power** in the *Payee* field, and **45.17** in the *Payment* field.

Now move down to the **Category** field. The check falls into the **Gas-Elec** subcategory of the **Utilities** category, and in the **Cabin** subclass of the **Home** class. As you know, category and class entries in the *Category* field should be separated by a slash (*/*). To separate a category from a subcategory, or a class from a subclass, use a colon (:). Thus, the entry you'll be making in the *Category* field for this transaction is **Utilities:Gas-Elec/Home:Cabin**.

Although you could type in the entry yourself, you can have Quicken fill out most of the field for you. With the cursor in the *Category* field, type **U**. Notice that QuickFill completes the **Utilities** entry for you. Now, carefully type : (if you hit a stray key, the highlighted portion of the category will be erased). QuickFill automatically enters the first subcategory under the **Utilities** category, which in this case is **Garbage**. Type a couple more letters of the correct category name, **Gas-Elec**, until QuickFill completes the entry correctly.

Now type a slash (*/*) and the letter **H**. Again, QuickFill steps in, completing the entry of the **Home** class. This time, however, don't type a colon just yet. Instead, press **Right Arrow** to move the cursor to the very end of the entry. Now type the colon, followed by **cabin**. (QuickFill won't make an automatic subclass entry, since the Class list doesn't indicate which classes you're using as subclasses.) You can now record the transaction.

Of course, there will often be more than one category or class that starts with the first letter you've typed. If QuickFill guesses wrong, you can just keep typing the correct entry. As soon as you've typed the second letter, QuickFill looks through the Category list again for another match. If necessary, type a third or fourth letter until you see the entry you'd like.

Alternatively, instead of typing additional letters, press **+** or **-** to have QuickFill switch to the next or previous match, in alphabetical order, among the categories or classes in your account.

If Quicken doesn't come up with a match for what you've typed, there are at least two possibilities: the category or class you wanted may not exist in the list, or it may be spelled slightly differently. If you're trying to enter a main category, another explanation can be that the entry you're typing is actually a subcategory.

No matter which of these situations prevails, the solution is the same. When QuickFill doesn't provide an expected match after typing a character or two, just scroll through the drop-down list of categories until you find the one you'd like. Choose it, and you're in business. If you can't find the desired category, pop up the Category & Transfer list (**Ctrl-C**) and create the category from scratch.

If you're entering a category and your partial entry matches a subcategory, Quicken enters the full subcategory as well as the main category it belongs to. If that's not what you intended, you can pop up the Category or Class list as appropriate and select from it—the highlight will be on the list entry that matches what you typed most closely.

Using Subclasses

Freedom can be a dangerous thing. The good news about the method Quicken uses to keep track of subclasses is that it gives you lots of flexibility. The bad news is that it may also lead to some confusion. As you've seen, Quicken doesn't distinguish subclasses from regular classes on the Class list. In other words, you're free to use a subclass as a main class and vice versa, if you so desire; all you have to do is enter the subcategory name first, a colon, then the category name, and the roles are reversed. In fact, if you enter a subclass by itself in a transaction's class field, Quicken interprets it as a regular class.

When you ask Quicken to prepare a report showing class-by-class breakdowns, the program simply reads whatever entries are recorded in the *Class* field. It does not check them to see whether they're in proper order according to their status as classes or subclasses. You don't even get a *Type* column in the Class list to help you keep track of which entries are subclasses.

NOTE	The bottom line is that you must be very careful to assign the class and subclass to each transaction in the proper order to get the results you really intend. If you're hastily entering checks one month and enter **Cabin** as the class for one of your checks, forgetting it's really a subclass, your report will show that payment in a separate class equal in importance to **Home**.

Handling Multiple-Item Transactions

In this age of one-stop shopping at giant food, drug, and discount warehouses, it's not uncommon to write a single check for a multitude of different kinds of purchases.

Let's say that one hectic weekend you emerge from your local JumboGiant store with a week's supply of food, a set of new tires for your car, a new computer for your business office, and some floppy disks and copier paper. For convenience, you paid for all these items with your new JumboGiant credit card. Since you have enough money in your checking account to cover the purchase, however, you plan to write a check for the entire amount as soon as you get the bill.

If you're using Quicken to its fullest, you've already set up one category for food, another for automotive expenses, another for depreciable business items, and yet another for miscellaneous business supplies. Now comes the tricky part: how to divide that one check you wrote for all those purchases among the categories. As always, Quicken turns recording a complex transaction into an effortless task.

The phenomenon of carrying out many transactions with one sum of money is even more common when you make deposits, particularly if you run a business. You probably make deposits only once a day at most, yet each deposit contains many checks (I hope). You'd like to somehow record the deposit as a whole, so that you can keep track of your daily income and easily match your deposit records with your bank statements. On the other hand, you want a record of each check in the deposit. Again, that's no problem for Quicken.

Quicken refers to transactions that cover multiple items as *split transactions*. You can split any transaction while you're entering it in the Write Checks window or the register.

Recording a Check as a Split Transaction

Let's use the example of the trip to the JumboGiant to see how the process of splitting a check transaction works. Your JumboGiant credit card bill has arrived, and you're sitting down in front of your computer to pay it in full. The check you'll be writing is shown in Figure 5.6.

Payee: JumboGiant Superstore
Amount: $1766.22

Here's the way the purchase went, divided by category.

Category	Memo	Amount
Groceries/Home	*Weekly groceries*	**$ 112.67**
Auto:Parts/Home	*Tires*	**$ 320.86**
Equipment/Business	*Computer*	**$1,310.44**
Supplies/Business	*Paper, misc. supplies*	**$ 22.25**

FIGURE 5.6

*A sample
check covering
several purchases.*

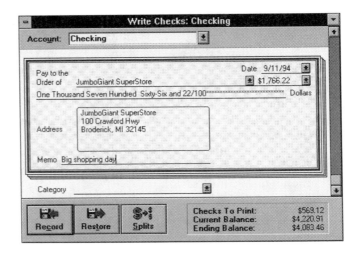

I'll assume you've already set up your Category and Class lists to match the sample lists shown earlier in this chapter. If not, you can modify your lists temporarily while you work through this example, or use the nearest categories and classes from your own lists.

Entering the Check to be Split

NOTE   If you were recording a check you had written by hand to cover this same purchase, you would enter it from the register. Otherwise, the procedure for splitting the transaction would be the same as described in the following section.

Start by writing the check to pay for your little trip to the store. Move to the Write Checks window if you're not already there (press the **Ctrl-W** keyboard shortcut, click the **Check** icon, or choose **Write Checks** from the Activities menu). Be sure a new blank check is on the screen; if not, press **End** to display one. Then fill out the fields in the screen check to match the one shown in Figure 5.6. Don't enter a category or class in the *Category* field, however, and don't record the check yet.

Splitting the Check

Now you're ready to split the check transaction. To do this, you can choose the **Splits** button (now you know what that button is for) or press **Ctrl-S**. You'll see the Splits window, which is shown in Figure 5.7.

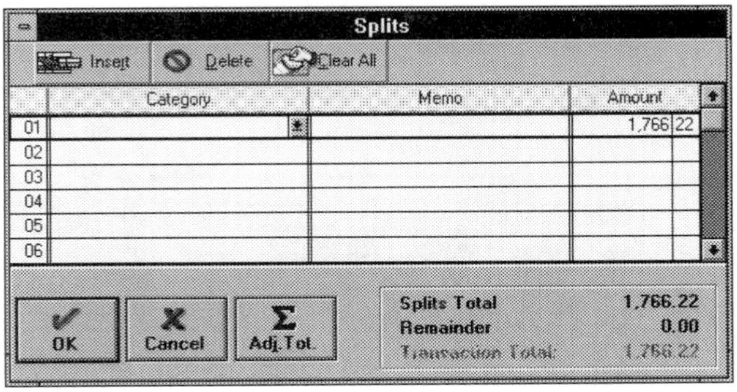

FIGURE 5.7

The Splits window.

The Splits window is empty except for the total amount of the check on the first line of the far-right column. If you had made an entry on the check in the *Category* field, that entry would have been copied to the top line of the Splits window as well.

As you can see, the Splits window comes equipped with several buttons along the top and bottom. The main part of the window consists of a simple table or grid. Each row in the table corresponds to one of the splits in your transaction. As the column titles suggest, you can assign each item to a category, class, or both, and enter an optional memo. Most important, you must fill out the third column labeled *Amount*.

NOTE

Quicken 2 lacks the top row of buttons. Also, the button on the bottom labeled **Adj Total** in Quicken 3 is called **Recalc** in Quicken 2—but it does the same job.

The cursor should be in the first row in the *Category* column. You make category and class entries in the Splits window just as you would on the check itself or in a register transaction—QuickFill and the Category & Transfer and Class lists work the same way.

Make the entries for the first part of the split, the one covering your food purchase at JumboGiant. Enter the category for your food purchase, **Groceries**. (QuickFill works within split transactions to automatically finish your entries so you only need to type a letter or two.) After typing /, enter the **Home** class. The completed entry in the *Category* field should read *Groceries/Home*.

Press **Tab** to move to the *Memo* column where you can type **Weekly groceries**. Then move to the *Amount* column by pressing **Tab** again. Type the dollar amount of your food purchase, **112.67**, over the total amount of the check now there. If you start typing before moving the cursor, Quicken will erase the previous entry in the column.

SHORTCUT	If you want to edit an entry in the *Amount* column without completely replacing it, move the cursor to the first digit you want to change before you type any new numbers.

Press **Tab** when you're through with the *Amount* column. The cursor will move to the *Category* column for split item 2. You'll see that the *Amount* column for this item now contains what's left of the original check total after the food expense has been subtracted.

SHORTCUT	In the *Category* column, you can press ' to copy the category and class information from the previous line of the split.

Enter the second item in the split, your tire purchase. The entry in the *Category* column should read **Auto:Parts/Home**.

Since the class for the tires is the same as for the food, you can use another shortcut to enter it if you'd like. After typing / to indicate you'll be entering the class, type ' to copy the class information from the above line to this entry. The word *Home* will appear on the second line. Press **Tab** to complete the entry and move the cursor to the next column.

In the *Memo* column, enter an appropriate note such as **Tires**, then press **Tab**. As in the *Category* column, you could have used ' (**single quote**) to copy the information from the previous line of the split.

The cursor should now be in the *Amount* column. Type in the dollar amount of your tire purchase, **320.86**. Press **Tab** to move on to the next line.

Complete the entries for the third and fourth parts of the split, the computer purchase and the office supplies, copying from the previous list. When you press **Tab** after entering the amount of the purchase that went for office supplies, your screen should look like Figure 5.8.

NOTE Note that there will be no entry in the *Amount* column for line 5. This shows that the total of all the lines equals the original check amount.

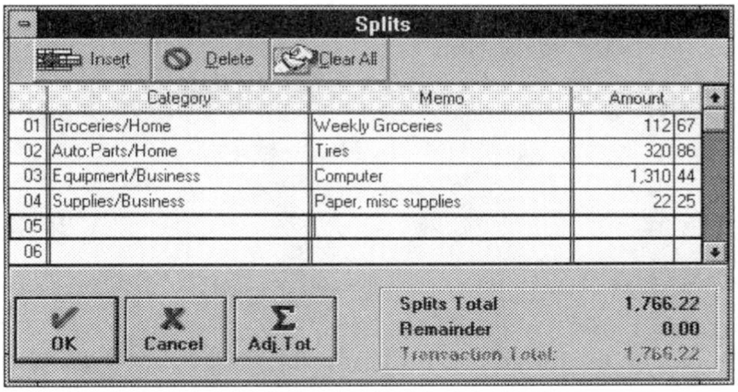

FIGURE 5.8

Make these entries in the Splits window.

When all four lines in the window are complete, choose **OK** to finish the entry. You'll be returned to the Write Checks window. The *Category* field will show the notation *-SPLITS-*. Press **Enter** to record the transaction.

To see how split check transactions look in the register, press the **Ctrl-R** keyboard shortcut to move to the register now. You'll see the new check in the register, again with *-SPLITS-* in the *Category* field.

Recording a Deposit as a Split Transaction

Now that you're in the register, you'll learn how to use the Split Transaction feature from this part of Quicken. Actually, the process is the same whether you're writing checks or recording register transactions, but you'll also learn how split transactions can be used to record subcategories as well as full categories.

Let's say you're an interior design consultant. It's after lunch, and you're back at your home office preparing to make your daily bank deposit. The day has been rather quiet so far. You collected three checks and one cash payment from your clients, and you also received a tax refund check in the mail. With Quicken's Split Transaction feature, you'll be able to record all these income items in one deposit, and the program will add them up for you as you proceed.

This time, we'll assume you've created your Quicken account for business use only, so you're not using classes. Instead, you've decided to group your consulting fees in the **Consultation** category, and further classify them into subcategories according to the type of problem you solved for your client.

Category	Memo	Amount
Consults:Color scheme	Tony Armano-chk #1675	**$100.00**
Consults:Windows	Sheila Tuliah-chk # 833	**$75.00**
Consults:Wall coverings	Hugh's Hobby House-chk#3226	**$50.00**
Tax refund:State	State income tax refund	**$345.89**
Consults:Bathroom	Mertha Wilson—cash	**$125.00**

Begin entry of the deposit transaction by pressing **End** four times to highlight the first empty transaction at the end of the register. Enter the date and put **Deposit** in the *Num* column. If you'd like, type the name of your bank in the *Payee* column.

Now you're ready to split the transaction. Press **Ctrl-S** or click the **Splits** button to pop up the Splits window. Your screen should look like Figure 5.9.

FIGURE 5.9

The Splits window showing your split deposit.

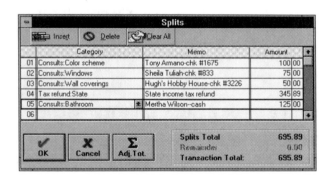

The Splits window will look just as it did when you split the check transaction, except that this time the *Amount* column will be empty on the first line, since you haven't entered an amount for the deposit yet. Copy the information from the list of items mentioned previously to the dialog box.

NOTE   To record split payment transactions in the register, enter the items with negative numbers in the *Amount* column of the Splits window.

In the *Category* column, you can use QuickFill, of course, so you don't have to type out the entries in full. In fact, all you need to do is start typing the subcategory name; QuickFill will fill in the full entry, including the main category, the colon, and the complete subcategory. (If your Category list doesn't exactly match the sample list in Table 5.1, you'll either have to create the categories and subcategories now, or use different ones that are already in your Category list.)

After typing in the memo and amount for the first split item, tab to the second line. Since the category entry is the same as for the item above, you could copy the previous category by typing ' and then add the subcategory information. Again, with QuickFill it's probably even easier just to start typing the subcategory name.

When you've entered all five items, choose **OK** to finalize your entries. Quicken will add up the amounts of the separate deposit items for you and place the total in the *Deposit* field in the register. Note also the notation *-SPLITS-* appears in the transaction's *Category* field. Now press **Enter** to record the split transaction in your account.

Viewing and Changing Split Transactions

Practice viewing and changing the details of the split from the register. The split deposit transaction should still be highlighted in the register, but if not, highlight it. Then choose the **Splits** button or press **Ctrl-S** to pop up the Splits window.

To make changes in any of the items in the window, use the standard Quicken techniques for moving the cursor and editing entries. Insert a new line above the one you're currently working with by choosing the **Insert** button. To delete an item in the window, move the cursor to the item's line and click the **Delete** button or press **Ctrl-D**. You can also restore a transaction to an "unsplit" condition by choosing the **Clear All** button or by pressing **Ctrl-D** repeatedly; this deletes every item in the Splits window.

When you're through making changes to the split items, finalize your work by pressing **Enter**. If you've deleted all the split items, the *Category* field will no longer contain *-SPLITS-*. To make this transaction a permanent part of your account, record the modifications by pressing **Enter** again.

Summary

In learning to use categories and classes, you've just mastered some of the most important Quicken techniques for tracking your finances. You now know the mechanics of working with categories and classes: how to set them up, how to assign them to transactions, and how to modify and delete them. Even more important, you know when to use categories, subcategories, classes, and subclasses to make your records more organized. You've also learned how to split a single transaction that covers two or more items, assigning each item to its own category and class.

The effort you've put into assigning transactions to categories and classes will pay off as you produce informative reports and graphs in Chapters 10 through 16. But next, in Chapter 6, you'll practice balancing your checkbook with Quicken.

Chapter Six
Balancing Your Checking Account

nce a month, your bank or savings and loan sends you a statement listing all the checks that have cleared your account that month, all the deposits you made, and any other transactions that affected your balance. If you're a responsible money manager, you're used to spending a few minutes comparing the statement to your own records, to see which checks have cleared and to catch any overcharges or unexpected fees. Most important, you want to make sure that the bottom lines match—that you and your bank agree about how much money you had in your account at the time the statement was issued. This is called *balancing* a checkbook. The more accurate term is *reconciling*, since you are checking your bank's records against your own and trying to iron out any discrepancies. Whatever you call it, it's one of life's trying little chores—but one that Quicken can help you dispense with almost effortlessly.

An Outline of the Balancing Process

Here, in a nutshell, is how balancing or reconciling your account works with Quicken. You start by making sure that Quicken has certain essential information from the bank statement, including the opening and ending balances for the period the statement covers. With this information on board, Quicken then displays a list of transactions taken from your register, and you mark the ones that have cleared on your bank statement.

Once you've marked all the cleared transactions, Quicken compares its balance, which is based on your cleared transactions, to the ending balance shown on your statement, and then displays the difference. If the numbers don't match, you can go on to correct mistaken entries in the register or take other appropriate steps. When Quicken and your bank statement agree, you have completed the reconciliation process. A printed report of your work is easily attainable.

With Quicken to do your calculations for you, the reconciliation process goes extremely quickly and accurately. Still, you should expect to spend at least half as much time as you would in doing it the old way, at least for the first month or two.

Now that you have the basic idea of how to balance your checkbook with Quicken, let's review the details. For this chapter, I'll assume that you've begun entering your own "real" checks into your account, and that you're working with your latest bank statement.

Balancing Your Account the First Time

When you begin work with Quicken, it's common to have discrepancies between the items and balance in your statement and the ones in your Quicken account. The problem is simply that when you jump into record-keeping with Quicken in midstream, you usually don't know what your actual balance is, nor which transactions have already cleared your bank. Let's study the situation in more detail, and then discuss the techniques for dealing with it.

The first time you reconcile, Quicken uses the balance you entered when setting up your account as the opening balance for the reconciliation. As you'll recall, Quicken strongly recommends when you set up the account that you use the closing balance from your last bank statement as your opening balance.

Here's the reason for this advice. The balance in your paper checkbook register is simply a running tally that reflects the checks you've written, not the ones that have cleared. Imagine that you buy Quicken one fine day just after you've received your latest bank statement. Going right to work, you enter the balance showing in your paper checkbook, **$950**, as the opening balance for your Quicken account. But the balance in your checkbook reflects all the checks that you've written up to that point, including one for $100 that hasn't cleared as of your last statement. Therefore, your latest statement's closing balance is $1,050, or $100 more than the balance you calculated in your checkbook.

That closing balance will be carried forward to become the opening balance in the next statement, indicating an apparent surplus of $100. This surplus is only apparent, however, because the new statement will probably show that the $100 has now cleared. But Quicken must still account for the discrepancy in the original balance, or all its future calculations will be off by $100.

To avoid this kind of trouble, just take Quicken's advice when you set up a bank account and enter as the opening balance the closing balance of your last statement. But even if you used another figure as your opening balance, you can still reconcile successfully, as you'll learn in the section "Handling an Opening Balance Difference."

But there's one more step to successful balancing when you're just getting started with Quicken. Remember those uncleared checks you wrote before you created your Quicken account? They will eventually appear on a future statement, and if you don't enter them into Quicken, they'll throw off your balance when they do appear.

Ideally, then, you should make an effort to enter all your uncleared transactions before you start reconciling by getting out your previous bank statements and searching for the uncleared checks. On many statements, the bank prints an asterisk or some other warning mark where it finds a break in a sequence of check numbers; this should help you find the uncleared transactions. When they do clear your bank—an event that will probably appear on the statement you're about to reconcile—you'll be able to mark them as cleared. You can also enter the uncleared transactions during the reconciliation process itself, as described in the section "Adding Missing Transactions" later in the chapter.

Beginning the Balancing Process

| WARNING | If you've created more than one Quicken checking account, before you start reconciling, you should take a moment to be sure that you're working with the account that matches your bank statement. If the account name shown at the top of the window isn't the right one, switch to the Account List window by pressing **Ctrl-A**, select the correct account, and then choose **Use**. |

To begin balancing, start with either the Write Checks window or the register as the active window, and choose **Reconcile** from the Activities menu or click the **Recon** icon on the Iconbar. You'll see the Reconcile Bank Statement dialog box, as shown in Figure 6.1.

FIGURE 6.1

Begin balancing your checkbook by filling in the Reconcile Bank Statement dialog box.

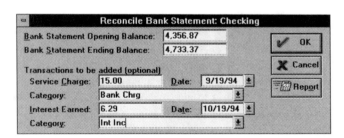

In the first field on the window, *Bank Statement Opening Balance*, Quicken displays the balance it thinks your bank statement will show as the opening balance for your account. Once you've reviewed the balancing process the first time, and if you do it regularly, this number should be correct. The first time you balance, though, the amount may not be correct, and it will be off if you haven't kept up the process month by month.

If the amount shown matches the opening balance on your statement, simply press Tab to advance to the next field. If the amounts are different, type in the opening balance from your statement, and then press **Tab**.

| **NOTE** | If you have to correct the opening balance Quicken displayed, you'll be asked to enter additional information later to account for this change. |

The cursor should now be on the field labeled *Bank Statement Ending Balance*. Copy the ending balance from your statement (it might be called the *Current Balance* or *New Balance*) into this field, and press Tab.

The next few fields record transactions initiated by your bank, that is, for service charges and interest earned. These fields are labeled *Optional*, but you should fill them in unless you don't have any charges or interest listed on your statement. When you enter transactions in these fields, Quicken automatically records them in your register, marking them as cleared for you.

| **WARNING** | If you started reconciling this statement during a previous session and filled out the *Service Charge* and *Interest* fields, but then canceled the reconciliation process, don't fill out these fields again; Quicken has already entered them into your account. |

At the *Service Charge* field, type in the total amount of all service charges listed on your statement. If more than one charge appears, add the amounts together and enter the total. To do the calculations, you may want to pop up the Windows Calculator by clicking the **Calc** icon or choosing **Use Calculator** from the Activities menu. It's up to you whether to include in this amount special fees or penalties such as overdraft penalties you've assessed; if you'd like, you'll be given a chance to enter these as separate transactions in a later step in the reconciliation process. When you've entered the amount, press **Tab**. Here, in the *Date* field, Quicken has already entered today's date. If you want to be more exact, change the date to that shown on the bank statement for the service charge.

Press **Tab** to move to the *Category* field. An entry here is truly optional when it comes to a minor expense like service charges. But if you do fill it in, you'll be able to see how much money you've paid in service charges over the course of a year—and who knows, the total might motivate you to shop for a new bank. Just as for any other transaction, you can type in a category, a class, or both, or use Quicken's Category and Class lists to insert the category and class names for you.

Next comes a set of fields for interest earned by the funds in your account. In the *Interest Earned* field, enter the total of all interest payments credited to your account on your statement, and press Tab. Again, make entries in the *Date* and *Category* fields if you like, pressing **Tab** after completing each field.

NEW IN 3 In Quicken 3, you can print a report summarizing the current status of your account, prior to this balancing session, by choosing the **Report** button. The report will include the number and dollar amount of any previously cleared transactions and of the yet-to-be-cleared transactions in your account, information you may find useful while balancing.

Using the Reconcile Bank Account Window

When you've completed all the fields in the Reconcile Bank Statement dialog box, choose **OK**. Quicken takes you to the main window for reconciliation, the Reconcile Bank Account window. As shown in Figure 6.2, this window provides a summary listing of all the transactions in your account that have not yet been cleared. I'll refer to it as the reconciliation window.

FIGURE 6.2

The Reconcile Bank Account window.

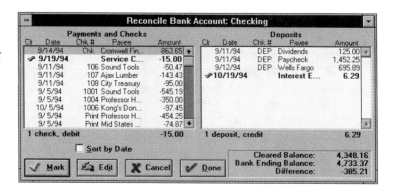

Before going any further, check the lower-right portion of the new window. No matter what, you'll see a line labeled *Difference*, which tells you the difference between the closing balance on your bank statement and the total of all the items you clear in Quicken. When this amount is zero, you've successfully balanced your account.

If you had to change the opening balance Quicken had calculated to match the opening balance on your bank statement, the difference between the two amounts appears on an extra line at the lower right, labeled *Opening Balance Difference*. If an opening balance difference is shown, remember that you'll have to account for the discrepancy later on (see "Handling an Opening Balance Difference," later in this chapter).

It's possible to interrupt the balancing process at any time by choosing **Cancel** in the reconciliation window. But this has repercussions for the next time you balance, as detailed in "Interrupting the Balancing Process," also later in this chapter.

Clearing Transactions

Now it's time to mark the transactions that show up in your bank statement as cleared. In Quicken 3, the reconciliation window lists transactions in two separate areas, one for debits like checks and withdrawals, and one for credits like deposits and interest payments. To mark an individual transaction as cleared, click on the transaction. Alternatively, you can move the highlight to the transaction either by clicking on it with the mouse or with the cursor keys, and then choose **Mark** or press **Enter** or the space bar. When you do, Quicken places a checkmark in the first column of the transaction list, the one labeled *Clr*. If you mistakenly mark a transaction as cleared, just click on it or press **Enter** or the space bar again to unmark it.

| NOTE | Quicken 2's Reconciliation window displays all transactions in one list, but otherwise works the same as Quicken 3. |

| SHORTCUT | Use a pen or pencil to check off each item on your bank statement when you mark it as cleared. |

Each time you clear a transaction, Quicken adds it to a running total and displays the result underneath the proper transaction list, with debits on the left and credits on the right, as shown in Figure 6.3. In addition, at the lower right of the window, Quicken adjusts your opening balance by the amount of the cleared transaction and computes the difference between the current balance and the closing balance in your statement.

FIGURE 6.3

As you reconcile, Quicken tracks your progress in the lower portion of the Reconciliation window.

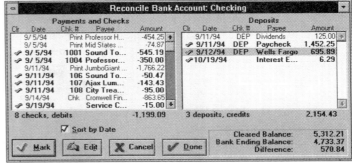

Clearing a Sequence of Transactions in One Step

If you see from your statement that a continuous sequence of checks has cleared, you can mark that whole range of checks as cleared in one step. With the mouse, point to the first transaction in the list, then just drag over the whole range, releasing the mouse button when the last transaction has been marked. Another way to do it is to click on the first check in the group, hold down the **Shift** key, and then click on the last check.

| NOTE | This quick method for clearing a range of checks in a single step can save you some work, but to avoid errors you should still |

compare the amounts listed in your statement with those in the list on your screen for each check in the range.

Interrupting the Balancing Process

Don't worry if something comes up that forces you to leave Quicken before completing the balancing process. Just choose **Cancel** in the reconciliation window.

At this point, you'll see a small dialog box asking whether or not you prefer to save your work (see Figure 6.4). If you choose **Save**, you can pick up where you left off at your next Quicken session.

| NOTE | In Quicken 2, if you cancel a reconciliation session your work is always saved, and asterisks appear in the *Clr* column of the register as described here. There is no Save Changes? dialog box. |

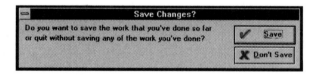

FIGURE 6.4

The Save Changes dialog box.

Before you make your choice, it's important to understand how Quicken handles an interruption in reconciliation. If you choose **Save**, Quicken enters an asterisk (*) in the register's *Clr* field for each transaction you marked as cleared. The asterisk means that the transaction has only been provisionally cleared; when the balancing process is complete, Quicken will change the asterisk to an x.

If you decide to save your work, don't change or delete the asterisks! When you're ready to resume reconciliation, display the Reconcile Register with Bank Statement dialog box again and enter the same amount in **Bank Statement Ending Balance** that you entered before—just copy it again from the same statement.

Then, when you choose **OK** to move to the reconciliation window, you should find that all the transactions you previously marked as cleared are still marked. You can now go on to complete reconciliation as detailed in this chapter.

On the other hand, if you choose the **Don't Save** button, Quicken leaves the *Clr* field blank for all transactions involved in this reconciliation. The next time you balance, you must mark each transaction again. With a complicated bank statement, this may actually be easier.

WARNING	One more point that applies whether or not you save an incomplete reconciliation: Quicken always saves any transactions for service charges or interest earned you entered in the Reconcile Bank Statement dialog box, the one that begins the balancing process. So when you balance again, don't enter the service charge or interest earned again—even if you chose not to save your work last time.

Adding Missing Transactions

Occasionally, you'll need to add transactions to your account as you reconcile. This will be obvious when your statement shows transactions that don't appear in your Quicken account. For example, if you're balancing your account for the very first time, or after skipping one or more months, you may well find that checks you assumed had cleared are only now showing up on this month's statement. Or you may have simply neglected to enter a transaction or two during the current cycle. You may also have been assessed a special penalty such as a returned check charge that you preferred not to enter as a service charge when you began the reconciliation process.

Quicken makes it easy to examine your account in detail and add new transactions while balancing. Begin from the Reconciliation dialog box, with the list of uncleared transactions on the screen. Choose **Edit** to display the register for the account you're working with. The Register window appears; the transaction that was highlighted in the Reconciliation dialog box will be selected in the register. You can also switch to the register by clicking on any visible part of its window, or by choosing **Bank Account** from the Window menu.

NOTE
The transactions you've checked as cleared in the Reconciliation window have been marked with an asterisk (*) in the *Clr* column of the register.

With the exception of special charges and the like, you can't assume that transactions appearing on your bank statement but not in the Reconciliation dialog box are actually missing from your Quicken account. Instead, they may have been entered already but marked as cleared, either by accident or during a previous reconciliation. (In the latter case, the bank has made an error in listing the transaction a second time.) For this reason, before you enter a "missing" transaction, be sure it doesn't already exist. You can browse through the register manually, or use the **Find** command to search for the transaction.

Once you're sure that the transactions in question are indeed missing from your Quicken account, enter them individually in the register. The only difference from the normal procedure is this: For each transaction, be sure to enter * in the column labeled *Clr* (for *Cleared*). You can do this either by tabbing over to the *Clr* field and typing *, or by double-clicking on the *Clr* field.

NOTE
Double-clicking a second time changes the * to an **x**, which means the transaction was cleared in a previous reconciliation—be sure not to do this unless you mean to.

When balancing your account for the first time, it's sometimes necessary to add earlier transactions that haven't yet appeared on your bank statement to resolve an opening balance discrepancy. You can enter such transactions in the register during reconciliation, but in this case, leave the *Clr* field blank, since these transactions haven't yet been cleared by your bank.

To return to the Reconciliation dialog box, choose **Reconcile Bank Account** from the Windows menu. (You can also click on any part of the window you can see, but if you click over a transaction in the Reconciliation list you'll change its cleared status, so be careful.) You'll see the transactions you've just entered in the Reconciliation list, each of them with a checkmark in the *Clr* column.

Correcting Mistaken Transactions

As you check off cleared transactions, you may find an occasional item in Quicken's list that doesn't agree with the corresponding entry in your statement. Quicken makes it easy to correct mistakes you've made in recording your transactions, but if it's the bank's fault, you've got your work cut out for you.

To correct an erroneous transaction, double-click on the transaction in the Reconciliation window. With the keyboard, highlight the transaction and choose **Edit** (**Alt-I**). Either way, you'll be taken directly to the register with the transaction you want to work with highlighted there.

| NOTE | In Quicken 2, choose **Go To** instead of **Edit**.

Edit the transaction using the techniques you've already learned (see the section "Making Changes in Existing Transactions" in Chapter 4 if you need a reminder). Once you've recorded the altered transaction, the changes are immediately reflected in the Reconciliation window. When you're through correcting transactions, return to the Reconciliation window by clicking on it or choosing **Reconcile Bank Account** from the Windows menu.

Checking Your Balance

You'll recall that as you progress through the balancing process, Quicken keeps and displays running totals of your cleared payment (debit) and deposit (credit) transactions. Likewise, it continuously updates the overall balance of all cleared transactions in your Quicken account, and then compares this adjusted balance to the closing balance on your statement.

This last number, the difference between Quicken's tally of your account balance and the closing balance on your statement, is the most critical. It's labeled *Difference*, and is displayed at the bottom right of the Reconciliation dialog box. When the dust settles and you've finished marking all your cleared transactions, the difference should be zero. If it is, Quicken and your bank agree about how much money you have and your account balances. You can celebrate—you won't have to look at a bank statement again for another month. Go on to the section "Concluding the Balancing Process" at the end of this chapter.

If *Difference* is not zero and doesn't equal *Opening Balance Difference*, your account hasn't balanced. See "What to Do When Your Account Doesn't Balance," later in this chapter. When the *Difference* amount equals the amount listed for *Opening Balance Difference*, you've successfully balanced your account. But you must still account for that opening balance discrepancy. Go on to the next section, "Handling an Opening Balance Difference."

Handling an Opening Balance Difference

| WARNING | Typically, your bank statement will show a larger amount for the opening balance than Quicken has calculated because you have checks that still haven't yet cleared. In this case, even if you can't find the missing uncleared checks in your recent statements, don't assume that you've just received an unforeseen windfall. Before you spend the extra money, make doubly sure that all your old checks have cleared. |

If you changed the opening balance when you filled out the Reconcile Register with Bank Statement window, Quicken displays the difference between its calculated opening balance and the one you copied from the bank statement on the line labeled *Opening Balance Difference* at the lower right of the Reconciliation dialog box. Short of a bank error, there are two situations in which Quicken's opening balance and the one on your bank statement will conflict:

- You are balancing your account for the very first time. That situation is covered in "Balancing Your Account the First Time" earlier in this chapter as well as here.

- You are balancing your account with your most recent bank statement, but you did not reconcile in one or more previous months.

When you balance for the first time, transactions recorded recently in your paper check register often don't appear on the current bank statement. Still, these transactions have figured in the balance you recorded in your paper check register. If, against Quicken's recommendation, you used the paper register balance as your opening balance in Quicken, you'll have an opening balance discrepancy the first time you reconcile.

The best way to handle this situation is to return to your register by choosing **Edit**, and then to correct the opening balance transaction so that it matches the closing balance on your last bank statement.

> | **NOTE** | When you record the changed transaction, Quicken will warn you that you're altering a cleared transaction. However, choosing **OK** will eliminate the opening balance discrepancy.

You have two alternatives to this approach: (1) you can let Quicken create a special transaction that adjusts the opening balance to match the bank statement's. This has the same effect as correcting the opening balance yourself, but it clutters up your register and might confuse you later. The section "Concluding the Balancing Process" explains how this option works. (2) Accept the balance discrepancy for now. As long as you've entered all the transactions that were outstanding as of the date of your opening balance, (recommended in "Balancing Your Account for the First Time") Quicken and your bank will agree on a balance after you reconcile a time or two.

You'll have a different problem—extra uncleared transactions in your Quicken account—if you've skipped reconciling for one or more months, assuming you've continued to enter all your transactions in Quicken. In this case, your account will contain a number of transactions that have cleared your bank on statements for the months you skipped, but that are not marked as cleared in Quicken.

To maintain accurate records, it's best to go back and reconcile consecutively every month you missed before you begin reconciling the current month's statement. However, if you've reached this point and have already started clearing transactions from the current statement, you still have a chance to square the opening balance difference and maintain the accuracy of your records with the techniques described in the next section, "Adding and Marking Previously Cleared Transactions."

Although this is the safest course, Quicken will let you start balancing with a new statement after you've skipped a month or more, much as if you'd started a new account. In this case, you can have Quicken adjust the opening balance to match that of the current bank statement. This saves you some work, but remember that you're unprotected from errors that may have occurred during previous months. If you choose this course, skip to "Concluding the Balancing Process" and follow the steps in "Adjusting the Opening Balance."

Adding and Marking Previously Cleared Transactions

When Quicken's opening balance differs from the one shown on your statement, and if you've reconciled your account at least once before, the probable reason for the discrepancy is this: You haven't reconciled for one or more months. Your Quicken account now contains uncleared transactions that have in fact cleared the bank as of the statements you skipped. To mark these transactions as cleared in the past—rather than on the current statement—switch to the register by choosing **Edit** (**Go To** in Quicken 2). There, enter an **X** in the *Clr* field of each previously cleared transaction. You can do this by typing the **X** in the *Clr* field, or by double-clicking on the field twice.

In the register, marking a transaction with an **X** means it cleared the bank as of an earlier statement. Quicken adjusts its opening balance accordingly. Marking a transaction with an asterisk (*), on the other hand, means the transaction has cleared as of this month's statement.

Of course, you'll need the earlier bank statements to guide you in the process. If the earlier statements include transactions you've neglected to enter at all, enter them as new transactions now (see "Adding Missing Transactions") and mark them with an **X** as well.

Transactions you mark with an **X** during reconciliation are added to the opening balance that Quicken calculates. As you mark them, if the lower-right corner of the Reconciliation dialog box is visible, you'll see the changes in the amount listed at *Opening Balance Difference*. When this amount is zero, you've entered all the previously cleared transactions.

What to Do When Your Account Doesn't Balance

If the amount at *Difference* in the Reconciliation dialog box is anything other than zero, and if it doesn't equal the amount listed at *Opening Balance Difference*, either you or the bank has made an error in figuring your balance.

There are two common reasons for a discrepancy: (1) Either you've marked the wrong number of payments or deposits as cleared; or (2) at least one of the transaction amounts in your Quicken account doesn't match the corresponding items on your statement. And you have two ways to deal with the problem: (1) The preferred approach is to find and correct the transactions on which your register and your statement don't agree; or (2) you can decide to have Quicken adjust its own balance arbitrarily to match the one on your statement—dangerous, unless the difference is tiny.

Finding and Correcting Mistaken Transactions

By far the best way to handle a discrepancy between Quicken's account balance and the one on your bank statement is to trace the source of the problem. Somewhere, there's been a mistake made in recording a check or deposit, or in marking the status of a transaction.

Before you go any further, check once more to be sure that the amount listed at *Difference* is not equal to the amount listed at *Opening Balance Difference*. If the two amounts are the same, you don't actually have a problem with reconciliation, you just began with the wrong balance. For instructions on how to proceed, see the section "Handling an Opening Balance Difference" earlier in this chapter.

SHORTCUT   Another quick check you can make is to see whether the difference listed is a multiple of 9 (that is, whether you can divide the difference amount evenly by 9). If so, you've probably transposed two digits in one of the transaction amounts. For example, you may have entered $45.62 as $46.52. This may help you to find the mistake more easily.

If you really do have an imbalance to contend with, you'll want to take methodical steps to locate the problem as quickly as possible. Begin by determining whether the discrepancy lies in the area of payments (checks and other debits) or in the area of deposits and other credits. Here's how to proceed.

Your bank statement should list separate totals for debits and credits for the period covered by the statement. Compare these amounts to the ones Quicken has calculated for the transactions you've cleared, displayed at the bottom left of the reconciliation screen. The problem lies with whichever category shows a difference.

If the debits don't tally, follow the instructions in the next section, "Correcting Debit Discrepancies." If the problem is in the credits category, skip to the "Correcting Credit Discrepancies" section. Of course, it might turn out that you have a mismatch in both categories. In that case, just proceed on through both steps.

Correcting Debit Discrepancies

If the total dollar amount for debits listed on your bank statements doesn't match the amount Quicken lists in the item labeled *Checks, Debits* at the lower left of the Reconciliation window, narrow down the problem as follows.

First, count the total number of debit items in your bank statement and compare it to the total that Quicken displays at *Checks, Debits.* When you count the debit items on your statement, be sure to include any transaction that reduces your balance. In addition to checks, look for service charges and other fees, wire transfers, withdrawals you made at an automatic teller or from the bank window, and payments that are deducted automatically from your account.

The number of debit items on your statement should match the number displayed by Quicken, except in one case: If you combined several different service charge transactions into one when you filled out the *Service Charge:* field in the Reconcile Register with Bank Statement dialog box (see Figure 6.1 on page 138). In that case, you should add the number of additional service charges to the number displayed by Quicken. For example, if you combined three service charges into one, add 2 to the total number of Quicken debit items.

If the adjusted debit item totals match, but there's a monetary discrepancy, someone made a mistake in recording the amount of one or more items. Skip to the next section, *When Debit Amounts Don't Match*. If your adjusted item totals don't match, follow these steps to locate the missing or extra items:

- If Quicken shows more debit items than your bank statement does, you marked one or more transactions as cleared by mistake. Review the list in the Reconciliation dialog box for items that you've marked, but that don't appear in your statement.

- When you find the culprit(s), move the pointer there and press the space bar, removing the asterisk in the *Clr* column.

- If Quicken shows fewer debit items than your statement, either you didn't mark a payment as cleared when you should have, or you didn't record a check or other payment in the register. Start by ticking off the cleared debit items on your statement against the items in the window. If you find one that you haven't yet marked on the list, mark it as cleared.

- If you find an item listed on your statement that doesn't appear at all in the list in the window, switch to the register by choosing **Edit** and then enter the missing transaction. When you're finished, switch back to the Reconciliation dialog box by choosing **Reconcile Bank Account** from the Windows menu.

When Debit Amounts Don't Match

If Quicken has a matching entry for every debit item on your bank statement, and vice versa, but the total debit amounts still don't match, there's an incorrect amount somewhere. Compare the amount of each transaction listed on the statement against the amount listed in Quicken for the corresponding transaction. If you find a mismatch, don't automatically assume it's your error; instead, get out your returned checks and see if the bank properly recorded the amount of the problem check on your statement.

If there is an error in your Quicken account, correct it in the register. Switch there by choosing **Edit**, make the change, and then return to the Reconciliation dialog box by choosing **Reconcile Bank Account** from the Windows menu.

If you believe the bank has made an error in recording the amount of one or more transactions, you should create a new transaction in the amount of the discrepancy. If the amount of the debit on your statement is larger than the amount in your Quicken account, record the amount of the adjustment in the *Payment* field; if the statement shows a sma*l*ler amount, record the adjustment in the *Deposit* field. Then assign the transaction to a category such as **Bank Error**, which clearly indicates the purpose of this adjustment. If Quicken and the bank statement agree after you enter the transaction, you've reached a reconciliation and can proceed now to the section "When Your Account Balances," near the end of this chapter.

NOTE	You can create the transaction to resolve the discrepancy by switching to the register and entering it there during reconciliation. Or, if you prefer, you can have Quicken create this transaction for you automatically, as described later in this chapter in the section, "If Your Account Still Doesn't Balance."

Your next step should be to report the problem to your bank's customer service department. Assuming the people there agree with your bookkeeping, they'll make the necessary adjustment in your account, which will appear in your next statement. The tricky part comes the next time you reconcile. The special transaction you entered to take care of the bank's mistake has already been cleared, in order to make the previous month's statement balance. But the adjustment recorded by your bank appears on the new statement, and it will throw off your balance by the same amount when you reconcile the next time. The only solution is to create another special adjustment transaction in Quicken at that time. It will be for the same amount as the first adjustment transaction, but in the other column. If you entered the original adjustment in the *Payment* field, the new one should go in the *Deposit* field, and vice versa.

Correcting Credit Discrepancies

If the total dollar amount for credits listed in your bank statements doesn't match the amount Quicken lists at *Deposits, Credits* (under the Deposits list on the right of the window), narrow down the problem as follows.

First, count the total number of credit items in your bank statement and compare it to the total that Quicken displays for *Deposits, Credits*. When you count the credit items in your statement, be sure to include any transaction that increases your balance. Count regular deposits at the teller window, those you made at automatic tellers, wire transfers to your account, interest payments, and so on.

The number of credit items in your statement should match the number displayed by Quicken, except in one case: If you combined several different interest payment transactions into one when you filled out the *Interest Earned:* field in the Reconcile Bank Statement window (see Figure 6.1 on page 138) you need to add the number of additional interest payments on your statement to the number displayed by Quicken. For example, if you combined two interest payments into one, add 1 to the total number of Quicken credit items.

If the adjusted credit item totals match, but there's a monetary discrepancy, someone made a mistake in recording the amount of one or more items. Skip to the section, "When Credit Amounts Don't Match." If your adjusted item totals don't match, follow these steps to locate the missing or extra items:

- If Quicken shows more credit items than your bank statement shows, you mistakenly marked one or more deposits as cleared. Review the list in the Reconciliation dialog box for items that you've marked, but that don't appear on your statement.

- When you find an item that you've cleared by mistake, unmark the item by clicking on it or by moving the highlight there and pressing the space bar.

- If Quicken shows fewer credit items than appear on your statement, either you didn't mark a deposit as cleared when you should have, or you didn't enter a deposit in the register. Start by ticking off the cleared credit items on your statement against the items in the window. If you find one that you haven't yet marked on the screen list, mark it as cleared.

- If you find an item listed on your statement that doesn't appear at all in the list on your screen, switch to the register by choosing **Edit** and then enter the missing deposit. When you're finished, switch back to the Reconciliation dialog box by choosing **Reconcile Bank Account** from the Windows menu.

When Credit Amounts Don't Match

If Quicken has a matching entry for every credit item on your bank statement, and vice versa, but the total credit amounts still don't match, there's an incorrect amount somewhere. Compare the amount of each credit transaction listed on the statement against the amount listed in Quicken for the corresponding transaction. If you find a mismatch, it might not be your error. If you've kept your deposit receipts (and you should have), get them out and see if the bank properly recorded the amounts on your statement.

If there is an error in your Quicken account, correct it in the register. Switch there by choosing **Edit**, make the change, and then return to the Reconciliation dialog box by choosing **Reconcile Bank Account** from the Windows menu.

If you believe the bank has made an error in recording the amount of one or more deposits, you need to enter a new transaction in the amount of the discrepancy, typing the amount into the appropriate *Deposit* or *Payment* field. If the bank statement shows the amount of the credit transaction to be larger than the one in your Quicken account, enter the difference in the *Deposit* field. If the statement shows a smaller amount, enter the difference in the *Payment* field. Assign the transaction to "Bank Error" or some other category that clearly indicates the reason for this adjustment. If Quicken and your bank statement agree after you've entered the transaction, you're done with reconciliation and can proceed to the section "When Your Account Balances," near the end of this chapter.

NOTE	As an alternative to adding the adjustment transaction manually, you can have Quicken create it for you automatically after reconciliation is complete (see "If Your Account Still Doesn't Balance," near the end of this chapter).

Next, report the problem to your bank's customer service department. If the people there agree with your conclusion, they'll make an adjustment in your real account, which will appear in your next statement. Since the special transaction you entered to take care of the bank's mistake has already been cleared in order to make the previous month's statement balance, you'll have to add another adjustment transaction in Quicken the next time you reconcile.

It will be for the same amount as the first adjustment transaction, but in the opposite category. If you recorded the previous adjustment as a *Payment*, this adjustment will be a *Deposit*, and vice versa.

Concluding the Balancing Process

Whether you arrive at this step the first time through or after painstaking double-checking of your records, you've succeeded in reconciling your Quicken account with your bank statement—or you've given up trying to track down a trivial discrepancy. In the Reconciliation dialog box, complete the reconciliation by choosing **Done**. What happens next depends on whether or not there is a difference between the opening balance in Quicken and the one in your bank statement.

If you had no opening balance discrepancy and if your account balanced exactly, you'll get a well-deserved congratulations from Quicken (see Figure 6.5 on the next page). As the message says, items that you checked as cleared during this reconciliation session will now be marked with an x in the register. A remaining option is to print a reconciliation report. (See "Printing a Reconciliation Report," later in this chapter.)

FIGURE 6.5

Quicken congratulates you with this message when you balance your account successfully.

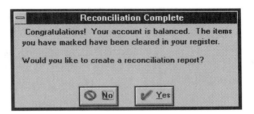

If any discrepancies remain, you'll see messages describing the remaining problem. Proceed to "Adjusting Your Opening Balance" or "If Your Account Still Doesn't Balance," or both, as appropriate.

Adjusting Your Opening Balance

If your account fails to balance, and if you have an opening balance discrepancy, Quicken displays the message shown in Figure 6.6 when you leave the Reconciliation dialog box. You're asked whether you want the program to adjust the opening balance by adding a new transaction in the amount of the discrepancy. Choose **Yes** if you want Quicken to go ahead and create the adjustment transaction, which will appear in the Quicken register, just like any you would enter yourself. After you return to the register, you can add a category such as "Open Bal Adj" to the adjustment transaction.

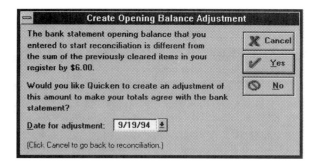

FIGURE 6.6

You'll see this message if you have an opening balance discrepancy.

Choose **No** if you don't want Quicken to adjust your opening balance. Take this option if you plan to return to your register to correct your account for earlier months and you expect to resolve the discrepancy in the opening balance that way. Otherwise, you'll face the same problem next time.

If Your Account Still Doesn't Balance

If your account still doesn't balance after you've tried all the methods we've discussed for identifying and correcting discrepancies, the mistake you or your bank has made has simply eluded your efforts to track it down. If the amount is small, it's probably safe to call it quits and let Quicken create a transaction that adjusts your final balance to match the bank statement's closing balance. This way, at least, your account's opening balance should agree with your bank statement the next time you reconcile.

In this situation, you'll see a message similar to the one in Figure 6.7 when you leave the Reconciliation dialog box. If you'd like, you can return to the Reconciliation dialogue box to try again at this point; just choose **Cancel**. If you do want to abandon your attempts to balance exactly, choose **Adjust Balance**. Quicken records the adjustment transaction in your register where you'll be able to examine it and add an entry such as **Balance discrep** or **Bank error** in the *Category* field. Depending on the amount of the discrepancy, you may decide to pursue the matter further with your bank, or simply to ignore it.

FIGURE 6.7

This message appears if your account isn't balanced when you finish reconciling.

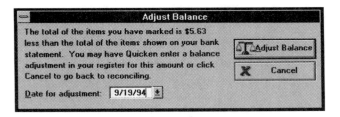

Printing a Reconciliation Report

After you've completed the balancing process, Quicken informs you that it has marked the items you cleared during reconciliation with an **X** in the *Clr* field of the register. As shown in Figure 6.8, you'll also be asked if you want to create a report summarizing your work.

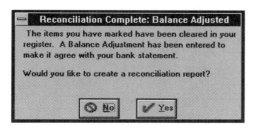

FIGURE 6.8

*A dialog box
like this one
appears when
you complete the
balancing process.*

Choose **No** if you want to return to the register without creating a report. If you want the report, however, choose **Yes**. The Reconciliation Report Setup dialog box will appear, as shown in Figure 6.9. In the top field, you can title the report yourself; otherwise, Quicken titles it *Reconciliation Report* for you.

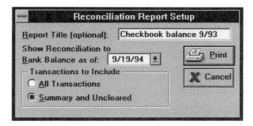

FIGURE 6.9

*The Reconciliation
Report Setup
dialog box.*

Two options are unique to the Reconciliation Report Setup dialog box.

The first is the field labeled *Show Reconciliation to Bank Balance as of*, which is a complicated way of asking for the date for the report. Quicken enters today's date in this field, but you can change it if you want to examine the cleared status of your transactions on another date.

The final field in the window lets you choose between a lengthy full report and a shorter summary format. The preset choice is **Summary** and **Uncleared** for the short report. If you want more detail, select the **All Transactions** radio button. In Quicken 2, you print the report directly from the Reconciliation Report Setup dialog box.

NEW IN 3 When you've filled out all the fields, ready your printer and choose **Print**. In Quicken 3, the standard Print Report dialog appears. To print the report on paper, just choose **Print**; other options in the Print Report window are covered in Chapter 10. A sample report as it appears on the screen is shown in Figure 6.10.

FIGURE 6.10

A sample reconciliation report.

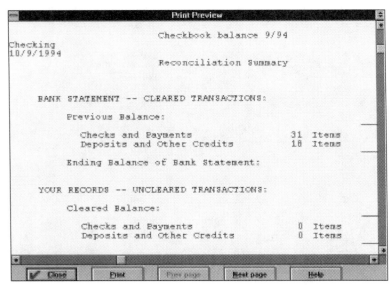

Entering Year-to-Date Financial Information

Suppose you started your Quicken checking account on April 12 with an opening balance of $5,000. To complete your records, you decide to go back and enter your records for the entire year beginning January 1. This requires some special handling to avoid problems the next time you balance your account.

Normally, you leave the *Clr* field empty when you enter transactions in your register, and then fill it in when you receive your bank statement and balance your account. However, if you enter transactions after the fact—after they've already been cleared on a previous bank statement, that is—the normal rule doesn't apply. In that case, you'll want to be able to mark the transactions as cleared at the time you enter them.

Before you do anything else, write down the current ending balance in your account. You'll need this amount to ensure that you enter the older transactions properly. Remember, the ending balance tells you how much should remain in your account when the transactions dated today or earlier have cleared (it does not include postdated transactions). The ending balance is always displayed in the lower right of the Write Checks window and the register.

Next, you need to know what your balance was as of the date of the first transactions you'll be entering, ideally as recorded in your bank statement from that time. Find the opening balance transaction in the register, and change its date and amount accordingly using the standard methods for editing register items. In our example, say your records show that the balance in your real-life checking account as of the first of January is $4,000. Before going any further, you would locate the opening balance transaction in your Quicken account, changing its date from 4/12 to 1/1 and the amount in the *Deposit* field from $5,000 to $4,000. You'd then re-record the transaction.

Now record all your transactions since the new opening balance date in the register, marking each one as cleared by entering x in its *Clr* field. When you're finished, be sure the ending balance at the lower right of the screen hasn't changed. If it has, you made a mistake in entering the transactions, either by leaving some out or by typing in the wrong dollar amounts. Try to find and correct the problem; if you can't, adjust the new opening balance to return the ending balance to what it was.

Once you've entered and cleared all the transactions accurately, Quicken's opening balance in the Reconcile Register with Bank Statement dialog box should match your bank statement the next time you balance your account. You can then proceed with balancing the standard way.

Summary

Although it's a bother, reconciling your checking account is essential. In this chapter, however, you've learned how to use Quicken to speed the process of checking account balancing considerably. You now know how to:

- Begin the reconciliation.
- Handle discrepancies in the opening balance amount between your bank statement and Quicken.
- Mark transactions as cleared.
- Identify the reasons for other disagreements between Quicken and your bank statement.
- Print a reconciliation report.

With these skills, you'll be able to forget the drudgery of reconciliation and finish the task in a few painless minutes.

The ability to manage your checking account makes Quicken well worth its modest cost, but the program has much more to offer. You can also monitor all the other components of your financial situation, as outlined in Chapters 8 and 9. And, as you'll learn in Chapters 10 through 16, you can use Quicken to create many kinds of reports and graphs to keep you constantly abreast of the trends in your personal or business finances. First, however, let's turn to Chapter 7 to learn how Quicken automatically fills out checks and other transactions that occur regularly.

Chapter Seven
Regular Bills and Deposits

L ike most people, you probably pay the same bills month after month. There's your car payment, the loan on that living room set you bought last year (or was it the year before?), and your rent or mortgage, of course. Why should you have to rewrite exactly the same check every month? With Quicken, you don't have to; the program will remember the information from any of your transactions, payments, and income items alike, and lets you reuse that information in new transactions whenever you need to.

Automatic Bill Paying with the Quicken Calendar

NEW IN 3 Quicken 3's new calendar makes scheduling payments or deposits extraordinarily convenient and helps you manage your finances as well. All you do is "pin" a transaction on the calendar, and Quicken remembers it for repeated use every month. The calendar shows you graphically, at a glance, your income and spending patterns over time and helps you anticipate cash-flow crunches. If you don't have a mouse, or just prefer working directly with the numbers, Quicken still offers simple manual methods for memorizing and reusing transactions individually and in groups. Quicken's calendar looks just like a wall calendar, with a space for each day of the month where transactions scheduled on that date are displayed. Depending on how you've set up the calendar window, you may also see a list of transactions and a graph comparing your income and expenses over a range of dates (amounts for future months are projected based on scheduled transactions and your budget).

In this chapter, you'll learn how to use the calendar for scheduling regular transactions. Chapter 13 shows you how the calendar can help you plan and budget using the calendar's graph.

Working with the Calendar Window

Let's get oriented to the calendar window, shown in Figure 7.1. When you first use the calendar, Quicken displays it in a fairly small window. You'll find it easier to work with the calendar if you enlarge the window (you have to do it by hand since there's no Maximize button). The calendar will be easier to read, and Quicken adds text to the buttons at the top of the window to help you remember what they're for.

On the calendar itself, today's date always appears in light blue; days from the previous or next month are shown in gray. A highlight of green indicates the day that's currently selected, that is, the day on which you're currently recording or editing transactions. The calendar displays all of the transactions you've recorded so far, each in the box for the appropriate date (these previously recorded transactions appear in black type, while transactions you schedule for future entry will appear in blue).

FIGURE 7.1

Quicken's financial calendar.

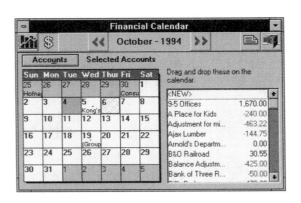

At the very top, just below the window's title, Quicken displays the current month and year. To either side are **Arrow** buttons; choosing either of these takes you to the previous or next future month.

Of the remaining buttons, the two at the upper left control the items displayed on the calendar window. Choosing the **Plan** button (the one with the chart graphic) shows you the graph of your income and expense patterns, whereas choosing **List** (the button with the dollar sign) displays or hides the list of transactions at the far right of the window.

Just below the **Plan** button, the **Accounts** button lets you select the accounts whose information appears on the calendar. At the upper right, the **Note** button lets you attach a memo to the current date, while the **Close** button (the one with the arrow and door) simply closes the calendar window.

Scheduling Future Transactions with the Calendar

When you open the Calendar window, a list of all the transactions from your accounts should appear at the right. If you don't see the list, pop it up by choosing **List** (the dollar sign button) in the calendar's button bar.

Scheduling a previously recorded transaction for a future date is as easy as dragging it from the list to the calendar. All you have to do then is tell Quicken how often you'll be paying the bill (or receiving the income).

For example, let's say you want to schedule your monthly utility bill for automatic payment. Assuming you've recorded a utility payment at least once before in Quicken, here's all you do:

1. Be sure the calendar displays the correct month. If the bill comes due next month, choose **Next** (the Arrow button to the right of the date) to advance the display.

2. Locate a previous example of the transaction you want to schedule in the list, using the scroll bar to display it if necessary. Or, to create a scheduled transaction from scratch, use the *New* item at the top of the list.

3. Drag the transaction to the date when you want to schedule the next payment. If it's due August 1, you might want Quicken to write the check on, say, July 24.

4. When you release the mouse button, Quicken displays the Enter into Register window. Here, type in the amount of the transaction.

5. The Set Up Scheduled Transaction window is shown in Figure 7.2 on the next page. Complete the window (details are covered below), choose **OK**, and the transaction appears in the calendar.

You can also create new scheduled transactions with the keyboard. Highlight the first future date for the new transaction and press **Enter**. Choose **New** in the small window that appears to pop up the Set Up Scheduled Transaction window.

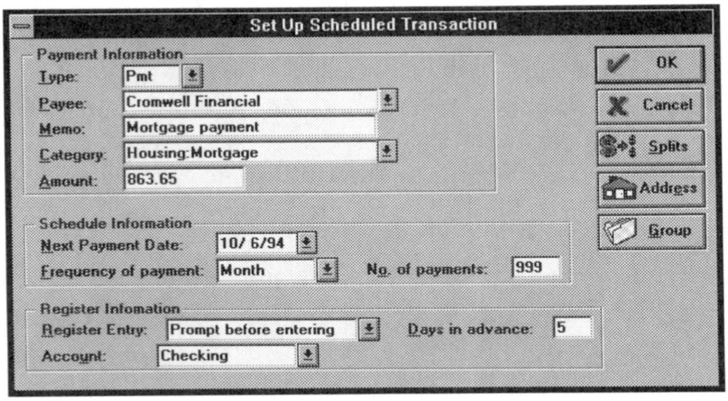

FIGURE 7.2

*The Set Up
Scheduled
Transaction
window.*

Filling Out the Set Up Scheduled Transaction Window

The fields in the top part of the window are for the same information you would use for any register transaction, but in fields arranged in a dialog box. If information in the earlier transaction doesn't apply, you can change or erase the entries.

In this case, for example, you don't know how much your utility bill will be each month, so you erase the entry in the *Amount* field. You can also change the entry in the *Type* field. For instance, you might decide to write a check by hand from now on, in which case you would change the item's type from a check to a payment. However, the address information would be lost; note that only check items can have addresses.

Scheduling the Transaction

Next, come a group of three fields labeled *Schedule Information*. Here is where you tell Quicken when to record this transaction, and how often—weekly, monthly, and so on. In the *Next Payment Date* field, enter the date for the very next time this transaction should be recorded—in our example, July 24.

In the *Frequency of Payment* field, Quicken has entered **Only Once** for you, meaning a one-time-only transaction. For recurring items, choose the appropriate option from the drop-down list.

> **NOTE**
> There's no "daily" option for scheduled transactions. Rather than enter each of your business' daily deposit or payments individually, you'll save time by recording a separate scheduled transaction for each working day of the week, choosing the **Week** option in the *Frequency* field. Unfortunately, you can't copy transactions on the calendar from one date to another, so you have to create each day's transaction separately.

The *No. of Payments* field tells Quicken how many times to enter the transaction into your account. Quicken automatically sets this field to **1** and the **Only Once** option is selected in the *Frequency* field. The automatic entry for any other frequency is **999**, meaning that Quicken will continue to record the transactions until you tell it to stop. That's appropriate for a utility bill, but for a payment on a car loan, you would set the *No.* field to **36**, **48**, or **60**.

Deciding How to Record the Transaction

The bottom group of fields, *Register Information*, tell Quicken how to handle the transaction in the register. The choices in the *Register Entry* field are:

- **Enter w/o Prompting**, for transactions you're sure you want Quicken to record automatically.
- **Prompt Before Entering**, for transactions you want to review first (perhaps you won't always have a credit card balance and therefore won't actually pay a "monthly" credit card bill every month).
- **For Planning Only**, for transactions you just want Quicken to include in the calendar's planning graph, so you can see their impact on your finances before you decide to commit to a new loan and so on.

In the *Account* field, select the name of the account where Quicken should record the transaction. Then enter a number in the *Days in Advance* field if you want Quicken to record the transaction in your account prior to the actual date you chose for the transaction. Quicken will record it as a postdated transaction. That way, the Billminder program and Quicken itself will start reminding you to print the check (or otherwise pay the bill) prior to the transaction date.

Scheduling Split Transactions

When you drag a split transaction from the Transaction list to the calendar, Quicken records the split details along with all the rest of the information. You can edit split transaction information for a scheduled transaction by clicking the **Splits** button in the Set Up Scheduled Transaction window. The familiar Split Transaction dialog box appears. You can make changes in any of the information here, or split a previously unsplit transaction, using the same techniques covered in Chapter 5. Press **Enter** to leave the dialog box.

| SHORTCUT | If you make regular payments on a loan, Quicken can automatically calculate the amount of each payment that goes to interest and the amount that goes to the principal, and will even keep a running total of the total amounts you've paid on the loan. The technique relies on memorizing a split payment transaction, then applying Quicken's **Amortization** feature to it. (See Chapter 9 for instructions.) |

Entering Address Information for Checks

If you're scheduling a check item, you can edit the address recorded for the check by choosing the **Address** button at the far right of the Set Up Scheduled Transaction window. When your changes are complete, press **Enter** to save them and exit the window.

*Using the **Groups** Button*

At the bottom of the column of buttons in the Set Up Scheduled Transactions window is one labeled **Groups**. You use this button to schedule an entire set of transactions, rather than individual ones, as you'll see in the section "Paying Bills Automatically with Transaction Groups" later in this chapter.

| WARNING | Don't choose the **Groups** button unless you really want to convert a scheduled transaction into a transaction group. Haphazard use of this button can destroy all the information about your scheduled transaction. |

Editing Scheduled Transactions

To make changes to a scheduled transaction, choose its date on the calendar (by clicking on it with the mouse, or by highlighting it with the cursor keys and then pressing **Enter**. A tiny window pops up listing all the transactions scheduled for the date. Highlight the transaction in the list, and then choose:

- **Edit** to display the Set Up Scheduled Transaction window again.
- **Delete** to remove the transaction from the calendar (this doesn't affect transactions already recorded in your account that were based on this scheduled transaction).
- **Register** to view transactions on this date that have already been recorded into your account. (Quicken won't let you choose the **Register** button if you're examining future dates, since those transactions haven't been entered in the register.)
- **Pay Now** to record the transaction right now, regardless of when the transaction was scheduled to be entered.

SHORTCUT	Use the **Pay Now** option if you'll be away the next time a scheduled transaction is due to be recorded. That way, you can write all your checks in advance without disturbing future scheduled payments.

Recording Scheduled Transactions in Your Account

When a date of a scheduled transaction rolls around, Quicken enters the transaction in your account automatically if you had selected **Enter w/o prompting** in the Register Entry field when you scheduled the transaction. If you selected **Prompt before entering**, you'll see a window informing you that it's time to record the transaction in your account. You can edit the transaction information if you'd like, including any transaction split or the address for a check. Then choose **OK** to go ahead and enter the transaction. Choose **Remind Later** if you don't want to enter it now, and **Skip Payment** if you want Quicken to cancel the transaction for this date.

Using the Calendar to Record Previous Transactions

NEW IN 3 In Quicken 3, the calendar provides an alternative to the register for entering transactions directly into your account. When you add a transaction to the calendar on a past date, Quicken records the transaction in the account immediately, just as if you'd typed it into the register.

To enter a past transaction this way, drag *New* or a previous entry from the calendar's transaction list to the proper date. When you release the mouse button, Quicken presents you with an Edit Register Transaction window, with the fields arranged in a form-like configuration (it's similar to the Set Up Scheduled Transaction window, but the fields pertaining to scheduling are missing). Complete the window and choose **OK** to record the transaction.

You can also enter a past transaction by double-clicking the correct date, or highlighting it and pressing **Enter**. In the tiny window that appears, choose the **New** button to display the window for the transaction details.

Attaching Notes to the Calendar

Quicken's calendar lets you attach memos to any date. Maybe you're scheduling a payment for six months from now, and you think you might forget why. Maybe you've given a customer a few extra weeks to pay off an old bill, but you want her phone number handy if the expected check doesn't arrive on schedule. In situations like these, here's how to leave yourself a reminder on the calendar:

1. Select the date on the calendar for the note.
2. Choose the **Note** button. A small Note window appears for typing in text (Figure 7.3).
3. Write your memo. To enter a **Tab**, press **Ctrl-Tab** (by itself, the **Tab** key moves to other parts of the dialog box).
4. Choose a color for your note. You can color code your notes, perhaps to keep business and personal notes straight.

WARNING Don't rely too heavily on the color-coding system for your calendar notes—you can only store one note per day.

5. Choose **Save** to finish the note and close the window. A small box of the color you choose appears in the selected date.

To read a note, just click on the colored box, or select the date and choose **Note** again. You can delete a note by choosing the **Delete** button on the Note window.

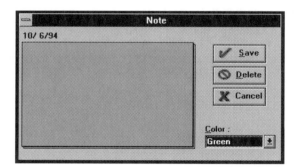

FIGURE 7.3

Attach memos to the calendar by typing them in this window.

SHORTCUT   If you work with the calendar a lot, you can use notes as effective reminders about any upcoming event or obligation, be it a dental appointment, the fall flower bulb-planting season, or your mother's birthday. If you want a stronger reminder message, or if you don't use Quicken that often, you can set up a scheduled transaction for each event. Drag the *New* item in the transaction list to the appropriate date. In the Set Up Scheduled Transaction window, type your message in the *Payee* field, and enter **0** in the *Amount* field. On the date of the transaction, a window appears when you start Quicken telling you it's time to enter the transaction. Choose the **Skip Payment** button, and consider yourself reminded. (If you set up Billminder to warn you in advance, you'll also get messages that there are scheduled transactions coming due when you start Windows.)

Memorizing Transactions

Quicken lets you store, or "memorize," any check or register transaction you enter into your account. Suppose you're writing a check and you realize you'll probably pay the same bill more than once in the future, but you don't know when. By memorizing the check now, you can recall all the information in a flash, type in a new amount, and have your check ready to go. Quicken stores all the details from a transaction except the date, including the split transaction details.

NOTE   Quicken does not memorize the date of the transaction, since it assumes you don't want to enter two identical transactions on the same day!

QuickFill relies on the list of memorized transactions to complete transactions automatically for you. When QuickFill is on, as soon as you start typing something in the *Payee* field, QuickFill searches the transactions you've memorized for a match. If the first letter you type matches at least one memorized transaction, QuickFill copies all the stored information for that transaction to the screen. If that's the wrong transaction, all you have to do is keep typing until QuickFill finds the correct one.

When you first install Quicken for Windows, the program is set up so that all transactions are memorized automatically as you record them in your accounts. If you like, you can turn off the automatic memorization of transactions. You might want to do this if you know that most of the transactions you record will be to unique payees. Then you can "manually" memorize the small number of transactions you expect to reuse regularly.

Even if you leave the automatic memorization turned on, you may occasionally want to memorize a transaction on your own. That way, you can create memorized transactions before you ever need them, and without throwing off your account balance.

NEW IN 3   In previous versions of Quicken, you could only schedule recurring transactions by storing them as memorized transactions, and then assigning these to transaction groups. While you can still use that technique, it's often simpler to schedule individual transactions on the calendar as described earlier in this chapter.

What's more, the manual method lets you memorize incomplete transactions, that is, ones containing only the information that will repeat each time you reuse (or recall) them. You might well want to memorize a "template" check containing a payee's name and address, but no amount. Then, each time a payment is due, you just call up this generic check and fill in the amount. Quicken stores all memorized transactions together, even if you created them in different accounts. Likewise, you can recall and reuse any memorized transaction and reuse it in any of your accounts.

Memorizing a Check

Manually memorizing a check is as simple as filling out the check and pressing a couple of keys. If you've already written the check you want to memorize, the process is that much easier.

WARNING

If you want to memorize a check transaction that you can print after recalling it, you must either memorize it from the Write Checks window or set the memorized transaction's type to "check" as described in "Editing a Memorized Transaction" later in this chapter.

To begin, switch to the Write Checks window. Display the check you want to memorize, or press **End** four times to display a blank check. Then type in the information you want memorized—the information that will be the same each time you reuse the check. To memorize the check, press **Ctrl-M** or choose **Memorize Transaction** from the Edit menu. Quicken beeps three times, copying the information in the check to the list of memorized transactions, and returns you to the check.

If you created this check from scratch, you can now decide whether to record it in your account. To do so, finish typing any missing information, and then record it the usual way. If you don't want to record the check in your account, press **Ctrl-D** to delete it from the screen (the memorized check information remains intact).

If a transaction you're memorizing has the same payee as one that's been memorized previously, Quicken notifies you with this message: *Transaction Already Memorized.*

Choose **Replace** if you want to replace the existing memorized transaction with the new one you're memorizing now; **Add** if you want to leave the previously memorized transaction intact as you place the new transaction on the memorized transaction list; or **Cancel** if you decide not to memorize the new transaction at all.

NOTE

When QuickFill is on and memorizing transactions automatically, you don't see this message. Instead, whenever you record a transaction with a payee you used before, QuickFill memorizes the new transaction separately, leaving the earlier transactions for that payee intact.

One other point: Once a transaction is memorized, Quicken stores the memorized transaction's details (payee, amount, etc.) separately from those of the original transaction in your account. Changing this original transaction in the Write Checks window or in the register has no effect on the memorized transaction at all. If you want to change the memorized transaction, use the technique detailed in "Editing a Memorized Transaction" later in this chapter.

You can also memorize a transaction from the Memorized Transaction list. Just choose **New** and you'll see the Create Memorized Transaction dialog box as shown in Figure 7.4.

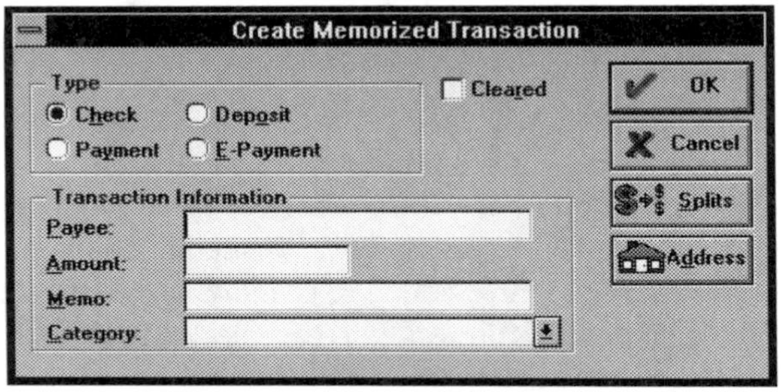

FIGURE 7.4

Enter information for a new memorized transaction in this window.

Memorizing a Transaction from the Register

You can also use Quicken's manual memorizing feature in your account register. You might memorize transactions that affect your account from time to time, but not on a predictable schedule—for instance, checks you sporadically write by hand or payments on an old loan you receive erratically from an underemployed relative. Or, if you're using transaction groups to record an entire set of regular register transactions, you must memorize the individual transactions first.

When memorizing a transaction from the account register, Quicken stores all the information entered in the transaction except the date and check number. The entry in the *Cleared* column (the one labeled *Clr*) is memorized. If you don't want the information in a particular field memorized, just leave that field empty when you memorize the transaction.

You can memorize either new or existing transactions from the register. Let's try it now. If you're not already there, switch to the register screen by pressing **Ctrl-R** or clicking on the **Register** icon. To create a new transaction to be memorized, start with an empty transaction (press **End** four times to move to the bottom of the register if you're not already there) and type in the information you want memorized in the various fields on the transaction. You can fill in as few or as many fields as you like. If you want to memorize a previously recorded transaction, highlight the transaction using the techniques for browsing through the register, which you learned in Chapter 4.

Now, just as when you memorized the check, either press **Ctrl-M** or choose **Memorize Transaction** from the Edit menu. You'll see a window message offering you a chance to cancel the memorization.

Choose **OK** to have Quicken go ahead and memorize the transaction. Quicken copies the information in the transaction to the list of memorized transactions and returns you to the register. If you started with a new transaction, it's time to ask yourself whether to record it in your account. If the answer is yes, finish typing any missing information, and then click **Record** or press the arrow button. If you don't want to record the transaction, press **Ctrl-D** to delete it from the screen. The information you've memorized remains intact even if you delete the transaction from the register.

Reusing Memorized Transactions

Whenever you use QuickFill to finish a transaction for you by copying the details from a previous transaction, you're reusing (recalling) a memorized transaction. But if QuickFill is turned off, or if you want more details on the memorized transactions than you get from the QuickFill drop-down list of payees, you can recall memorized transactions from a separate window. Whichever way you recall a memorized transaction, you can make any changes you like in the transaction before recording it in your account.

NOTE	For even greater efficiency, you can recall entire groups of memorized transactions in one step, as you'll see in the section "Using Transaction Groups," later in this chapter.

Generally, you'll want to start with a new empty check or transaction, although it is possible to replace an existing transaction with the information from a memorize transaction.

The easiest way to recall a memorized transaction is with QuickFill. After entering the date of the new transaction, move the cursor to the *Payee* field. Then just start typing the payee name. QuickFill immediately completes the field with the first matching memorized transaction.

If the payee name QuickFill enters isn't the right one, press [-] or + on the numeric keypad (or **Ctrl-Up Arrow** or **Ctrl-Down Arrow**) to bring up the payee names from other memorized transactions one at a time in alphabetical order. Once the right payee name appears, press **Tab**. QuickFill recalls all the remaining information from the corresponding memorized transaction. (If you don't want QuickFill to complete the rest of the transaction for you, don't press **Tab**. Instead, move to the next field by clicking on it with the mouse.)

QuickFill will fill in the remaining fields only if you start with a new, empty transaction. If you use QuickFill to change the payee of an existing transaction, the other fields remain as they are. To completely replace a current transaction with a memorized one (rarely a good idea, by the way), you need the alternate technique for recalling memorized transactions described next.

Recalling Transactions from the Memorized Transaction List

SHORTCUT — If you recall a specific memorized transaction very often, you can set up a button on the Iconbar to recall it for you with a single mouse click. When you first install Quicken, one of the iconbar buttons (shown here in the margin) is assigned to this purpose. However, you must set up the button for the specific memorized transaction you want it to recall. You can add additional buttons for other memorized transactions if you' like. See the section on customizing the Iconbar in the Appendix for details.

Besides QuickFill, your other main option for recalling memorized transactions is to pick them from the Memorized Transaction list. First, move to the transaction you want to fill with the recalled information. Then press **Ctrl-T** or choose **Memorized Transaction** from the Lists menu.

You'll now see a list, similar to the one in Figure 7.5, of all the transactions you've memorized. The transactions are listed alphabetically according to the entry in the *Payee* field in the register and the equivalent *Pay to the Order of* field on a check. In this window, however, these entries appear in the column labeled *Description*.

FIGURE 7.5

The Memorized Transaction List dialog box.

Next, find the transaction you'd like to recall in the list. If it's not visible, you can move to it either with the **Down Arrow** and **Up Arrow** keys, or by pressing the first letter of the transaction's entry in the *Description* column. Once the transaction is in the window, recall it by double-clicking on it, or by highlighting it and choosing **Use**. You'll be returned to the Write Checks window or the register, whichever you started from, with the information from the recalled transaction on display.

Fill in the empty fields and make any revisions you want. When the new transaction is correct, record it just as you always do.

Locating a Transaction in the List Quickly

If you've memorized a large number of transactions, it's often quickest to recall the one you want with a combination of **QuickFill** and the Memorized Transaction list. After you type the first letter or two of the Payee's name, pop up the Memorized Transaction list. The highlight will be on the first entry in the *Description* column that begins with the letters you've typed. Assuming this isn't the correct transaction, use the **Up Arrow** or **Down Arrow** keys or keep pressing the first letter of the payee name to locate the desired memorized transaction. Then choose **Use** to recall it.

Memorizing Split Transactions

When you memorize the information in a split transaction, Quicken records the split details as well as the entries in the regular fields of the transaction.

| SHORTCUT | If you make regular payments on a loan, Quicken can automatically calculate the amount of each payment that goes to interest and the amount that goes to the principal, and will even keep a running total of the total amounts you've paid on the loan. The technique relies on memorizing a split payment transaction, then applying Quicken's **Amortization** feature to it. (See Chapter 9 for instructions.) |

Editing a Memorized Transaction

| SHORTCUT | You can use the method outlined as follows to enter new memorized transactions from scratch, without memorizing them from |

transactions already in your account. This might be appropriate if you'd like to set up your account at one sitting in anticipation of future transactions rather than memorize transactions as you enter them. To do this, display the Memorized Transaction list and choose **New**.

Suppose one of your regular payees has changed his or her address, or has raised his or her prices. Instead of creating a new memorized transaction from scratch, you can edit the old one.

To edit a memorized transaction, you start by displaying the Memorized Transaction list. Highlight the item you want to edit and choose **Edit** to pop up a special window for this chore. Let's try this with the check transaction you memorized before.

1. Call up the Memorized Transaction list by pressing **Ctrl-T** or by choosing **Memorized Transaction** from the Lists menu.

2. Highlight the check transaction that you memorized earlier in the chapter.

3. Choose **Edit** or press **Ctrl-E** to call up the Edit Memorized Transaction dialog box, shown in Figure 7.6.

FIGURE 7.6

Use this dialog box to edit memorized transactions.

4. The *Type* field contains a set of radio buttons specifying whether the item is a check, deposit, payment, or electronic payment. If you decided to write the memorized check by hand from now on, you could change the item's type from a check to a payment. However, the address information would be lost; note that only check items can have addresses.

5. Make whatever changes you want in the other transaction information (in the *Payee, Amount, Memo, Category,* and *Cleared* fields). In the most common case, you'd just change the amount of a monthly payment.

6. You can edit split transaction information for the memorized transaction by clicking the **Splits** button; the familiar Splits window appears. You can make changes in any of the information here—or split a previously "unsplit" transaction—using the same techniques covered in Chapter 5. Press **Enter** to leave the dialog box.

7. If you're editing a check item, you can edit the address recorded for the check by choosing **Address**. When your changes are complete, press **Enter** to save them and exit the window.

8. Once the information on the Edit Memorized Transaction dialog box meets your approval, choose **OK** to save the modifications. You're returned to the Memorized Transaction List dialog box.

9. Close the Memorized Transaction list by pressing **Esc**.

Deleting a Memorized Transaction

After you've held your mortgage-burning party, it's time to delete the memorized transaction that you've been using to pay your bank or finance company for all those years. Deleting the transaction is a lot easier than paying off the mortgage!

To prove that bold assertion to your own satisfaction, press **Ctrl-T** or choose **Memorized Transaction** from the Lists menu. The Memorized Transaction list will appear.

Highlight the transaction you want Quicken to delete, and choose **Del** or press **Ctrl-D**. Quicken will display a message warning you that a deletion is imminent. Choose **Yes** to complete the deletion, or, if you decide not to delete the transaction, choose **Cancel**.

Printing a List of Your Memorized Transactions

See Chapter 3 for information on setting up your printer. The printout of the memorized transaction list uses the Report/Graph printer setup, covered specifically in Chapter 10.

To print the list of all the transactions you've memorized, start from either the register or the Write Checks window. Press **Ctrl-T** or select the **Recall Transaction** command from the Quick Entry menu. The Memorized Transaction list will appear.

Now press **Ctrl-P** or choose **Print List** from the File menu to begin the printing process. The Print Memorized Transactions List window will appear. Decide whether to print the list on paper or on disk, make the appropriate **Radio** button selection, and choose **OK**. If you've selected disk output, you'll be asked to type in the name for the file to contain the list. When the printout is complete, you'll be returned to the Memorized Transaction list.

Paying Bills Automatically with Transaction Groups

In Quicken, a *transaction group* is a set of transactions that you regularly post to your account at the same time. It's not hard to come up with examples of transactions that always occur together once a month or at some other interval. You probably pay several bills related to your home or apartment at the same time each month. If you own rental property, you might receive and deposit rent payments from several tenants at about the same time each month. By collecting these transactions into a transaction group, you can have Quicken remind you when it's time to print and mail the checks (if the group includes checks) or otherwise take care of the transactions. And Quicken will record all the transactions in the group into your account in a single step.

As you can imagine from this description, transaction groups work much like transactions you schedule with the calendar. But because they let you record multiple transactions automatically, transaction groups go even farther than individual memorized transactions to help you increase your efficiency and prevent errors.

A group can contain any number of transactions. After you've defined a transaction group, you can modify the definition, adding or removing transactions from the group, or even deleting the entire group.

NOTE   Of course, each time Quicken records the transactions from a group into your account, you can modify the individual transactions as needed. For example, you might want to fill in missing dollar amounts, make up a name for a class left empty, or even delete one or more of the transactions.

Creating a Transaction Group

Creating a transaction group is a little more complicated than setting up an individual scheduled transaction. That's because you can't just drag transactions from the list in the calendar to a group. Instead, you have to "memorize" each transaction first, then assign it in a dialog box to the group.

NOTE   Before you can create a transaction group, you must have Quicken memorize the transactions you want to include in the group. Any transaction you want Quicken to write and print as a check must be memorized as a check type transaction, as described in "Memorizing a Check" at the beginning of this chapter.

Still, the process is really quite painless and goes quickly. Once all the transactions you want to include in your transaction group have been memorized, you're ready to create the new group. Press **Ctrl-J**, or choose **Scheduled Transaction** in the Lists menu. You'll see the Scheduled Transaction List window. Now choose **New** to display the Set Up Scheduled Transaction dialog box, as shown in Figure 7.7.

SHORTCUT   Working from the Quicken calendar you can bypass the Scheduled Transaction list. Choose a date (click on it or highlight it and press **Enter**). In the small window, choose **New** to display the Set Up Scheduled Transaction dialog box.

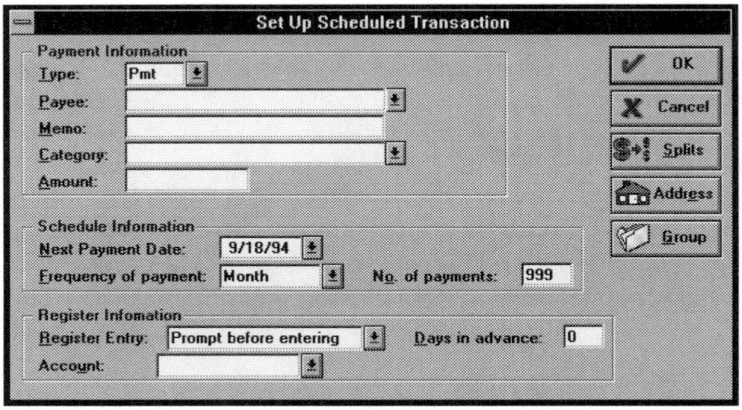

FIGURE 7.7

The Set Up Scheduled Transaction dialog box (also used to schedule individual transactions from the calendar).

Choose the **Group** button to set up a transaction group. Quicken displays the Set Up Transaction Group dialog box (Figure 7.8).

FIGURE 7.8

*The Set Up
Transaction
Group
dialog box.*

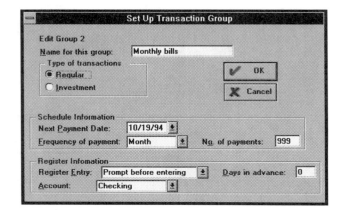

In the *Name* for this group field, type in whatever name or description you like to indicate the transaction group's purpose. The next field, *Type of Transactions*, should be left set to *Regular* unless you're working with investment transactions; Quicken keeps investment transactions in separate groups.

The remaining fields are the same as the corresponding ones in the Set Up Scheduled Transaction dialog box, described earlier in this chapter in the section *Filling out the Set Up Scheduled Transaction window.*

When all the fields are complete, choose **OK** to complete the dialog box. You'll now see the Assign Transactions to Group dialog box. As you can see, this dialog box lists all the transactions Quicken has memorized. Use the **DownArrow** and **UpArrow** keys to highlight the first memorized transaction you want in the group, then press the space bar or choose the **Mark** button to assign it to the group. You'll notice that the number of the transaction group you're setting up appears in the column labeled *Grp* (for *Group*).

WARNING

Again, in order to print checks from a transaction group, the transactions must be memorized as checks. Memorized transactions that meet this requirement have the notation *Chk* in the *Type* column of the Assign Transactions dialog box, shown in Figure 7.9. You can change the type of a memorized transaction with the method described in "Editing a Memorized Transaction" earlier in this chapter.

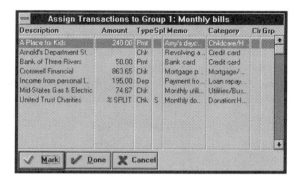

FIGURE 7.9

The Assign Transactions dialog box.

Repeat this process for each transaction you'd like to add to the new group. If you mistakenly assign the wrong transaction to the group, just press the space bar again to cancel the assignment.

NOTE   You can only assign a memorized transaction to one group. If you want to assign a transaction you've already assigned to a second group, you must memorize the transaction again and assign this new copy to the other group.

When you've assigned all the transactions you want in the group, choose **Done** to finish the setup process and close the window. You'll be returned to the Scheduled Transaction List dialog box.

Using a Transaction Group

Quicken will place the transactions from a group into your account automatically if you tell it do so when setting up the group. Depending on your entry in the *Register Entry* field, Quicken will tell you before it actually carries out the procedure, giving you a chance to cancel it.

NEW IN 3 On the other hand, you can have Quicken enter any group (whether or not it's scheduled at regular intervals) into your account any time you'd like. To do this, open the Scheduled Transaction list (**Ctrl-J**), highlight the desired group, and choose **Pay Now** (or just double-click the group name).

In Quicken 2, the process of automatically recalling all the memorized transactions in a transaction group and recording them in your account is referred to as "using" the transaction group. The Enter Scheduled Transaction dialog box is titled *Use Transaction Group*.

If Quicken is set to inform you before recording a transaction group, or if you manually "pay" a group, you'll see the Enter Scheduled Transaction dialog box (Figure 7.9). Here, you can change two of the choices you made when setting up the group. If you'd like, you can:

- Choose a different account where Quicken should enter the new transactions.
- Assign a different date to the transactions Quicken records (you can change the date with the + or - keys, use the date shortcut keys you learned in Chapter 2, or display the pop-up calendar by clicking on the arrow in the *Date* field).

FIGURE 7.9

The Enter Scheduled Transaction dialog box.

SHORTCUT   If you use a transaction group frequently, you can add a button to the Iconbar that lets you execute the group with one quick click of the mouse. The icon you'll see in the button is shown in the left margin. (See the section on customizing the Iconbar in the Appendix.)

After a Transaction Group is Activated

After you use a transaction group and its transactions are in place in your account, you'll be returned to the register. You're then free to edit or add to any of the individual transactions that have just been entered. For example, you may need to add or edit the dollar amounts of the payments or credits in one or more of the newly recorded transactions. You can also print any checks in the group, as long as they were originally memorized from the Write Checks window.

If there are any checks to be printed in the transaction group you've just executed, you can print them immediately if you'd like. If you're not already at the Write Checks window, press **Ctrl-W** to move there. Then press **Ctrl-P** to begin printing. See Chapter 3 if you need more information on printing checks.

Editing and Deleting a Transaction Group

Once you've set up a transaction group, you can modify particulars such as the description or scheduled date, add or remove transactions, or delete the entire group.

Editing a Transaction Group

In essence, all you're doing here is repeating the setup process you went through earlier to set up the group. If you'll be adding more transactions to the group, the new transactions must be memorized first. If they haven't been, start by memorizing them following the steps outlined earlier in this chapter.

You have two choices for actually editing the group:

- Starting from the calendar, choose any date on which the group is scheduled. In the little window that you see, highlight the group and choose **Edit**.
- From anywhere in Quicken, **Ctrl-J** or choose **Scheduled Transaction** from the Lists menu. You'll see the Scheduled Transaction List dialog box. Highlight the transaction group you want to edit and choose **Edit**.

At this point, the Edit Transaction Group dialog box pops up (it looks just like Figure 7.8 on page 184). If you want to change the group description, the scheduling frequency, or the next scheduled date, enter your changes here. When the group definition is correct, choose **OK** to confirm your changes, if any.

You'll now see the list of your memorized transactions. Just as when you first set up the transaction group, you can assign additional transactions by marking them, then pressing the space bar. You can also cancel an existing assignment in the same way. After all the new transactions are added to the group, choose **Done**. You'll return to the list of transaction groups.

Deleting a Transaction Group

To delete a transaction group, use either of the two methods listed above to display the name of the group in a Quicken window. Highlight the group you want to delete and choose **Del**. You'll see a warning that you're about to delete the group permanently (the memorized transactions included in the group are not deleted, however). To proceed, choose **OK**; the group will be deleted.

Transaction Group Reminders

Quicken and the Billminder program inform you when you should post the transaction group to your account—you'll see a little reminder window on the screen. These reminders appear before the actual date on which the transactions are scheduled to be entered into your account; how far in advance depends on an adjustable setting that you can alter with the Preferences menu (see the Appendix).

Summary

Congratulations! You've just completed the basic course in using Quicken to keep your checking account records. In the first five chapters, you learned how to start Quicken accounts; write, record, and print checks; enter other transactions in your checking account register; and organize your account by assigning transactions to categories and classes. In this chapter, you learned how to speed up repetitive entries with memorized transactions and transaction groups.

From now on, you'll be applying these fundamentals to practical financial management. In later chapters, you'll learn how to keep track of other parts of your financial situation with additional Quicken accounts; how to produce informative financial reports; and how to use Quicken effectively in your overall financial strategy, whether at home or in your business.

Chapter Eight

Working with Quicken Accounts: Keeping Track of Cash, Credit Cards, and More

 or many people, a single Quicken checking account will suffice for recording all income and expenses, including cash and credit card transactions. If your financial affairs are more complicated, though, a Quicken checking account by itself may not allow you to keep adequately detailed records of other kinds of transactions. That's why Quicken provides a total of six different accounts.

For example, if a lot of cash passes through your hands—whether it's because you prefer to make most purchases with cash, or because you're paid in cash—you may be better off accounting for your cash transactions separately. Similarly, if you use your credit cards frequently, you may want to monitor the purchases you charge and the payments you make in more detail than a checking account easily permits.

Besides, your net worth undoubtedly depends on more than the payments and deposits recorded in your checking account. Aside from your checking account balance, you may have additional assets that don't appear in your monthly bank statement and simply don't belong in a checking account at all: a savings account or an IRA, investments of various types, rental property, the tax basis of your home, business equipment, or your business's accounts receivable, for instance. And your financial picture may include liabilities, such as your mortgage or a large loan, or your business's accounts payable, which you need to track separately and in detail.

| NOTE | Net worth is the dollar value of everything you own minus everything you owe. It's equal to how much cash you'd theoretically have if you converted all your assets to cash and paid off all your debts. |

In this chapter, you'll learn techniques for accounting for your cash, credit cards, savings accounts, and money market funds. You'll also learn to juggle multiple Quicken accounts and entire files containing many accounts. (Chapter 9 covers the complexities of investments and loans.)

About Quicken Accounts and Files

Quicken has an account suited specifically to every type of financial transaction you conduct. Quicken's cash, credit card, and other specialized accounts all work very much like the checking account you've been using, except that each is tailored to the particular type of transactions for which it's intended.

To account for every nickel of your net worth, you can create as many separate accounts as you need in your Quicken file. In the real world, funds often flow from one type of account or asset to another; you withdraw cash from your checking account to make a purchase, for example, or sell some stocks and place the proceeds in your checking account. As you'd expect, Quicken has the know-how to make transfers between the accounts in your account file almost automatically. And when it's time to prepare a budget, cash flow statement, or tax summary, Quicken has access to all the accounts in a file as it draws up the report on it.

One Quicken file should provide ample room for monitoring all your assets and liabilities. Just in case, however, Quicken lets you set up and maintain as many separate files as you'd like. You might want to divide your business and personal finances into two account files, or keep each year's records in a different file. The final section in this chapter covers the techniques for managing your account files.

Working Through the Examples

I recommend that you enter all the example accounts and transactions in this chapter, even if you don't plan to use all the available account types. Since all the account types work in similar fashion, you'll learn and refine useful skills that you'll be able to apply to whatever accounts you do use. In particular, you'll get plenty of vital experience in transferring funds between accounts.

Keeping Track of Cash

With electronic pay points popping up at the corner gas station, and those little plastic cards in our wallets and purses, we may be on the road to a brave new cashless society. But it hasn't materialized yet, and most of us want a little folding money in our pockets. Quicken makes it easy for you to track your cash transactions accurately no matter how you use cash. If you make cash purchases or receive cash income only occasionally, you can record them in your checking account. If you use cash more extensively, however, you may want to set up a separate account for your cash transactions.

Keeping Track of Cash in Your Checking Account

Unless your cash transactions are very numerous and important, the easiest way to account for them is to record them in your regular checking account.

Recording Cash Purchases in your Checking Account

NOTE   If you need to record a purchase made with cash that you received directly as income, see the next section, "Recording Cash Income in Your Checking Account."

When you withdraw cash from your checking account, you record it as a withdrawal in your register by entering the amount of the withdrawal as a payment. If you'd like to record what you spent the money on, just enter a description of your purchase in the *Memo* field and assign the transaction to a category, class, or both in the *Category* field.

If you spent the cash on more than one type of item, you can use one of Quicken's split transactions to record the items as separate parts of the one withdrawal transaction. Imagine you've withdrawn $80 and have spent $60 on office supplies for your business and $20 for a trip to the movies. To record this transaction, switch to the register and start a new entry by pressing **End** three times. Type **Cash Withdrawal** in the *Payee* field and then enter the amount of the withdrawal, $80, in the *Payment* field.

Now you're ready to split the transaction. Choose **Splits** or press **Ctrl-S** to pop up the Splits dialog box. On the first line, Quicken will have entered *$80*, the total amount of the withdrawal. Enter the first item, your supplies purchase, by typing **Supplies/Business** in the *Category* field and **60** (over the existing entry) in the *Amount* field. (If you prefer, you can use whatever category and class names you want from the ones in your own account.)

Move to the second line and enter your movie expenses as **Entertainment** or **Misc** in the *Category* field. Quicken has already calculated the remaining amount of your withdrawal as *$20*, so that completes your entry. The window should now look like the one in Figure 8.1.

FIGURE 8.1

A checking account withdrawal for two cash purchases entered as a split transaction.

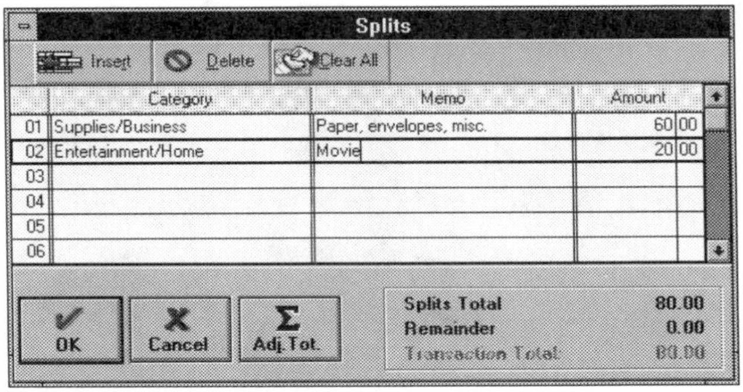

Don't worry about associating every cash purchase with the right withdrawal. If you don't know which withdrawal gave you the cash you used for a purchase you want to itemize, just pick any cash withdrawal from around the time of the purchase, as long as it covers at least the purchase amount. If the withdrawal was larger than the purchase amount, enter the remaining amount as a miscellaneous expense by assigning it to the appropriate category in the Splits dialog box.

Recording Cash Income in your Checking Account

If you're like most people, the bulk of your income comes from your regular paycheck, but you also have cash income from time to time. Waitresses and waiters collect tips, of course. When you hold a garage sale, most of your customers probably pay in cash.

If you deposit the cash you've received into your checking account, all you need do is record it as a deposit in the register, as you learned to do in Chapter 4. But if you spend the cash without depositing it, and want a record of your purchases, things get a little trickier. If you simply record your purchases, Quicken will think that you've made a withdrawal or written a check, and will reduce your account balance accordingly.

Instead, record the cash income and your purchase as a deposit—even though you don't actually deposit the money—again using a split transaction. To practice this technique now, let's say your garage sale was very successful and brought in $300. You took $150 of the money and bought a new typewriter for your business, spent $80 on groceries, and took your family out to a $50 meal. You'll spend the remaining $20 on miscellaneous items over the next few days.

To record this flurry of spending, begin by switching to the register and pressing **End** to start a new transaction. In the *Payee* field, enter something like **Cash inc/purchases**, and then choose **Splits** or press **Ctrl-S** to pop up the Split Transaction dialog box (do not make an entry in the *Payment* or *Deposit* field).

On the first line, enter **Cash inc** for the category name, or the name of the category you've created for cash income in your account. Press **Tab** to confirm the entry and, if the category you've entered isn't already part of your account, create it with the steps you learned in Chapter 2. Then press **Tab** until you've moved to the *Amount* column. Here, type in the amount of your garage sale earnings, **$300**.

Now move to the second line in the split transaction. Here and on the following lines type in your purchases shown as follows (be sure to enter the minus sign in front of each amount).

Category	*Amount*
Equipment/Business	-150.00
Dining/Home	-50.00
Groceries/Home	-80.00
Misc/Home	-20.00

When you've finished typing, the completed split transaction should look like the one shown in Figure 8.2. Choose **OK** to complete the split and return to the register. Notice that there is no entry in the *Payment* or *Deposit* field, and that your balance is unchanged.

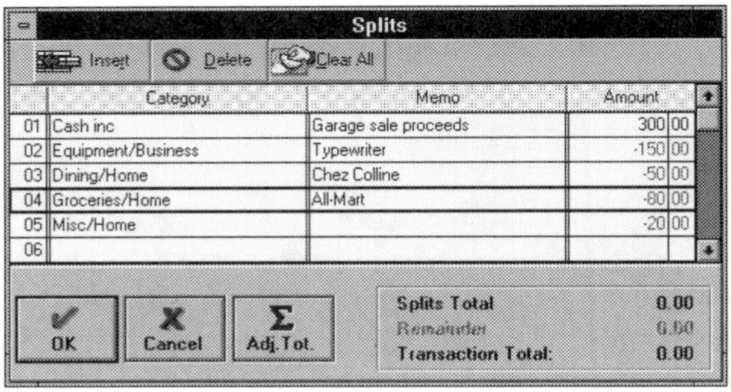

FIGURE 8.2

Recording cash income and spending in the checking account register as a split transaction.

Recording "Less Cash" Deposits

When you deposit a check from which you get some cash back, type **Deposit** in the *Payee* field, and place the actual amount of the deposit—after the cash you've kept has been subtracted—in the *Deposit* field. Then choose **Splits** or press **Ctrl-S** to split the transaction. In the *Category* column on the first line of the Split Transaction dialog box, enter the category for the source of your income. Then, in the *Amount* column, type the total amount of the income, before the cash was withheld, over the amount displayed.

On the next line or lines, enter your purchases (the ones made with the cash you've kept) as items in the split. In the *Amount* column, enter a minus sign before the amount of each purchase, and be sure the total of all the purchases is equal to the amount of cash you withheld from the deposit.

Figure 8.3 shows an example of such a split transaction for a "less cash" deposit.

FIGURE 8.3

A "less cash" deposit prepared as a split transaction.

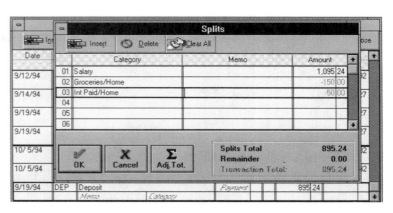

Keeping Track of Cash with a Cash Account

If you want detailed records of all of your cash purchases or income, you can set up a separate account devoted strictly to cash transactions. A cash account works almost exactly like your Quicken checking account, so you should feel right at home.

Quicken doesn't force you to record every $2 magazine or book of stamps you buy in your cash account. Instead, you can enter the important cash expenditures, and have Quicken automatically adjust the balance to cover miscellaneous amounts.

The procedure for setting up a cash account is essentially the same as the one you used when setting up your checking account. To begin, display the Account List window by pressing **Ctrl-A**, clicking on the **Accts** icon, or choosing **Account** in the Lists menu. The Account List window (Figure 8.4) contains a list of all the accounts in the current file. If you're working through this book in sequence, you only have one account so far, the checking account.

FIGURE 8.4

The Account List window.

With the Account list active, choose **New** or press **Ctrl-N**. The Select Account Type dialog box will appear, as illustrated in Figure 8.5. Then take the following steps:

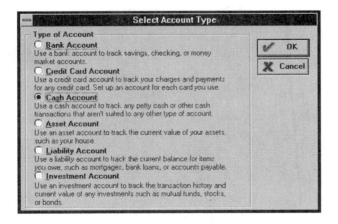

FIGURE 8.5

The Select Account Type dialog box.

1. Select the **Cash Account** radio button and choose **OK**. The New Account Information dialog box appears (Figure 8.6 on the next page).

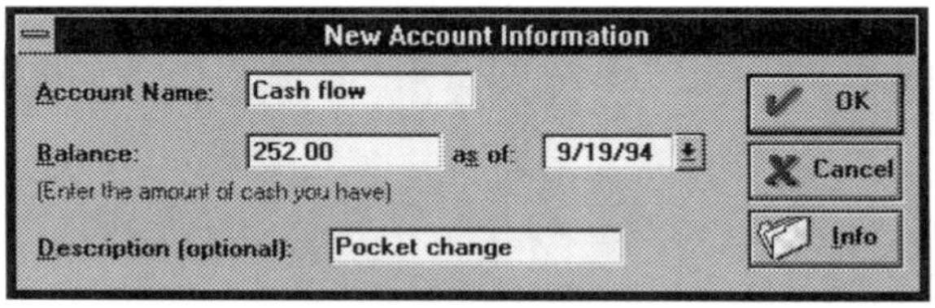

FIGURE 8.6

The New Account Information dialog box.

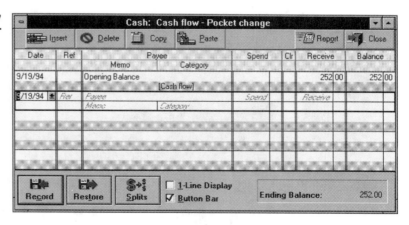

2. In the *Account Name* field, type **Cash Flow** as the name for the new account.

3. At the *Balance* field, enter the amount of cash you now have on hand. If the balance you're entering reflects a date other than today's, make the necessary change in the *As of* field.

4. Type in a description if you like in the final field, then choose **OK** to create the cash account. You'll be returned to the Account List window with the new cash account visible in the list.

To work with any Quicken account, you must first select it in this window. To select the cash account, double-click on its name in the list, or move the highlight to the name and choose **Use**. You'll immediately be "deposited" at the cash account register, shown in Figure 8.7.

FIGURE 8.7

The cash account register.

Notice that this register looks almost identical to the one in your checking (bank) account. There are a few differences, however. Some of the columns at the top of the register have different names. Instead of a *Num* field, there's one labeled *Ref*; instead of *Payment* and *Deposit*, there's *Spend* and *Receive*. Naturally, the account name at the top of the window has also changed. And if you have a color screen, you'll notice that the background color is green instead of yellow. Of course, you can't write checks on a cash account.

Switching Between Accounts

Before you go any further, practice switching between the new cash account and your checking account. You can use this same method to select any Quicken account. From the register, the easiest course is to press **Ctrl-A** (*A* for *account*) in order to pop up the Account List window—the same one shown in Figure 8.4. Alternatively, you can click on the **Accts** icon or choose **Account** in the Lists menu to display this window.

In the Account List window, choose your checking account to move directly to the checking account register, showing all the transactions you recorded earlier. You can use the Account list at any time to move directly to any account you want to work with.

Once an account window is open, though, you don't need the Account list to switch to the account. In this case, the cash account window should still be on the screen—the checking account's register appears to cover up much of the cash window, but you should be able to see a portion of it. If you have a mouse, click on any visible part of the cash account's window. The window comes to the top, activated for further use.

With the keyboard, you can cycle through all the open windows one by one. Press **Ctrl-Tab** to move from the cash window to the Account list, then to the checking account window, and finally back to the cash account (if any other windows are open, they'll be included in this cycle as well). Pressing **Shift-Ctrl-Tab** cycles through the open windows in the reverse direction.

| **NOTE** | Quicken lets you set up the Iconbar so that you can switch to a particular account with the click of a mouse, using the Iconbar button labeled **UseAcct**. However, you must set up the button for the specific account you want it to bring up. You can add additional buttons for other accounts if you like. See the section on customizing the Iconbar in the Appendix for instructions. |

Recording Cash Transactions

| **NOTE** | If you're planning to keep a cash account, plan to save all the receipts of your cash purchases and other cash transactions. That |

way, you'll be able to enter the amounts by copying them in directly.

Of course, your cash account doesn't represent a formal account in real life (unless perhaps your spouse serves as your personal banker!). When you receive cash, you simply put it in your wallet or purse, and when you spend it, out it goes again. Nevertheless, in a cash account you record all the coming and going just as you do in your Quicken checking account. While you don't have to record every minuscule expenditure, your records will be seriously in error unless you do enter all the cash you take in.

In your cash accounts, as in all Quicken accounts, you can enter transactions in two ways. First, and most common, you can simply type them in yourself. In addition, you can have Quicken transfer amounts to and from other accounts as needed.

Let's review the process of entering transactions in the cash account register by recording the following transactions:

Payee	Spend	Receive	Memo	Category
Jerry's Kids	$50		Donation	Charity/Home
Luigi's Restaurant	$65		Dinner w/client	Entertain-ment/Business
Jim Smith		$100	Sold old lawnmower	Cash inc/Home

For each transaction, enter the information into the register fields, just as you did when entering transactions into the checking account register. Assign them to categories and classes just as you do checking account transactions. When each entry is complete, record it by pressing **Enter**. When you've finished, your register should resemble Figure 8.8.

FIGURE 8.8

The cash account register after entering several transactions.

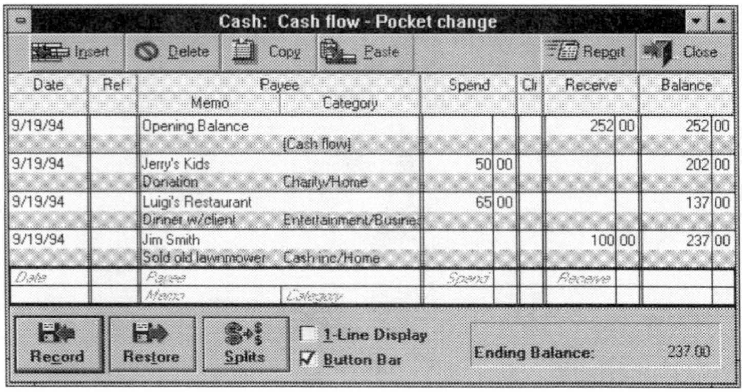

NOTE   Use the *Ref* column for entering a reference number for the transaction. This is handy when you're keeping track of petty cash for your business.

Transferring Cash to and from Your Checking Account

Although there are times when you receive cash directly, the cash in your possession usually comes from a bank withdrawal. Instead of entering the transaction twice—once as a withdrawal from your bank account, and again as a **Receive** item in your cash account—you can have Quicken transfer the funds directly.

What Quicken actually transfers, of course, is a record of the funds, not the funds themselves. You enter a transaction in one of the accounts affected by the transfer, and Quicken automatically creates a parallel transaction in the other account. We'll use the term *transfer transaction* to refer to either of the transactions involved in a transfer—the one you create to initiate the transfer, or the one Quicken creates for you in the other account.

By now, you're ready for a typical but fairly complicated example to illustrate how this process works. Let's say you've just gone to the bank with your weekly $1,000 paycheck. You deposit most of it in your checking account, but take $200 in cash for day-to-day expenses. Here's how to record this "less cash" deposit in your checking account and automatically transfer the cash to your cash account.

1. Switch to your checking account register. Click on the window if it's visible, or press **Ctrl-A**, highlight the checking account in the Account list, and choose **Use**.

2. In the *Payee* field, type **Deposit-Salary**; enter the amount you actually deposited into your account, **$800**, in the *Deposit* field.

3. Now split the transaction by choosing **Splits** or pressing **Ctrl-S**. On the first line of the Split Transaction dialog box, type in a category for your salary income (**Salary** should do); and in the *Amount* column, enter the total amount of the check, **1000** ($1,000), typing it over the entry that Quicken made for you.

4. With the cursor in the *Category* column of the second line, press **Ctrl-C** or choose the **Category List** button to pop up the Category List window, and press **End** to move the pointer to the bottom of the list. As shown in Figure 8.9 on the next page, Quicken adds all your accounts to the end of the Category list, just for the purpose of transferring funds between

them. In the *Type* column for each account in the Category list you'll see an entry reflecting the type of account. The possible entries are **Bank** for bank accounts, **Cash** for cash accounts, **CCard** for credit card accounts, **Oth A** for asset accounts, and **Oth L** for liability accounts.

FIGURE 8.9

Your accounts are added to the end of the Category list.

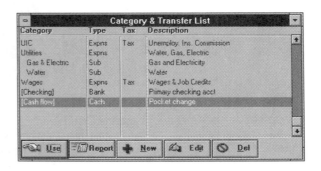

SHORTCUT   If you prefer, you can type in the name of the account to or from which you're transferring funds, using QuickFill to minimize your typing. Type a left bracket, then the first letter or two of the account name (in this case, QuickFill fills in the full name of the account, including the closing bracket.

5.   In the Category list, choose your cash account by double-clicking on it or by highlighting it and pressing **Use**. You'll be returned to the Split Transaction dialog box with the name of the cash account in brackets in the *Category* column, as shown in Figure 8.10. Quicken has already calculated the amount of cash you received.

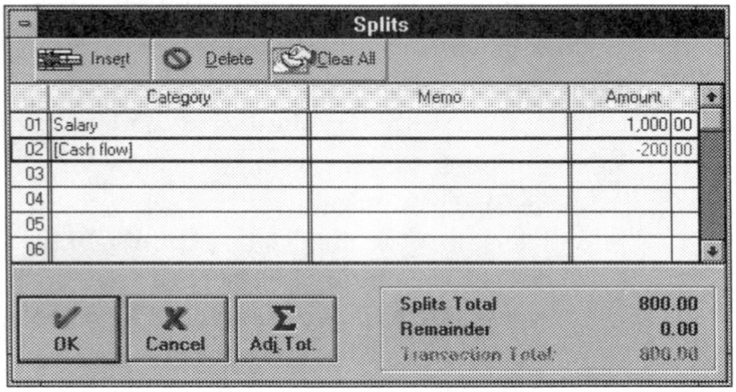

FIGURE 8.10

Transferring funds from the checking account to the cash account in the Split Transaction dialog box.

NOTE Because transfer transactions represent the movement of funds within your own financial "universe," not income or outflow, they don't usually require categorization. However, you may prefer to assign all transactions to "real" Quicken categories, not account names. In this case, you can't use the automatic transfer feature, but you can still track funds that flow from account to account by manually creating parallel transactions in each account.

6. Choose **OK** to leave the Split Transaction dialog box, and record the transaction in your checking account by pressing **Enter** again.

SHORTCUT You can switch directly from a transaction in one account to the corresponding transfer transaction in another. Press **Ctrl-X** or choose **Go to Transfer** from the Edit menu. You'll switch instantly to the parallel transaction in the other account.

Because you listed your cash account as the category for the cash you received, Quicken has added the cash automatically to that account for you. To confirm that the transfer has taken place, switch to the cash account (click on its window or choose it on the Account list). You'll see a new transaction highlighted in the cash account register, a transaction that is a duplicate of the one you just made in the checking account—except that this one increases your balance.

As you can see, when Quicken creates a transfer transaction in the second account, it copies the date, payee, dollar amount, and memo of the transaction, and automatically records the account of the original transaction in the *Category* field.

NOTE The new transaction doesn't include the check number. You can add this if you like, or make other changes as detailed in "Modifying a Transfer Transaction."

Using the same technique, you can record a withdrawal from your checking account by entering the amount you withdrew in your cash account, letting Quicken make the transfer for you. Just enter a notation such as **Withdrawal** in the *Payee* field and the amount in the *Receive* column. Then in the *Category* field, pop up the Category List dialog box and select your checking account as the category. When you record the transaction, it will be transferred automatically to your checking account, and the balance there will be reduced accordingly.

Transferring Cash Between Other Accounts

You can transfer funds between your cash account and any other Quicken account in just the same way you've learned here. For example, if you obtain a so-called cash advance—that is, a high-interest loan—from your credit card, you can enter the transaction in your credit card account as a charge, and transfer the cash automatically to your cash account by assigning the transaction to the **Cash Account** category. We'll run through the procedure in more detail in a moment, after you've opened a credit card account.

Modifying a Transfer Transaction

If you find it necessary to modify a transfer transaction, you generally only have to make the changes once, since Quicken will automatically adjust the corresponding transaction in the other account to match. Any modifications you make to the date or dollar amount in either transfer transaction will be passed along to the corresponding transaction in the other account. If you delete a transfer transaction in one account, Quicken will delete the corresponding transaction in the other account for you. On the other hand, entries or changes you make in the *Num (Ref)* field are not copied to the parallel transaction.

Things get a little tricky when you're working with split transactions that contain one or more transfers. As you've already seen, you can use an account name as the category entry in any line of a split transaction. Only that line of the split will show up in the parallel transfer transaction created in the other account. The other lines of the split show only in the current account.

To prevent you from making mistakes due to this complicated arrangement, Quicken will let you change a transfer created by a split transaction only in the account where you originally recorded the split. In the example you just worked through, for instance, you would be able to modify the "less cash" transaction only in your checking account, not in the cash account.

To test this out, start from your cash account and highlight the transfer transaction Quicken just created during your "less cash" deposit to your checking account. In the *Receive* field, type in a new amount, then try to record the modified transaction. You'll get the message shown in Figure 8.11. As the message advises, to change the transaction, you must choose **OK**, then press **Ctrl-X** to move to the parallel transaction in the checking account. There, Quicken automatically pops up the Split Transaction dialog box, and you can go ahead and make your modification.

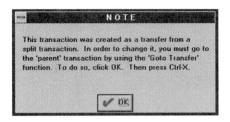

FIGURE 8.11

*Quicken displays
this message when
you try to change
a transfer transaction
that was created in
another account.*

Adjusting the Balance in your Cash Account

Periodically, you should adjust the balance in your cash account to reflect the minor purchases you've made and not recorded. As long as you record all the cash you receive, you won't need to increase the account balance.

Quicken handles the adjustment for you in typically streamlined fashion, automatically creating a single transaction that changes the balance to agree with the amount of cash you now have on hand. To make the adjustment, be sure the cash account's window is active, then choose **Update Balance** followed by **Update Cash Balance** in the Activities menu. You'll see the Update Account Balance dialog box, shown in Figure 8.12.

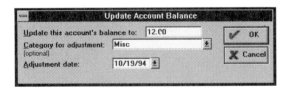

FIGURE 8.12

*The Update
Account Balance
dialog box.*

All you have to do then is total up your cash on hand and type in the amount in the window. If you like, you can assign the transaction to a specific category, such as **Misc expenses**. If you don't enter a category, Quicken will group the amounts of these adjustment transactions in your reports under the heading **Expense-Other**. Quicken has entered today's date for you; if you want to make the adjustment apply to a different date, enter it in the last field.

When you've finished filling out the window, choose **OK** to execute the adjustment. Quicken will figure out the difference between your actual cash on hand (the amount you just typed in) and the existing balance, and enter a transaction in this amount in the register, as shown in Figure 8.13 on the next page.

FIGURE 8.13

*Quicken
calculates
a balance
adjustment.*

Keeping Track of Your Credit Cards

Most of us use credit cards regularly, and some of us use them too often. If you're trying to keep tabs on your credit-card spending habits, Quicken can make the work a good deal easier.

Just as with cash, Quicken lets you handle your credit cards in two ways. If you don't need detailed credit card records, you can simply record the credit card payments you make in your checking account. On the other hand, if you want to monitor your credit card usage closely, you can set up one or more special credit card accounts, and record each credit card purchase and payment there. Quicken for Windows even offers a new service called *IntelliCharge* that, coupled with a special Quicken credit card available through Intuit, automatically records all your credit card transactions in Quicken.

Keeping Track of Credit Cards in your Checking Account

Some rare souls use their credit cards only in emergencies and always pay off their entire credit card balance each month. If you are one of these, you may not want to bother with a separate credit card account. Instead, simply record the checks you write to your credit card company in your check register, and use the split transaction feature if you want to indicate the separate charges covered by your payment. If you don't want to itemize the charges separately, just assign the whole transaction to the category corresponding to most of the purchases, or to a catchall category such as **Credit card exp**.

Here's an example. Let's say that last month you made three charges on your major bank card, as listed here:

Purchase	Category/Class	Amount
Shoes	Clothing/Home	$45
FAX transmissions	Office/Business	$12
Magazine subscription	Education/Home	$25

NOTE
If you have two or more purchases in a single category, you can make one entry for the entire category. To figure the total, put the cursor in the *Amount* column for that entry, then pop up the Windows Calculator by pressing **Alt-Tab** to switch to Program Manager and double-clicking the **Calculator** icon. Add the separate purchase amounts, choose **Copy**, and switch back to Quicken and choose **Paste** to enter the result automatically in the transaction. The Quicken calculator doesn't work when the Splits window is open.

To simplify things, we'll assume that you paid off your account in full last month, and that your credit card company doesn't post a finance charge until the second billing period. Your total charge, then, is the same as the cost of the purchases, $82. You can record all the purchases as you write one check to cover the balance, as follows.

1. Start with a new blank check in the Write Checks window (press **End** three times to display a new check if one is not already on the screen). Make the check payable to your credit card company, fill in the amount of the check as $82, and enter the address.

2. Choose **Splits** or press **Ctrl-S** to split the transaction. Enter the category and the amount of each purchase in the dialog box. When the Splits window is complete, it should look like the one in Figure 8.14.

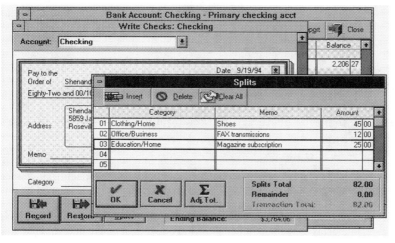

FIGURE 8.14

Splitting a check transaction covering a credit card payment.

3. Choose **OK** to return to the check. You can then go on to record the check in your account and print it.

Keeping Track of Credit Cards in a Credit Card Account

For those of us who depend on our credit cards too much, a separate Quicken credit card account offers the kind of close-up detail that's needed in a sensible financial management program. While it won't enforce discipline over spending, a credit card account will make it easier to spot your credit purchase patterns. If a crunch comes, it can tell you your current balance and, more importantly, how much of your credit limit is left. In addition, when your payment is due, the program can automatically write your check. And you can have Quicken transfer transactions in your credit card account to and from other accounts.

Quicken provides two types of credit card accounts: (1) the ordinary kind, in which you enter all your purchases, interest charges, and other transactions yourself; and (2) IntelliCharge accounts, which record all credit card transactions automatically, either by modem via the telephone lines or with a special update disk you receive each month. IntelliCharge accounts only work with the Quicken credit card, which you can apply for through Intuit, Quicken's publisher.

| **NOTE** | In general, it's best to create a separate account for each of your credit cards. That way, you'll be able to know what your remaining credit limit is on each card, and you'll be able to use Quicken's Automatic Payment feature, as well. |

Starting a Credit Card Account

Setting up either type of credit card account involves essentially the same procedure. The details given in the following steps are for regular credit card accounts; see "Using IntelliCharge" later in this section for the variations for setting up an IntelliCharge account.

To start a credit card account, follow these steps:

1. Press **Ctrl-A** or click the **Accts** icon to display the Account List window.
2. Choose **New**. You'll see the Select Account Type dialog box.

3. Select the **Credit Card Account** radio button and choose **OK**. The New Account Information dialog box appears. As shown in Figure 8.15, this dialog box looks a little different than it does for bank and cash accounts.

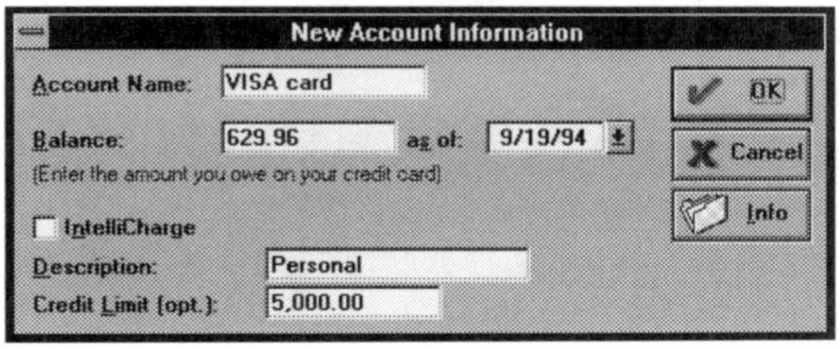

FIGURE 8.15

The New Account Information dialog box as it appears when you're starting a credit card account.

4. Type in the name you want to use for the account, then press **Tab**. In credit card accounts, the *Balance* field indicates the amount you currently owe on your card (this is different from the way checking and cash accounts work, where the balance is the amount of money you have). Type in the amount you currently owe, as indicated on your last statement. Change the date in the *As of* field to that of the statement.

5. Leave the *IntelliCharge* field unchecked since you're starting a regular credit card account. You can enter anything you like in the final field, *Description*. For example, if you use a different credit card for home and business purchases, you could enter that in the *Description* field.
    If you have more than one credit card, enter the interest rate for this card in the *Description* field. When you pay your bills each month, you can decide which card to pay off first by comparing rates in the account list (of course, you want to pay off the card with the highest rate).

6. The *Credit Limit* field allows you to enter the dollar limit on your card. If you want Quicken to tell you how much credit you have left at any time, be sure to type an entry here and choose **OK**.

7. You can choose the **Info** button to open the Additional Account Information dialog box where you can enter the name of the bank, the account number, the interest rate, and so on.

8. Choose **OK** to finalize the dialog box.

You should now be back at the Select Account to Use window. To activate the new credit card account, choose it from the Account list. When you do, you'll be taken to the credit card account register. The credit card register shown in

Figure 8.16 already has a few sample transactions added; yours will be empty at this point except for the opening balance transaction.

FIGURE 8.16

The credit card account register.

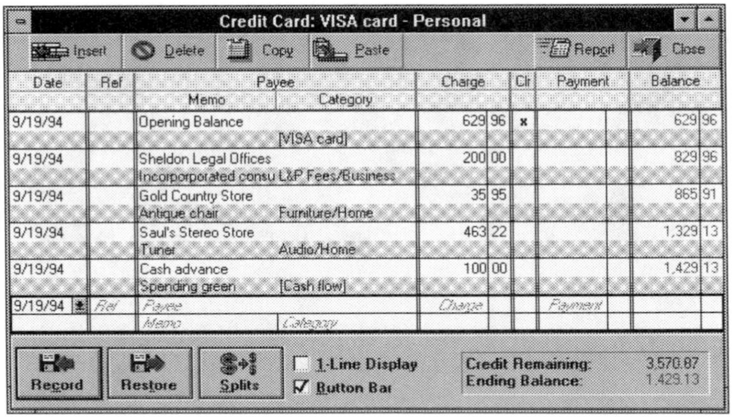

The credit card register looks and works much as the checking and cash account registers do. As you'd expect, a few details vary. There are *Charge* and *Payment* fields instead of *Payment* and *Deposit* or *Spend* and *Receive* columns. The amount of your remaining credit line appears just above the account balance at the bottom right. Just as in a cash account, you can't write checks from your credit card account.

Entering Credit Card Transactions

You can follow either of two strategies for entering charges in a Quicken credit card account. If you want to know what your balance is at any time during the month, or if you want to be able to compare your records against your monthly statement, you should enter your credit purchases as you charge them. Just copy the amounts from the receipts you receive from the sellers. Alternatively, if knowing your day-to-day balance isn't critical, you can enter transactions once a month from the statement.

With either approach, enter transactions into your credit card account just as you would into a checking or cash account. For transactions that you have to pay for, such as purchases, finance charges, or membership fees, place the amount of the transaction in the *Charge* field. In the *Payment* field, enter the amounts of any transactions that reduce what you owe on the account, such as direct payments, credits applied to the account, and returned merchandise. If you're copying the transaction from your monthly statement, type * in the column labeled *Clr* as you enter the transaction.

Transferring Credit Card Transactions to Other Accounts

Quicken's ability to transfer funds between accounts will certainly come in handy with your credit card account. In all likelihood, you pay your credit card bills from your checking account, so you'll want the checks you write to show up in both accounts. You may also use your credit card to obtain cash advances, which both increase the balance you owe on your credit card and increase your cash balance.

Let's use the second scenario to illustrate the point, and say you obtain a cash advance of $100 against your credit card. In the credit card register, enter the transaction by typing **Cash Advance** in the *Payee* field and **$100** in the *Charge* field. In the *Category* field, use QuickFill to help you enter the name of your cash account as the destination for the new cash. Type a left bracket, [, then the first letter or two of the account name. When QuickFill has the remaining characters right, record the transaction. (If you don't recall the name of your cash account, you can scroll to the bottom of the drop-down list of categories, or press **Ctrl-C** to pop up the Category list and select it from the bottom of that list.)

To confirm that the transaction has also been entered into your cash account, leave the transaction selected and press **Ctrl-X**. You'll be delivered immediately to your cash account register with the corresponding transaction selected and the balance adjusted to reflect the cash advance.

Making Payments and Reconciling your Account

Once a month you receive your statement from your credit card company, and once a month you should balance your credit card account against the statement. The steps are much like those you learned for balancing your checking account in Chapter 6, but they are less complex. You simply check off the transactions in your account when they agree with the ones on your statement. Quicken creates a transaction for the finance charges for the month, and will write a check for your payment automatically if you want it to.

If you're entering transactions into the credit card account directly from your statement, you can enter them before or after you start the process of balancing your account. With either method, mark the transactions as cleared by typing * in the *Clr* column as you enter them.

To start the account balancing procedure, choose **Pay Credit Card Bill** from the Activities menu or click on the button labeled **Recon** on the Iconbar. You'll see the Credit Card Statement Information dialog box, shown in Figure 8.17.

FIGURE 8.17

The Credit Card Statement Information dialog box.

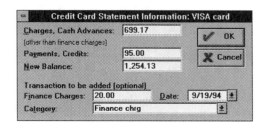

Use your credit card statement to fill out the dialog box. Copy the total amount of new charges and fees (except finance charges) to the first field, *Charges, Cash Advances*. You must enter a number in this field, even if it's **zero (0)**. In the next field, enter the total amount of all the payments and credits applied to your account during the period covered by the statement. In the *New Balance* field, enter the total balance now outstanding on the statement.

NEW IN 3 Next, if your statement shows finance charges, enter them in the appropriate field. Although the *Finance Charges* field is labeled *Optional*, you should fill it in if your statement shows any finance charges. However, don't include other fees in this field. Quicken automatically creates a transaction covering your finance charges. If you like, use the final fields to assign this transaction to a category, so that you'll see the charges separately on your reports, and to a date. Unless you can think of a better category name, **Finance Charges** seems a good candidate.

| NOTE |
Unlike Quicken 3, Quicken 2 combines charges and payments into a single list.

With all the fields complete, choose **OK** to proceed to the list of uncleared items, as shown in Figure 8.18. Like the Reconciliation window for bank accounts, items are listed in two columns, one for charges, the other for payments. If you entered a finance charge in the previous dialog box, you'll find that Quicken has created the transaction and added it to the charges list, marking it with a check as cleared.

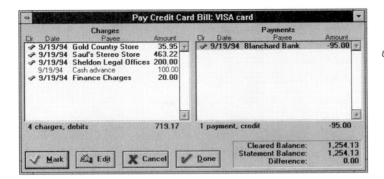

FIGURE 8.18

The list of uncleared items in your credit card account.

Now just mark off the items on the screen that also appear in your statement. To mark an item, click on it or highlight the item and press the space bar. Quicken places a checkmark in the *Clr* column of each transaction you mark as cleared. As you mark transactions, note that Quicken keeps a running tally of the number of transactions marked and compares their total to the balance showing on your statement.

If there are transactions on your statement that don't appear in your account—for example, credit card insurance charges—you can add them now, if you wish, by switching back to the register. Choose **Go To**, or click on any visible part of the Credit Card Register window.

In the register, be sure to mark each transaction with an asterisk in the *Clr* field as you enter it. If you prefer not to enter all your transactions, you don't have to; Quicken will adjust the account with a special transaction to cover them if you want it to. To return to the list of uncleared items, choose **Pay Credit Card Bill** from the Windows menu, or just click on the Pay Credit Card Bill window (try not to click on a line containing a transaction, because doing so will change the item's cleared status).

When you've entered and marked all the transactions, look at the bottom right of the screen. You'll find that Quicken has calculated the difference between the transactions you've marked and the balance on your statement. If the difference is 0, you've successfully reconciled the account, and you're ready to pay your bill. Choose **Done** to complete the balancing process, and go on to the section "Having Quicken Make Your Payment," which follows.

If there's a difference remaining between your account and your statement, it may be simply because you have chosen not to enter all the transactions in your statement. If that's the case, you're ready to have Quicken adjust your account balance for the unentered transactions, described as follows. If you think you've entered all your transactions, or if you're concerned that there's a genuine discrepancy, you'll have to hunt down the transactions that are erroneous or still missing. Use the same techniques described in Chapter 6 in the section "Finding and Correcting Mistaken Transactions."

Adjusting your Credit Card Account Balance

When a discrepancy remains between your account in Quicken and your credit card statement after you reconcile, you can have Quicken create one or more transactions to adjust your account. To make the adjustment, finish reconciling by choosing **Done**. Quicken will display a window similar to the one shown in Figure 8.19. There may be fewer entries on the window you see, depending on the types of discrepancies Quicken has detected.

FIGURE 8.19

Use this window to adjust the balance in your credit card account to match your statement.

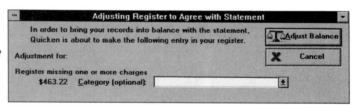

Quicken can create three types of adjustment transactions, corresponding to the three types of mismatches that can occur.

- If the new balance shown on your statement was different from that calculated by Quicken, the program will create a transaction to adjust your account balance to match the statement.

- If one or more payments or other credits applied to your account on the statement are missing from your Quicken account, Quicken will record a transaction to reduce your balance (here, the amount you owe) by the amount of the missing credits.

- If one or more charges listed on the statement are missing from your register, Quicken will create a transaction to increase your balance by the amount of the missing charges.

Having Quicken Make Your Payment

Once you've finished balancing your credit card account, Quicken will offer to fill out a payment transaction, either by writing the check for you or by entering the payment amount as a record in the register of your handwritten check. You'll see the Make Credit Card Payment dialog box, shown in Figure 8.20. If you don't want Quicken to complete a transaction for your credit card payment, just choose **Cancel** at this point.

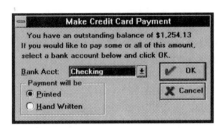

FIGURE 8.20

The Make Credit Card Payment dialog box.

In the window, Quicken has entered the name of the checking account on which it thinks your credit card payment will be drawn. If you have more than one checking account, you can change the account name here by selecting it from the drop-down list. Then choose the radio button that corresponds to the kind of check transaction you want Quicken to record, **Printed**, **Handwritten**, or **Electronic** (you'll only see the first two of these if you haven't set up any accounts for CheckFree—see Chapter 17).

If you selected a printed check or an electronic payment, you'll be taken directly to the Write Checks window, where you'll find a new check filled out in the amount of the entire balance of your credit card account. Change the amount to the actual amount you're planning to pay, add the payee's name and address and any memo or category assignment you wish to make, and then record the check as usual. You can now print it out and mail it in or transmit it to CheckFree. Everything you type in the check at this point except the date and amount will be memorized in your credit card account and filled in for you when you next make a payment.

If you chose a handwritten payment, you'll be taken to the register of your checking account with a payment transaction started for you in the amount of your credit card balance. Again, change the amount to match your actual payment and fill in the rest of the details, then record the transaction. Whichever type of credit card payment you make, it's recorded in your checking account as a transfer to your credit card account. With the transaction selected in your checking account, you can press **Ctrl-X** to move to the parallel transfer transaction in the credit card account.

Using IntelliCharge

Quicken for Windows offers a new feature designed to cut down further on your computerized "paperwork": IntelliCharge, a system for keeping credit card records automatically. To use IntelliCharge, you must apply for a special credit card available through Intuit, Quicken's publisher.

The Quicken credit card lets you make purchases and get cash advances as you would with any other card. The difference comes when it's time to record these transactions in Quicken. Instead of typing in the transactions individually, you use IntelliCharge to add them for you from a computerized statement once a month. To make your Quicken records really complete, each transaction even gets assigned to a category automatically.

After you check the statement against your paper receipts, Quicken records the new transactions in your account and automatically writes your payment check. The whole process is quick and painless.

Setting Up an IntelliCharge Account

The procedure for setting up an IntelliCharge account is much like that for a regular credit card account (see *Starting a Credit Card Account* earlier in the chapter), but there are few differences in detail.

If you plan to update the account by modem, you'll need one important piece of information before you begin using the account: The phone number you modem must dial to access the IntelliCharge service. IntelliCharge connections are handled by CompuServe, a leading electronic information service, so you use your local CompuServe access number.

If you don't already use CompuServe, it's easy to get the local access number. Get pen and paper ready, then dial (800) 848-8980 with a TouchTone phone. When you hear the recorded message, press **2** on your phone. You'll be asked to type in the phone number you'll be calling from and the speed of your modem. Based on this information, the system gives your access number.

Now you're ready to set up the IntelliCharge account. Begin by displaying the Account List window (click on the **Accts** icon or press **Ctrl-A**). After choosing **New**, follow the basic steps for starting a credit card account as outlined earlier. At the *Balance* field in the New Account Information dialog box, enter 0 for now—IntelliCharge will enter the correct amount for you. The exact date you enter in the *As of* field doesn't matter, but choose one prior to the time you obtained your Quicken credit card.

Then check the box in the *IntelliCharge* field. In the next field, *Credit Card Number*, you must enter the account number of your special Quicken credit card.

The completed dialog box should look something like Figure 8.21. Choose **OK** to finalize the entries. A new IntelliCharge Account Information dialog box appears (Figure 8.22). Check the Statement Delivery on Modem box if you plan to update your account electronically, by modem; leave the box unchecked if you plan to use update disks. Enter your social security number, the same one you gave on your Quicken credit card application and the security password for the account. Choose **OK** to close the dialog box.

FIGURE 8.21

The New Account Information dialog box filled out for an IntelliCharge account.

FIGURE 8.22

Use this dialog box to set up your IntelliCharge account.

If you indicated you'll be updating by modem, you must set up Quicken for your modem and give Quicken the phone number your modem should dial to reach the IntelliCharge service. You do this in the Modem Preferences dialog box, available on the Preferences menu. (See the Appendix for details.)

Recording Credit Card Transactions

The beauty of the IntelliCharge service is that you need never enter another credit card transaction by hand. In fact, you should actively avoid doing so—if you make a minor mistake, you may wind up with duplicate entries in your account, and an incorrect balance.

Updating Your IntelliCharge Account

You'll get two versions of your Quicken credit card statement every month: an ordinary paper statement and a special computer version that either comes to you by mail on a floppy disk or is made available to you by modem. The computer statement is identical to the paper one, containing all transactions that have affected your credit card balance over the previous month: purchases, cash advances, charges, credits—and your payments.

When it's time for monthly reckoning, all you have to do is put the disk in your computer or have Quicken dial the IntelliCharge service. Quicken reads the information in the computer account statement and adds it to your account automatically.

Here's the procedure. Begin at the register of your IntelliCharge account. Choose **Get IntelliCharge Data** from the Activities menu.

- If you're updating from a disk, Quicken will ask you to type the letter of the disk drive containing the statement disk; put the disk in that drive.

- If you're updating via modem, Quicken reminds you to get your modem ready (it should be turned on and connected to the phone line).

Choose **OK**. Assuming you've inserted the disk or prepared your modem properly, Quicken handles the rest of the update process automatically.

However, this process stops temporarily whenever the category assigned to the current transaction doesn't match an existing category in your account. A message states that the category can't be found and asks you either to add the transaction's current category to your account (choose **Set Up**) or to select a different category for the transaction from the Category list (choose **Select**).

Using the Statement Window

After all the transactions have been added to your account, a Statement window appears, listing all the new transactions along with the statement date, your balance, and the minimum payment you must make and its due date. In other words, the Statement window has all the same information you get on your paper statement.

Examine the list of transactions to make sure they're accurate, comparing them to your paper receipts if you like. Notice that payments and credits are listed as negative amounts, since they reduce your credit card account balance.

If you notice any transactions that are inaccurate, that you want to check against your records, or that need additional work (e.g., you might want to add a memo or split the transaction), you can mark them in the Statement window. To mark a transaction for future action, click on it or highlight it in the list and press the space bar. Either way, a *?* shows in the left-hand column.

As you know, each transaction has already been assigned a category. After you've verified the crucial payee and amount entries, look over the category assignments as well, since inaccurate categorization will skew your reports. You can change a transaction's category right from the Statement window—just highlight the transaction and choose the **Categorize** button or press **Ctrl-C** to pop up the Category list. To erase the category entry from the highlighted transaction, choose **Delete Cat** or press **Ctrl-D**.

When you've completed your transaction review, leave the Statement window by choosing **Record All**. Quicken adds all the transactions to your credit card account. You'll now see the Make Credit Card Payment dialog box, described earlier in this chapter.

NOTE	If you can't finish your review in the current session, you can cancel the update by choosing **Cancel**. In this case, none of the transactions get recorded in your account, and you can restart the update process later. Be sure not to choose **Record All** until you're really finished reviewing the statement, since you'll add duplicate transactions to your account if you then repeat the update.

When you eventually return to the credit card account register, you'll find the new transactions marked as cleared—that is, each has an *X* in the *Clr* field. You can identify any transactions marked for further review easily—each has five question marks in the *Ref* field. To find them, press **Ctrl-F** to pop up the Find window, type **?????** in the *Find* field, and select **Check Number** from the drop-down list in the *Search* field. Then choose **Previous** or **Next** to search forward or backward through the register.

Working with Categories in IntelliCharge Accounts

As you've seen, IntelliCharge automatically categorizes each credit card transaction in your statement. Here's how the process works: As Quicken reads in each transaction in the statement, it compares the payee information to transactions already recorded in the account. If there's a match, Quicken assigns the new transaction to the same category as the most recent transaction with that payee.

NOTE
If the register transaction with the matching payee is split, Quicken uses the category assignment from the first line of the split.

If Quicken can't find a matching transaction in your register, it uses a predefined list of categories to make the assignment. Each credit card payee has an identification number that corresponds to the payee's type of business. Quicken includes a list that matches each type of payee to a category. When reading a new transaction, Quicken uses the payee's code number to find the appropriate category in this list.

If you don't like the category assignment Quicken makes for a particular payee, just change it, either in the Statement window, or later, in the register. The next time that payee appears in an account statement, Quicken will use the category you entered.

Dealing with Disputes

Occasionally, just as with any credit card account, you may run into mismatches between your own records and your IntelliCharge statement. If you disagree with a merchant or the bank about how much you owe for a purchase or how much you've paid, you should mark the transaction in the Statement window as previously described. Then, even though you think it's inaccurate, go ahead and record it with the other transactions.

When you get back to the register, locate the transaction for reference, but don't delete it from your account—you'll need it at least until you and the bank work things out. Contact the sponsoring bank at (800) 772-2221 and follow their instructions for dealing with a disputed transaction. Remember that you must notify them in writing as well as by phone.

Keeping Track of Savings and Money Market Accounts

If you maintain a passbook savings account or have a money market account with your bank, savings and loan association, or a money market fund, you can keep track of the account by starting a new Quicken bank account for that purpose. To set up the account, display the Account List window and choose **New**. In the Select Account dialog box, choose **Bank Account**, then choose **OK**. In the next dialog box, New Account Information, enter an appropriate name for the account, and type in the current balance of your funds in the account in the *Balance* field. Add a description if you like, then choose **OK** to confirm your entries and create the account.

Use the new account's register to record deposits and withdrawals just as you've done in your Quicken checking account. If your account allows you to write checks, you can order Quicken checks for it and have the program print them using the methods you learned in Chapters 2 and 3.

> **NOTE** To track a tax-sheltered savings plan such as an IRA or 401(K) account, you should set it up as an *investment* account, designating it as tax-deferred so that Quicken won't lump its earnings with taxable interest from other accounts. See Chapter 9 for details.

Modifying and Deleting Your Accounts

> **NOTE** At some point, you'll want to delete all the example transactions you enter while working through this book. Chapters 10 through 12 make use of the samples, so you may want to wait until you're finished with them before deleting the samples. When you're ready to delete the samples, just delete the entire accounts that you've created for them—unless you've mixed in transactions you want to keep, in which case you'll have to delete the sample transactions individually.

Modifying your accounts is easy in Quicken. If you want to change an account's name, its description, or, in credit card accounts, your credit limit, you just type in the new information over the old. You can even delete an entire account any time you decide it has served its purpose. For example, if you consolidate two accounts into one using Quicken's **Export/Import** feature (see the Appendix), you'll no longer need one of the accounts.

To make any of these changes, start by displaying the Account List window by pressing **Ctrl-A** or clicking on the **Accts** icon. Highlight the account you wish to modify, then choose **Edit** if you want to edit the name, description, or credit limit; choose **Del** if you want to delete the entire account.

If you're just making modifications in the account, you'll see the Edit Account Information dialog box, with fields for you to type in a new account name and description. Changing the account's name or description is simply a matter of typing the new information into the appropriate field. Once you've completed all the fields, choose **OK**.

WARNING I'm obligated to caution you that deleting any genuine financial records is contrary to all accepted standards of accounting practice. However, you might justifiably delete an account in Quicken after exporting its transactions to another account, and you'll certainly want to delete the practice records you've created in working through the examples in this book.

If you're deleting an account, be sure to proceed with caution. The deleted information will be excised from your Quicken records permanently, with no chance for recovery. To drive this point home, Quicken presents you with a special warning after you've started the deletion. If you really want to proceed with the deletion, you must type out **yes** in full. When you then choose **OK**, Quicken erases all traces of the account and returns you to the Select Account dialog box. If you decide not to go through with the deletion, press **Esc**.

Moving Data to Another Account

Rarely, you may find it necessary to duplicate in one account information you've already entered into another. This situation may arise if, for instance, you decide to combine two accounts. Thus, if you invest in stocks you might want to have a separate asset account for each stock while you own it, but a single account for all the stocks that you've sold. Each time you sell your entire holding in a particular stock, you'll need a way to move all the information from the individual stock account into the account covering the stocks you've previously owned. Another reason you might want to move records from one account to another is if you've entered a series of transactions in the wrong account; after all, the registers all look very similar.

Quicken doesn't provide a direct way to move or copy transactions from one account to another. Instead, you must export data to a file on disk, and then import it into the new account. With this technique, you can move or copy transactions to another account within the same account file or in different account files. See the Appendix for information on the export/import process.

Managing Account Files

As you've learned, your Quicken accounts are organized into files. As the name implies, a file represents a file on your disk—actually several related files.

Although a single file can hold many separate accounts, you can only work with one file at a time. Within a file, you can transfer funds between any of the accounts and create reports on them. On the other hand, your transfers and reports cannot cover transactions from different files. Quicken lets you create as many separate files as you need.

A single Quicken file provides plenty of record-keeping flexibility—and room—for the vast majority of people. After all, you can have multiple separate accounts in one file, you can create a myriad of categories and classes with which to organize your transactions, and you can limit your reports to any subgroup of accounts you're interested in. About the only situation in which separate files are almost essential is when you're using Quicken to keep the books for several independent individuals or companies. Still, you can set up separate files to suit your taste and needs. If you yourself are involved in two or more different business ventures and want to set up an individual account file for each one, you can.

Actually, though, the one common scenario in which you may really need to create separate account files involves your computer rather than your financial situation. Since Quicken expects to find all the data from a file on a single disk and directory, a file is limited in size to the space available on your data disk. If you're using a floppy disk to store your files, that means that any one file can be no larger than the capacity of a single floppy disk. Even if you have a hard disk, space on it may be limited, especially if you use many other programs and keep extensive and detailed Quicken records.

If you do run into this kind of space limitation, you can overcome it by dividing your records into separate files and storing each file on a separate disk. If this becomes necessary, try to break up your records into files along logical dividing lines; for instance, you might have one file for each calendar or fiscal year, or one for your business finances and another for personal finances. You'll learn how to specify the disk Quicken uses for a file's data in a moment.

Creating a New File

To start a new file, choose **New** in the File menu. In the little window that appears, leave the **New File** radio button selected and choose **OK**.

You'll now see the Create Quicken File dialog box, shown in Figure 8.23. This window shows you a list of the files in the current disk drive and directory, and lets you change to any other disk and directory if you want to store the new file elsewhere.

FIGURE 8.23

The Create Quicken File dialog box.

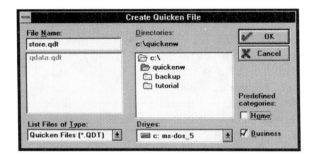

Make the disk/directory selection, then type in the name for the new file in the *File Name* field. Quicken will use the name you enter as a DOS file name for your account group files, so you can enter no more than eight characters and you cannot use spaces and certain punctuation marks in the name. Quicken won't let you enter invalid characters, so you don't have to worry about this.

Now look at the lower-right corner of the dialog box. There, you'll see two checkboxes with which you tell Quicken which of its standard categories to include in the new file. You made the same choice, though in a different window, when you started your first Quicken account in Chapter 1. Your choices are home-related categories and business-related categories; you can check either or both boxes, or leave both unchecked.

NOTE   No matter which of the built-in Category lists you select, it's a good idea to customize your Category and Class lists before you start entering transactions. See Chapter 5 for detailed instructions.

When you're through defining the new file, choose **OK** to create it. Quicken closes all the windows of the file you were working with and presents you with the Select Account Type dialog box to get you started with your first account in the new file.

Working with a Different File

To switch from one account file to another, choose **Open** from the File menu. This displays a dialog box much like the one used to start a new file (Figure 8.23). If necessary, switch to the disk drive and directory where the file you want to work with is stored. When the file name appears in the list at the left of the dialog box, select it, then choose **OK**.

If the file you've chosen contains only one account, you'll be taken directly to the account's register. If the file has more than one, you'll have the opportunity to select the account you want to use first from the Account List window.

Modifying Files

To change the name of a file, make an exact or a modified copy of an existing file, or delete the file entirely, start by choosing **File Operations** from the File menu. This displays a cascading menu listing the choices **Copy**, **Rename**, **Delete**, and **Restore** (this last choice is covered later in the section "Restoring a Backup").

Copying a File

Copying a file is the most complex of these operations. To copy a file, you must have the file already open in Quicken (see *Working with a Different File*). When you choose **Copy** on the File Operations cascading menu, a dialog box with a variety of options appears (Figure 8.24). In the top field, type in the name for the new copy of the current file. Next, type the path (disk drive and directory) where you want Quicken to store the copy.

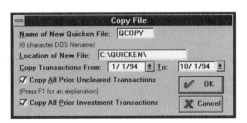

FIGURE 8.24

Use this dialog box to make a copy of the current Quicken file.

Then come two *Date* fields, allowing you to narrow the range of transactions included in the copy by date. Finally, there are two checkboxes that allow you to specify exceptions to the date range you already set.

When *Copy all prior uncleared transactions* is checked, Quicken includes uncleared transactions dated prior to the first date in the range, since they're likely to show up on a future statement from your bank or credit card company. Uncheck this box if you want to exclude earlier uncleared transactions despite this possibility.

A checkmark in the **Copy All Prior Investment Transactions** box tells Quicken to add to the new file all investment transactions in the original file, even those dated prior to the beginning of the date range. The record of your past investment buys and sales can weigh heavily on investment decisions you make today; hence, this exception to the date range. If you don't want the old investment transactions in the copy, uncheck the box.

After you choose **OK** and Quicken has created the new copy of the file, you're given a choice: whether to reload the original file or load the new copy. Select the appropriate **Radio** button and choose **OK** to return to work.

Renaming a File

When you choose **Rename**, you'll see the dialog box shown in Figure 8.25. Here, you can locate the file you want to rename by choosing its disk drive and directory in the appropriate fields. Select the file in the list at the left of the dialog box, then type its new name in the field at the bottom right. (As always, the file name must satisfy DOS naming conventions—no more than eight characters and no invalid characters.) When you choose **OK**, Quicken completes the rename.

FIGURE 8.25

The Rename Quicken File dialog box.

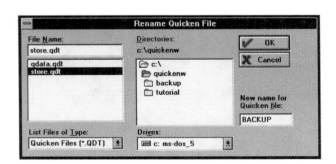

Deleting a File

To delete a file, choose **File Operations** and **Delete** from the File menu. The Delete Quicken File dialog box appears. After switching to the disk drive and directory where the file is stored, select the file by name in the list at the left of the dialog box. When you choose **OK**, you'll be warned that the deletion will erase your data permanently. If you want to proceed anyway, type out **yes** in full, then choose **OK** again. The account file will be deleted from your disk.

Backing Up the Current File

In "Backing Up Your Account," in Chapter 4, you learned how to make backup copies of your checking account to protect your records against accidental erasure or damage, or loss of your computer. The simple backup techniques you learned then (choosing **Back Up** from the File menu or pressing **Ctrl-B**) will back up an entire file for you in a single step.

NOTE

If you'd like to back up only the current account, rather than the entire file, you can do so using the export technique outlined in the Appendix. To restore the backup account data, you would import it—again, you'll find details in the Appendix.

Choose the disk drive where you want to store the backup from the little drop-down list in the *Backup Drive* field.

If you have more than one file and want to back up a file you're not currently using, you can do just that. In the backup window, select the **Radio** button labeled **Select From List**. When you choose **OK**, Quicken presents you with a dialog box from which you can pick the disk drive, directory, and file name of the file you want to back up.

If the disk drive you choose is not a floppy drive, before going ahead with the backup, Quicken asks you to type in the name of the directory where you want the backup stored. Once you've made this entry and chosen **OK**, the backup begins. Follow the instructions on the screen telling you when to insert your backup disk.

In the next section, you'll learn how to revivify all or most of your records from your backups should disaster strike.

Restoring a Backup

If your primary data disk is damaged, your backups will be your salvation. But should your hard disk lose data, you must *restore* your accounts before you can use them again.

Once the hard disk has been repaired or replaced, you may need to reinstall Quicken according to the steps outlined in the Appendix. Then, to restore a file, choose **File Operations** and **Restore** from the File menu.

Following the instructions on the screen, place your backup disk in one of your floppy drives and tell Quicken which drive you've used. Quicken searches the disk for data files, displaying those it finds in a moment or two. Select the account file you wish to restore from the list, then choose **OK**. Quicken will copy the account data from your backup disk to the hard disk.

If there's already a file with the same name on the hard disk, Quicken will ask you whether you want to overwrite the existing file, erasing it and replacing it with the backup copy. If the backup file covers more than one floppy disk, Quicken will instruct you when to change disks.

Making a Year-End Copy of a File

It's often convenient for record-keeping and tax purposes to separate transactions by calendar year. Quicken can automatically store last year's records in a special archive file for safekeeping. Or, if you prefer, Quicken can remove old transactions from the current file, leaving only this year's information.

Start either procedure by choosing **Year-End Copy** from the File menu. In the dialog box that appears, choose one of the two **Radio** buttons:

- **Archive** if you want Quicken to copy all transactions prior to the first of the year to a separate file. As the message says, this won't affect the current file at all.
- **Start New Year** if you want to create a new file containing only this year's transactions. (Don't worry, you won't lose any records—Quicken makes a copy of the entire current file before proceeding).

When you OK the box, Quicken presents you with a new dialog box. If you chose **Archive**, you'll enter the name of the archive file containing old transactions. If you'd like, you can change the cut-off date (Quicken copies all transactions dated earlier to the archive file).

If you chose **Start New Year**, you're asked to name the new file that will hold all the transactions; older transactions will be removed from your existing file. Again, you can change the date for removing old transactions.

Summary

In this chapter, you've learned how to keep track of cash, credit cards, and savings, whether your finances are simple or complex. You know how to record transfers of funds between two accounts. Using split transactions and transfers, you can also keep track of transactions involving your checking account as well as your cash or credit card accounts. Chapter 9 details Quicken's facilities for tracking investments, mortgages, and so on.

Chapter Nine

Keeping Track of
Investments and Loans

uicken can't guarantee fat profits on Wall Street or find you a no-money-down, low-interest mortgage, but it can help you keep close tabs on the money you've invested and borrowed. With Quicken's special accounts for market investments, long-term assets, and loans and other liabilities, you'll always know how well your investments are performing, how much equity you've accumulated, and how much loan interest you'll be able to deduct on your taxes.

Tracking Stocks, Bonds, and other Securities with Quicken

Quicken offers a complete system for keeping track of investments such as stocks, bonds, and mutual funds. Using Quicken investment accounts, you can easily record purchases and sales of investment securities and track their value as market prices change.

NEW IN 3 Quicken 3's new Portfolio View window serves as a master control center for all your investment accounts, allowing you to enter new investment transactions, record price changes, and monitor the performance of your investments.

In this chapter, you'll get practice in setting up investment accounts and entering transactions in them. In Chapters 10 and 12, you'll learn how to analyze the information in your investment accounts with reports and graphs that track your investment performance or provide tax-related information. Once you have these fundamentals under your belt, you can proceed to the tips on overall strategies for monitoring investments in Chapter 14.

Understanding Investment Accounts

Quicken investment accounts are tailor made for securities such as stocks, bonds, real estate trust shares, and so on, whose prices vary frequently. Commodities that have a variable price per unit, such as precious metals, fall into this category as well. But you can also use Quicken investment accounts to track brokerage accounts and similar conglomerations of investments that may include cash or other fixed-price instruments in addition to stocks, bonds, and so on.

| NOTE | Actually, Quicken offers two separate subtypes of investment accounts, one specifically designed to track a single mutual fund, the other for all other types of securities. |

On the other hand, you wouldn't ordinarily use an investment account to keep track of a certificate of deposit (CD), a money market fund, or any other investment whose price or price per share remains constant. Nor are investment accounts appropriate for investments such as some retirement accounts that may fluctuate in value, but in which you don't own a specific number of shares (or if you do, you don't know the price per share). You're better off setting up investments like these in bank or asset accounts (see "Keeping Track of Loans and Other Assets and Liabilities," later in this chapter). Asset accounts also are the best place to store information on items of value such as real estate, collectibles, and so on.

| NOTE | Of course, the total value of a fixed-price investment does change, since you can withdraw funds and receive interest payments. These changes can be recorded in asset or bank accounts. |

The exception to this rule of thumb has to do with tax-sheltered savings plans. With Quicken 3, you should use investment accounts to track IRA, 401(K), and tax-sheltered annuity holdings. See "Using Tax-Deferred Investment Accounts," later in this chapter.

Planning an Investment Monitoring Strategy

The best strategy for organizing your investments in Quicken investment accounts depends on the types of securities you hold and your record-keeping goals.

For ordinary securities that you own outright (not through a mutual fund), you can either set up a separate investment account for each stock, bond, and so on, or group them into one or more accounts. If you hold long-term positions in two stocks and a single treasury bond, for instance, a single account for all three securities would be convenient and might well provide all the record-keeping power you need.

On the other hand, if you trade regularly in various types of investments, you'll probably want to group them into accounts by type. You might have stocks in one account, bonds in another, or keep separate accounts for different industries (high-tech stocks, transportation issues, etc.). And if you do a great deal of short-term trading, you'll find it easier to get up-to-the-minute data on a given issue if you track it separately in its own account.

If you own one or more mutual funds, you'll want to decide whether to enter them in "regular" investment accounts or the special type for mutual funds. The regular type of investment account allows you to keep track of a cash balance in the account as you sell shares, receive dividends or interest payments, and so on. And it lets you follow as many separate mutual funds as you'd like in the same account, mixing them with other securities if that's your preference. However, an ordinary investment account won't tell you how many shares you own of each security.

SHORTCUT Quicken lets you switch the type of an investment account from regular to mutual fund or vice versa at any time, so don't worry too much about deciding which type it should be. Also, it's possible to use mutual fund accounts for other types of investments if you want the benefits of automated cash transfers to and from other accounts and don't need to lump multiple investments in combined accounts.

By contrast, each mutual fund investment account accepts entries for only one mutual fund. You can't accumulate cash in the account, but this can be a plus—cash transfers to and from other accounts are automatic as you buy and sell shares. And you always get to see the total number of shares you own of the mutual fund from the Account register.

You should set up a separate investment account in Quicken for each of your real-life brokerage accounts or similar managed accounts. Since you can maintain a cash balance in an investment account, you'll have no trouble monitoring your balance of uninvested cash or money market fund deposits right along with your other securities.

Handling Past Investment Records

Once you've come up with a plan for dividing up your investments among Quicken investment accounts, your next decision involves how much past information to enter about your investments. The easiest and quickest option is simply to list your current positions in each security—how many shares you own and how much they're worth. As you record future transactions, you'll start reaping the benefits of Quicken's ability to report raw income and analyze your rate of return, but you won't be able to generate tax-related reports until you enter a full calendar year of transactions.

Since taxes figure so heavily in the life of the investor, it may make sense instead to enter the historical data Quicken will need to help you with your next tax return. In this case, you'll simply enter all the transactions pertaining to each investment from the first day of the current tax year until the present. For each investment, you'd start by entering a transaction indicating the number of shares you owned and the share price on the last day of the previous year.

Unfortunately, even a year's worth of records won't be enough when you sell the security. For the most complete reports possible, the remaining alternative requires that you enter all past transactions for the investments you're tracking, beginning with your purchase of each security. Gathering and typing in all your old records makes for tedious work, but you will then be able to produce reports that span the entire period during which you held the investment.

In particular, you'll be able to quickly produce capital gains reports from which you can transfer your gain or loss to Schedule D on your federal tax form. Obviously, Quicken has to know how much you actually paid for a given investment and when you bought it before it can calculate the gain or loss you realize when you sell the investment. Although you can enter the total cost of all the shares of an investment (the *cost basis*) you own as a so-called artificial transaction, you may not get accurate capital gains results if you sell only part of your holdings at a time.

By the way, the term *realized gain* refers to the amount of money you actually gain or lose after selling an investment. An *unrealized gain* is the theoretical amount you would make if you sold the investment at a particular moment—since you haven't sold it, the gain is unrealized.

Setting Up an Investment Account

With these strategic decisions behind you, it's time to assemble your investment records and set up the new accounts. For practice, let's say that you've chosen to start a new regular investment account to track two securities, a stock and a bond, plus your modest holdings of gold bullion. Because you want help with your income tax, you'll be entering past transactions starting from the first of the year.

NOTE	When you set up your first investment account, Quicken automatically adds a set of investment-related categories to your file for use with miscellaneous income and expense transactions. See "Recording and Categorizing Miscellaneous Transactions," later in this chapter.

By now you're familiar with the Quicken procedures required to activate a new account—use the method that is the easiest for you to display the Select Account Type window. After choosing the **Investment Account** radio button, OK the window to display the New Account Information dialog box for investment accounts, shown in Figure 9.1.

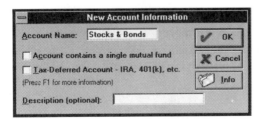

FIGURE 9.1

The New Account Information dialog box for investment accounts.

In the dialog box, enter a name for the account (perhaps **Stocks and Bonds**), then press **Tab** to skip over the *Account Contains a Single Mutual Fund* field (its box should remain unchecked).

Check the **Tax-Deferred Account** checkbox only if the earnings from this account won't be taxable (at least until you actually have the income in your hands). This feature tells Quicken to exclude the account from your tax reports. When you've entered a description in the final field, choose **OK** to confirm your entries.

NEW IN 3   Tax-deferred investment accounts are a new feature in Quicken 3. In Quicken 2, you must exclude them yourself from tax-related reports.

You will then see a warning message reminding you that investment accounts are an advanced Quicken feature. Choose **OK** to return to the Account List window (if you were setting up a mutual fund account, you'd see an interim window first—see "Setting Up a Mutual Fund Account," which follows).

NEW IN 3   The first time you create an investment account, Quicken will ask you if you want to add a **Portfolio View** icon to the Iconbar. New in Quicken 3, the Portfolio View is a special window that lets you monitor the performance of all your investments efficiently. Choose **Yes** to add the icon so that you display the **Portfolio View** with one quick click. It's fine if you prefer not to add the icon now—you can always change your mind later (see the Appendix for instructions on customizing the Iconbar).

Using the Investment Account Register

NEW IN 3   Quicken 3 investment accounts have a button bar, which Quicken 2 lacks.

Choose the new account by clicking on it or highlighting it and choosing **Use**. As you can see, the Investment Account register (see Figure 9.2) looks very similar to the other registers you've worked with. Some of the column headings have changed. In addition, there isn't a **Splits** button or a **1-Line Display** checkbox at the bottom of the register, and there are some unfamiliar buttons in a button bar at the top of the window. As always, Quicken has selected the first empty transaction in the register, indicating that it's ready to accept an entry.

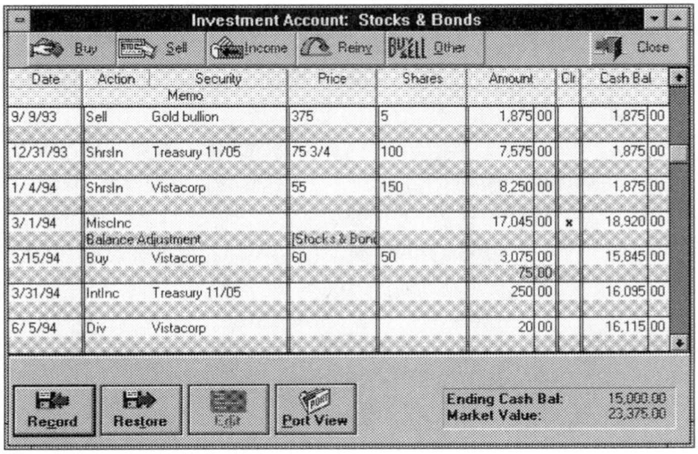

FIGURE 9.2

*The Investment
Account register
where several
sample transactions
have already been
recorded.*

The sample transactions listed below assume you buy investments with cash you had previously "parked" for that purpose in a special real-life brokerage or money market account. However, since you haven't yet entered a cash balance for your Quicken investment account, the register will show a negative balance when you enter the sample purchase transactions. Don't worry about this for now—you'll correct it later in the section "Adjusting Cash and Share Balances."

Entering Stock Transactions

To practice entering transactions in your investment account, let's start with some sample transactions for a hypothetical stock. The samples cover the most common types of transactions you'll be recording. Some of the fields in each sample are empty, either because the field doesn't pertain to that type of transaction, or because Quicken calculates the correct value for you from the other entries.

Here's the first sample transaction:

Date: **1/1/94**
Action: **ShrsIn**
Security: **Vistacorp**
Price: **55**
Shares: **150**
Amount:
Commission:

Since you'll be entering data back to the beginning of the year for this practice investment, your first step will be to change the date that Quicken has entered for you in the *Date* field to December 31 of the previous year. Press **Enter** to move to the *Action* field where you indicate the type of the transaction. For example, when you buy shares of a security, you'd record the transaction by entering **Buy** in the *Action* field; if you're recording interest or dividend earnings, the entry would be **Div**.

You can make an entry in the *Action* field by typing it in, allowing QuickFill to complete the entry for you. Or you can choose the action you want from the field's drop-down list. If you need more information about the action choices, press **F1** from the *Action* field to call up the Help menu on that topic. Also refer to Table 9.1 for a complete list of types of actions and what they do.

TABLE 9.1   *Types of Actions on the Action List*

Action List Types	Action Items	Explanation
Add/Remove Shares	ShrsIn	Add shares without accounting for cash used
	ShrsOut	Remove shares without accounting for proceeds
Buy shares	Buy	Shares purchased with cash in investment account
	BuyX	Shares purchased with cash transferred from another account
Capital gain distr	CGLong	Long-term capital gains
	CGLongX	Long-term capital gains transferred to another account
	CGShort	Short-term capital gains
	CGShortX	Short-term capital gains transferred to another account
Dividend	Div	Dividend income
	DivX	Dividend income transferred to an other account
Interest	IntInc	Interest income
	MargInt	Interest paid on margin loan (broker loan)

Other Transactions	MiscExp	Miscellaneous expense
	MiscInc	Miscellaneous income item
	Reminder	Used to remind you to enter a transaction later
	RtrnCap	Cash received from return of capital
	StkSplt	Change in number of shares owned due to a stock split
Reinvest	ReinvDiv	Additional shares purchased with dividend or income distribution
	ReinvInt	Additional shares purchased with interest distribution
	ReinvLg	Additional shares purchased with long-term capital gains distribution
	ReinvSh	Additional shares purchased with short-term capital gains distribution
Sell shares	Sell	Sell shares, with income from sale remaining in current investment account
	SellX	Sell shares, transferring income to another account
Transfer cash	XIn	Transfer cash to investment account from another account
	XOut	Transfer cash from investment account to another account

Since the transaction you're entering represents shares that you already owned on the date indicated, you should enter **ShrsIn** rather than **Buy** as the action for this transaction. The entry **ShrsIn** tells Quicken not to require a source of cash for the shares you're adding to the account. In this case, since two action items begin with **Shrs**, it's probably quickest to choose the **ShrsIn** item from the drop-down list rather than typing it with QuickFill's help.

In the next field, type the name of the security, **Vistacorp**, and press **Tab**. Quicken will display the Set Up Security dialog box (see Figure 9.3 on the next page). You'll see this dialog box every time you add a new security to an investment account.

FIGURE 9.3

*The Set Up
Security
dialog box.*

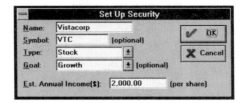

NOTE   You can also add new securities to your account or edit existing securities using the Security list, described later in this chapter.

Quicken has already filled in the *Name* field with your entry, but you can edit this if necessary. Then enter the security's symbol as printed in newspaper stock tables.

In the *Type* field, select the type of security you're working with, **Stock**, from the drop-down list. The entry in the *Type* field is important, since Quicken groups securities by type in the Portfolio View window for easier entry of share prices, and since you can make focused reports covering only specific types of securities.

Quicken allows you to set up a total of 16 different security types, four of which (Bond, CD, Mutual Fund, and Stock) are set up for you in advance. You can edit these four types or set up new types of your own from the list of types, much as you would add a new category or class. You'll learn to set up new security types soon.

The *Goal* field offers its own list of descriptive words (not dollar amounts!) for your purpose in buying the security. Again, make your selection of a goal from the drop-down list. The goals supplied by Quicken include generic objectives such as *growth* and *income*, but you're free to create a *Tahiti vacation* goal if you'd like (I'll cover the steps to set up a new goal shortly). If you want to keep track of your exact dollar amount projections for the investment, Quicken also gives you a field in which you can fill in your own estimated annual profit. You can generate reports and graphs that track your investments by goal as described in Chapters 10 and 12.

SHORTCUT   If you're using an investment account to track a money market fund or a fixed-price instrument like a CD, you would enter the total value of the security in the *Price* field and the number **1** in the *Shares* field. You handle tangible assets such as collectibles in the same way unless you own several identical items that all have the same value. Again, it's better to use a bank account for money market funds and another asset account for CDs or collectibles.

The final field in the Setup Security dialog box is for the income you expect each share of the security to earn per year. If you enter an amount here, Quicken will use it to calculate measurements such as investment yield in the Portfolio View window.

After completing the Setup Security dialog box, choose **OK** to return to the register. In the next field, *Price*, type in the security's price per share on the date of the transaction. The price of the first sample entry includes a fraction, which you must enter by leaving a space after the dollar amount—type **55 1/ 4**. As long as the price you enter follows this format, Quicken will display its calculation in the *Amount* field in the same format.

NOTE	If you'd prefer, you can enter securities prices as dollars and cents, as **$72.50**. If the decimal part of your entry equals a multiple of 1/ 16, Quicken will convert it to a fraction when you move out of the *Price* field. You can control the way Quicken displays the price— as a fraction or a decimal number—by editing the security type as described later.

Move to the *Shares* field by pressing **Tab**. When you enter the number of shares owned as of this transaction date, Quicken automatically calculates the total value of all your shares in the *Amount* field.

To complete the entry, move to the *Memo* field and type in a brief comment about this transaction. Then record the transaction.

Using the Investment Account Button Bar

Now enter the second sample transaction, shown here:

Date:	**3/15/94**
Action:	**Buy**
Security:	**Vistacorp**
Price:	**60**
Shares:	**50**
Amount:	
Commission:	**75**

This transaction is a new purchase of additional shares of the same security, bought with cash "parked" in this investment account. For transactions of this type, the entry in the *Action* field should be "Buy." But this time, instead of typing the transaction directly into the register, you'll enter the information in a separate dialog box.

NEW IN 3 To enter transactions in this way you need the investment account register's special button bar (a new feature in Quicken 3). Choosing the **Buy**, **Sell**, **Income**, or **Reinv** buttons displays a window for that type of transaction similar to the one in Figure 9.4. When you choose the **Other** button, you'll get a list of miscellaneous transaction types; after picking the type you want from the list, you'll see the appropriate window. Instructions for using all the different types of transactions are given in the section "Strategies for Investment Tracking," later in this chapter.

> **NOTE** Quicken 2 lacks the button bar, so you must enter all investment transactions directly into the register.

> **NOTE** The **Close** button at the right side of the button bar simply closes the Investment Account register.

For this transaction, start by moving to a blank transaction at the bottom of the register (when an existing transaction is highlighted, the button bar is unavailable, appearing in gray). Then choose the **Buy** button. You'll see the window shown in Figure 9.4.

FIGURE 9.4

*You can enter
investment
transactions
in dialog boxes
like this one.*

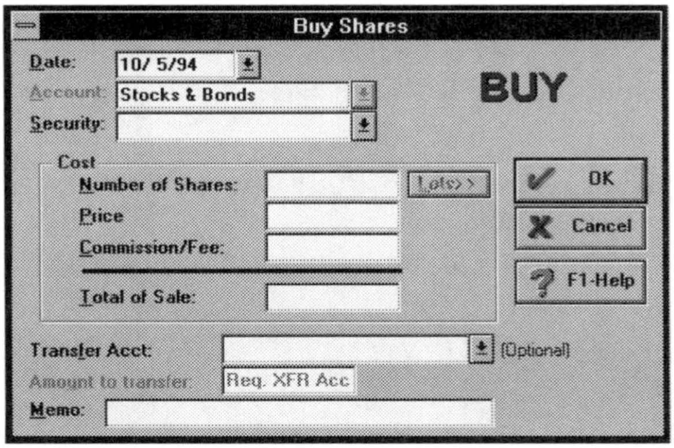

Fill in the remaining transaction details from the previous sample. Notice that the *Account* field displays the name of the current investment account. When you enter a transaction from the register, you can't change this entry even if you have more than one investment account. But when you enter transactions from the Portfolio View window, this field determines which account Quicken records them in.

In the *Security* field, instead of typing in the full name again, you can use QuickFill or choose the name from the drop-down list. QuickFill also works in the *Security* field when you enter transactions directly into the register. Enter the price, number of shares, and the commission amount for the transaction. Quicken calculates the total amount of the transaction for you.

NOTE	If you prefer, you can have Quicken figure the commission for you. In this case, you would make a manual entry in the *Total of Sale* field, copying the total price of a purchase or your net proceeds from a sale. You must then press **Tab**. Whenever your entry in this field is different from the calculated value of a purchase or sale, Quicken assumes that the discrepancy represents commissions and fees, and enters this amount on the *Commission/Fee* line automatically.

Down at the bottom of the window, type in a memo if you'd like. Ignore the *Transfer Acct* field for now—you'll use it later when you buy shares with money from another account. Choose **OK** to record the transaction and to return to the register.

More on How the Investment Register Works

Quicken copies your entries in the Buy Shares dialog box to the corresponding columns of the register (the value in *Total of Sale* appears in the *Amount* column). With the transaction you just entered highlighted in the register, notice that the display is slightly different for this transaction. In particular, since this is a **Buy** transaction, Quicken has added a second line labeled *Comm Fee* in the *Amount* column. If you had typed the transaction into the register directly, that's where you would have entered the commission and other fees for the purchase.

Pay attention to other ways the register columns and fields change depending on the entry in the *Action* field. Quicken displays columns for *Price* and *Shares* in all transactions that move shares in or out of the account (**Buy**, **BuyX**, **ShrsIn**, and **Sell**, **SellX**, and **ShrsOut**). On the other hand, these columns are blank in transactions that list dividends, interest on bonds, and miscellaneous expenses.

NOTE	Note that Quicken keeps a running total of the cash in the account in the far-right column, labeled *Cash Bal*. So far, this is a negative

number: The money you just used to buy the Vistacorp shares came from this account, but you haven't yet entered a transaction to tell Quicken how much cash you had on hand. You'll do that a little later, in the section "Adjusting Cash and Share Balances."

Recording a Dividend

The third sample transaction represents a dividend you received on your holdings of Vistacorp stock:

Date:	**6/5/94**
Action:	**Div**
Security:	**Vistacorp**
Price:	
Shares:	
Amount:	**$20**
Commission:	

You can enter the transaction with either of the two methods you've already learned. To enter it with the button bar, choose the **Income** button. After changing the date and entering the correct security, type the amount into the *Dividend* field. (The remaining fields above the heavy line are for other types of investment income; Quicken records a separate transaction for each field in which you make an entry.) Type a memo in the bottom of the window, then choose **OK** to record the transaction and to return to the register.

If you type the transaction into the register directly, enter **Div** in the *Action* field. After you enter the security name and press **Tab**, the cursor will jump all the way over to the *Amount* field. Again, dividend transactions have blank columns where you entered price and share information in the earlier transactions, and Quicken won't accept entries there.

Entering a Sale of Stock

The fourth and final of our sample stock transactions records a sale of half of your imaginary holdings:

Date:	**9/20/94**
Action:	**Sell**
Security:	**Vistacorp**
Price:	**65**

Shares:	**100**
Amount:	
Commission:	**120**

Again, you can enter this transaction either by typing it directly into the register, or by choosing the **Sell** button and filling out the dialog box that appears.

Selling Vistacorp shares brings up an accounting question: Since you bought the stock on two separate occasions—in two different "lots"—from which lot do you want to sell shares? The answer has tax implications.

Tracking Separate Lots of the Same Security

For example, suppose you've held the first lot for longer than a year but the second lot only three months. Selling shares of the first lot gives you a long-term capital gain, taxed at lower rates than the short-term gain you'd realize on sales of the second lot.

Or what if you paid twice as much per share for the first lot as the second? If the price has since rebounded from its bottom but is still below what you originally paid, you can sell shares of the first lot at a capital loss, offsetting profits in other securities that would otherwise be taxed. If you sell from the second lot instead, you'll pay additional capital gains taxes on those shares.

NOTE Quicken 3 automatically keeps track of separate lots of the same security and offers you a chance to indicate which lot you used when you record a sale of that stock, bond, and so on. If you enter the **Sell** transaction in the register, Quicken asks whether you want to identify the lot the shares came from when you record the transaction. If you use the **Sell** button bar to record the transaction, the dialog box that appears has a button labeled **Lots**.

NEW IN 3 Quicken 2 lacks the ability to automatically track separate lots during purchases and sales, though it can display them together on the Update Prices window. To track multiple lots of the same security, you must set up each lot as a separate Quicken security, assigning each lot a different name but exactly the same symbol.

To tell Quicken which lot to use for the sale, choose **Yes** to Quicken's question or choose the **Lots** button in the Sell Shares window. You'll see a special window for identifying the source of the shares you sold (see Figure 9.5 on the next page).

FIGURE 9.5

Use this window to tell Quicken the lot of a security from which you sold shares.

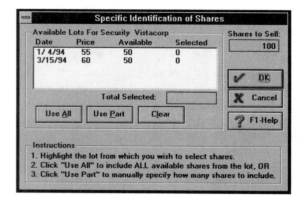

The main section of the window lists all available lots of the security, showing you when you bought each lot, how much you paid, and how many shares you now hold. At the top right, it displays the number of shares you sold.

If all the shares sold came from one lot, just highlight the lot and choose the **Use All** button. If you sold shares from more than one lot, there's an extra step for each lot. Highlight the lot and choose **Use Part**. In the tiny dialog box that appears, type in the number of shares sold from that lot and choose **OK**. Repeat this process until you've accounted for all the shares you sold.

Entering Bond Transactions

The next set of sample transactions pertain to an imaginary bond investment:

Date:	**12/31/93**
Action:	**ShrsIn**
Security:	**Treasury 11/02**
Price:	**75 3/4**
Shares:	**100**
$Amount:	
Commission:	

Date:	**3/31/94**
Action:	**IntInc**
Security:	**Treasury 11/02**
Price:	
Shares:	
$Amount:	**$250**
Commission:	

Date:	**6/15/94**
Action:	**Buy**
Security:	**Treasury 11/02**
Price:	**74 1/2**
Shares:	**100**
$Amount:	
Commission:	**45**

> **NOTE**   Note that 11/02 after "Treasury" in the *Security* field indicates the date the bond matures (November 2002).

The only important difference to be aware of when entering bond purchases and sales concerns the way you record monetary values and number of shares. Bonds are usually listed in the newspaper at one-tenth of their actual value. For example, a bond quoted at "83-1/8" actually costs $831.25. Since Quicken isn't smart enough to adjust for this oddity, you'll have to compensate yourself. You have two choices: You can multiply the price by 10 and enter this number in the *Price* field, or you can enter the price per bond as listed in the paper in the *Price* field, then enter 10 times the number of bonds you actually own in the *Shares* field.

In the first sample bond transaction, you owned 10 bonds each valued at 75-3/4 at the end of the previous year. Since each bond was actually worth $757.50, you must enter 100 in the *Shares* field to make the total in the *Amount* field come out correctly. Enter the remaining transactions in the same way.

Creating New Security Types and Goals

The third set of sample transactions illustrates how you record the purchase and sale of precious metals or similar investments. Before you enter the sample transactions, however, you'll need to set up a new security type for them, since Quicken's built-in types don't include metals. While you're at it, you might as well learn how to set up new investment goals as well.

To create a new security type, choose **Security Type** from the Lists menu. A small Security Type List dialog box appears, listing the types currently available in your account. Choose **New** to display the Set Up Security Type dialog box (see Figure 9.6 on the next page). Enter a name for the new type in the *Type* field—here, type in **Precious metal**—then tell Quicken whether to display prices for this security type in decimal form or as fractions. Choose **OK**. You can change an existing security type from the Security Type List dialog box by highlighting it and choosing **Edit** or pressing **Ctrl-E**.

FIGURE 9.6

*The Set Up
Security Type
dialog box.*

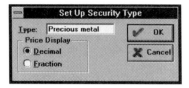

Creating a new investment goal is just as simple. Choose **Investment Goal** from the Lists menu to display the Investment Goal list. Then choose **New** to pop up the supremely simple Set Up Investment Goal dialog box (see Figure 9.7). Here, just type in your name for the goal, and then choose **OK**. The new goal appears on the list. To change an existing goal, highlight it in the list and choose **Edit** or press **Ctrl-E**.

FIGURE 9.7

*The Set Up
Investment
Goal dialog box.*

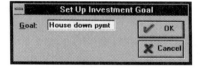

Entering Commodities Transactions

You're now ready to enter your third set of sample investment transactions, those relating to gold purchases and sales. The key point here is that you enter the number of ounces of the metal you bought or sold in the *Shares* field. This would be true for any type of commodity—if you were recording a purchase of soybean futures, you'd record the number of bushels in the commodity contract here.

Date:	**12/31/92**
Action:	**ShrsIn**
Security:	**Gold bullion**
Price:	**$350**
Shares:	**10**

Date:	**9/9/93**
Action:	**Sell**
Security:	**Gold bullion**
Price:	**$375**
Shares:	**5**

Adjusting Cash and Share Balances

As you'll remember, you have a choice regarding how much past information about your investments to enter when you set up an investment account. In that exercise, you entered past transactions beginning from the first of the current year.

If you had entered all past transactions, including those from prior years, the cash balance at the bottom of the register would have been correct. In this case, though, you didn't create a separate cash entry to start the account. Because the funds for our hypothetical transactions have come from your investment account, Quicken displays a significant negative cash balance representing the amount you spent on investments subtracted from your dividend earnings and the amount you took in from sales of some of your Vistacorp stock and gold bullion.

Let's assume that your account actually contained more than enough cash to cover this shortfall. Fortunately, Quicken gives you a way to adjust the account's cash balance so that it equals the cash that's really in your investment account.

Choose **Update Balances** and **Update Cash Balance** from the Activities menu. In the dialog box that appears (see Figure 9.8), enter **$15,000** as the actual cash balance in the account. Change the date to one prior to your first buy or sell transaction. When you choose **OK**, Quicken creates a special transaction adding or subtracting cash so that the current balance is correct.

FIGURE 9.8

Use this dialog box to adjust the cash balance in your account to match what is actually in your brokerage account.

Similarly, you can have Quicken reset the number of shares of any given security the account holds. Choose **Update Balances** then **Update Share Balance** from the Activities menu. In the window, enter the date on which you want Quicken to make the adjustment. In the next field, type the name of the security whose share balance you'd like to change. Finally, enter the total number of shares of the chosen security that should be in your account after the adjustment (don't enter the number of shares you want to add or subtract—Quicken does the math for you). Then choose **OK**.

Setting Up a Mutual Fund Account

Earlier, you learned that Quicken offers a special subtype of investment account expressly designed for mutual funds. You can only track one mutual fund in each of these mutual fund accounts, but in return you get a running total on the number of shares you own and automatic transfers of cash into and out of the account.

Here's how to set up a mutual fund account:

1. Use one of the standard methods for starting a new account.
2. In the Select Account Type dialog box, select the **Investment Account** radio button, and choose **OK**.
3. In the Create New Account dialog box, type in a name for the account.
4. When you get to the *Account Contains a Single Mutual Fund* field, check the box.
5. If you will not pay taxes on the earnings from this account until you take possession of them, select the **Tax-Deferred Account** checkbox.
6. Enter a description in the final field if you like.
7. Click **Info** if you want to enter additional information about the account. This is optional and only for your own reference.
8. When you're done filling out all the fields, click **OK**.
9. You'll now see the Set Up Mutual Fund Security dialog box (Figure 9.9). Type in the fund's name, its trading symbol, its type (mutual fund is entered for you, but you can use other types to describe the investments the fund holds), and the investment goal. Choose **OK** to record your responses.

Back in the Account list, double-click on the new account (or highlight it and choose **Use**) to open the register. You'll be greeted by the Create Opening Share Balance window, which instructs you to give the account an opening balance. If you plan to enter all past transactions for this mutual fund, choose **Cancel** to bypass this window. Otherwise, type in the total value of your mutual fund investment as of the first date the account will cover (usually either today's date or December 31 of the previous year). If necessary, change the date shown for the opening balance as well.

When you choose **OK**, Quicken creates a transaction for the opening balance amount and takes you to the register. Notice that the notation in the *Action* field is **ShrsIn**, indicating that these are shares you already owned and that you don't have to account for the cash used to purchase them.

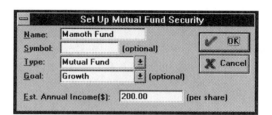

FIGURE 9.9

The Create Opening Share Balance dialog box for setting up a mutual fund account.

Using Tax-Deferred Investment Accounts

NEW IN 3   Tax-deferred investment accounts are new in Quicken 3.

As you've seen, you can specify investment accounts as tax deferred by checking the relevant box when you first set them up (see Figure 9.1 on page 233). Do this if your earnings from this account will be tax free until you withdraw them. Tax-deferred accounts include IRAs, 401(K) plans and 403(K) plans, annuities, and Series EE and HH U.S. Savings Bonds.

When you specify an account as tax deferred, Quicken excludes it from Tax Summary and Tax Schedule reports, and from records it exports to tax preparation software, such as TurboTax. That way, you won't overestimate the amount of taxable income you've earned.

You can transfer funds to and from a tax-deferred investment account and any other Quicken account. Quicken will include transfer transactions in tax reports if they involve non-tax-deferred accounts. That way, you'll have a record of contributions to IRAs and the like so you can enter these amounts on your tax forms (and subtract them from your taxable income).

For tips on tracking retirement investments, including tax-deferred accounts, see Chapter 14.

Tracking Your Investments

Once you've set up your investment accounts, you can use them to monitor the health of your investments on a regular basis and to prepare reports whenever you need them for tax purposes or portfolio analysis.

Monitoring Market Value in the Register

At the lower-right corner of the Investment Account window, Quicken lists two items of bottom-line importance: the dollar amount of the cash currently in your account (*Ending Cash Bal*) and the current market value of the entire account, including the cash balance (*Market Value*). If your cash balance is zero, the market value displayed represents the amount you would realize if you sold the investments in your account. If you do have cash in the account, you must subtract the cash balance from the market value shown to obtain the value of your securities or other investments.

Of course, the accuracy of the information Quicken displays on these two lines or provides in reports and graphs depends on how complete and up to date you keep your investment accounts. Whenever a significant change in your portfolio takes place, you'll want to record the new information by adding corresponding transactions to your accounts (see "Recording New Transactions") or by updating the market prices of your holdings (as described later, in "Updating Market Prices").

Using Portfolio View

The Portfolio View window (presented earlier in this chapter) gives you a central control panel for managing all your investments. Shown in Figure 9.10, the Portfolio View window lists any combination of securities from any or all your investment accounts. Open the Portfolio View window by choosing the **Port View** button in the Investment Account register. If you installed the **Portfolio View** icon on the main Iconbar when you set up the account, you can display the window at any time, even when no investment accounts are in use.

| NOTE | Quicken 2 provides much of the same information in the Update Prices window, although you can't enter new transactions and Customization options are limited. |

FIGURE 9.10

The Portfolio View window.

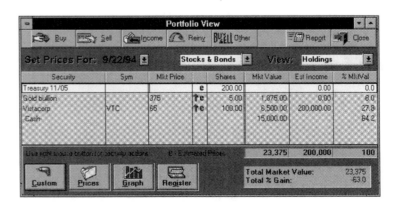

Portfolio View lets you enter new transactions into any account, edit existing transactions, and record market price changes. It also provides crucial information on how well your investments are doing overall. In fact, you can decide exactly what information to display from a wide assortment of calculated measures of performance.

The Portfolio View window is equipped with a button bar across the top, a set of three fields just below the button bar, and several big buttons at the bottom right. Choose the **Close** button at the top right to close the window, of course.

The **Register** button lets you move directly to the register for the investment account currently on display in Portfolio View. If more than one account is displayed, you can't access the **Register** button. We'll cover the functions of the other controls as we proceed.

Tracking Market Prices

If you're serious about investing, keeping track of your "paper wealth" is probably one of your major pastimes. Fortunately, Quicken makes it easy to follow the current market value of your holdings as their prices fluctuate from day to day and month to month. So grab the latest Wall Street Journal and get ready to update your account.

The main section of Portfolio View lists your investment holdings by type (stocks, bonds, and so on), organizing them alphabetically within these groups. Reading along any row from left to right, the first two columns in the window display the investment name and its type. The next three columns show the investment's current market price per share, an arrow indicating whether the current price is higher or lower than the last recorded price for that security; and the total number of shares you own.

NOTE	Quicken 2 displays an asterisk (*) rather than an *e* to indicate "estimated" market prices.

About that narrow column between *Mkt Price* and *Shares*, containing the arrows—Quicken lets you enter the market price every day, but you don't have to. If you haven't entered a price for a given date, Quicken supplies it for you, copying the most recent price available. The small *e* next to the entry indicates that Quicken has "estimated" the market price in this way. Again, the little arrows in this column tell you whether the price shown is higher or lower than the previous price.

The information in the last three columns depends on which "view" you've chosen. At the top-right corner of the window, the drop-down list labelled View lets you select from several built-in profiles and two custom ones that you can build yourself. When you select a view, the headings and data in the last three columns change accordingly. Table 9.2 explains what you'll see in each view.

TABLE 9.2   *The Built-in Views Available in Portfolio View*

View	First Column	Second Column	Third Column	Purpose
Holdings	Mkt Value	Est income	%MktVal	Shows you the value of your investments, and their estimated income both in dollar terms and as a percentage of their value.
Performance	$ Invested	$ Return	ROI	Shows you how much income your investments are earning on a percentage basis over the period you specify.
Valuation	$ Invested	$ Return	Mkt Value	Shows you how much you've invested, how much return you've realized over the specified period, and the current market value of the investments.
Price Update	Last Price	Mkt Value	MktVal Chg	Shows you how the current price of the investments has changed their market value since you acquired them.

Below the list of individual investments, Quicken figures your overall percentage gain or loss and totals the market value of all the investments shown.

NOTE   Quicken enters asterisks for %Gain if your portfolio includes any short sales. This calculation refers to the percentage gain or decrease in the actual price of the security, not to the change in your portfolio's value. In a short-sale situation, a decreasing security price indicates a gain in your portfolio's value; but Quicken isn't able to display this complication clearly. See the section "Recording Short Sales," later in this chapter.

Quicken fills in all this information for you. However, you can change one entry yourself: the market price per share. That's how you update your account to bring it into line with the current prices of your real-life investments.

Displaying Other Dates

But before you start changing market price entries, note the date above the list of securities (where it says *Set Prices For*). You can use Portfolio View as a daily record of the ups and downs of your portfolio. Whenever you want to see how the price of an investment has fluctuated over the past weeks or months, you can browse through the records for those previous dates.

Try changing to a different date now. If you click on the **Arrow** button beside the date, you can choose a new date from the familiar pop-up mini-calendar. You can also type in the date you want to display. Click anywhere else in the *Date* field or press **Ctrl-G** (the shortcut for **Go to Date** in the Edit menu). Type the date in the small dialog box that appears and choose **OK**. (You can also change the date shown using the Price History dialog box, but we'll get to that a bit later.)

If you go back far enough in time, you'll probably notice that your investments have disappeared from the window. Unless you change the Portfolio View layout (see "Customizing Portfolio View"), Quicken displays market value information for a given security only if you owned that investment on the date currently shown.

Entering Daily Market Prices

There are two ways to supply a market price for a Quicken security on a given date: by entering a **Buy** or **Sell** transaction in the register for that date, or by specifying the price on the Portfolio View window.

If Quicken has estimated the market price in the Portfolio View window, as indicated by a small *e* in the column between *Mkt Price* and *Shares*, this means there is no **Buy** or **Sell** transaction for that date. To add a price, move to the line for that investment whose price you want to change, either by clicking on the line or with the cursor keys. Then just type in the current price of one share (if you're working with a bond holding, remember to adjust the "share" price as discussed in "Entering Bond Transactions").

You can increase or decrease the price by 1/8 of a point ($0.125) by pressing the + or - keys. If the actual price on the current date is the same as Quicken's estimate, confirm it as a valid actual price by typing an asterisk yourself (you don't have to move the cursor to the column containing the asterisk). The asterisk already there will disappear. To restore the estimated price, eliminating anything you've typed in so far, type an asterisk again.

NOTE	In Quicken 2, you must choose **Record Prices** to confirm a new entry in the Update Prices window.

As soon as you move the cursor out of that row, Quicken recalculates the figures for that investment in the last three columns and the totals shown at the bottom of the window.

Viewing Price History

Although you can get an idea of the variation in an investment's price by browsing through various dates on the Portfolio View window, Quicken provides an easier way to review the price history. In Portfolio View, highlight the investment you want to work with. Then choose the **Prices** button (**Price History** in Quicken 2), or choose **Edit Price History** from the Edit menu. As shown in Figure 9.11, you'll see a dialog box listing each market price change you've entered for that security.

FIGURE 9.11

This dialog box displays the changes in price you've recorded for a single security.

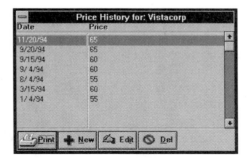

You can enter price changes from this dialog box as well. Choose **New** to display a small window in which you can enter the date of the price change (or accept today's date as already entered for you) and then type in the updated price. Choose **OK** to get back to the Price History window.

SHORTCUT | From the keyboard, **Alt-N**, **Ctrl-E**, and **Ctrl-D** work to create, edit, and delete price history entries, respectively.

You can also change the price of an existing entry in the price history list. Highlight the item, choose **Edit**, and enter the new price. To delete the price change for a given date, highlight the entry and choose **Del**. If the **Require Confirmation** setting in the General Preferences dialog box is turned on, you'll see a warning before Quicken deletes the price. You can print the list of prices by choosing the Print button.

When you're through with the Price History dialog box, there are two ways to return to the Portfolio View window. If you simply press **Esc** or double-click the control box, you'll go back to the Portfolio View window without changing the date it displays. To return to the window at another date, move the highlight to the price history entry with the date you want, and then choose **View Date**.

Customizing the Portfolio View

NOTE | Quicken 2 only lets you select which accounts and securities the Update Prices window displays.

To control the type of information shown on the Portfolio View window, choose the **Custom** button. The window that Quicken displays, shown in Figure 9.12, lets you decide which investment accounts and specific securities appear in Portfolio View, how much information about each security it shows, and the calculated investment measurements displayed in the three columns on the right of the Portfolio View. In addition, you can choose the date range Quicken considers in making its investment analysis calculations.

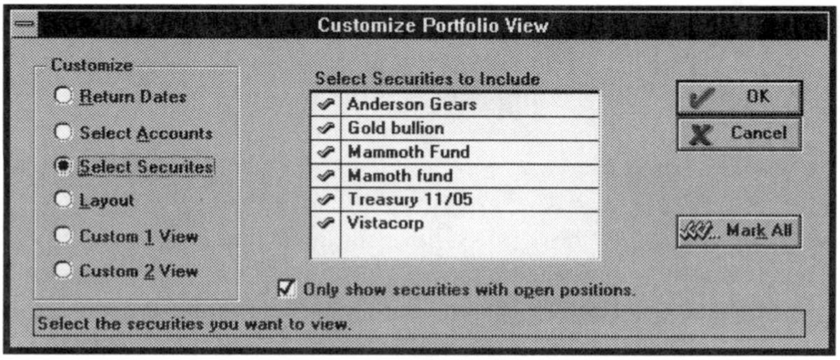

FIGURE 9.12

Customize Portfolio View using this window.

On the left side of the Customize Portfolio View window are six radio buttons. The fields you see in the middle of the window change depending on which of these buttons you select.

Use the top radio button, **Return Dates**, to choose which dates Quicken uses to calculate the return on your investments shown in Portfolio View. (When you choose the built-in Performance views, the last two columns display the overall return in dollars (*$ Return*) and the rate of return as a percentage of the amount invested (*ROI*) for the chosen period.

Choose **Select Accounts** radio button to display a list of your investment accounts. On the list, check off the accounts you want to see in Portfolio View by clicking on each account name or highlighting it and pressing the space bar. The **Mark All** button marks or unmarks all the accounts in turn.

SHORTCUT If all you want to do is choose the accounts to be displayed, it's quicker to use the field at the top center of the main Portfolio View window. The drop-down list lets you pick any of your investment accounts individually, an **All Accounts** choice, or **Selected Accounts**. If you choose the latter, you're taken to the Customize window with the **Select Accounts** radio button already chosen.

Choose the **Select Securities** to specify which of your securities will be displayed in Portfolio View. You can only select from the securities listed in the accounts you picked with the **Select Accounts** button. Again, your securities appear in a simple list; you mark them with a checkmark to include them in Portfolio View. Check the box below the list if you want to display securities only if you hold open positions on the date at the top of Portfolio View. If you don't check the box, the security will appear, even if you don't currently own any shares.

WARNING The **Display** setting for a security in the Security list overrides your selection on the Customize Portfolio View window. If you set a security's display option in the Security list to **Never**, you won't see the security in the Portfolio even if you select it in the Customize window. See "Using the Security List," later in this chapter for details.

Choose **Layout** to specify how much information Portfolio View gives you about each security. You can set it up to show anything from the name of the security only to the name, its type (stock, bond, or etc.), and symbol.

Choose either of the **Custom View** buttons to pick the investment analysis measures that Portfolio View will display in the three right-most columns. You can pick from close to 20 different calculations. The formula for each is displayed in a list in the middle of the window. To select a calculation, choose the **Radio** button for that column above the list, then pick the formula from the list with the mouse or by highlighting it with the cursor keys. When you've chosen calculations for all three columns, you can type a name for your customized view in the field below the list. This name appears in the list of views at the right of the Portfolio View window.

Entering Investment Transactions from Portfolio View

If you'd like, you can use Portfolio View to record investment transactions in your accounts—in fact, you never need to look at the register if that's your preference. Note that Portfolio View's button bar has the same buttons as an investment account, for entering **Buy**, **Sell**, **Income**, **Reinvestment**, and **Miscellaneous** transactions. When you choose one of these buttons, you'll see the same dialog boxes you get in the investment accounts, such as the one back in Figure 9.4 on page 240.

The only difference in entering a transaction from Portfolio View is that you must specify the account where Quicken will record the transaction. Use the second field, *Account*, for this purpose.

Graphing Price and Value History

If you think better with the right side of your brain—visually—you can use the Portfolio View window to see a graph charting a given security's price and its value in your portfolio over time. Highlight the security name in the list and choose **Graph**. You'll see a combination line and bar graph like the one in Figure 9.13.

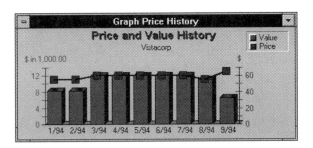

FIGURE 9.13

This is an example of what you'll see when you graph a security's price and its value in your portfolio.

SHORTCUT If the graph is too small to see the details clearly, you can resize its window with the mouse or by using the standard keyboard commands for that purpose.

In the graph, the line represents the market price of a share of the security. Each larger square along the line stands for its price on the last day of the month shown. The bars represent the total market value of your security, that is, the amount of cash you'd have if you sold all your holdings of that security at the then-current price.

The graph is snazzy enough, but there's more here than meets the eye. You can "inspect" it to get numeric details on individual months' price and values, or to see a quick report covering the entire period shown on the graph.

Notice that whenever you move the mouse pointer over one of the bars, it turns from an arrow into a magnifying glass with a Z (for *Zoom*) in its center. Clicking with the right mouse button with this pointer over a bar displays a tiny window containing the dollar amount of the value represented by the bar (see Figure 9.14). Similarly, clicking with the right button over any of the squares on the price line shows you the exact price at that time.

FIGURE 9.14

When you click over a bar in the Investment graph with the right mouse button, you'll see a little window showing the dollar value the bar represents.

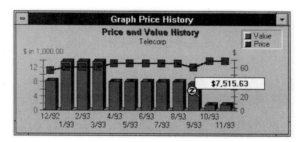

To display the report of price and value history, double-click the Magnifying Glass pointer (using the left mouse button) on any of the bars. You'll see a report titled "Price and Value History," as shown in Figure 9.15. The report shows every recorded change in the price of the security and the total value of your holdings in that security. The column headings should be self-explanatory.

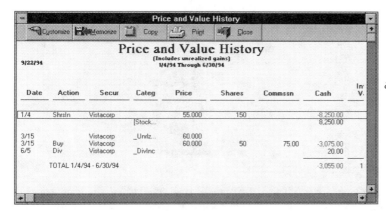

FIGURE 9.15

You get this report of the security's price and value history when you double-click over any of the bars in the Investment graph.

You can also produce a report listing all the transactions for a given security by highlighting the security in the main Portfolio View list and choosing the **Report** button.

I won't go into details about how to work with these reports here—Chapters 10 and 11 cover reports in full. Suffice it to say that you can move around in the report with the scroll bars and print it out by clicking the small **Print** button at the top of the Report window (or by choosing **Print Report** from the File menu or by pressing **Ctrl-P**).

Printing Market Price Information

To print the market price information shown on the Portfolio View window, press **Ctrl-P** or click the **Print** icon. You can also print the price history for a given investment. After highlighting the investment, open the Price History window by choosing the **Prices** button, then choose **Print**.

Using the Security List

If you want to set up securities before you actually start entering them in your investment accounts, use Quicken's Security list. The Security list also lets you control the display of your securities in Portfolio View.

Pop up the list by pressing **Ctrl-Y** or by choosing **Security** from the Lists menu. Figure 9.16 on the next page shows the Security List window.

FIGURE 9.16

The Security list.

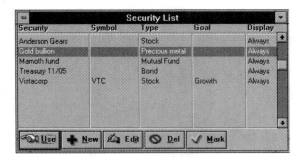

To create a new security, choose the **New** button. The dialog box that appears is the same one you used when setting up securities from the register (see Figure 9.3 on page 238). You can edit an existing security just as easily by highlighting it in the list and choosing **Edit**; or you can choose **Del** to delete a highlighted security.

You can also start a new transaction from the Security list. Highlight the security that figures in the transaction and choose **Use**. Quicken takes you immediately to the register of the investment account you last used, transferring the security name to the proper field. You fill out the rest of the transaction as usual.

Note the far-right column of the Security list, labeled **Display**. For any given security, the entry here determines when that security will be displayed in the Portfolio View window. You can select one of three options:

- **Always**, which displays the security at all times.
- **Open**, which displays the security only if you have an active long or short position in the security—in other words, if you currently own shares or have not yet covered a short sale.
- **Never**, which keeps the security off the Portfolio View window.

To change the entry in the *Display* field, highlight the security in the list and press the space bar or choose **Mark** until the entry you'd like appears. Setting the *Display* column to **Never** or **Open** overrides whatever display choice you make for that security in the Customize window for Portfolio View.

Strategies for Investment Tracking

You've already learned how to enter the basic types of investment transactions as you worked through the imaginary "past" transactions in setting up your practice first investment account in this chapter. You'll use exactly the same methods to record new purchases or sales of securities, dividend income, fees and commissions, and so on. This section covers some of the fine points about recording various types of investment transactions. Of course, when you record any real-life transaction, remember to enter the date on which the transaction actually took place.

Recording Buy Transactions

When you purchase or sell shares of a stock or a set of bonds, Quicken expects you to account for the cash that you pay out or receive. For example, when the money for a securities purchase comes from the same account in which you track securities, you should choose the **Buy** button.

NOTE   To transfer money between an investment account and another account, you use the same transferring techniques you learned earlier in this chapter. In the *Transfer Account* field enter the name of the account from which you'll be transferring the funds. To switch back and forth between two parallel transactions linked by a transfer, highlight the transaction in one account and press **Ctrl-X**.

On the other hand, if you buy the securities with cash from a different account—probably your regular checking account—your entry in the *Action* field should be **BuyX**. In this case, Quicken will transfer the cash out of the other account to pay for your purchase.

There are two ways to enter **BuyX** transactions: in the Investment Account register or in the register of the account that holds the cash. If you wrote the check for the purchase by hand, it's easiest to record the transaction from the investment account, entering **BuyX** in the *Action* field. As soon as you make this **Action** entry, Quicken automatically adds two new fields on the second line of the transaction: *Xfer Acct* (where the *Category* field would be in other accounts) and *Xfer Amt* (below the *Shares* field), as shown in Figure 9.17 on the next page. When you get to the *Xfer Acct* field, enter the name of the account from which the cash for the purchase came.

In the *Xfer Amt* field, enter the amount of funds transferred from the other account. If this is less than the full amount of the **Investment** transaction, Quicken subtracts the remaining cost from the cash balance of the investment account.

You can also use your checking account to start the entry for an investment purchase involving a transfer. This is especially convenient when you're buying shares of a mutual fund that you track in a Quicken mutual fund account. All you have to do is make out the check in the amount you want to invest in your mutual fund purchase. Based on the last recorded share price in your mutual fund account, Quicken calculates the number of shares you're purchasing and automatically enters a linked **BuyX** transaction in the mutual fund account. If it turns out that the share price you enter is different from what you paid at the time your purchase went through, you can revise the **Transaction** entry when you receive a statement from the mutual fund or broker.

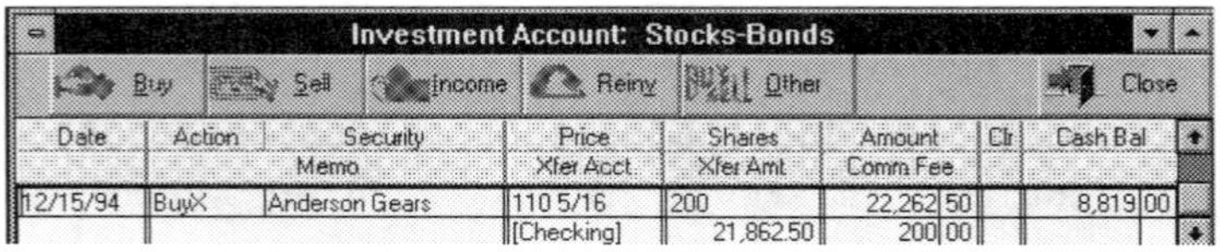

FIGURE 9.17

*Quicken adds Xfer Acct and Xfer Amt fields to **BuyX** and other types of transactions that transfer money into or out of an investment account.*

Date	Action	Security	Price	Shares	Amount	Clr	Cash Bal
		Memo	Xfer Acct	Xfer Amt	Comm Fee		
12/15/94	BuyX	Anderson Gears	110 5/16	200	22,262 50		8,819 00
		[Checking]		21,862.50	200 00		

Recording *Sell* Transactions

Sell transactions work essentially the same as purchases. If the proceeds from the sale stay in the account, you type **Sell** in the *Action* field; if you'll be transferring part or all of the cash to another account, you record the sale as a **Transfer** transaction by typing **SellX** in the *Action* field. You then enter the name of the account to which the transfer is going in the *Xfer Acct* field, and the amount of funds to be transferred in the *Xfer Amt* field.

Recording Investment Income

When your investment earns dividends or interest, you should record the earnings as transactions in Quicken. If the cash will stay in your investment account, you list the income in the *Action* field as either a **Div** (**Dividend**) or **IntInc** (**Interest Income**) transaction. If you're transferring the funds to another account, you must enter **DivX** in the *Action* field whether you're recording dividend or interest income. For **DivX** transactions, Quicken will automatically include an Xfer Acct field in the transaction so that you can select the account to which the earnings are destined.

Mutual funds may pay you two types of income: *income distributions* and *capital gains distributions* (Quicken allows only these types of income transactions in a mutual fund account). Income distributions are essentially just dividends pooled from all the securities in which the mutual fund has invested; treat them as any other dividend.

Capital gains distributions are paid when the mutual fund sells some of its shares at a profit. Since short-term and long-term capital gains receive different tax treatment, Quicken provides separate **Action** entries for each type of income. If you keep a short-term distribution in your investment account, enter **CGShort** in the transaction's *Action* field; if you transfer the funds to another account, the **Action** entry should be **CGShortX**. For long-term capital gains distributions, use the corresponding entries **CGLong** and **CGLongX** in the *Action* field.

If you funnel your dividend, interest, or capital gains earnings back into an investment, rather than keeping or spending the cash, Quicken lets you record the income and the reinvestment) as a single transaction. For reinvested dividend or interest income, the *Action* field entry should be **ReinvDiv**. When you reinvest short-term capital gains, you should enter **ReinvSh**; for reinvested long-term capital gains, enter **ReinvLg**. With all three types of transactions, enter the number of shares you purchased with the reinvestment in the *Shares* field, and the amount of your reinvestment earnings plus commissions or fees in the *Amount* field. Quicken will calculate for you the price per share you paid.

NOTE	These **Reinvestment** entries work best for securities with a low price per share, because you can reinvest almost all your earnings in an even number of shares with very little cash left over. With high price-per-share securities, your reinvestment earnings probably won't be close to an even multiple of the share price. In other words, you'll have a significant amount of cash left over after the reinvestment (but not enough for additional shares). In this case, you'd have to create a **Cash Update** transaction to keep your cash balance accurate, an inconvenience that defeats the purpose of these **Reinvestment** entries.

Handling Loads

Instead of charging a separate commission, some mutual funds make you pay a purchase price higher than the actual market value of the shares. The difference between what you pay per share and what you could sell it for at the same moment is the *load*.

When you record a load fund purchase in Quicken, ignore the load—simply enter the price you actually paid for your new shares. If you want to follow the actual market value of your purchase, you should then adjust the share price, as discussed later.

Recording Stock Splits

In a *stock split*, you receive one or more additional shares of the stock for each share you already own. The price of each share is reduced proportionally, so that the total value of your holding in the stock remains the same. For example, let's say you own 100 shares of a stock selling for $45 with a total value of $4,500. If the company that issued the stock declares a "three-for-one" split, you'll end up with 300 shares at $15 each; your holding still has a total market value of $4,500.

To record a stock split in Quicken, enter it as a separate transaction. In the *Action* field, enter **StkSplit**. Type in the security name, but leave the *Price*, *Shares*, and *Amount* fields empty. Move over to the column that's usually labeled *Shares*. Here, Quicken now provides two fields, *New Shares* and *Old Shares*. Type in the number of shares you now have, after the split, in the *New Shares* field, and enter the number you started with in the *Old Shares* field.

Recording Gifts

If you give away shares of an investment, record the transaction by entering **ShrsOut** in the *Action* field and the number of shares you give away in the *Shares* field. Quicken records the capital gain from the "sale" as zero. Similarly, when you receive shares as a gift or inheritance, enter **SharsIn** in the *Action* field. In the *Price* field, type in the cost basis per share, including commissions and other fees (the cost basis depends on the type of gift you received—you'll probably need an accountant's help to figure it). Quicken records either type of transaction without changing the cash balance in any of your accounts.

One caveat: Giving away shares of a security reduces the average annual rate of return listed in an Investment Performance report (see Chapter 10 for a description of this report). If you want to track this measure accurately, you must record two more transactions beside the initial **ShrsOut** transactions. First, calculate the gain you would have realized on the shares you donated if you had sold them instead (subtract what you originally paid from their current market price). Enter offsetting transactions for this amount, as in this example:

Action	Security	Amount
MiscInc	TLC Ltd.	$950
MiscExp		$950

Recording Margin Purchases

Buying an investment "on margin" means that you pay for part of the purchase with a loan from your broker. Handle the purchase itself by recording just as you normally would. Quicken will subtract the cash for the entire purchase price from your investment account (if you record the transaction as a **Buy** entry) or another account (if you record it as a **BuyX** entry). If you want to maintain an accurate record of your cash on hand, you must then enter the loan in a liability account, transferring the cash generated by the loan to the account used to purchase the investment.

Recording Short Sales

Although it sounds crazy, you can make money in a declining market by selling borrowed shares of stock at a high price, then buying shares to replace those you borrowed at a lower price later. To record such a short sale, enter it just as you would an ordinary **Sale** transaction (use a **Sell** or **SellX** entry in the *Action* field). Because you haven't recorded a prior purchase, Quicken recognizes that you're entering a short sale (you'll get a warning to that effect). Later, when you buy back the borrowed shares, enter an ordinary **Buy** transaction (**Buy** or **BuyX** in the *Action* field).

If you can stand a little extra work, you can include accurate information on short sale profits and losses in your capital gains reports (these reports are described in Chapter 10). In addition to the transactions already mentioned, enter a second pair of Buy and Sell transactions for the same security. The trick is simply to list the amount of the original short sale in the *Amount* field for both of the new transactions.

Tracking Savings Bonds and T-Bills

U.S. savings bonds and Treasury bills are issued at a price less than their face value. If you hold the savings bond or T-bill to maturity, the difference between the sale price and the price you payed is interest. Record it by entering **IntInc** in the *Action* field of the register, or by choosing the **Income** button and filling out the window that appears.

If you sell a T-bill before it matures, the sale price will probably reflect a capital gain or loss since interest rates fluctuate on the secondary market. In this case, subtract the amount representing interest from the total you receive on the sale, and enter the result as a **Sell** transaction.

Tracking Zero-Coupon Bonds

The value of a zero-coupon bond increases as you hold it, reflecting the accumulated interest it earns. You receive a yearly report of the taxable interest earned on the bond, even though you don't receive the money. Record the annual interest amount as you would any interest income, entering **IntInc** in the *Amount* field, or by choosing the **Income** button. At the same time, record the increased value of the bond itself by entering the same number as a negative amount in a separate transaction. Enter **RtrnCap** in the *Action* field, or to enter the transaction in a window, choose **Other**, then **Return Of Capital**. After you enter the two transactions, the cash balance of your account remains the same, and the cost basis of the bond is increased.

Tracking Non-taxable Bond Income

If you receive tax-exempt income from a bond, create a new category for it—use a name like *_Non-taxable int*, including the underscore at the beginning. To record the income transaction, enter **MiscInc** in the *Action* field, then enter your new category in the Category field. Alternatively, you can enter the transaction in a window by choosing **Income**, entering the interest amount in the *Other* field, and adding the category assignment. See the next section for details on how Quicken handles such transactions.

Recording and Categorizing Miscellaneous Transactions

Occasionally, you may have miscellaneous income or expenses associated with your investment account. When you buy a bond, for example, you may owe "accrued interest" to the previous owner. Similarly, when you sell a stock short, you pay dividends to the owner of the "borrowed" shares you sold. There are a variety of miscellaneous fees you may have to pay associated with the maintenance of an account, as opposed to a specific transaction.

To record miscellaneous income and expense items, enter them as transactions in your Investment Account register, entering **MiscInc** or **MiscExp** in the *Action* field as appropriate. When you enter either of these actions, Quicken automatically adds a *Category* field to the transaction (where it would be in noninvestment accounts). You'll recall that Quicken enriched your file with a set of investment-related categories as soon as you set up your first investment account. These categories, shown in Table 9.3, are intended for **MiscInc** and **MiscExp** transactions.

TABLE 9.3 *Quicken's Built-in Investment Categories*

Category	Description
Income	
_DivInc	Dividend
_IntInc	Investment Interest Inc
_LT CapGnDst	Long-Term Cap Gain Dist
_RlzdGain	Realized Gain/Loss
_ST CapGnDst	Short-Term Cap Gain Dist
_UnrlzdGain	Unrealized Gain/Loss
Expense	
_Accrued Int	Accrued Interest
_IntExp	Investment Interest Exp

Categorize a **Miscellaneous Income** or **Expense** transaction the same way you would a transaction in another type of account. In an *Investment Category* field, the **Investment-Related** transactions appear at the top of the drop-down list so you can find them easily. They all begin with an underscore, as in **_DivInc**, so type that first if you're using QuickFill.

Recording Accrued Bond Interest

Generally, when you purchase a bond on the secondary market (that is, after it was originally issued), you must pay to the previous owner any interest the bond has accrued since the last interest payment. To record the purchase of a bond with an accrued interest payment, begin by recording the bond purchase itself in its own transaction. Then create a separate transaction for the interest payment, assigning it to **MiscExp** in the *Action* field and adding an explanatory memo. If the funds for the interest payment came from another account, document this by setting up a third transaction listing the amount of the transfer. Assign the **XIn** action to this transaction, and place the name of the account from which the funds came in the *Xfer Acct* field to create an Automatic Parallel Transfer transaction in the other account.

Recording Repeated Transactions

You can memorize and recall investment transactions and transaction groups just as you can in other types of Quicken accounts. This is probably most often useful for entering automatic stock purchases you make as part of an employee stock ownership plan and for regular dividends you receive. You'll find details on memorizing and recalling transactions in Chapter 7. Remember that Quicken is usually set so that transactions are memorized automatically so they can be recalled by QuickFill. To memorize a transaction yourself, select it in the register and press **Ctrl-M**. To recall the transaction, press **Ctrl-T**, and then choose the transaction from the window that appears.

Importing Price Data from Disk Files

If you have access to security price information in a spreadsheet or database—perhaps you download prices to your spreadsheet from an on-line Vistacommunications service—you can transfer the new prices to Quicken without retyping them.

To make this work, the information must be stored on disk in a *comma-delimited* ASCII file, a simple standard for data exchange. Each line of the file must list one security's symbol, price, and date, in that order, with a comma between each of these items (you can omit the date, in which case Quicken assigns the date you specify). Any of the three items may be enclosed in double quote marks, but there must be no spaces within the quotes, and the commas must be outside the quotes. The first item is the security's symbol (not its name) and must be identical to the symbol you've entered for that security in Quicken.

Here are examples of valid entries:

```
IBM     150.45   10/15/93
CBS     123.75   10/20/93
```

Once you've created the price information file, import it from the Portfolio View window by pressing **Ctrl-I** or choosing **Import Prices** from the File menu (you must start from the Portfolio View window or you'll import a Quicken data file, which is not what you'd like). In the window that appears, type in the file name, including the path if the file isn't in your Quicken directory. If you have items in the file that don't include a date, you can type in a date to which Quicken will assign them during the import process. Choose **OK** to proceed with the import.

Keeping Track of Loans and other Assets and Liabilities

Aside from the balance in your checking and savings accounts and your cash on hand, your net worth may well include a variety of other important assets, such as the equity in your home. Likewise, if you do own your own home, your outstanding mortgage balance probably dwarfs the amount you owe on your credit cards. In addition, you may be paying off loans on your car or your college education.

| SHORTCUT | When you're comparing competing loan packages or deciding whether it makes sense to refinance a mortgage, call on Quicken's specialized calculators designed just for these situations. See "Using the Loan and Refinance Calculators," at the end of this section. |

Quicken makes it easy to keep track of all these assets and liabilities and just about any other kinds with special asset and liability accounts. These differ in only minor ways from checking, cash, and credit card accounts. You can assign the transactions in them to categories and classes and create detailed reports or summaries of their activities whenever you need to do so. As with any type of Quicken account, you can also transfer funds between asset or liability accounts and any other Quicken account as necessary.

Whether or not you make use of these additional types of accounts, however, is often a matter of personal taste and judgment. Since most mortgages and other major loans have fixed payment schedules, you may be content to make your monthly payments knowing that the loan will eventually be paid off. In that case, you can record the payments in your regular checking account.

<table>
<tr><td>

NOTE

</td><td>

For most people, though, that won't be enough—especially when Quicken can automatically *amortize* your loan for you, showing you just how much you're spending on both principal and interest each month. That's perfect for tax-deductible interest payments, and it's a good way to watch your equity grow. Quicken 3 requires you to use a separate liability account for each amortized loan.

</td></tr>
</table>

Similarly, although the value of your collection of rare recordings or fine wines may vary from month to month, you may prefer just to follow price trends in your trade magazines rather than keep a running balance of your entire investment in Quicken. But if you have a substantial investment portfolio that plays a major role in your overall financial picture, you may want to use Quicken to assess its total value regularly.

The range of assets and liabilities you might want to monitor with a Quicken account is considerable. On the asset side, you can track your IRA, the value of your home and the improvements you make to it, investment real estate, antiques, fine art, collectibles, and, for a business, accounts receivable or capital equipment. Liabilities that justify their own Quicken account include your mortgage, any other major loans, and business liabilities that accrue over time. (Ordinary accounts payable should be part of your business checking account, however, as described in Chapter 15.)

Tracking Assets

Let's practice by setting up an asset account for your investment in a curio collection, currently worth $1,000. To start the new account:

1. Click on the **Accts** icon or press **Ctrl-A**, and then choose **New**.

2. In the Select Account Type dialog box, choose the **Asset Account** radio button and choose **OK**.

3. Next comes the Create New Account dialog box, where you should type in a name such as **Curios** for the account and enter the current value of the investment, **$1,000**, in the *Balance* field.

4. Choose **OK** to create the account.

<table>
<tr><td>

NOTE

</td><td>

If you were setting up a single asset account to encompass several different existing investments, you would type **0** in the *Balance*

</td></tr>
</table>

field, and then enter separate transactions for the current values of each investment in the Account register. You could then delete the **Opening Balance** transaction.

When the Select Account dialog box reappears, choose the new account in the list to display its register, shown in Figure 9.18. In this register, the columns for recording transaction amounts are labeled *Decrease* (i.e., transactions that decrease the asset's value) and *Increase* (those that raise it).

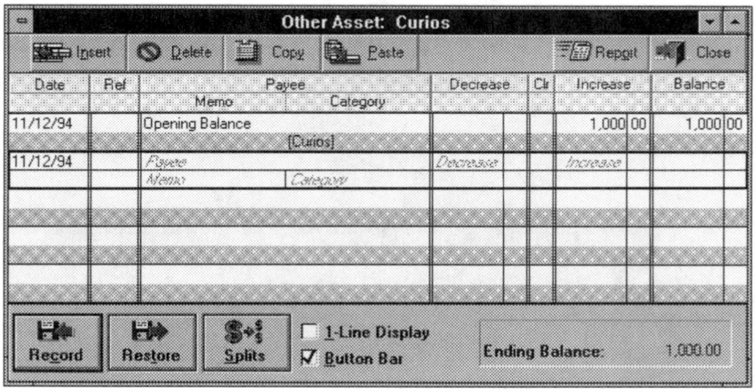

FIGURE 9.18

The register of a new asset account.

The only transaction in the account so far, the one showing the initial value of your curio collection, is recorded as **Opening Balance** in the *Payee* field. If you like, edit the **Payee** entry to read something like **Initial value of collection**.

NOTE   Notice that Quicken has entered the name of the curio account in the transaction's *Category* field. If you can't think of a more useful category name, listing a transaction as a **Transfer** from the same account is a safe way to ensure that it will be included in the analysis when you prepare a category-based report on the asset account.

Let's say that a month after you've started the account, you decide to buy a second lot of curios from another dealer. This time, the price is $1,250. You write a check for the purchase from your regular checking account.

You could record this transaction directly into your asset account, transferring the necessary funds from your checking account to cover the purchase. But that won't work if you want Quicken to write the check for you. So let's switch to the checking account and write the check there. Press **Ctrl-A** to move to the Account List window, select the checking account, and choose **Use**. Then press **Ctrl-W** to display the Write Checks window. Next, enter the following information on your screen check:

Payee: **Whitted Antiques, Inc.**
Amount: **$1,250**
Address: **1212 Kneller Drive, La Cienega, NM 52432**
Memo: **Northwestern trinkets**

In the *Category* field, open the drop-down list and move to the bottom where your accounts are listed. Choose the name of your curio account. Quicken will place the name in brackets in the *Category* field and transfer the funds to the curio account. The completed check should look like the one shown in Figure 9.19.

FIGURE 9.19

Writing the check to cover the curio purchase described in the text.

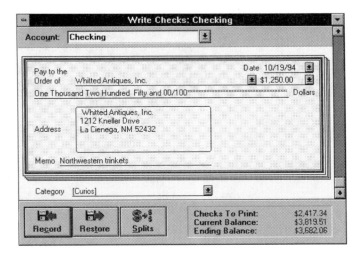

Record the check, and then press **PgUp** to redisplay it. Now press **Ctrl-X** to move immediately to the corresponding transaction in your curio account, as shown in Figure 9.20. Because the value of your total curio collection has been raised by the purchase, the purchase amount is shown in the *Increase* column.

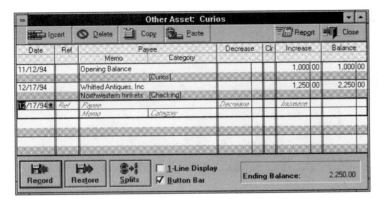

FIGURE 9.20

The transaction has been transferred to the asset account used to track the curio collection.

Adjusting the Value of an Asset or a Liability

Many of the assets you're likely to track with asset accounts vary in value according to market conditions. This means that even if you don't buy or sell portions of an asset, you may still need to enter transactions that will change your account balance to reflect the asset's current market value. That would be the case if the curios you bought with your first purchase, rose in value by $400 since you started the account.

To change the value of an asset, you can use one of two methods. If you like, you can simply enter the adjustment as a transaction in the register, typing an appropriate notation such as **Manual balance adjustment** in the *Payee* field and placing the amount of the adjustment in the *Decrease* or *Increase* field as appropriate.

NOTE You can use these same techniques to adjust a liability account balance. Although it's uncommon for liabilities to change in value in the absence of an actual transaction to account for the change, this can happen when you sell an investment "short."

If you prefer, you can have Quicken enter the adjustment transaction for you instead. Here, we'll use the latter method, on the next page.

WARNING Use the Automatic Account Adjustment technique only if the account covers a single investment. If you use a single account to track several different types of collectibles, for instance, you should enter a separate adjustment manually for each type of collectible in the account.

1. Choose **Update Balances** and **Update Cash Balance** from the Activities menu. You'll see the Update Account Balance dialog box, shown in Figure 9.21.

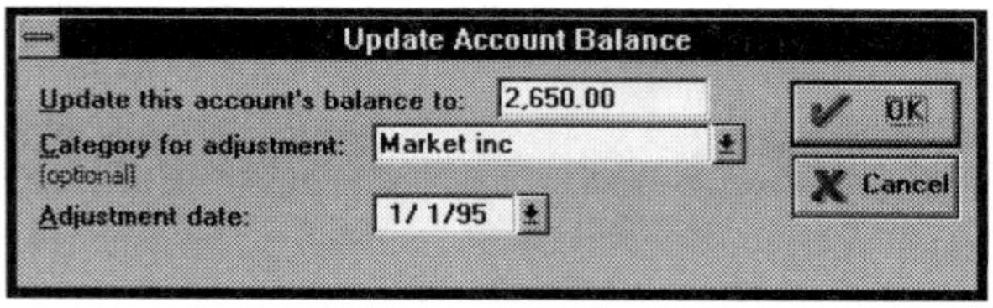

FIGURE 9.21

The Update Account Balance dialog box.

2. In the first field, enter the current balance of the account—in this case, the value of the entire curio collection. Since the total value of the curios is now $2,650 ($1,400 for the revalued first lot, $1,250 for the second lot), type **2650** in the field.

| **SHORTCUT** |

Remember, if you're adding up a series of numbers to determine the new balance, you can pop up the calculator by clicking the **Calc** icon or by choosing **Use Calculator** from the Activities menu.

3. Assign the transaction Quicken is about to create to a category indicating that the adjustment was due to a market value increase—**Market inc** is fitting. Since this category doesn't yet exist in your account, you'll have to create it when you leave the field.

That done, you'll be returned to the register, where you'll see the **Adjustment** transaction Quicken has created. As shown in Figure 9.22, Quicken has calculated the difference between the new and old balance as $400 and placed that amount in the *Increase* column.

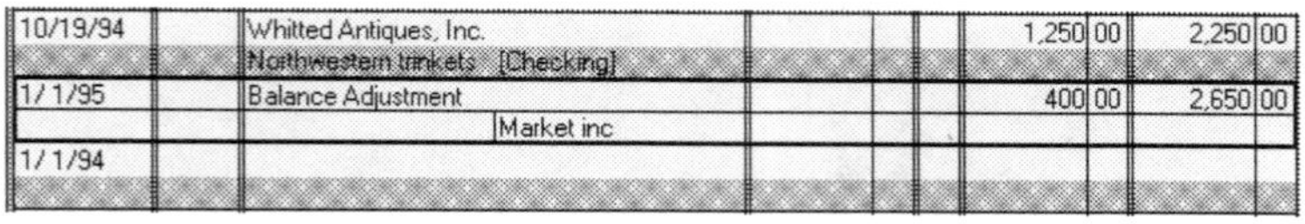

FIGURE 9.22

*A **Balance Adjustment** transaction added to the curio asset account to reflect an increase in the market value of the collection.*

10/19/94	Whitted Antiques, Inc.			1,250 00	2,250 00
	Northwestern trinkets [Checking]				
1/1/95	Balance Adjustment			400 00	2,650 00
		Market inc			
1/1/94					

Splitting a Transaction after a Transfer

Most often, when a transfer of funds between accounts involves a split transaction, you'll create the split in the account where the transfer originates. For instance, earlier in this chapter you transferred cash you received from a split, "less-cash" deposit in your checking account to your cash account.

NOTE For simplicity, this example transaction doesn't include a commission, which you might pay to the broker or store owner who sells your collectibles. You'll find more complete coverage of how to keep track of investment income and expenses, including commissions, in Chapter 14.

If the need arises, however, you can also split the transaction created by a transfer. Again, an example will help to illustrate how this might be useful. Let's say that after another month, an article in a national magazine extols the virtues of curio collecting. This sudden response has driven up demand for curios similar to yours, raising the value of your collection to $4,000. You believe the price has peaked, so you decide to sell your holdings and transfer the proceeds to your checking account, where you'll hold them for reinvestment. On the same day you sell the collection, you also receive your paycheck for $1,000 and deposit the entire amount in your checking account.

To record these financial events, you'd start by creating a transaction in your curio account to cover the sale. Enter **Collectibles Sale** as the payee and type the proceeds, **$4,000**, in the *Decrease* field. Then, in the *Category* field, enter the name of your checking account from the Category list. When you record the transaction, Quicken creates a matching deposit in the checking account for you.

NOTE You could also have entered the split transaction for the deposit first, transferring the proceeds of the sale from your curio account. Quicken would then have created the sale transaction in your mutual account fund for you. Either method works equally well.

That's all well and good, but what about your $1,000 paycheck? It was part of the deposit, too. Here's what you do: With the sale transaction in your mutual fund account highlighted, switch to the check register by pressing **Ctrl-X**. Press **Ctrl-S** to split the transaction, and enter **$1,000** in the *Amount* column on the second line of the window. Recalculate the total amount of the transaction by choosing **Recalc** and close the window by choosing **OK**. Then record the new version of the transaction.

NOTE	If you want the final balance of your account to be zero after recording the sale of your mutual fund investment, you would enter another **Balance Adjustment** transaction reflecting the increase in value of your collection from $2,650 to $4,000 (the entry in the *Increase* field should be $1,350).

Marking Closed Assets and Liabilities

Now that you've sold off your curio collection, what about the account? Since you should keep your records of your purchase and sale for your own review and tax purposes, you don't want to delete the account. On the other hand, since you've sold your shares, you don't need to see entries for the account on all your monthly reports.

To handle this situation, type * in the *Clr* column for all the transactions in the account. In checking and credit card accounts, an asterisk in the *Clr* column would signify a cleared transaction, but here you can interpret it as indicating a closed item. Then, when you make your monthly Investment reports, customize the reports to limit them to uncleared items by filtering the transactions as explained in Chapter 11. If you need to produce a report that does cover your curio-collecting venture, just remove the "filter."

SHORTCUT	Use the same technique to indicate liabilities that you've paid off in full. Just type * in the *Clr* column in the corresponding liability account.

Tracking Liabilities

If you want to monitor closely a major liability such as your mortgage, you'll need one of Quicken's liability accounts. Liability accounts work just like asset accounts, except that the balance reflects the amount you *owe*, not what you *own*. Most often, liability accounts are used to monitor large loans. In business, you can also use them to keep tabs on liabilities such as payroll taxes that accrue over time.

Liability accounts are most often used to track mortgages. Though this chapter covers the mechanics of using liability accounts to track mortgages, Chapter 14 discusses an overall strategy for mortgage record-keeping.

To see how liability accounts work, let's set up one for a hypothetical mortgage with a current principal balance of $115,000. Monthly payments on the mortgage total $1,046.31. To set up the account, use the same methods you used to create all your accounts (refer to the previous section "Tracking Assets," if you need to review the techniques for setting up an account). In the Select Account Type dialog box choose **Liability Account**, and in the New Account Information dialog box type **Mortgage** for the account name, and enter the amount of the liability—in this case, the principal balance of the mortgage, $115,000—in the *Balance* field. When you complete the dialog box, and then choose the account in the list, you'll see the Liability Account register, as shown in Figure 9.23.

NOTE   Use a Quicken asset account to track the value of your home, including any improvements you make, for tax purposes. See Chapter 14 for details.

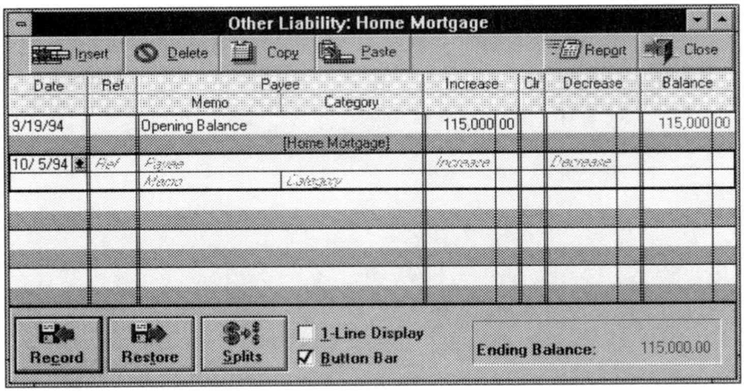

FIGURE 9.23

The register of a liability account.

Notice that the *Increase* and *Decrease* columns are reversed from their order in asset accounts. You'll see why this is so as you enter a sample mortgage payment. Since you'll be using Quicken to write the check for the payment, switch to your checking account by pressing **Ctrl-A** or clicking on the **Accts** icon, selecting the account, and choosing **Use**. Then press **Ctrl-W** to display the Write/Print Checks screen. Enter the following information on the check:

Payee: **Caldwell United**
Amount: **$1,046.31**
Memo: **Mortgage payment**

Since the payment will be divided between interest and principal, you need to split the transaction. Choose **Splits** or press **Ctrl-S** to pop up the Splits dialog box. On the first line, enter **Mortgage:Interest** as the category and **$968.11** as the amount of the payment to be applied to interest. Now you're ready to enter an item covering the mortgage payment—and, in the process, automatically transfer the funds to your mortgage account. With the cursor in the *Category* field on the second line, type a left bracket, [, followed by the first letter or two of your mortgage account's name. When QuickFill completes the entry correctly, press **Tab**. At this point, your screen should resemble the one shown in Figure 9.24.

FIGURE 9.24

Making a mortgage payment.

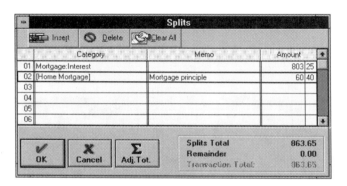

Choose **OK** to leave the Split Transaction dialog box. Record the check, then press **PgUp** to recall it to the screen. Now press **Ctrl-X** to move to the mortgage account. You'll see the transferred transaction selected in the register, as shown in Figure 9.25. Notice that only $78.20, the portion of the payment that pays down the principal balance has been transferred, and that Quicken has adjusted the balance accordingly.

FIGURE 9.25

The portion of the mortgage payment applied to the principal is transferred automatically to the mortgage account.

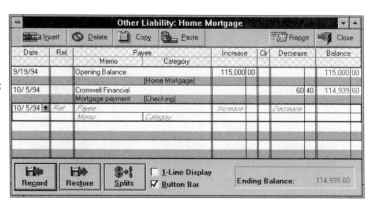

Whether you track your mortgage "manually" with the above technique, or use Quicken's loan amortization feature (described in the next section), you should create a separate liability account for each mortgage (first, second, and third) you have on the property.

Keeping Track of Amortized Loans

NEW IN 3 Quicken's automatic loan setup process is new in version 3. In Quicken 2, you could track amortized loans in ordinary bank accounts, but the process required you to first memorize a Split Mortgage Payment transaction.

Although you can track loan payments yourself in a regular Quicken bank account, why not let Quicken handle it for you? Quicken's automatic amortization capability calculates for you the amount of each payment that goes to interest and the amount that goes to the principal. As a result, you can keep close tabs on the growth of your equity and your tax-deductible interest payments.

Quicken's Amortization feature is highly capable. You can amortize adjustable-rate as well as fixed-rate loans. You can make prepayments whenever you like; Quicken takes them in stride, recalculating the loan amortization instantly. And Quicken can generate a single transaction for each check you write for the loan, even if it includes impound items such as insurance or taxes in addition to the loan interest and principal.

NOTE For simplicity, the instructions given here assume you're the borrower of the loan you're tracking. Quicken 3 can monitor loans you make to others equally well. Once you tell Quicken you have lent, rather than borrowed the money, you use exactly the same steps given here to set up the loan and record payments.

Here's how to set up an amortization schedule to track your loan payments:

Choose **Set Up Loan** from the Activities menu. You'll see the View Loans window, shown in Figure 9.26 on the next page.

The View Loans window gives you access to all the loans you set up in Quicken from the list in the *Loan* field at the top left. At the moment, the field is probably empty, since you haven't yet set up any loans.

FIGURE 9.26

The View Loans window.

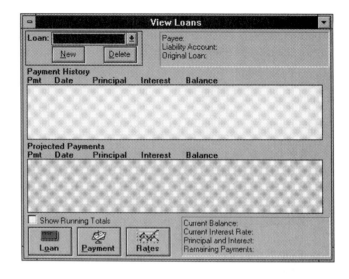

Choose the **New** button just under the *Loan* field. The Set Up Loan Account window appears (Figure 9.27). Since Quicken 3 requires a separate account for each loan, it sets up one for you automatically, using your entries in this window.

FIGURE 9.27

The Set Up Loan Account window.

First, choose the **Borrow Money** radio button if you're taking out a loan such as a mortgage or car loan; in this case, Quicken sets up the loan in a liability account. Choose the **Lend Money** button if you're lending the money to someone else; Quicken starts an asset account for this situation.

Use the lower section of the window to select the account where Quicken will set up the loan. To create a brand-new account, choose **New Account** and type in the account name; to use an account you already have, choose **Existing Account** and pick the account from the drop-down list (the list only shows accounts of the type you're setting up, liability or asset).

When you choose **OK**, the Set Up Loan dialog box appears, as shown in Figure 9.28. The entries you'll make here require some explanation.

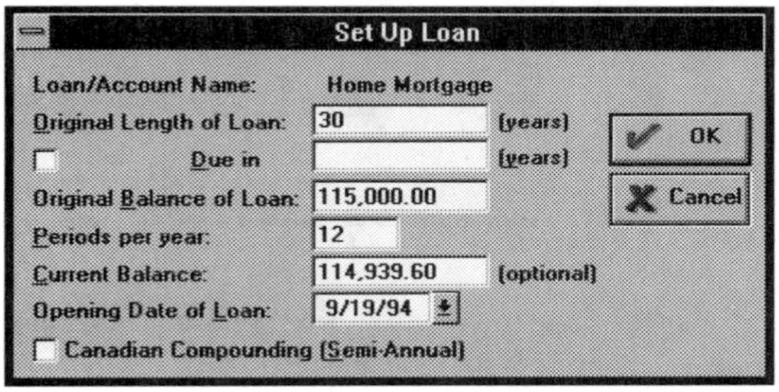

FIGURE 9.28

The Set Up Loan dialog box.

In the top field, type in the amortization period used to calculate your loan payment amount. The instructions say to enter the loan length in years, but this is a bit misleading for loans that are due sooner than the amortization period.

But Quicken does provide for such loans in the next two fields. These days, it's common to have one of those *30/5* loans (meaning the amortization period is 30 years, but the remaining loan balance is due in a balloon payment at the end of 5 years). If that's your situation, check the box below the *Length of Loan* field, then use the field labeled *Due In* to enter the number of years from the time the loan began that the balloon is due.

Enter the original amount of the loan, the number of periods per year (12 if you pay monthly), and the date the loan was issued (even if that was many years ago). The field for the current balance is marked optional, but again, this is misleading. If you're setting up your loan in Quicken any time after the loan was issued, you *must* enter the current loan balance for accurate amortization and payment schedule calculations.

When the Set Up Loan window is complete, OK it to display the Set Up Loan Payment dialog box, shown in Figure 9.29 on the next page. Fill out the top field of this window with the loan's interest rate (use the current rate if you have an adjustable loan).

FIGURE 9.29

*The Set Up
Loan Payment
dialog box.*

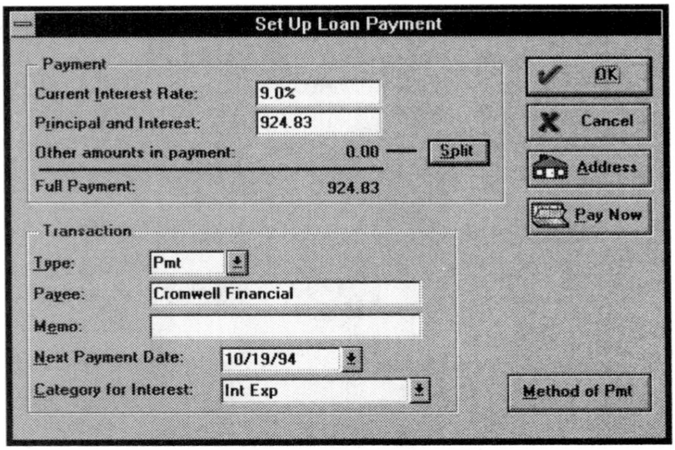

```
┌─────────────────────────────────────────────────────────────┐
│ ─                    Set Up Loan Payment                      │
│ ┌─ Payment ──────────────────────────────┐  ┌─────────────┐  │
│ │ Current Interest Rate:    │9.0%      │  │  ✔   OK      │  │
│ │ Principal and Interest:   │924.83    │  └─────────────┘  │
│ │ Other amounts in payment:      0.00 ── Split             │
│ │                                            ┌─────────────┐│
│ │ Full Payment:                  924.83     │  ✘  Cancel  ││
│ └────────────────────────────────────────┘  └─────────────┘│
│ ┌─ Transaction ──────────────────────────┐  ┌─────────────┐│
│ │ Type:      │Pmt  ±│                       │  🏠 Address  ││
│ │ Payee:     │Cromwell Financial      │   └─────────────┘│
│ │ Memo:      │                        │   ┌─────────────┐ │
│ │ Next Payment Date: │10/19/94  ±│        │ 💳 Pay Now │ │
│ │ Category for Interest: │Int Exp     ±│  │Method of Pmt││
│ └────────────────────────────────────────┘  └─────────────┘│
└─────────────────────────────────────────────────────────────┘
```

Quicken then calculates the total of amount you pay each time for interest and principal (excluding impounds such as taxes and insurance), entering this figure for you in the next field. When Quicken creates a Payment transaction, it will automatically split it and enter the amounts for principal and interest on separate lines.

At any rate, the amount Quicken calculates probably won't match exactly your actual loan amount because of minor discrepancies in amortization methods, but it should be quite close. If the payment your loan company expects differs from Quicken's calculation by a few cents, enter that actual amount here instead. If the difference is larger, you should check your previous entries for accuracy. If there's still a discrepancy, you may want to review the numbers with your loan company.

Suppose you're required to pay impounds every month along with the payment on the loan itself. In that case, choose the **Splits** button. In the standard Splits window, enter the amount of your regular payment that goes for each impound on a separate line. OK the Splits window when you're through. Quicken adds the impound amounts to the *Principal and Interest* field, showing you your total payment.

Now it's on to the Transaction section of the Set Up Loan Payment window. In the *Type* field, select the type of payment you want Quicken to make each time you pay the loan: **Pmt** for a Standard Register transaction,

Chk for a Quicken check, or **Epmt** for a CheckFree electronic payment (CheckFree is covered in Chapter 17).

Enter the payee, the name of the lender, in the next field. If you'll be paying the loan with Quicken checks, choose the **Address** button to enter the payee address as well.

After typing in a memo, if you'd like, enter the date that your next loan payment is due in the next field. At the bottom of the window, select the category to which you'd like to assign the interest portion of your loan payment when Quicken enters the payment in your register. This accounts for all the fields. Your final step is to choose the **Method of Pmt** button. In the dialog box that appears (see Figure 9.30), choose the radio button for the way you'd like Quicken to store your payment information, either as a:

- *Memorized transaction*, so you can recall it whenever you pay it.
- *Scheduled transaction*, so Quicken will automatically enter it for you every month.
- *CheckFree fixed payment*, so CheckFree will pay it for you every month, much like a scheduled payment in Quicken.

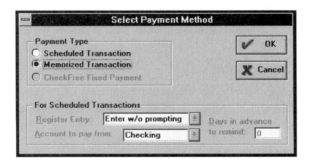

FIGURE 9.30

Choose the type of transaction you want Quicken to record for your loan payment.

If you choose a scheduled transaction, you must also complete the fields at the bottom of the dialog box, just as you would for any other scheduled payment. (See Chapter 7 if you need a refresher on scheduled payments.)

Choose **OK** to return to the Setup Loan Payment window. When you choose **OK** there, you'll be back at the View Loans window, which should look something like Figure 9.31 on the next page.

FIGURE 9.31

The View Loans window after you've set up a loan.

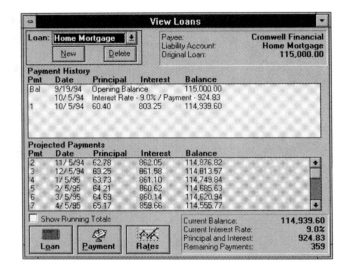

Using the View Loans Window

The upper section of the window lists all the payments you've made on the loan to date. Immediately after you set up a loan, all you'll see are a line for the interest rate and loan payment amount and a line for the current loan balance.

The bottom section of the window contains a schedule of your loan payments. You can scroll through it to see how much of each payment goes to interest and principal. If you check the *Show Running Totals* box below the schedule, Quicken displays cumulative amounts that you've spent for interest and principal.

Changing the Loan Setup

You can edit the loan setup any time you need to with the buttons at the bottom of the window. For example, to change the payee—perhaps your loan has been sold to another financial institution—choose the **Payment** button to display the Setup Loan Payment window again. The only reason to change items such as the loan amount and term is if you made a mistake when you originally entered them—but if so, just choose the **Loan** button to pop up the Set Up Loan window again.

SHORTCUT   If you make a mistake in entering the loan specifications, you should delete the transactions Quicken has already entered in the loan account. Otherwise, Quicken will include them in its amortization and payment schedule calculations, which will give you erroneous results.

But the most common reason to edit the loan details is to change the interest rate on a variable rate loan (you'll learn how to do this in the next section).

Handling Adjustable Loans

The steps for setting up a adjustable-rate loan amortization are the same as those for fixed-rate loans. Whenever the interest rate changes, you simply inform Quicken of the new rate and your amortization schedule is adjusted automatically.

Just be sure that if you're setting up an existing loan—one that you've been already making payments on—you enter the current principal balance in the appropriate field. Quicken amortizes this amount, not the original amount of the loan, over the time remaining on the loan term.

There are two ways to handle a change in the loan's interest rate. To change the interest rate in the Set Up Loan Payment window, choose the **Payment** button in the View Loans window. Alternatively, highlight the loan payment in the Memorized Transaction or Scheduled Transaction list (depending on how you set up the payment) and choose **Edit**. Either way, the window that appears looks just like the one you originally used to set up the loan (see Figure 9.28 on page 281). Type the new interest rate in the first field and choose **OK** to confirm the change.

If you want to avoid the clutter of the Set Up Loan Payment window, you can also make interest rate changes by choosing **Rates** in the View Loans window. A list showing each change in the loan's interest rate appears. To enter a new rate change, choose **New** and type in the rate as well as the date on which the rate took effect.

However you change the interest rate, Quicken calculates a new amortization schedule based on the current principal balance and the number of months left to go on the loan. Repeat these steps each time your lender adjusts the interest rate on your loan.

Handling Loans with Negative Amortization

Because you can set the payment amount independently of the interest rate, Quicken can handle negatively amortizing loans. These are loans whose principal balance can actually grow larger from month to month because the required payment amount is fixed, or cannot rise above a specified cap. Once the interest rate hits a certain value, the payment becomes too small even to cover the monthly interest you owe. When this happens, the unpaid interest gets tacked onto the principal balance.

To account for this unpleasant situation, change the payment amount Quicken calculates in the Set Up Loan Payment window to the amount you actually pay. When you return to the View Loans window, the schedule of payments there indicates that the loan balance increases every month.

With loans of this kind you're either expected to pay an early balloon payment (by refinancing) or to increase the regular payment at some later time to cover the larger amount you owe. In the latter case, when it's time to increase the payment, just change the payment amount in the Set Up Loan Payment or Insert an Interest Rate Change window.

Amortizing Loans on Which You've Already Made Prepayments

If you've made prepayments previously on the loan you want Quicken to amortize, just be sure you enter the current remaining principal balance accurately when you set up the loan.

Handling Extra Prepayments and other Loan Balance Changes

As you'll see in the following section, Quicken's amortizer can account for prepayments on a loan's principal balance that you add to your regular payment. But if you write a separate check for a principal prepayment, you must enter the transaction manually in the *bank* account (not the account for the loan) you used to make the payment. This transaction should be set up as a transfer of funds to the liability account for the loan (enter the loan account's name in brackets in the *Category* field). The amortizer is smart enough to read the new transaction and adjust its amortization schedule accordingly.

Handling Interest-Only Loans

Tracking a loan on which you're only paying interest is simple, since the loan requires no amortization. Each month, you entire payment goes toward interest. You can track this kind of loan in a bank account or a liability account; in either case, assign the entire amount of your payment to your **Interest** category.

Making Payments on an Amortized Loan

Once you've set up an amortized loan, you can record payments in the Quicken loan account in a variety of ways. From the View Loans window, display the loan information, and then choose **Payment** to pop up the Setup Loan Payment dialog box. Choose **Pay Now**.

If you stored the loan payment as a Memorized transaction, you can make the payment by highlighting it in the Memorized Transaction list and choosing **Use**.

For automatic payment, you can assign the loan payment to a transaction group that Quicken will place in your account at regular intervals.

If you set up the payment as a Scheduled transaction, Quicken is already set to record it automatically. Depending on the setting in the set-up window, you'll be asked whether or not to proceed with the automatic entry.

No matter which of these methods you use, the endpoint is the same. Before Quicken actually enters the transaction, you'll be given an opportunity to change the amounts you're paying for interest and principal. If you've included a prepayment of principal with your monthly check, you then enter the extra funds in this window.

When the amounts are to your satisfaction, choose **OK**. Quicken places the transaction in your checking account (where the money for the payment came from) and recalculates the loan balance and schedule according to the new payment plan.

Once the amortized transaction reaches your account, record it. You can then split the transaction by choosing **Splits** or pressing **Ctrl-S**. Verify that Quicken has properly apportioned your payment to principal, interest, and impounds. If you like, switch to the Parallel transaction in the liability account where you track your mortgage balance: with the Split Transaction dialog box open and the cursor on the first line, press **Ctrl-X**.

Using the Loan and Refinance Calculators

Quicken offers two special-purpose calculators to help you make informed decisions about borrowing money. The Loan calculator tells you how much your monthly payments will be based on the loan amount and the interest rate; if you already know your monthly payment, the calculator can figure what the original loan balance was. The Refinance calculator helps you decide whether you should refinance and existing mortgage. It compares the savings in your monthly payment to the cost of the new loan, calculation how soon you'll break even.

To call up either Loan calculator—or any of the other specialized Quicken calculators—start by choosing **Financial Planners** from the Activities menu. This brings up a Subsidiary menu listing the special calculators. Here, choose **Loan** or **Refinance** to see the desired calculator.

Using the Loan Calculator

Shown in Figure 9.32, the Loan calculator is self-explanatory. First, tell the calculator whether you'd like to calculate the amount of each payment or the loan principal using the radio buttons at the bottom left. You can't change the value in the field Quicken calculates.

FIGURE 9.32

The Loan calculator.

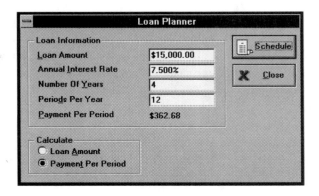

NOTE	To get a very close approximation of the payment on an *interest-only* loan (one on which you only make interest payments until the balance comes due), set the loan term to **100 years** or longer. You can calculate the actual amount with the regular calculator, but using the Loan calculator is easier, and the payment it calculates is off by only about 50 cents on a $250,000 loan.

Next, just fill in the loan details: the interest rate, the loan term in years, and the number of payments you'll be making per year. If you're calculating the monthly payment amount, type in the total loan amount in the *Loan Amount* field. On the other hand, if you're calculating the principal amount, type your payment amount in the *Payment per Period* field. The Loan calculator recalculates the result each time you move from one field to the next.

Using the Refinance Calculator

NEW IN 3   Quicken's Refinance calculator, new in version 3, will tell you when it makes sense to refinance your mortgage or when your existing loan is really the better deal. Even if you can get a significantly lower interest rate by refinancing, a new loan may cost more—in fees, points, and appraisal charges—than the realized interest savings.

Which of the two options is better depends partly on how much lower the new loan's interest rate is and how much the loan will cost. However, your final decision also turns heavily on how long you plan to keep the property. The new loan's costs amount to a one-time charge, but with each payment you'll save an additional amount of interest. Sooner or later you'll reach a break-even point, the point when your interest savings equal the original cost of the loan.

The Refinance calculator figures out this critical break-even point for you. Just plug in the details of the two loans, the existing mortgage and the refinance, and let Quicken tell you how many monthly payments it will take to break even. If you plan to keep the property longer than that, the refinance looks like a winner.

Using the refinance calculator is simple. Display it by choosing **Financial Planners** followed by **Refinance** from the Activities menu. (See Figure 9.33 on the next page.)

FIGURE 9.33

The refinance calculator.

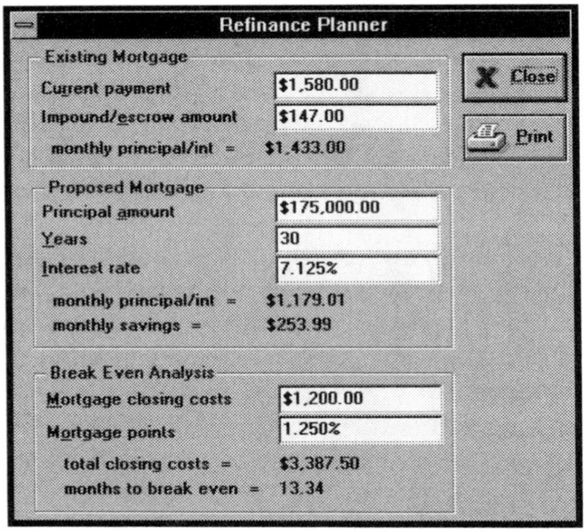

```
┌─────────────────────────────────────────────────┐
│ ═                 Refinance Planner                │
│  ┌─ Existing Mortgage ──────────────┐  ┌────────┐ │
│  │ Current payment    [$1,580.00  ] │  │ X Close│ │
│  │ Impound/escrow amount [$147.00 ] │  └────────┘ │
│  │   monthly principal/int = $1,433.00 │ ┌───────┐ │
│  └──────────────────────────────────┘  │ 🖨 Print│ │
│  ┌─ Proposed Mortgage ──────────────┐  └────────┘ │
│  │ Principal amount   [$175,000.00] │             │
│  │ Years              [30         ] │             │
│  │ Interest rate      [7.125%     ] │             │
│  │   monthly principal/int = $1,179.01 │           │
│  │   monthly savings    = $253.99   │             │
│  └──────────────────────────────────┘             │
│  ┌─ Break Even Analysis ────────────┐             │
│  │ Mortgage closing costs [$1,200.00] │           │
│  │ Mortgage points        [1.250%  ] │            │
│  │   total closing costs  = $3,387.50 │           │
│  │   months to break even = 13.34    │            │
│  └──────────────────────────────────┘             │
└─────────────────────────────────────────────────┘
```

The top section of the calculator is for details on your current loan. In the first field, type in the total amount of each payment you make (the dollar figure on the check you write). In the next field, enter the portion of the payment that goes for fees, taxes, insurance, and other impounds. Quicken calculates the amount you actually pay toward the loan (principal and interest) in the *Monthly Principal/Int* field.

The next section is for the refinance you're considering. In the first three fields, type the amount you'll be refinancing, the new loan's interest rate, and the number of years it will run. Quicken figures the monthly payment you'll be making and how much it saves you compared to your current payment in the next two fields.

The calculator's final section, Break Even Analysis, determines when the new mortgage actually starts saving you money. Type in the total of all the miscellaneous fees you'll pay to get the loan in the *Mortgage Closing Costs* field; enter the points you'll be charged in the *Mortgage Points* field (as a percentage such as 1.5, not as a dollar amount). When you press **Tab**, Quicken calculates the total cost of the loan and displays the bottom line result: how many months it will take you to break even.

Summary

With the experience you've gained in using all the different types of Quicken accounts, you now know how to keep detailed records of every facet of your financial situation. In this chapter, you've learned how to set up accounts for investments, other assets such as your home and your collectibles, and liabilities such as your mortgage.

In Chapters 10 through 12, you'll learn how to put together the "raw" records in all your accounts into clearly organized, informative reports and graphs that spotlight the specific trends you want to monitor. Then, in Chapters 13 through 16, you'll learn how to bring all of your Quicken skills to bear in meeting the demands of common financial management situations.

Chapter Ten
Fast Financial Reports

 o matter how accurate and detailed your financial records, they're not going to be very useful in managing and planning your finances until you organize them into an easily understandable form. Specifically, you need a way to collect all the different kinds of records into reports that highlight trends in income and expenses and summarize what you need to know.

Quicken comes complete with a reporting system that makes it even easier for you to generate useful reports than to enter transactions in the first place. The program provides about 20 predefined report setups that cover the most common reporting needs in personal and business finance. All you need to do is select which of these "standard" reports you want to use and tell Quicken the dates you want it to cover. Quicken does the rest for you, producing a clearly laid out report that you can view on the screen or print on paper. You'll learn to use these built-in report setups in this chapter.

If none of the standard report setups suits your needs, you can modify them accordingly. In fact, you can design new report setups from the ground up if you'd prefer. Customizing reports is the subject of Chapter 11. In Chapters 13 through 16, you'll learn when and how to use all your reporting skills to solve many specific challenges in personal and small business finance.

Types of Built-In Reports

Quicken's report setups are listed on the **Reports** menu. The preset reports are divided into three groups, for home, business, and investment uses (in Quicken 2, the first group is referred to as "personal" rather than "home" reports).

The Home Reports menu offers the following options:

- **Cash Flow** helps you make reports that show total income and spending for each category over the period of time you want the report to cover. Cash Flow reports summarize the transactions from all bank, cash, and credit card accounts in the account group that you're currently using.

- **Monthly Budget** helps you compare the amount you've received or spent in each category with the amount you've budgeted on a month-by-month basis. As with Cash Flow reports, all bank, cash, and credit card accounts are included in monthly budget reports.

- **Itemized Categories** is the option to choose for reports that list all the transactions from all your accounts individually, but group and subtotal them according to category.

- **Tax Summary** is the setup for reports that show the same kind of transaction-level detail as the itemized categories reports, but only for transactions assigned to tax-related categories.

- **Net Worth Report** calculates your net worth by presenting the balances from all your accounts on a given date.

- **Tax Schedule Report** lists only the transactions you've assigned to categories associated with specific tax schedule line items, grouping the transactions by item within each schedule.

- **Missing Checks** lists all the checks recorded in your account in order, indicating where breaks in the check number sequence have occurred.

- **Comparison** gives you a category-by-category comparison of your income and spending this year versus last.

The options on the Business Reports menu include the following:

- **P & L Statement** is for profit and loss statements that summarize income and expenses category by category for all the accounts in the current account group.

- **Cash Flow** creates reports that are identical to personal cash flow reports, showing total income and spending for each category over the time period you select.

- **A/P by Vendor** is for *Accounts Payable* reports that present the total amount of all the unprinted checks you've written to each payee in your bank accounts. See Chapter 13 for instructions on how to use Quicken for accounts payable.

- **A/R by Customer** is for *Accounts Receivable* reports that list unpaid balances owed to you as shown in your "other asset" accounts, which is where you should keep such records. Again, Chapter 13 gives details on using Quicken for accounts receivable.

- **Job/Project Report** shows your income and expenses by category (in rows) and class (in columns).

- **Payroll Report,** as its name implies, reports on your payments to your employees and other payroll-related transactions. A Quicken Payroll report has sections totalling the income, expense, and transfer transactions for each payee. However, only transactions assigned to a category beginning with the word *Payroll* are included in the totals.

- **Balance Sheet** reports list the balances from all your accounts on a given date, and calculate your business's overall net worth.

- **Missing Checks** and **Comparison** reports provide the same information for business accounts as they do for personal ones.

Finally, here are the options on Quicken's Investment Reports menu:

- **Portfolio Value** generates information about individual investment holdings on a given date, including the number of shares you own, the most current price per share, their cost basis, your "paper" gain or loss, and the market value of the holding.

- **Investment Performance** reports on the annual return from your investments, taking into account income such as dividends and interest, as well as changes in market value.

- **Capital Gains** summarizes the actual gain or loss of investments that you purchased and sold.

- **Investment Income** summarizes the income your investments have generated from all sources, including dividends, interest, realized gains or losses, capital gains distributions, and if you'd like, the unrealized "paper" gain or loss due to changes in market price of investments you still own.

- **Investment Transactions** lists the transactions in your investment account, showing their impact on your cash balance and the value of your holdings.

| NOTE | The **Other** item on Quicken 3's **Reports** menu lists the generic report types you can use for customizing, as described in Chapter 11. In Quicken 2, these report types are listed under the item labelled **Custom**. |

Practicing with Quicken Reports

By this time, you've been using Quicken long enough to have entered many transactions into one or more accounts. You've probably experimented extensively with entering self-created transactions, and you may well have begun using Quicken for your actual financial records. In this chapter and in Chapter 11, you'll simply use these accumulated transactions as the raw data for your practice reports. The figures and labels that appear in your practice reports may vary from those shown in the examples, but the illustrations will give you a good idea of what you can expect to see. And you won't have to type in numerous practice transactions to see how the reports work.

Preparing a Cash Flow Report

Let's say you've just looked at your checking account balance and once again found less money remaining than you'd hoped. You decide that it's finally time to draw up that budget you've been meaning to create. Of course, to build a realistic budget, you'll need a good idea of the source of your money, and where it is being spent. In other words, you want a report of your cash flow. As you now know, the Cash Flow report is one of Quicken's built-in report formats. All you have to do is enter the months you want included in the report, and the program does the rest for you.

Figure 10.1 shows an example of how one of Quicken's cash flow reports looks when you "print" it on the screen. The report you're about to create will look similar, but the sample report is simplified so the entire report will fit on one page. As you can see, the report is laid out with the cash-flow figures for each category in a separate row. Income items, or *inflows*, are listed at the top of each report; then come expenditures, or *outflows*. There's a total for each section.

A Cash Flow report lumps the figures for the entire period covered by the report in a single column. If any transactions covered by the report are assigned to subcategories, this column will be quite wide, since Quicken aligns the subcategory amounts to the left of the amounts for the overall categories. This is illustrated in the sample report in Figure 10.1. At the bottom of the report column, Quicken subtracts your expenses from your income to give you a total. If you spent more than you earned, the total will be printed with a minus sign.

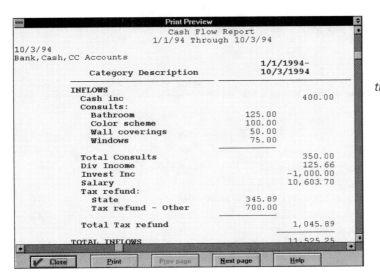

FIGURE 10.1

A sample Cash Flow report that is "printed" on the screen, which will look even sharper when you actually print it out.

Starting the Report

You can find all of Quicken's reporting functions on the Reports menu. To start the sample Cash Flow report, choose **Home** and **Cash Flow** from the Reports menu. Quicken pops up the Create Report window, shown in Figure 10.2.

NOTE

Quicken 2 has different windows for the fields you must fill out to create and customize a report, but the fields themselves are essentially the same.

FIGURE 10.2

The Create Report window.

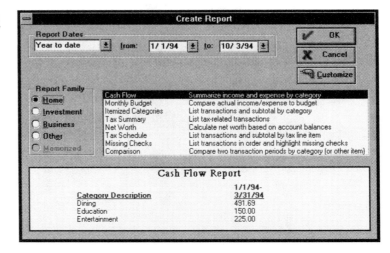

The Create Report window gives you access to all the Quicken reports—no matter which type of report you choose from the Reports menu, you can select any report type Quicken offers. At the left, the selected radio button indicates which general category of reports you're working with; to switch categories, just choose a different radio button. By the way, the radio button labelled **Memorized Reports** lets you reuse customized reports you've designed; you'll learn how to memorize reports in Chapter 11.

The middle of the window lists the individual report types in the group you've selected. You can pick an individual report type from the list whenever you like. If you try it, notice that the sample report excerpt at the bottom of the window changes to match. For some reports, the *Date* fields at the top of the window change as well.

To create the Cash Flow report, choose the range of months that will be covered by the report. The report will show each month in a separate column. There are three *Date* fields at the top of the window. The first lets you pick a range of months for the report by a description, such as **Current Year** or **Include all dates**. If none of the standard date ranges fit, you can enter any dates you like in the from and to fields (when you change either of these fields, the entry in the *Report Dates* field changes to **Custom Date**.

When you OK the box, Quicken sorts through the transactions in your file, producing an on-screen report like the one in Figure 10.3.

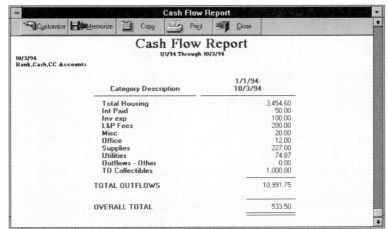

FIGURE 10.3

The Cash Flow report as it looks on your screen before being printed.

Viewing the Report

As you can see, the Cash Flow report you've just produced is set up just like the sample printed report you saw earlier in Figure 10.1. Unlike Figure 10.1, however, this version of the report doesn't show the fonts and spacing that you would get on paper. You see this window before printing the report (even to the screen).

Depending on the size and resolution of your screen and the number of categories in your accounts, the entire report probably won't fit in its window. It's easy, though, to see any part of the report: just use the scroll bars or the cursor keys. **Down Arrow** moves to the next line down on the report, **Up Arrow** moves back up a line, **PgUp** and **PgDn** display a new group of lines at a time. To move the display to the top-left corner of the report, press **Home**; to move to the bottom-right corner, press **End**. In wide reports, you can shift left or right by a window-ful of information by pressing **Ctrl-Left Arrow** or **Ctrl-Right Arrow**. Spend a few moments scrolling through the report until you've seen the whole thing.

Using the Report Screen Button Bar

NOTE | The button bar for reports in Quicken 2 has more buttons, corresponding to the additional dialog boxes for customizing Quicken reports. Still, all the fields you eventually fill out to customize a report are essentially the same.

Notice that there's a button bar at the top of the report screen. As with most Quicken buttons, you can activate them either with the mouse or the keyboard by clicking on the button or pressing **Alt** along with the key for the underlined letter.

You'll learn how to use the Customize and Memorize buttons in Chapter 11. In this chapter, you'll work with the three buttons on the right:

1. **Copy**, for copying report information to the clipboard, and then to other Windows programs.
2. **Print**, for printing the report (of course).
3. **Close**, for closing the report window.

Using QuickZoom to See Transaction Detail

Before you print the report or close the window, try out QuickZoom, Quicken's way of letting you examine the details that make up the report numbers. Say you notice that the total for the **Gasoline** category is unexpectedly high. To find the responsible transactions, use QuickZoom.

NOTE | QuickZoom only works in noninvestment reports, and then only in Summary, Budget, and Transaction reports. In transaction reports QuickZoom works a bit differently from the way it's described here—again, you'll find details in Chapter 10. (Don't worry, you don't have to memorize what these categories of reports mean. If QuickZoom is available, you'll know, because the Magnifying Glass mouse pointer appears).

- With the mouse, point to the dollar amount for the category. The pointer becomes a magnifying glass with a Z in the center, then double-click.
- With the keyboard, move the rectangular outline over the dollar amount for the category and press **Enter**.

Either way, you'll now see a QuickZoom report, a list of all the transactions that figure in the total for the **Gasoline** category shown in the report (Figure 10.4). You can scroll the new report just as you did the Cash Flow report if there are too many transactions to fit in the window.

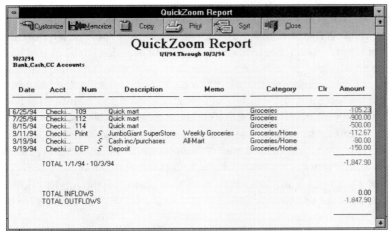

FIGURE 10.4

The QuickZoom report.

NOTE

The QuickZoom report is a just another Quicken report (a customized Transaction report, to be exact). Like any other report, it has the Report button bar and can be further customized or memorized for automatic recall. See Chapter 11 for details on customizing and memorizing reports.

If you identify a transaction that seems incorrect, or about which you want more detail, you can use QuickZoom on the new QuickZoom report. When you choose a specific transaction, Quicken moves you directly to the register where that transaction is recorded. Quicken selects the transaction, or, if it's a split transaction, displays the Split Transaction dialog box—either way, you're instantly ready to edit the transaction. Once you're back at the register, you're free to make changes in the "zoomed" transaction.

NOTE

By the way, Quicken immediately updates any open reports when you make changes in your accounts. In this case, for example, the QuickZoom and Cash Flow reports will automatically reflect any revisions you record to the zoomed transaction. Of course, you won't see those changes until you activate the report window so you can see it again. Read on.

Working with Report Windows

At this point, you should have two reports on your screen: the original Cash Flow report and the QuickZoom report Quicken created for you. Now is a good time to try manipulating report windows.

Once you've created a report, it functions as a Quicken window much like the Register or Write Checks windows. You can move to or from a report and any other window with the standard methods (by pressing **Ctrl-Tab**, clicking on another window, or choosing the window you want from the Window menu). You can minimize the report to an icon by clicking the Minimize button at the top right of the Report window. To restore a Minimized report, double-click on its icon. (You can't maximize Report windows, however.)

Again, when you edit or add any transactions in the Register or Write Checks window while one or more Report windows are open, Quicken updates all the reports automatically to reflect the new data.

To close a Report window, choose the **Close** button on the report's button bar, or just press **Esc** when the window is active. But don't do that yet for the sample Cash Flow report.

Printing Reports

Now that you've looked over your report on the screen, it's time to print it out for more careful study and for your records. But before you actually make that paper copy, you'll need to set up your printer for reports.

Setting Up the Report Printer

In Chapter 3, you learned the basics of how to set up printers in Quicken. Go back and reread the first part of that chapter for a refresher.

To set up your printer for reports, choose **Printer Setup** and **Report/Graphs Printing Setup** in the File menu to display the dialog box shown in Figure 10.5. Choose the particular machine you want to use for printing reports (if you have more than one printer) and if necessary, change the Paper Feed setting (see Chapter 3).

The Report Printer Setup window has several fields that weren't present on the the window for setting up to print checks:

- The checkbox in the middle of the window lets you tell Quicken whether to print your reports in "color," if you have a color printer. (Actually, checking this box simply prints negative dollar amounts in red—the rest of the report still comes out in basic black.)
- Four fields let you set the margins for each page of your report.

More Setup Choices

When planning your printed report, you have to keep in mind the fact that many reports are either too long, too wide, or both, to fit on a single sheet of paper, at least with the standard printer settings.

Of course, Quicken will automatically split the report across as many sheets of paper as are needed to print the entire report—you'll be able to view wide reports by placing the printed sheets for each report "page" side by side. Still, you can use two strategies for fitting more information on each page.

If the report is wide, and assuming your printer permits, you can choose to print the report sideways, in a *landscape* orientation. In Landscape mode, the long edges of the paper become the top and bottom of the report.

To switch your printer into Landscape mode, choose the **Settings** button. In the next dialog box that appears, select the choice labelled **Landscape** or **Sideways** (usually it's a radio button). If you don't find this choice in the first Printer Settings dialog box, navigate through the other available dialog boxes for your printer using the buttons labelled **Options**, **More**, or the like, until you do find the **Landscape** setting. After selecting **Landscape**, choose **OK** (more than once, if necessary) until you return to Quicken's Report and Graph Printer Setup dialog box.

| WARNING |

When you use Quicken to set your printer to Landscape mode, <u>all</u> your Windows programs will print sideways until you reset the printer to the normal Portrait mode (except those programs that override the Windows control panel setting). You return the printer to Portrait mode via the same Printer Setup dialog box you used to select Landscape mode. You can access this window from Quicken as just described, via the Windows Control Panel, or using another program's **Print Setup** command; by the way, setting your printer to Landscape mode has no effect on check printing in Quicken.

Another way to get more information on each page is to select a smaller font for printing the report. In addition, of course, you'll want to select fonts that make your reports look good. Quicken lets you select two different fonts for report printing: one for the title, and one for the remainder of the report.

To pick a new font for either of these uses, choose the corresponding button, **Head Font** or **Body Font**. You select the specific font and size you want just as you did when setting up for printing checks in Chapter 3. You can only select the customary (nonbold, nonitalicized) style. However, Quicken automatically prints row and column labels in bold type using the font you've chosen for the report body.

Printing the Cash Flow Report

To print the Cash Flow report, be sure its window is active, and then choose the **Print** button or press **Ctrl-P**. Then the Print Report dialog box appears.

The *Print to* field at the top of the dialog box should be set to **Printer**, the first and obvious choice. But if you have Quicken 3, you can preview the report on your screen before printing it, to make sure your font and margin choices will give the results you expect. Choose the radio button labelled **Screen**.

| NOTE | The other choices are discussed in the appendix, in the section "Transferring Data to Word Processors, Spreadsheets, and Databases." |

Since you can print on paper from the preview window, go ahead and complete the rest of the box now (there's not much to it anyway). For top-quality printouts, check the boxes **Print in Color** and **Print in Draft Mode**; for quicker paper reports, uncheck either or both boxes.

| NOTE | In Quicken 2, the Print Report dialog box has a checkbox at the bottom labelled **Use Graphic Line Drawing**. When this box is checked, Quicken draws solid lines on reports rather than "faking" them with dashes and equals signs for a sharper-looking report. |

Choose **OK** to start the printout. After a pause for Quicken's calculations, the Preview report appears in its own window, looking much like the one back in Figure 10.1 on page 297. You can maximize this window so it fills the whole screen. Flip from one page of the report to the next with the **Next Page** and **Prev Page** buttons; use the scroll bars to see other parts of the current page.

When you're satisfied with the report's appearance, make sure your printer is on and ready to go, then choose **Print** to go ahead and make a paper copy. The screen version of the report closes automatically (of course, the **Close** button closes the screen report without printing it).

Now you can close the Cash Flow Report window on your screen by pressing **Esc** or choosing the **Close** button.

Using Other Built-In Reports

All of Quicken's standard reports are just as easy to prepare as the Cash Flow report. All you do is select the report type from the Reports menu (or from the Create Report window), tell Quicken which dates you want covered, and choose **OK**. When the Report window appears, you can scroll around in the report, use **QuickZoom** to get more information on specific sections or individual transactions, and print out the report on your screen or on paper.

If the report doesn't give you quite the right perspective on the information in your account, you can customize the report and then memorize your custom settings for future use (see Chapter 11).

| WARNING | Most of the built-in reports are set up to report on only one account, the last one you used before creating the report. If you have Register or Check windows open from more than one account, switch to the correct account before opening the Create Report window. If you don't get the results you're expecting, check the note at the upper left of the report listing the accounts covered in the report—it may be you've reported on the wrong account. |

Preparing a Budget Report

A vital part of financial management is preparing and sticking to a budget. Disciplined financial management involves comparing the amounts you've budgeted with what you've actually taken in and paid out. For this, you need more than a summary of your income and expenses; you need a budget report, one of Quicken's built-in report formats, which you can get by choosing **Home** and **Budget** from the Reports menu.

But before you can prepare a Budget report, you first have to enter your budget into Quicken. Since the process of budgeting and financial planning is an important one, Budgeting and Budget reports are covered separately in Chapter 13.

Itemizing Your Transactions by Category

When the Cash Flow report doesn't supply enough detail about your income and spending patterns, you can turn to a third report format built into Quicken, the *Itemized Category report*. This report displays or prints all the transactions in your account register sorted by category; within each category, the transactions are further sorted by date. Unlike Cash Flow reports, Itemized Category reports also include transactions from any other asset and liability accounts in the current account group.

NOTE	The Itemized Transaction report is an example of Quicken's Transaction reports. Quicken provides some special features for Transaction reports, as detailed in Chapter 11.

Figure 10.5 shows an example of an Itemized Category report prepared by Quicken. The report gives you overall totals for income and expenses, as well as subtotals within each of the categories, just as the Cash Flow report does. But it also has a separate line for every individual transaction recorded for the period of the report. However, you don't get the monthly breakdown by columns of the activities in each category that you do in a Cash Flow report.

FIGURE 10.5

An Itemized Category report.

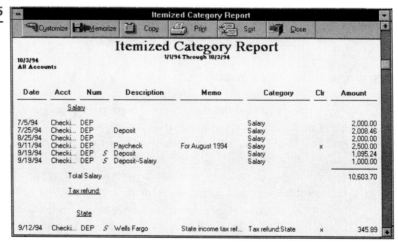

Date	Acct	Num	Description	Memo	Category	Clr	Amount
		Salary					
7/5/94	Checki...	DEP			Salary		2,000.00
7/25/94	Checki...	DEP	Deposit		Salary		2,008.46
8/25/94	Checki...	DEP			Salary		2,000.00
9/11/94	Checki...	DEP	Paycheck	For August 1994	Salary	x	2,500.00
9/19/94	Checki...	DEP	S Deposit		Salary		1,095.24
9/19/94	Checki...	DEP	S Deposit--Salary		Salary		1,000.00
		Total Salary					10,603.70
		Tax refund:					
		State					
9/12/94	Checki...	DEP	S Wells Fargo	State income tax ref...	Tax refund:State	x	345.89

Itemized Category Report
1/1/94 Through 10/3/94
10/3/94
All Accounts

To prepare an Itemized Category report, you'll follow essentially the same steps you used to produce the Cash Flow report. Choose **Home** and **Itemized** Categories from the Reports menu. In the window, enter a custom title for the report if you'd like, then enter the months you'd like to include in the report. Then choose **OK** to begin the report.

Preparing a Tax Summary Report

With income taxes levied by the federal and state governments consuming a third or more of most people's gross income, you're certainly not alone if you feel the need for a tax-reducing financial strategy. Quicken's *Tax Summary report* will lighten the burden of combing your records for tax-related income and expenses.

A Tax Summary report is simply an Itemized Category report that includes only transactions from tax-related categories. Otherwise, it's identical in every way to an ordinary Itemized Category report. Just as in an Itemized Category report, the Tax Summary report combines transactions from all the accounts in your current account group.

Let's take a look at the Tax Summary report shown in Figure 10.6. It's quite similar to the Itemized Category report in Figure 10.5. The only difference, in fact, is that most of the expense transactions are missing from the Tax Summary report, since expenses for your personal transportation and entertainment can't be deducted.

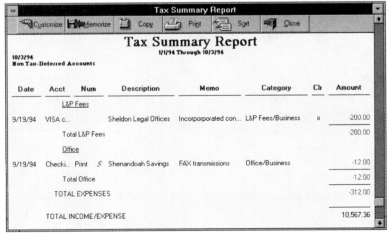

FIGURE 10.6

A sample Tax Summary report.

Preparing a Tax Summary report requires exactly the same steps as producing an Itemized Category report, except that you should choose the **Tax Summary** option on the Home Reports menu.

Preparing a Net Worth Report

If you're working with more than one Quicken account, there'll be times when you want nothing more than an overall summary of all the assets and liabilities recorded in all your accounts. To get up-to-date information on the balance in each account, and on your total assets and liabilities, use the *Net Worth report*.

As you can see from the sample in Figure 10.7, a Net Worth report is a model of simplicity, ignoring the trees (the individual transactions) so that you can clearly see the forest (your overall account balances). Unless you have an unusually large number of accounts, the entire report will fit onto a single printed page. To create an Net Worth report, choose **Home** and **Net Worth** from the Reports menu. Title the report if you like, then enter the date for which you want Quicken to calculate your balances. Quicken should have filled in today's date for you, so if you just want to know what your balances are today, leave it unchanged. Choose **OK** to create the report.

FIGURE 10.7

A sample net worth report.

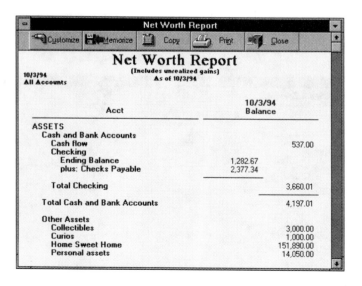

Preparing a Tax Schedule Report

The Tax Summary report described earlier gives you an idea of how your tax-related income and expenses are shaping up, but for details at tax time, you need the Tax Schedule report. Instead of listing your transactions by descriptive category, it groups them by IRS tax form, breaking them down further within each form according to individual line items on the form. You can transfer the summary totals for each line item to the corresponding field on your tax form by hand, or save the report in a disk file to transfer the data to tax preparation software.

To prepare the report, choose **Home** and **Tax Schedule** from the Reports menu. Type in the time period you want the report to cover and choose **OK** to display the report.

Preparing a Missing Checks Report

Quicken can show you any gaps in the sequence of checks you've written with a *Missing Checks report*. This report is especially useful when you use Quicken to record handwritten checks. To be sure you've actually entered all your checks, run a Missing Checks report by choosing **Home** and **Missing Checks** from the Reports menu. Or, if your bank statement shows "missing" checks, you can see whether or not you actually wrote checks with those numbers with this report.

Enter the dates you want covered in the report and choose **OK**. If the check number in question is listed as missing in the report, you haven't recorded a check with that number.

Preparing a Comparison Report

Quicken's built-in *Comparison report* format compares the activity in your account in each category for two time periods. When you choose **Home** and **Comparison** from the Reports menu, the Create Report window offers two sets of date fields, so you can decide exactly which two periods to compare. The resulting report lists the total amount of income or spending in each category in side-by-side columns, one for each of the time periods.

Using the Built-In Business Report Formats

If you run a small business, Quicken's built-in report formats should give you most of the day-to-day and month-to-month financial information that a hands-on owner or manager needs in order to make sensible business decisions. Quicken won't replace the services of a well-trained bookkeeper or an accountant (for a discussion of this point, see the first section of Chapter 15). But the knowledge you acquire from having your own business reports should make your accountant's reports and advice much more meaningful.

In any case, by working through the practice personal reports earlier in this chapter, you've already learned how to generate the built-in business reports. As you'd expect, all the business-related reports are on their own cascading menu. After you choose the report format you'd like, a window will pop up so that you can enter the report's title, and in some cases, select the dates it will cover. When you then choose **OK**, Quicken displays the report.

NOTE

Quicken's standard business reports have nothing to do with the sample class called **Business** you set up back in Chapter 2. The standard business reports assume that you've devoted your entire file to business-related transactions. Thus, these reports work on all the transactions in your file, regardless of the class assignment. The point of the sample **Business** class is to separate business from personal transactions when both are recorded in the same file. As described in Chapter 11, you can use custom reports to cull out transactions assigned to the **Business** class.

Let's take a few moments, then, to go over each of the available business report types just to get a feel for what each one does. You'll learn in Chapters 15 and 16 how to put these reports to work in practical business situations.

Preparing a Profit and Loss Statement

Quicken's profit and loss statement, called *P & L Statement* on the Business Reports menu, simply shows your income and expenses by category for the period you specify when you set up the report. This is very similar to what you get with a Cash Flow report, but there are a few differences. The most important contrast is that the profit and loss statement covers all your accounts, while the Cash Flow report is limited to your bank, credit card, and cash accounts. Therefore, when you're using "other asset" and "other liability" accounts to keep track of your payroll taxes, accounts receivable, capital equipment, and other noncash assets and liabilities, you'll choose **P & L Statement** if you want a summary of your overall income and expenses. If, on the other hand, you only want to see the inflow and outgo of spendable funds, you'll choose **Cash Flow**.

Preparing a Business Cash Flow Account

Knowing where your money is coming from and where it's going is important in managing your personal finances, but it's even more critical when you're trying to keep a small business running. Cash Flow reports are thus a staple of business accounting and, as you've already learned, Quicken makes them easy to prepare. In fact, there's no difference whatsoever between Quicken's personal and business Cash Flow reports. The Cash Flow reports you generate from either the Personal or Business Report menus will be identical, provided you base the reports on the same accounts. The way to produce a business-oriented Cash Flow report, then, is to set up your Quicken accounts to record business-related transactions.

Preparing an Accounts Payable Report

An Accounts Payable report—**A/P by Vendor** on the Business Reports menu—is simply your business's current liabilities for goods and services. Of course, Quicken doesn't know what your bills themselves are, but it can read your Checking Account register to find the checks you've written but not yet printed. This is the basis of Quicken's built-in Accounts Payable report. The report lists the total amount of all the unprinted checks you've written to each payee, or vendor, and then sums up the total of all your unprinted checks to give you a grand total for your accounts payable.

Of course, this report will normally only cover the checks you enter into your account from the Write Checks window, because Quicken doesn't ordinarily keep track of whether your handwritten checks have been sent yet or not. However, if you don't use Quicken to print your checks, you can still produce Accounts Payable reports by entering the amounts of your bills as check transactions in the register. The trick is to fill the *NUM* column with asterisks when you enter these transactions, since that's the notation Quicken uses to indicate unprinted checks. Your Accounts Payable report will now show the unpaid bills as you'd expect. Then, when you write and send the checks in, enter the check numbers in the *Num* field to indicate the transactions have been paid.

When you create a Quicken Accounts Payable report, you don't need to fill in a date range. That makes sense, since you're asking Quicken to find all your current accounts payable. Quicken will automatically read the dates on the unprinted checks and create a column for each month between the first and last dates the checks cover.

Preparing Accounts Receivable Reports

Accounts receivable are the amounts owed to you by your customers. A Quicken Accounts Receivable report—*A/R by Customer* on the Business Reports menu—lists the balances owed you as recorded in your "other assets" accounts, which is where you should record your accounts receivable. The report shows the amount of debt each customer has incurred each month, and then presents an overall total for the customer and a grand total of all your accounts receivable.

As with accounts payable, you don't need to specify a date when setting up a Quicken Accounts Receivable report. Quicken creates a column for each month covered by the transactions listed in your other asset account or accounts. Since you may well have additional other asset accounts besides the one in which you record your accounts receivable, you can customize the report to include the particular account on which you want to base the report. You'll find customization details in Chapter 11, including instructions for defining which accounts to include in a report.

Preparing Job/Project Reports

Reports produced by the **Job/Project** option summarize your income and expenses by transaction category, subtotalling the amounts in each category according to class. Figure 10.8 shows how such a report might look if you were a building contractor working on two or more construction projects at the same time. In that case, you'd have similar kinds of expenses at each site for lumber, hardware, and so on. To keep your spending for each project separate, you would create a class for each project. Then, to quickly produce a report that breaks down your total spending for lumber, hardware, and all the rest into the amounts you've spent on these items at each site, you'd simply choose **Job/Project Report** on the cascading Business Reports menu.

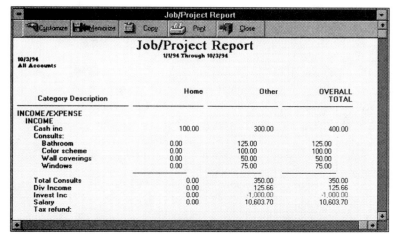

FIGURE 10.8

A sample Job/Project report.

Preparing Payroll Reports

Quicken creates Payroll reports by extracting all transactions assigned to any category that begins with the word *Payroll* from all of your accounts and totalling them in rows for each payee. In the columns, the payee totals are broken down into subtotals by category. As you'll see in Chapter 16, a payroll report usually lists employee names and the agencies to which you pay payroll taxes in the rows, with the different types of payroll payments (for wages, social security taxes, and so on) in the columns.

Preparing Balance Sheets

Except for the name, the **Balance Sheet** option on the Business Reports menu is identical to the **Net Worth** option on the Personal Reports menu. Either lists the balances from each of your accounts on a given date and will generate a report that combines the balances from the accounts to come up with a figure for your business's "owner's equity" (equivalent in concept to personal net worth).

Preparing Missing Checks and Comparison Reports

The Missing Checks and Comparison reports on the Business submenu work exactly like their counterparts among the Home reports, described earlier in this chapter.

Using Quicken's Built-In Investment Report Formats

Quicken includes five built-in report formats that should satisfy most investors' need to know about the health of their holdings in stocks, bonds, mutual funds, and so on. These investment reports work just like the personal and business reports you've already experimented with earlier in this chapter.

To begin the report, choose **Investment** from the File menu, and then choose the specific built-in investment report format you want. Fill out Create Report window with the dates that will be covered, and then choose **OK** to generate the report.

Preparing a Portfolio Value Report

The *Portfolio Value report* is intended to show you where your portfolio stands on a particular date. For each security or other holding listed in the report, you'll be shown the number of shares you own, the market price for a share on that date (or at least the price you recorded most recently), the investment's cost basis, your unrealized gain or loss, and the total market value for the holding. These figures are similar to those you can see on the Update Prices and Market Value dialog box. However, in the Portfolio Value report, you get a total dollar value for the cost basis of each holding (instead of the average price per share) and for your unrealized gain or loss (instead of a percentage).

Preparing an Investment Performance Report

Every investor wants to know how much money his or her portfolio is earning on a percentage basis. After all, if you can't generate a higher rate of return than you could by parking your money in a bank account, why bother with the complexities of stocks and bonds? Quicken's *Investment Performance report* will tell you in a few moments how well each security in your portfolio is doing in terms of its average annual return. The calculation for each security is based on dividends and interest earned, any other payments you received, and on the change in the market value of your holdings.

Preparing a Capital Gains Report

With Quicken's built-in *Capital Gains report* format, you can produce a breakdown of the actual gains you've realized from sales of your investments over a given period of time (usually a taxable year). You can have Quicken divide the report into subtotals for your short-term and long-term capital gains, ideal for tax preparation purposes.

Of course, for those subtotals to be accurate, you must enter the actual cost basis of the security, and the date you actually purchased it. If you haven't previously done so, you can add this information to your account register even after you sell off the security in question (just postdate the transactions).

Preparing an Investment Income Report

When you want to know how much money you're making from your investments in raw dollars, Quicken's *Investment Income report* is for you. This report simply summarizes all your sources of investment income and all your investment-related expenses over a given period of time, and then gives you a grand total of your earnings. Included in the accounting are dividends, interest, capital gains distributions, your actual capital gains (realized gains), and, if you'd like, unrealized paper gains and losses. Expenses such as margin interest (the interest you pay on a broker loan) are included in the expense breakdown, but commissions associated with purchases and sales of securites are omitted.

The *Investment Income report* is great for putting together Schedule B on your federal income tax return. Set the dates to cover a full tax period, and then subtotal the report by security (an easy customization—see Chapter 11); you've instantly got a list of your dividend and interest earnings from each of your investments. If you have both taxable and reportable tax-exempt earnings, you'll need to run the report twice using filters (also covered in Chapter 11) to obtain separate totals of your taxable and tax-exempt investment income.

Preparing an Investment Transactions Report

Use the *Investment Transactions report* for a detailed look at the history of your investment account. This report prints each transaction, listing its monetary impact on your account in terms of your cash balance, the value of your noncash investments, and the total of both cash and the investment value, as shown in Figure 10.9 on the next page.

For example, for a transaction in which you bought 100 shares of stock for $1,000 using cash in the investment account, the report will show a negative $1,000 entry in the *Cash* column, a positive $1,000 entry in the *Investment Value* column, and no entry at all in the *Cash + Invest* column (since the overall impact on the account's worth is neutral). If you recorded a $50 quarterly dividend, there will be a positive $50 entry in the *Cash* column, no entry in the *Investment Value* column, and a positive $50 entry in the *Cash + Invest* column.

In addition, an Investment Transactions report calculates the realized capital gain or loss on any securities sales that take place during the period covered by the report. Of course, you must have entered the original purchase price for the security in question if you want an accurate gain/loss calculation.

FIGURE 10.9

An Investment Transactions report.

	Investment Transactions Report								
Customize	Memorize	Copy	Print	Close					

Investment Transactions Report
1/1/94 Through 10/3/94

10/3/94
Stocks & Bonds

Date	Action	Secur	Categ	Price	Shares	Commssn	Cash
	BALANCE 12/31/93						1,875.00
1/4	ShrsIn	Vistacorp		55.000	150		-8,250.00
			[Stock...				8,250.00
3/1	MiscInc	-Cash-	[Stock...				17,045.00
3/15	Buy	Vistacorp		60.000	50	75.00	-3,075.00
3/31	IntInc	Treasury 11/...	_IntInc				250.00
6/5	Div	Vistacorp	_DivInc				20.00
6/15	Buy	Treasury 11/...		74 1/2	100	45.00	-7,495.00
9/20	Sell	Vistacorp		65.000	100	120.00	5,500.00
			_RlzdGain				880.00

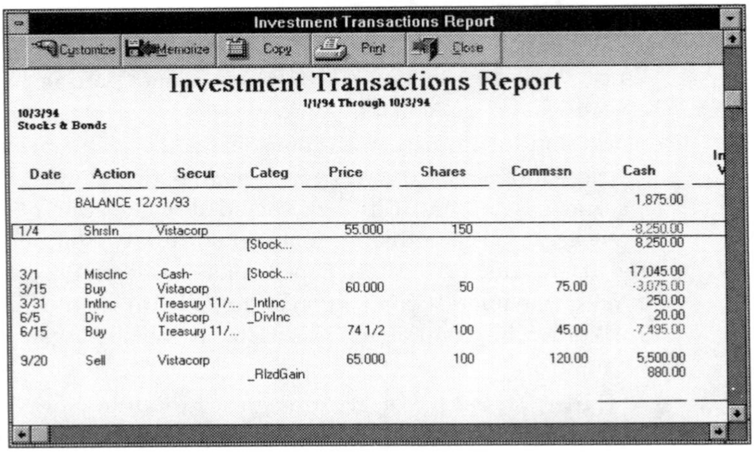

Summary

You've now learned how to use Quicken's built-in report setups for generating reports based on the information in your accounts. You've practiced using the Reports menu and seen how Quicken offers two groups of built-in report setups: five setups for reports on personal finances, and seven for business reports. You've created several sample reports, and learned in the process how to choose a report title and indicate the range of dates you want a built-in report to cover. Finally, you've seen how to display different parts of a report on your screen, and how to print out the report on paper. In Chapter 11, you'll discover techniques for customizing reports to suit special needs that aren't met by the built-in reports.

Chapter Eleven
Customizing Financial Reports

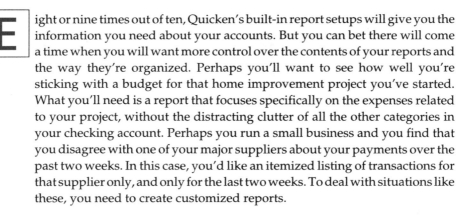

E ight or nine times out of ten, Quicken's built-in report setups will give you the information you need about your accounts. But you can bet there will come a time when you will want more control over the contents of your reports and the way they're organized. Perhaps you'll want to see how well you're sticking with a budget for that home improvement project you've started. What you'll need is a report that focuses specifically on the expenses related to your project, without the distracting clutter of all the other categories in your checking account. Perhaps you run a small business and you find that you disagree with one of your major suppliers about your payments over the past two weeks. In this case, you'd like an itemized listing of transactions for that supplier only, and only for the last two weeks. To deal with situations like these, you need to create customized reports.

NOTE	Don't think customizing a report is difficult; whereas there are a few more steps required than for the standard reports, you only have to make several additional choices from a few windows. Everything is spelled out on the screen for you.

With a couple of exceptions, every Quicken report is based on one of five main types of reports. For the built-in report setups covered in Chapter 10, Quicken has simply chosen some of the options for you ahead of time. To create a customized report you can start from scratch with one of the five basic types, or modify any existing report—including any of the standard reports. Either way, the basic steps are identical.

Here are the five main types of Quicken reports:

- *Transaction reports* detail individual transactions from one or more account registers. You decide which transactions are to be listed in the report, and whether to group and subtotal them by *category, class, payee, account,* or *time period.*

- *Summary reports* present totals for *categories, classes, payees,* or *accounts* in the rows of the report, without listing the individual transactions. If you like, you can break down these totals further into subtotals presented in columns according to *time period, category, class,* or *account.*

- *Comparison reports* compare amounts for a given *category, class,* and so on over two different time periods in side-by-side columns. You can subdivide the main columns to break out the amounts for shorter lengths of time within them.

- *Budget reports* compare the income and spending recorded in your accounts against the amounts you had budgeted over a specific time period on a category-by-category basis.

- *Account Balances* reports calculate the overall balance in any group of accounts at any one time. If you have recorded all your assets and liabilities in Quicken accounts, an Account Balances report covering all the accounts will indicate your net worth.

Although the details vary on each type of report, the process of creating a custom report is very similar for all of them. You fill out the similar fields no matter which type of custom report you're generating—as you'll see when you generate several practice custom reports in this chapter.

SHORTCUT   You can record or "memorize" any customized report definition for reuse later. See "Using Memorized Reports," later in this chapter.

How to Create a Custom Report

You can customize a report before you create it, or you can modify it after it's already on the screen.

- To create a new, customized report, start from the Create Report window and choose the **Customize** button.
- To modify an existing report after Quicken displays it on the screen, choose the **Customize** button at the top left of the button bar at the top of the report.

You'll practice both methods in this chapter. Either way, you use the same techniques to choose the report specifications you'd like.

Creating a Custom Transaction Report

Transaction reports are the most detailed type of report available in Quicken; they list the individual transactions in your accounts. In this section, you'll learn step by step how to create a customized Transaction report. In later sections, you'll learn to apply these same techniques to other types of custom reports.

Since a Transaction report details individual transactions, at first glance it looks much like a register printout. But several things are different: The Transaction report groups transactions by time period, category, or another classification, rather than simply listing them chronologically, and it gives you a subtotal for each group. At the end of the Transaction report, you also get overall totals of your income and outflow during the period, rather than just an ending balance.

Actually, if you worked through Chapter 10, you already have experience in creating a Transaction report. Quicken's built-in *Itemized Categories report* is a Transaction report that is based on all the categories in all your accounts, and that groups transactions according to categories. But perhaps you want to see your transactions itemized according to class or payee instead of category, and also to include only business-related items, or only items that have cleared your account. In that case, you'll need to customize a Transaction report to match your specifications. Figures 11.1 and 11.2 on the next page show a pair of sample Transaction reports, each one customized differently.

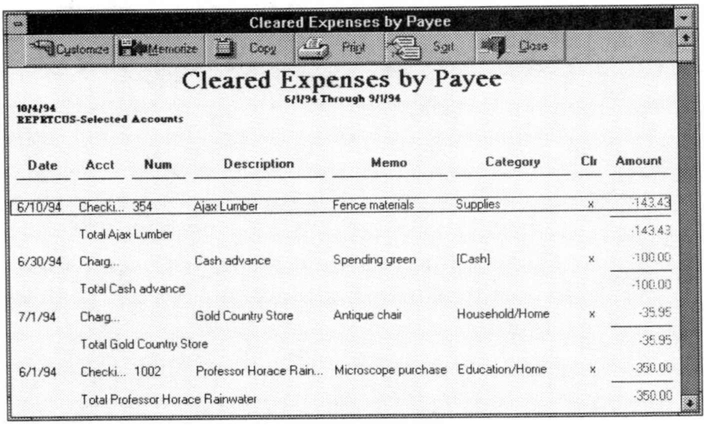

FIGURE 11.1

A Transaction report organized by payee and showing only expense items that have cleared the bank.

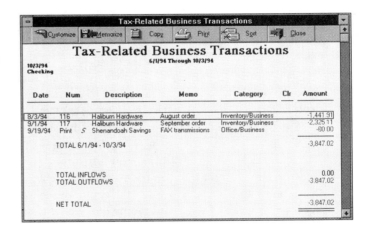

FIGURE 11.2

A Transaction report of business-related items grouped by tax-related categories.

To develop a custom Transaction report similar to the one shown in Figure 11.1, start by choosing **Other** in the Reports menu. The five basic report types appear on a cascading menu (see Figure 11.3).

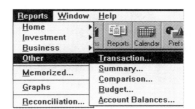

FIGURE 11.3

*The "Other" Reports
cascading menu.*

Choose **Transaction** from this menu. You'll see the Create Report dialog box, shown in Figure 10.2. As Usual, Quicken has entered a range of dates for you in the *Date* fields; change them as appropriate. Now choose **Customize** to open the Customize Transaction Report window, shown in Figure 11.4.

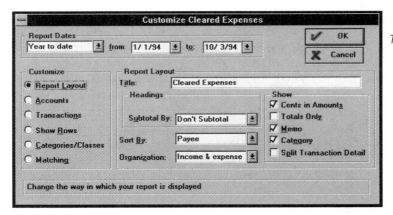

FIGURE 11.4

*The Customize
Transaction
Report
window.*

Choosing the Report Layout

The Customize Report window looks similar for all report types. At the top are *Date* fields, giving you another opportunity to modify the dates covered in the report. The fields you see in the main part of the window depend on which **Radio** button is selected in the *Customize* area to the left. Try choosing different radio buttons—when you switch from **Layout** to **Accounts**, for example, the *Title* field and its partners are replaced by a list of your accounts and a set of buttons, one for each type of account (bank, cash, etc.).

When you're finished testing the **Radio** buttons, choose the **Layout** radio button again. Start by giving your new report a title such as "Cleared Expenses by Payee."

The *Subtotal By* field is critical because it determines how Quicken will group your transactions when calculating the subtotals shown on the report. You have 12 choices in this field, available in a drop-down list. If you choose the **Don't Subtotal** option, already entered for you, Quicken simply reports the transactions in chronological order. The next seven choices offer various time periods by which you can group transactions in the report. If you wanted to itemize and subtotal your transactions on a quarterly basis, for instance, you'd select **Quarter** at the *Subtotal By* field.

NOTE	If you leave the *Report Title* field empty when creating a report, Quicken will title it for you according to the report type and the entry you make in the *Subtotal By* field in the Create Transaction Report dialog box. In the report you'll be creating, for example, the program would assign the title "Transaction Report by Payee," because that's how you'll fill out the *Subtotal By* field for the sample report. The remaining options for this field let you subtotal the report by **category**, **class**, **payee**, **account**, or **tax schedule**. Since the sample report you're developing is to be organized by payee, choose **Payee** in the *Subtotal By* field, and press **Tab** to continue.

Next, the *Sort by* field determines how Quicken sorts the transactions within each subtotal group. Three of the options, **Acct/Date**, **Date/Acct**, and **Acct/Cnum**, sort the transactions twice. If you choose **Acct/Date**, for example, the transactions in each subtotal group are first sorted by account, and then those for each account are sorted by date. The **Acct/Cnum** choice sorts first by account and then by check number. Other available options include sorting by **payee**, **amount**, or **category**, and the standard choice, **None** (for no sorting at all).

Of course, your choice of sorting options depends partly on the type of subtotals you've requested. If you're already subtotaling the report based on categories, it wouldn't make sense to sort by categories, too.

At the bottom of the window, the *Report Organization* field offers two alternatives for listing transfer transactions in the report. If you select **Income**

and Expense, the final report will first list all income transactions that were not transfers, then all nontransfer expense transactions, then all transfer transactions. This is a good choice when you want to see clearly how you've been managing your money among your various accounts.

The second choice, **Cash Flow Basis**, creates a Cash Flow report with separate groups for income and expense items only. In this case, transfer transactions are listed together with other income and expense transactions in sections titled "Inflows" and "Outflows." This type of report shows you more clearly how much you've received and spent.

The other choices in the *Report Layout* section of the Customize Report window depend partly on which type of report you're preparing and what sort of accounts you've set up.

Uncheck the **Cents in Amounts** checkbox if you want round dollar amounts only in your reports. Next comes the *Totals Only* field. This is one of several fields, which pertain to individual transactions and are therefore displayed only when you're creating a Transaction report.

If you check the **Totals Only** box, the report will list only the totals and subtotals of the groups you've defined, not the individual transactions. For instance, checking this box in the sample report would produce a report show-ing the subtotal for each payee and the overall total for all the payees, but not separate transactions. Instead, leave the box unchecked for this practice report.

Use the *Memo* and *Category* fields to determine how much information from each transaction to show in the report. Check *Memo* if you want a column showing memo entries, *Category* if you want a column listing the category and class assignments, and check both boxes if you want columns for both items.

NOTE	In Quicken 2, the equivalent choices are provided in a single drop-down list labeled Memo/Category Display. The choices are **Memo Only**, **Category Only**, and **Display Both**.

Check the bottom box, labeled *Split Transaction Detail*, if you wanted the report to include the details of each of the items within split transactions. If you leave this field unchecked, you'll see just the total amount of each split transaction. You can decide which way to set this field for the practice report. (Obviously, if you've set the previous field to show totals only and not individual transactions, your entry here has no effect on the report.)

NOTE	If you subtotal a Transaction report by category or class, or if you filter the report so that it only includes specific matching or

selected categories or classes, Quicken always shows split transaction details (filtering is discussed in the next section).

Selecting Accounts to Include

In Quicken 2, you select accounts to include in your report in a separate list. Instead of a checkmark, you'll see the word **Include** in the list for selected accounts. There's no way to select all your accounts of a given type. Otherwise, the process is the same.

When you've completed the fields in the Report Layout section of the dialog box, choose the next **Radio** button, **Accounts**. The middle part of the Customize Report changes to show a list of all your accounts. At the right, there are six new buttons, one for each type of account (Figure 11.5)

FIGURE 11.5

*The Customize Report window looks like this when you choose the **Accounts** radio button.*

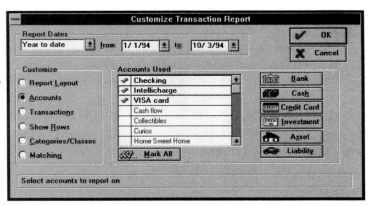

In this case, let's assume that you have several accounts, but that all of the expenses you want to report on are recorded in your checking and credit card accounts. The easiest way to select these accounts is to choose the **Bank** and **Credit Card** buttons. As you choose each button, Quicken marks the accounts of that type with a checkmark in the list.

To mark or unmark an individual account, click on it with the mouse, or move the highlight to the account with the cursor keys and then press the space bar. The **Mark All** button doesn't always mark all the accounts—if any are already marked, it unmarks them all.

Deciding Which Transactions to Include

Choose the **Transactions** radio button to display yet another set of fields in the Customize Report window. Here, you'll decide which types of transactions Quicken includes in the report.

WARNING	*All* of the criteria you define here must be met by every transaction to be included in your report.

The *Amounts* field actually consists of two related fields; together, they let you restrict a report so it only covers transactions within a range of dollar amounts. For this sample report, leave the first field in the pair set to **All**. You'll see how this field can be useful in the second sample report you prepare.

The checkbox labeled **Include Unrealized Gains** only pertains if you have investment accounts. Check this box if you want Quicken to temporarily create transactions corresponding to the price changes in the investments you've recorded via the Update Prices and Market Value dialog box (see Chapter 9).

When checked, the box **Tax-Related Transactions Only** limits the report to transactions assigned to tax-related categories. Again, you'll see how this works in the second sample report.

Your next order of business is to restrict the report to expense items. At the bottom of the window, notice the field labeled *Transaction Types*. In the drop-down list for this field, select **Payments**. When Quicken prepares the report, it will include only those transactions with dollar entries in the *Payment* column in your checking account, or in the equivalent field in other types of accounts—*Charge* in credit card accounts, *Spend* in cash accounts, *Decrease* in asset accounts, *Increase* in liability accounts, and *Security* in investment accounts. The other available choices in the *Transactions Types* field are **Deposits, Unprinted Checks**, and **All transactions**.

NOTE	Quicken 2 has a *Payments/Deposits/Unprinted checks/All* field rather than a *Transaction Types* field, but it works the same way. The **Reconciled** checkbox is labeled **Cleared** in Quicken 2.

Recall that the report you're creating is to be limited to transactions that have cleared your account. Notice the three checkboxes at the right of the window labeled **Blank, Newly Cleared**, and **Reconciled**. All of these pertain to the cleared status of the transactions. Since all transactions that have cleared the bank or credit card company have an entry in the *Clr* field of the register, you want to exclude transactions with no entry there. Therefore, uncheck the **Blank** box, meaning that transactions whose cleared status is blank will *not* be included in the report.

<table>
<tr><td>NOTE</td><td>To report only on transactions that you have been fully cleared after reconciling your account, you would uncheck the *Newly Cleared* field also, so that only the *Reconciled* field is checked.</td></tr>
</table>

Leave the other two boxes checked since transactions that have cleared the bank or credit card company have either an asterisk or an *x* in the *Clr* field. The completed window should look like Figure 11.6. Then choose **OK** to close the Filter Report Transactions dialog box, returning to the Create Transaction Report dialog box. Notice that the title bar now tells you that you've added filters to the report.

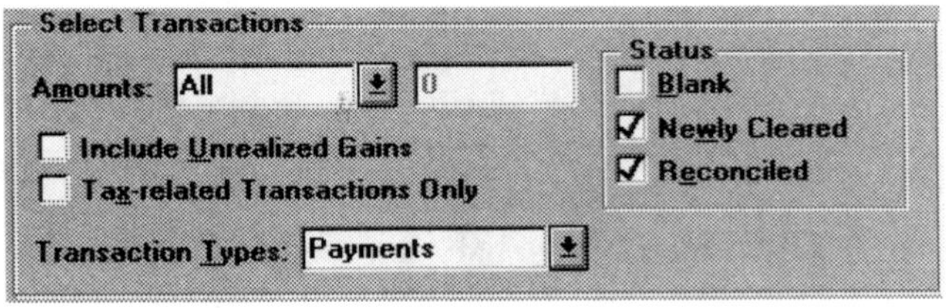

FIGURE 11.6

The Transactions section of the Customize Transaction Report window completed for the sample report.

Displaying Transfers and Subcategories

Choose the mysteriously named **Show Rows** radio button to display two fields that also affect the kinds of transactions shown on your report.

The first of these, *Transfers*, indicates which transfer transactions you want to include in the report. On the drop-down list, the **Exclude All** and **Include All** choices are self-explanatory. The third choice, **Exclude Internal**, tells Quicken to list only those transfers involving accounts that won't appear in the report. Choosing the best option is complicated, but don't worry if you're not entirely clear on how all this works—the most important information will still get to your report.

At any rate, your choice in this field depends partly on what you have already entered in the *Report Organization* field back in the Report Layout section. If you chose **Income and Expense** there, you should select **Include All** in the *Transfers* field to have Quicken list all transfers in a third group after income and expenses. If you chose **Cash Flow Basis**, however, you would select **Exclude Internal** here, since in the cash flow format the transactions among the accounts you are reporting on would cancel out each other. Finally, whatever your choice in the *Report Organization* field, if you simply want to focus on the transactions within the account and don't want to include any transfers, choose **Exclude All** in the *Transfers* field. Clear as mud?

The next field, *Subcategories*, lets you decide what kind of information to show about transactions assigned to subcategories:

- The standard option, **Show All**, groups subcategories within main categories and subclasses with main classes.

- To eliminate subcategories and subclasses from a report, select **Hide All** from the drop-down list.

- To reverse the order of the category/subcategory breakdowns in the report, so that items are grouped first by subcategories, then by main categories, choose **Show Reversed** in this field. This can be useful if you have two or more similar subcategories under different main categories, and want to combine amounts for the related subcategories in a report. For example, if you have separate categories for truck and car expenses, each with a **Gas** subcategory, you could use this option to report on how much you spent on gas for both vehicles.

Remaining Customization Options

For this report, you won't use the last two radio buttons on the Customize Report window, **Categories/Classes** and **Matching**. You'll see how these parts of the customizing process work when you create the next Custom report.

Producing the Report

With the customization settings complete, OK the Customize Report window to return to the Create Report window. Choose **OK** again to create the report.

Within a few moments you'll see the report on your screen, similar to the one shown in Figure 11.7.

FIGURE 11.7

A sample Custom Transaction report displayed on the screen.

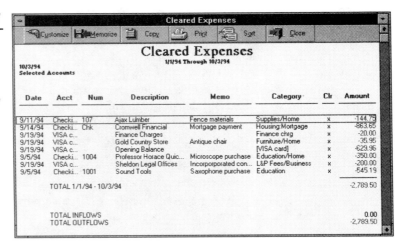

Working with the Transaction Report on the Screen

From this point on, you can work with the report just as you did with the built-in reports you produced in Chapter 10. To move the display one column at a time, use the four **Arrow** keys. Use **PgUp** and **PgDn** to move vertically by a screenful. The **Home** key moves you to the top of the report, while **End** moves you to the bottom.

The width of the Report window determines the width of the individual columns. When the report first appears, it's likely that some of the entries in the *Description*, *Memo*, and *Category* columns will be shortened to fit. If you want to see the full entries for these columns, resize the window (drag the right border to make it wider).

The **QuickZoom** feature works a bit differently in Transaction reports than in other report types. When you double-click on a transaction with the Magnifying Glass mouse pointer (or select a transaction and press **Enter**), you don't get a secondary report. Instead, Quicken moves you directly to the register. The transaction you started with in the report is selected for editing in the register.

Printing the Custom Transaction Report

If you want to print the report, press **Ctrl-P** or click on **Print** on the report's button bar. The Print Report dialog box gives you three options for outputting the report to your printer or to a file on disk. To print a paper copy of the report, select the **Printer** radio button. If you'd like to see an on-screen preview of the report before actually printing it, select the **Screen** button instead (see Chapter 10 for details on working with Preview reports).

| NOTE | See the Appendix for details on how to transfer report information with other programs using the three **Disk File** buttons to "print" the report as a file. |

After the printout is completed, your report will still be on the screen. Before leaving it, proceed to the next section where you'll learn how to store your customized reports for later use.

Memorizing Reports for Later Use

Whether you customize one of the built-in report setups or design your own Custom report, you can have Quicken memorize all of the report's characteristics—the report title, the row and column headings, the accounts that appear in the report, and so on. Then, whenever you want to analyze a new set of report data with the same report, you simply recall the memorized report by name. Of course, you'll be given a chance to alter any of the memorized report's characteristics each time you use it.

| NOTE | In Quicken 2 you could also memorize reports from the Create Report window. This is one feature that is no longer possible in Quicken 3. |

With the customized transaction report you just created still on the screen, choose the **Memorize** button in the report's button bar, or press **Ctrl-M**. Quicken offers you the chance to choose a different title for the memorized version of the report in the Memorize Report dialog box (see Figure 11.8 on the next page). You can also decide whether the memorized report should cover a fixed range of dates; if you select the **None** radio button, Quicken chooses a date range for you the next time you generate the report. In either case, you're free to select a new date range or enter a new title each time you generate the memorized report.

FIGURE 11.8

The Memorize Report dialog box appears when you first memorize a report.

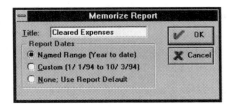

Once you have made all your choices in the Memorize Report dialog box, choose **OK** to go ahead and memorize the report. You'll hear three quick beeps as Quicken records the report setup.

Recalling a Memorized Report

The next time you need to use one of your memorized report definitions, just recall it and rerun the report. To recall a memorized report definition, choose **Memorized** from the Reports menu to pop up the Memorized Reports list, shown in Figure 11.9. Choose the memorized report you'd like to use again by highlighting the report title and choosing **Use**, or by double-clicking on the title with the mouse.

FIGURE 11.9

The Memorized Reports list displays a list of your memorized reports.

You'll see the standard Create Report window at this point, ready to go for the report you choose (notice that your report's title is highlighted in the middle of the window. If you like, change the dates at the top of the window; you can further customize it as well by choosing the **Customize** button. When you're ready, OK the window to re-create the report.

<table>
<tr><td>

SHORTCUT

</td><td>

Don't think you can edit the settings for a memorized report with the **Edit** button in the Memorized Reports list. The **Edit** button only lets you change the name of the memorized report you select. (See the next section.)

</td></tr>
</table>

Memorizing a Report Again

Any changes you made to a memorized report's setup in the Create Report or Customize Report windows apply only to the report you're currently generating and don't affect the memorized version of the report. Of course, if you like the new version, you can memorize it, too.

Once the new report is on your screen, choose **Memorize**. The Memorize Report dialog box you previously used (see Figure 11.8) comes up again. If you want to keep the original version of the memorized report, change the name here; if you want to replace the original with your new settings, leave the name the same.

Choose **OK** to proceed and memorize the new setup. If the name you've chosen is identical to that of an existing memorized report, Quicken asks you whether you want to replace the existing setup with the one you've just created. If that's all right, choose **Replace**. If you decide to keep the original, choose **Cancel**, then rename the report setup before you memorize it again.

Changing the Memorized Report List

You can make two simple changes in the Memorized Report List without recalling the report:

- To delete a memorized report, select its title in the list, and choose **Del**.
- To change the title of a memorized report, select the report name, and choose **Edit**. Type in the new name in the small window that appears, choosing **OK** when you're through.

Creating a Second Custom Transaction Report

To make sure that you have a firm grasp of the key steps in customizing Quicken reports, let's review the process again with a second Transaction report; this time, you'll be duplicating the report already shown in Figure 11.2 on page 320. This report is drawn from a single checking account that includes both business and personal transactions, using class assignments to differentiate the two as you've done in earlier chapters. (If you need to review how classes are used, see Chapter 5.)

In creating this report, you'll learn how to use Quicken's powerful Matching features to include only the transactions you want the report to show. In addition, to drive home the point that the standard, built-in report setups are nothing more than customized reports with options chosen for you, you'll use the Itemized Categories report format as a starting point.

Before you begin the new Transaction report, be sure the current account is the checking account on which the report will be based. If you're not already working with the correct account, switch to it by clicking on the **Accts** icon or by pressing **Ctrl-A**.

Now choose **Home**, then **Itemized Categories** in the Reports menu. You'll see the Create Report dialog box. As always, the only fields in this window are for the range of dates the report will cover. If you want to narrow the report to cover another period, you can change the dates shown here.

Now choose **Customize** to customize the report. Fill in your own title for the report, something like **Tax-Related Business Transactions**. In the *Subtotal by* field, Quicken has already entered the **Category** option (after all, you started with an Itemized Category report). Since your Custom report will also be subtotaled by category, you can skip over this field.

NOTE	When a Custom Transaction report is subtotaled by category, Quicken automatically displays sub-subtotals for any subcategories you've defined. Likewise, if you subtotal the report by class, you'll automatically see subclass sub-subtotals.

Most other fields can be left as they are. For example, *Organization* should remain set to the *Income and Expenses* format, and the **Show Totals Only** box should be unchecked, since you want a detailed report showing all the individual transactions.

As you did last time, however, you'll want to check the box labeled *Split Transaction Detail* at the right. Some of the split transactions might cover both home and business items, and you only want the business items to show up in this report. Uncheck the **Category** box so that the report will have a *Memo* column but not one for categories; after all, the transactions are already going to be grouped according to categories because you chose to subtotal by category.

Reporting on the Current Account

This Custom report focuses on your checking account. To exclude information from your other accounts, choose the **Accounts** radio button.

The list of your accounts shows all of them marked with a check. Choose **Mark All** to remove the checkmarks, then click on the checking account name in the list (you can highlight it with the cursor keys and press the space bar instead).

Including Transactions of Interest in your Reports

Now it's time to define exactly which transactions will be shown in the report, so choose the **Transactions** radio button.

In the pair of fields labeled *Amounts* you can tell Quicken to report on only those transactions falling in a given dollar range. With the first of these fields set to **All**, all transactions will be included in the report, regardless of their dollar amount (of course, transactions may be excluded from the report by other settings in the Filter window).

The other options for the first of the *Amounts* field include less than, equal to, and greater than. If you choose, say, the **Less Than** setting for the first field, and type **500** into the second *Amounts* field, you would read the two fields together as "Transactions less than $500." You could report on only the large transactions in your account by setting the first field to **Greater Than** and leaving the second field set to **500**. And if, for some reason, you wanted to see only those transactions in which you spent or received exactly $500, you'd change the first field's setting to **Equal To**.

The next field, *Tax-Related Categories Only*, is especially important for this report. Instead of going through the list of categories yourself to pick out those that are tax related, just check this box to have Quicken do the sorting for you.

Remember that you specify whether a category is tax related when you create the category. Quicken can use this information to collect only the transactions in tax-related categories for your report.

You worked with the remaining fields when you designed the previous Custom report. For this report, you want to see all the transactions, regardless of whether they were deposits or payments, and regardless of their cleared status. Leave the *Transaction Types* field set to **All Transactions**, and all three **Status** checkboxes (pertaining to cleared status) checked.

Reporting on Transactions in Specific Categories

Quicken lets you restrict a report to any group of categories and/or classes you specify. Choose the **Categories/Classes** radio button. A list of all your categories appears, as shown in Figure 11.10. All the categories are marked with a check, meaning that they will be included in the report.

FIGURE 11.10

The Customize Report window showing a list of your categories.

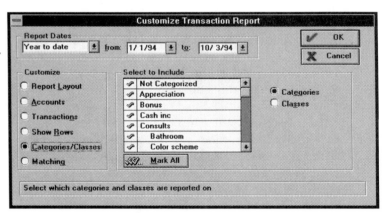

Notice that two additional radio buttons appear to the right of the Category list; one for categories, the other for classes. If you choose the **Class** button, Quicken displays a list of your classes instead.

To select a custom set of categories, choose **Mark All** to unselect all the categories. Then go through the list marking each category to include by clicking on the name or highlighting it with the cursor keys and pressing the space bar.

Reporting on Transactions Involving Specific Payees

Your Quicken reports can be tailored to show you only very specific information. If you like, you can restrict a report to transactions having a particular payee, or even to transactions that have a specific entry in the *Memo* field.

Here's how you do it: choose the **Matching** radio button in the Customize Report window. You should see four new fields in the window. If you make an entry in one or more of these fields, Quicken will include in your report only those transactions that match your entries.

NOTE You can use special characters to change the way Quicken decides whether a transaction matches the search criteria you specify in these four fields. See "Using Wildcard Matches," later in this chapter.

Say you want a report to be focused on the transactions involving T. F. Finch, your stock brokerage firm. You would enter the brokerage name in the *Payee Contains* field. Assuming you don't add any other specifications, the resulting report would show all the checks you've written to the brokerage firm, and all the payments you've received for dividends and stock sales.

SHORTCUT QuickFill works in the first three fields, completing your entries as you type them. You can select an entry from a drop-down list by clicking on the **Arrow** button at the right of the field.

In exactly the same way, you can enter a match for memos, so that the report shows only the transactions with that matching entry in the *Memo* field.

Similarly, you can specify matches for categories and classes. This has the same results as selecting a single category or class in the list displayed by the **Categories/Classes** radio button; the exception being if you use the special "wildcard" characters in your entry.

The report you're developing now is restricted to business-related transactions. Assuming you've assigned all the transactions in your account to one of two classes, **Home** or **Business**, all you have to do is type **Business** in the *Class Contains* field.

When preparing the report, Quicken looks for transactions that *contain* your entries in these first four fields, even if the corresponding entry in the transaction is longer than what you typed here. For example, if you type **inc** in the *Category Contains* field, Quicken will include all transactions in which the letters inc appear in any part of the assigned category. Transactions assigned to the **Inc-Salary**, **Inc-Bonus**, and **Divided Income** categories would all qualify.

Remaining Setup Steps for the Sample Report

That takes care of your setup for this report. Choose **OK** twice to start the report. After a few moments, you'll see the report on your screen, and you'll be able to move around in the report to see different parts, or print it out.

Creating a Summary Report

If you are like most Quicken users, you will take advantage of Summary reports more often than any other type. Summary reports give you just enough detail for most financial planning needs. Unlike Transaction reports, they don't obscure trends in your income and spending with a myriad of individual transactions. However, they do summarize the kinds of income and spending recorded in your account, providing the information you need to make wise week-by-week and month-by-month financial management decisions.

For your next practice report, then, you'll develop a Summary report. As the name implies, Summary reports don't show individual transactions, but instead list the totals for each category, class, account, or payee by row. In addition, you can further subdivide these primary groupings by a second classification scheme, breaking out subtotals for time period, category, class, payee, or account into separate columns. Overall, the report is divided into separate sections for income items and expense items. At your request, a Summary report can also include a third section for transfers.

Figures 11.11 and 11.12 show a pair of related sample Summary reports similar to the ones you're about to put together. They are very typical Summary reports, showing categories in the rows and months in the columns. These reports are based on a set of Quicken accounts that cover income from a salaried job, a part-time business, and miscellaneous sources, and both personal and business expenses. Note, however, that the report in Figure 11.11 has been customized to show only income from sources other than the business, while the one in Figure 11.12 shows only nonbusiness expense amounts. Notice too that in both reports income and spending are presented as "Inflows" and "Outflows," and that there is no section for transfers, indicating that this report follows the Cash Flow format. You'll design your practice reports to have these custom features.

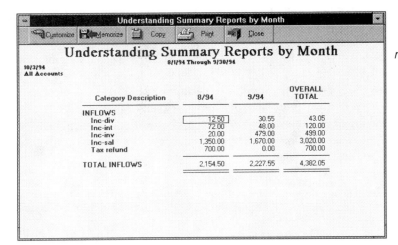

FIGURE 11.11

A Summary report showing income from nonbusiness sources.

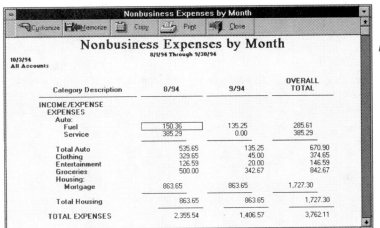

FIGURE 11.12

A Summary report showing only non-business expenses.

If you look closely at the reports, you'll also see that the row titles consist of the full description of each category, rather than just the category name. Often, you're forced to abbreviate a category's full name to fit it into the 15-

character limit Quicken imposes. For better readability, however, Quicken uses the long category description in reports (if you haven't entered a description of the category, the program uses the category name instead).

NOTE   If you'd prefer, you can have Quicken print the category name instead of or in addition to the category description by changing a setting via the Preferences menu. (See the Appendix for details.)

Finally, note that the Summary report in Figure 11.12 gives separate subtotals in each column for subcategories. For example, there are separate subcategory subtotals for gasoline and parts within the **Automobile Expenses** category, with an overall total for the entire category shown after the subcategories.

To generate these sample reports, you will need to add some new categories and a few transactions to your account. The following list contains the categories you should enter:

Category	Description
Inc-div	Dividend Income
Inc-int	Interest Income
Inc-inv	Investment Income
Inc-sal	Salary Income
Bus inc	Business Income

Now enter the following transaction pairs in the register. To get results similar to those in the reports shown here, you'll have to date them properly. First, decide on which two months the report will cover, choosing months for which you have already entered at least a few other transactions. Then, for each pair listed here, date the first transaction in the first month of your report, and the second transaction in the second month. (Use the same **payee** and **category** entry for both members of each pair).

Payee	Deposit	Category
B&O Railroad	12.50	
Inc-div	30.55	
First National Bank	72	Inc-int
	48	
Bill's Brokerage	20	Inc-inv
	479	
9–5 Offices	1350	Inc-sal
	1670	
Consultant fees	275	Bus inc
	450	

If you don't already have **Home** and **Business** classes, add these as well.

By now you should already be quite comfortable with the steps required to set up a Custom report. To get your practice Summary reports started, choose **Other** and **Summary** in the Reports menu to pop up the Create Report dialog box, and then choose **Customize**.

Notice that the fields in the Customize Summary Report window are a bit different than for Transaction reports (see Figure 11.13). Instead of a single *Subtotal* by field you have two equivalent fields, one each for row and column headings. Also, the window has only two checkboxes in the area marked **Show** at the right (we'll get to these in a moment). Enter a report title and the dates you want covered by the report.

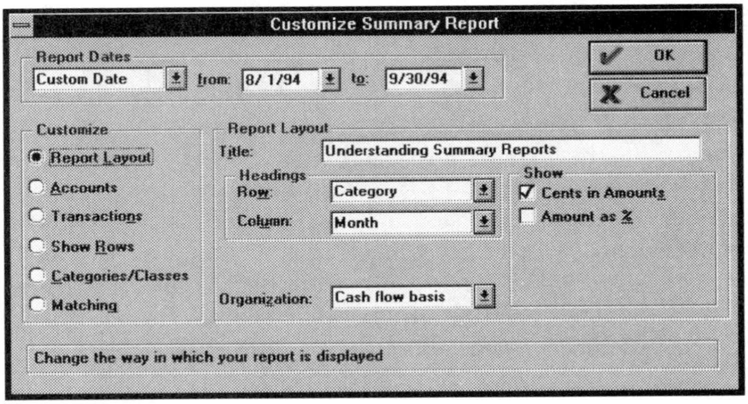

FIGURE 11.13

The Customize Summary Report dialog box.

For this example, you want to see a month-by-month breakdown of the activity in each category. The entry in the *Row Headings* field should be **Category**, meaning that the report will list category-by-category totals on its rows. Next, select **Month** in the *Column Headings* field to produce monthly columns. Since this is a Cash Flow report, choose **Cash Flow Basis** at the *Report Organization* field.

You want the summary to cover all your accounts. That's easy—choose the **Accounts** radio button and select **Mark All** so that all the accounts are checked.

Now choose the **Show Rows** radio button. As you'll recall, the *Transfers* field should be set to **Exclude Internal** for Cash Flow reports—that way, only transfers to accounts that have been excluded appear in the report. (In this case, since the report will cover all your accounts, you could choose **Exclude All** instead—either choice will eliminate transfer transactions from the report.)

Using Wildcard Matches

| NOTE | Wildcard characters work something like wildcards in poker; they can stand for any other characters. |

Now it's time to customize the first report to cover only the transactions you're interested in. Choose the **Matching** radio button. For this report, you'll use Quicken's special search characters to specify matches with greater precision. In addition, you'll see how you can have Quicken *exclude* from the report transactions that match what you type in any of the four fields.

As you've seen, the way each of these fields usually works is this: Quicken includes in the report all transactions that contain the entry you make in the field. Your entry only has to match any part of the corresponding field. In this case, however, we want only transactions with categories that *begin* with the letters *inc*. Move the cursor to the *Category Matches* field in the Filter Report window and type in **Inc..** as your entry.

The two periods are the wildcards. They indicate that you want Quicken to include in the report all categories that begin with the first three letters *inc*, no matter what the remaining characters in the category name are. The first four sample categories you just added meet this criterion, so all of them will be included in the report. Income categories with other names, such as **Bus inc** among the new sample categories, will be excluded from the report, even if they contain the letters *inc* elsewhere in the category name.

If you want to match categories that *end* with a particular word or sequence of characters, you need to type the two periods in front of the characters. If you enter **..income**, for example, your report will include the **Interest Income** and **Salary Income** categories. The wildcard double periods stand for text of any length containing any characters. You can even place them *between* regular characters; an entry such as **in..c..** would match both **Inc-Salary** and **Interest Charges**.

Now choose **OK** twice to start the report. The results on your screen should resemble the example report from Figure 11.11 on page 337.

For more information on using wildcards, read through the next section.

Modifying Reports Using the Report Button Bar

There's no need to go all the way back to the Reports menu if you find that some aspect of the report setup needs changing. Instead, you can customize a report after it's already on screen by choosing the **Customize** button at the top of the report button bar. The familiar Customize Report window appears. When you're through making changes, Quicken immediately reconstructs the report to your new specifications.

Let's say that, after studying the report you've just prepared, you decide you don't need to print it. Instead, you now want to put together a report like the one in Figure 11.12.

NOTE	In Quicken 2, you access **Customization** options for reports already on the screen with the **Settings**, **Options**, and **Filter** buttons on the report button bar. In Transaction reports, there's an additional button labeled **Sort**, which duplicates the *Sort Transactions by* field.

More on Wildcards

To alter the report so that you get the results shown in Figure 11.12 on page 337, all you have to do is change the matching criteria. From the window of the last report, choose the **Customize** button to display the Customize Report dialog box again.

Move to the *Category Matches* field and erase the **Inc..** entry you made previously. Then move on to the *Class Matches* field. Here, you'll use a new method to exclude business-related expense transactions from the report. Let's assume that you've assigned all expense transactions to one of two classes, **Business** or **Home**. To have Quicken do a sort of reverse match and include only the classes that *don't* match your entry, type a tilde (~) in front of the class name. In this case, by entering **~Business** in the *Class Matches* field, you'll be excluding transactions assigned to **Business**, thus automatically including the transactions assigned to **Home**.

SHORTCUT	You can even combine the tilde with the wildcard characters. For example, the entry **~Inc..** would cause Quicken to exclude all categories starting with *inc*.

After making the entry in the *Class Contains* field, choose **OK**. Quicken regenerates the report, which should now look something like the one in Figure 11.12 on page 337.

Uses for Summary Reports

It's easy to come up with useful applications for custom Summary reports. Quicken's standard Job/Project report, for example, is based on the Summary Report format, set up with category totals in the rows and subtotals for classes in the columns. The built-in Job/Project report automatically includes all accounts and all classes and categories, which is great for keeping tabs on each separate financial activity. But to focus the report on a specific part of your financial picture, you need to customize it.

Let's say you're managing a multicity fund-raising drive. You've created categories for each type of expense and income item, with separate classes for each city. A standard Job/Project report would show your overall income and expenses by category, with subtotals in each of the categories for each city. But if you want to see the numbers for a single city, you have to customize the report. In the Customize Report window, choose the **Matching** radio button, then enter the class for that city in the *Class Contains* field.

Likewise, you could customize the report to restrict it to a particular account or group of accounts. Or, if you want to know the subtotals for each week or month, just create a separate report for each time period you want to study.

Similar Category/Class reports are commonly used to summarize income and spending for multiple rental properties, and for other projects, such as building a home, that can be divided easily into separate areas of responsibility. You'll see more detailed examples of Summary reports in such real-life applications in Chapters 13 through 16.

Creating a Budget Report

When you choose a Budget Report format, Quicken automatically groups your transactions according to category. It then compares the income or expense recorded in your accounts for each category to the amount you had predicted for that category in your budget. For each category, the report displays the actual and budgeted amounts side by side in separate columns, followed by a third column for the difference between the two.

When you create a custom Budget report, your most important choice is the time period you want to use for these comparisons. The standard Budget report automatically compares your actual records to your budget a month at a time. With a custom report, however, you can budget by almost any interval, from a week to an entire year. In addition, of course, you can customize the report to focus on specific budget items, reporting only on the transactions in a particular group of accounts, or in a given category or class.

WARNING

In order to create a Budget report, Quicken must have something to compare against the actual category totals. In other words, you have to tell the program how much you've budgeted for each category. (See Chapter 13, which covers budgeting in detail.)

Figure 11.14 illustrates a portion of a Budget report divided into quarters instead of months. To create this report:

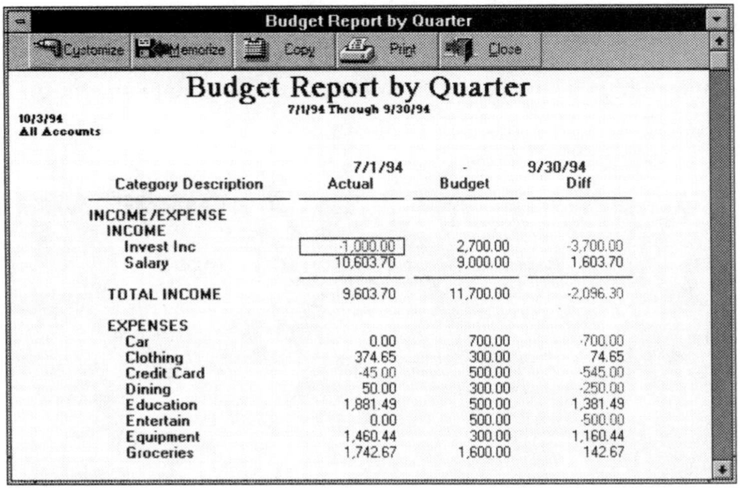

Budget Report by Quarter

7/1/94 Through 9/30/94

10/3/94
All Accounts

Category Description	7/1/94 Actual	- Budget	9/30/94 Diff
INCOME/EXPENSE			
INCOME			
Invest Inc	-1,000.00	2,700.00	-3,700.00
Salary	10,603.70	9,000.00	1,603.70
TOTAL INCOME	9,603.70	11,700.00	-2,096.30
EXPENSES			
Car	0.00	700.00	-700.00
Clothing	374.65	300.00	74.65
Credit Card	-45.00	500.00	-545.00
Dining	50.00	300.00	-250.00
Education	1,881.49	500.00	1,381.49
Entertain	0.00	500.00	-500.00
Equipment	1,460.44	300.00	1,160.44
Groceries	1,742.67	1,600.00	142.67

FIGURE 11.14

Part of a sample Budget report showing quarterly budgeting.

1. Choose **Other** and **Budget** from the Reports menu.
2. Choose **Customize** in the Create Report window or from the finished report to pop up the Customize Budget Report window.
3. Enter the name you want for the report and the dates it should cover. In the *Column Headings* field, select **Quarter** for a quarterly budget report.
4. Choose the **Accounts** radio button. The Monthly Budget report on the Home reports menu includes only bank, cash, and credit card accounts, whereas the basic Budget report from the Other menu includes all accounts. Mark or unmark accounts as necessary, so only the ones that you want to study in your Budget report are checked.
5. Choose **OK** to generate the report.

Creating an Account Balances Report

When you simply want to know how much money you have in your accounts, ask Quicken to prepare an Account Balances report. You can customize the report to see the balances of a selected group of accounts or to see how your financial status has changed over time.

As illustrated in Figure 11.15, an Account Balances report lists the balances of your accounts in two groups: one for your assets, showing bank, cash, and asset accounts; and one for your liabilities, showing credit card and liability accounts. The idea of this report is to give a "snapshot" financial profile of your accounts at a particular moment in time. Although you can prepare Account Balances reports that cover a number of different dates, the amounts listed for each date represent the balances that you had in each account on that date, not the change in the balances since the previous date shown on the report.

FIGURE 11.15

A sample Account Balances report listing month-by-month totals from all accounts.

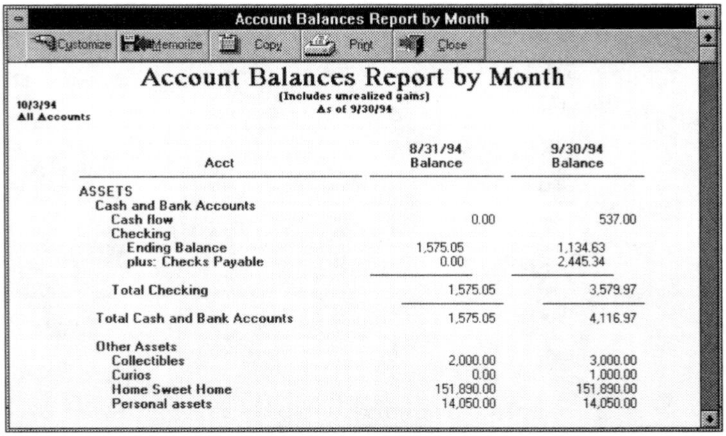

Account Balances Report by Month
(Includes unrealized gains)
As of 9/30/94

10/3/94
All Accounts

Acct	8/31/94 Balance	9/30/94 Balance
ASSETS		
Cash and Bank Accounts		
Cash flow	0.00	537.00
Checking		
Ending Balance	1,575.05	1,134.63
plus: Checks Payable	0.00	2,445.34
Total Checking	1,575.05	3,579.97
Total Cash and Bank Accounts	1,575.05	4,116.97
Other Assets		
Collectibles	2,000.00	3,000.00
Curios	0.00	1,000.00
Home Sweet Home	151,890.00	151,890.00
Personal assets	14,050.00	14,050.00

Two of Quicken's built-in reports are based on the Account Balances format: Net Worth, on the Home reports menu, and Balance Sheet, a Business report. The difference between these two reports is the way they display the totals.

NOTE

The total given for assets in an Account Balances report will be a negative number if the balances in the relevant accounts are less than zero—for example, if your checking account is overdrawn.

In a Net Worth report, amounts for all your checking, cash, asset, and investment accounts are detailed in the Assets section of the report. Then comes a liabilities section for totals from any liability and credit card accounts. The overall total shown at the bottom combines the total assets and total liabilities.

By contrast, the Balance Sheet format gives no overall total. Instead, it breaks out matching totals for assets and the total of your liabilities and equity. This format is typical of business balance sheets. The amount listed at the bottom of the report, labeled *Liabilities & Equity*, is actually just the figure for total assets brought down from the top section of the report. Just above this, *Equity* gives you the difference between the asset and liability totals—in other words, your net worth.

The simplest way to choose between these two formats for a customized Account Balances report is to start with the appropriate standard report, either Net Worth or Balance Sheet. However, you can switch any Account Balances report from one format to the other by customizing the report and changing the setting in the *Organization* field.

To prepare the report shown in Figure 11.15, choose **Other** then **Account Balances** from the Report menu, and then choose **Customize**. Enter a title, then move on to the first *Date* field. The dates you specify here work a little differently than they do in other types of Custom reports—Figure 11.16 shows the Customize Report window for Account Balances reports.

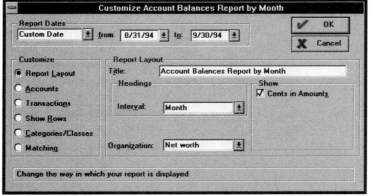

FIGURE 11.16

The Customize Account Balances Report window.

Remember that Account Balances reports do not report amounts over a range of dates, but on a particular date. As Figure 11.15 shows, if you report on more than one date, each date gets its own column. But again, the amounts in each column are the balances for that particular date, independent of the amounts shown for earlier or later dates.

The first of the two *Date* fields signifies the date to be reported in the first column of the report. This date is ignored, however, if you select the **None** option in the *Interval* field, indicating that you want the report to cover a single date. Since the practice report does show several columns for separate dates, enter the date you started the account here, or another date early in the account's history. The date you enter here also begins a range of dates for the report.

The date you enter in the second *Date* field will be the one shown in the report's last column; it serves as the end of the date range. This is the only date reported if you enter **None** in the *Interval* field. Enter today's date here (the quickest way is to type **t**).

Next, in the *Interval* field, select **Month** from the drop-down list to indicate that you want your account balances reported at monthly intervals. Then choose **OK** to generate the report.

Creating an Investment Report

You can customize the reports in any of Quicken's built-in Investment Report formats. As shown in Figure 11.17, the options in the Customize window are different from those for other types of reports.

When you choose the **Matching** radio button, you'll see only one or two fields, not four as with other reports. You can use the *Security Contains* field to enter a single security, confining the report to that investment. If you've set up separate lots of the same security, you can report on all the lots of that one security by entering the part of the name the lots have in common. Alternatively, if you have multiple lots and want to report on only one, precede the entry with an equals sign (as in **=IBM1**) to force Quicken to search for exact matches only.

There's another way to choose which securities appear in the report: by choosing the **Select to Include** radio button. As shown in Figure 11.18, Quicken displays a new set of **Radio** buttons on the right of the Customize window for investment actions (such as Buy, Sell, and so on); **Categories**; **Securities**; **Security Types**; and **Investment Goals**.

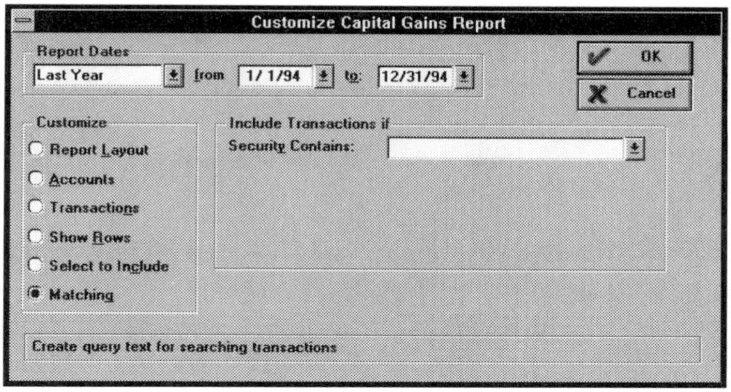

FIGURE 11.17

*The Customize dialog box for Investment reports with the **Matching** radio button selected.*

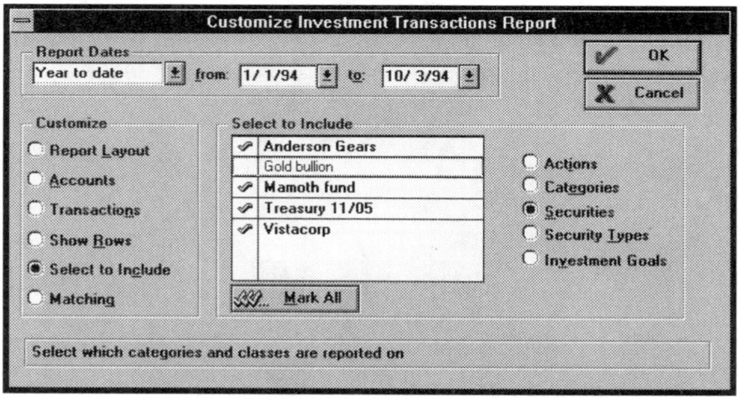

FIGURE 11.18

Customizing an Investment report.

When you select any of these radio buttons, you'll see a list of the available choices for that item in the middle of the window. You'll then be able to select any set of specific actions, securities, and so on by marking them with the mouse or the space bar. You can select arbitrary combinations of options (securities, security types, and goals) from any of these lists for a report tailored exactly to your needs.

Other customization options for Investment reports are similar to those of regular Quicken reports, with a few exceptions. For instance, you're given investment-related choices for row and column headings. Capital Gains reports provide a special field for specifying the limit, in days, for short-term capital gains—that way, you can set up Quicken to reflect any change in the tax-law definition of the maximum holding period for short-term gains.

Summary

In this chapter, you've learned all the skills you need to produce reports that contain exactly the information you want to know about your finances. You have practiced setting up all the types of Custom reports you can produce with Quicken: Transaction reports, Summary reports, Budget reports, and Account Balances reports. You have also worked through the process of choosing Custom Report options and seen how to filter a report to limit it to transactions that meet certain criteria.

In Chapter 12, you'll go on to learn how to create graphs that convey the same kind of summary information you learn from reports, but in a compellingly visual way.

Chapter Twelve
Financial Overviews at a Glance: Quicken Graphics

When you'd like an overview of the important trends in your financial situation, graphs and charts are the best way to grasp the big picture.

Graphs complement Quicken's reports well. You can display a chart to get a visual idea, say, of your monthly income performance over the past year, and then generate a report to see the exact dollar amounts in specific income categories.

Types of Quicken Graphs

You can create four types of graphs:

1. *Income and Expense:* These graphs show you the level of and the source of your income, as well as how much you're spending and what you're spending it on.
2. *Budget Variance:* These graphs show how well you're meeting your budget targets month by month and category by category.
3. *Net Worth:* These graphs give you a snapshot view of your overall net worth by comparing total assets against total liabilities. You can also get

an idea of the relative contributions of each type of asset or liability to the totals.

4. *Investment:* With these graphs, you can tell how your total investment portfolio is divided among different securities or types of securities. You can also see how the prices and overall value of your investments have changed from month to month.

In each graph type, Quicken actually displays several separate charts, using pie charts, double-bar graphs, stacked-bar graphs, and line graphs as appropriate to depict most clearly the information. (See Figure 12.1 for an example.)

FIGURE 12.1

A sample Quicken income and expense graph.

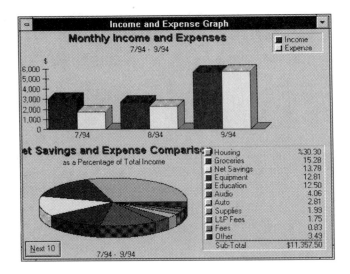

Just as in a report, you can control how much information actually appears on a given graph. For instance, you can decide which months the graph will cover, which accounts it will include, and which categories, classes, or securities to display.

Once the main graph is on your screen, you can get more detail about any item shown by using Quicken's fairly amazing QuickZoom feature. A quick click or two of the mouse conjures detail graphs, dollar values, and even full reports covering the item in which you're interested. And you can print any graph you see on the screen.

Limitations of Quicken Graphs

Keep in mind that Quicken doesn't allow you to design your own graphs. You can use only the predetermined types of graphs available on the various graph menus. You can't change the colors or patterns Quicken assigns to different parts of the graph, the text on the graph screen, or the location of the legend.

Of course, there's a positive side to having a limited number of options: You get useful graphs immediately, with a minimum of fuss.

Creating an Income and Expense Graph

The basic steps required to create a stock Quicken graph are extremely simple—you just pick the type of graph you want from a series of menus, type in the dates you want the graph to cover, and click the mouse or tap **Enter**.

To see how the process works, let's create a sample income and expense graph. You'll use essentially the same procedure for all other types of graphs in Quicken.

To begin the graph, either:

- click the **Graphs** icon, or
- choose **Graph** and **Income and Expense** from the Reports menu.

NOTE	In Quicken 2, the steps required to create a graph are only slightly different from the procedures described here. The graphs themselves contain the same information and look and work the same on the screen.

Quicken presents you with the Create Graphs dialog box (see Figure 12.2 on the next page). The window offers **Radio** buttons for the four types of Quicken graphs; in this case, the **Income and Expense Graph** radio button should already be selected.

NOTE	No matter what type of graph you create, it's usually a good idea to limit it to a fairly short date range. Quicken will obligingly create graphs that cover many years, but the bars will be minus-

cule and hard to see, and they'll represent more than one month's data. Occasionally, you might use such a graph to spot long-term trends, but in general, stick with a maximum of one year.

FIGURE 12.2

*The Create Graphs
dialog box.*

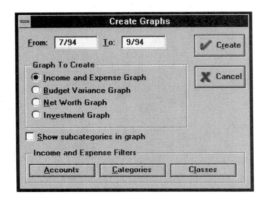

At the top of the dialog box, type in the range of the months you want to include in the graph in the *From* and *To* fields. Choose a range of at least three months for the sample graph, selecting a period for which your register has plenty of income and expense transactions. (For your own graphs, you can type in whatever range of dates makes sense for you.) The graph will cover the months you specify in their entirety, as well as all the time between.

For Income and Expense and Budget Variance graphs, the checkbox labeled **Show Subcategories in graphs** is available. Check this box if you want to graph subcategories separately. If you choose this option, subcategories are graphed independently; that is, nothing on the graph itself indicates which category they belong to, although the legend makes this clear.

You then have three buttons at the bottom of the window to consider before generating the graph. Each allows you to narrow the information that goes into the graph. For example, to limit the graph to a particular account or group of accounts, choose the **Accounts** button. You will be presented with a list of accounts as shown in Figure 12.3. Pick the accounts you want in the graph by double-clicking on the item name, or highlighting it and pressing the space bar. When an account is marked for graphing, the word *Include* appears in the column titled *Include in Graph*.

Similarly, to restrict the graph to a specific set of categories or classes, choose the corresponding button in the Create Graphs window. For each button, a list appears that is much like the one for choosing accounts.

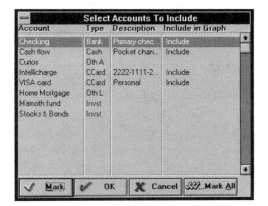

FIGURE 12.3

The Select Accounts to Include dialog box.

Displaying the Graph

After you choose **OK** in the Create Graphs dialog box, Quicken displays a pair of graphs in a single window—you should see something like the picture in Figure 12.1.

The top part of the graph represents a month-by-month breakdown of your income and expenses totaled for all the categories, classes, and accounts you've elected to include in the report. For each month, Quicken displays two adjacent bars, one for that month's income and one for expenses. It's easy to see how the two figures compare from month to month, and you get a quick general sense of how much money is coming in and going out.

The bottom part of the graph is a pie chart covering the entire period you specified. Here, each pie slice stands for one category of expenses, so you can easily see the relative importance of each type of expense to your cash flow. You can identify each slice using the legend at the right.

| WARNING | The colors used in the pie chart don't correspond to those in the bar chart. In the bar chart, blue stands for income and yellow represents expenses; in the pie chart, both colors are used for individual categories. |

The whole pie represents your total income (not, as you might think, your total expenses). If you spent less than you took in, Quicken creates a special slice that represents your *net savings*; that is, the amount of money you had left over after the expenses you recorded in Quicken (whether you actually saved this money is another matter, of course).

If the rough sense of relative size you get from the pie chart isn't enough, look at the legend. There, Quicken tells you exactly what percentage of your total income each expense category accounted for.

Now, to be meaningful, a pie chart should have a limited number of slices—with too many small slices, it's hard to gauge their sizes relative to one another, and they clutter up the "big picture" perspective you're supposed to be getting from a graph.

That's why Quicken automatically limits the pie chart to a maximum of 11 slices: 10 for individual categories, plus an eleventh slice that lumps together all the remaining, smaller categories. When you first display the Income and Expense graph, the pie chart shows slices for the 10 expense categories with the largest total dollar amounts.

The size of the "other" slice depends on how many additional categories it represents and the expenses they include. If it's relatively large, you may want to investigate further the expenses it represents. Here's how: Choose the **Next 10** button at the lower left of the graph window. Quicken redraws the pie chart so that it shows the 10 next-largest expense categories (in this case, the total size of the pie simply represents the total amount of all the categories shown). In the legend, however, you still see the percentage of your total income represented by each category's slice.

If there are still more categories than will fit on the new pie chart, the remaining categories are lumped into yet another "other" slice, which you can break down still further by choosing the **Next 10** button again. Eventually, when the graph shows the very smallest categories, the button's label becomes **First 10**. Choosing the button now takes you back to the original pie chart showing the 10 largest categories.

Inspecting Graph Details with QuickZoom

NOTE

Inspecting graphs with QuickZoom is the only time you absolutely must have a mouse in Quicken.

The basic Income and Expense graph is very informative by itself, but it also serves as a gateway to a whole range of detailed information, both graphical and numeric, about the money that has flowed in and out of your accounts. Whenever you want to know more about almost any part of a Quicken graph, you just point to the item in question, click the mouse a time or two, and you'll have your answers.

To see how this works, move the mouse pointer so that it's over one of the income bars in the top graph (the income bar is to the left in the pair of bars for each month). The pointer becomes a magnifying glass with a Z in it, just as when you used QuickZoom in reports (Chapters 10 and 11). With graphs, what happens when you use QuickZoom depends on the type of graph you're working with.

Double-click with the Magnifying Glass pointer over the income bar you've picked out. You'll see a new QuickZoom graph, a pie chart that gives you a breakdown of your income for that month by category. (See Figure 12.4.) You can print out the new graph if you'd like by clicking the **Print** icon or by pressing **Ctrl-P**.

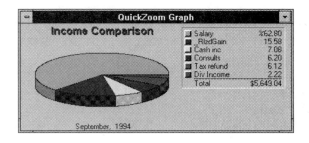

FIGURE 12.4

A QuickZoom graph showing the composition of your income for a particular month.

But you can go still farther with QuickZoom. If you now click over one of the pie slices in the new graph, Quicken automatically prepares a Transaction report listing the individual transactions that make up the category total for that slice (see Figure 12.5 on the next page.)

This report, Income Comparison, is a standard Quicken Transaction report just like the ones you created in Chapters 10 and 11. As with any other Quicken report, you can now modify the report settings via the Report window's button bar, memorize the report for future use (without having to create the graph first), or print the report on paper or to disk. And as with any other Transaction report, you can use QuickZoom to go straight to the corresponding register. Just double-click with the Magnifying Glass pointer on any row of the report, and you'll be taken to the register transaction it's based on.

Once you've navigated this sequence of graphs, a report, and the register, return to the original Income and Expense graph. To do this, you can click on any visible part of the graph window, but if you can't see the window at all, choose **Income and Expense Graph** from the Windows menu.

FIGURE 12.5

A QuickZoom report showing the transactions making up the category's total income for the month.

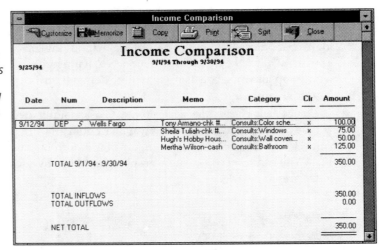

Now try QuickZoom in the pie chart. Double-clicking on any slice (except the "other" slice) brings up a bar graph that breaks down your expenses in that category by month, over the period covered by the main graph. Double-clicking on any of these bars produces a report listing the transactions in the category for the month covered by that bar.

If you use QuickZoom on the "other" slice, however, you get a new pie chart, which breaks down the slice into its component categories. In fact, this is exactly the same pie chart you got earlier when you chose **Next 10** from the original pie. Of course, you can analyze any of the individual categories in the new pie chart with QuickZoom.

> **NOTE**
>
> By the way, QuickZoom also works in the legends. If a pie slice is too small to point to accurately, it may be easier to double-click on the corresponding item in the legend, although the legend items are pretty small themselves.

To see the actual dollars-and-cents amount represented by any graphical element (e.g., a bar, a pie slice, or a point on a line), point to it with the magnifying glass pointer and hold down the mouse button for a moment (or press the right mouse button). Figure 12.6 is an example of what you'll see.

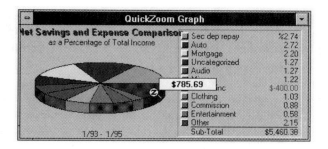

FIGURE 12.6

*Holding down the
mouse button over
a graphical element
pops up the
numeric value
represented by
that part of
the graph.*

Printing Graphs

To print a Quicken graph, open the **File** menu and choose **Print Graph**. Before you do, though, it will pay to know something about the process.

Quicken prints graphs using the same printer settings you chose for reports (see Chapter 10). Text appears in the font you selected for body text in the Report Printer Setup window. In general, you should leave blank the box labelled **Print reports and graphs in color** unless you actually have a color printer. However, if you find that printing a graph takes too long, you can try checking this box. This is especially helpful with PostScript printers, which can represent colors as shades of gray faster than they can reproduce fine patterns.

Another speed-up tip for laser printers: Printing at a lower resolution can be significantly faster, and may actually give you nicer-looking output. To try this, choose **Settings** in the Report Printer Setup window and set the resolution to a lower value.

Understanding the Other Graph Types

Now that you've reviewed one graph type thoroughly, you're ready to try out the other graphs at your pleasure. They all work in basically the same way, although a few of the options vary for setting them up, and each has a unique look.

Seeing How Well You Met Your Budget Goals

Create a budget variance graph if you want to assess your performance in meeting your budget targets. After starting things rolling by clicking the **Graphs** icon and selecting the **Budget Variance** radio button, or simply by choosing **Graphs** and **Budget Variance** in the Reports menu, you'll see a dialog box for creating the graph.

Type in the range of dates you want to study, and check the appropriate boxes if you want to narrow the report to specific accounts, categories, classes, or any combination of these. Again, if your income is fairly stable, you might want to look only at expense categories. Choose **OK** when you're through with the dialog box, and then, if you've checked any of the boxes, pick the items you want to include from the lists Quicken presents.

> **NOTE**   Unless you restricted the graph to particular categories, Quicken charts your actual "net income" (i.e., the amount left after subtracting your expenses from your income) to your budgeted net income. If you've excluded income or expense categories, the term *net income* isn't really accurate, but the basic meaning of the chart bars remains the same for the categories included.

Budget Variance graphs look like the example in Figure 12.7. The chart at the top shows you how well you met your budgetary goals overall, from month to month. If the bar for a month is above the line, you exceeded your goals by spending less or earning more or both. A red bar below the line tells you that you spent too much or earned too little for the month. Either way, the height of the bar evaluates your performance at a glance.

FIGURE 12.7

A sample budget variance graph.

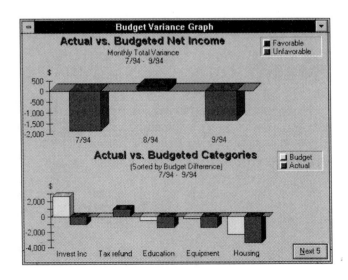

To see a category-by-category breakdown of how well you met your goals for an individual month, use QuickZoom on the bar for that month in the top chart.

WARNING	Don't compare the relative sizes of the bars in the lower chart except when they're visible at the same time. The graph labels often change when you display a new set of five categories.

The lower chart uses paired bars to compare the amount you actually took in or spent with the amount you budgeted for each category over the entire period of the graph. You see five categories at a time. Choosing the **Next 5** button shows you, obviously, the next five categories. Be sure to watch the labels on the graph's y-axis each time you bring a new set of categories into view—the axis usually changes, showing smaller amounts.

Use QuickZoom on either bar in a pair to see a month-by-month breakdown of the difference between actual and budgeted amounts for that category. You can go on from the QuickZoom graph to a report showing the transactions involved in each month.

Charting Your Net Worth

A Net-Worth graph makes it glaringly obvious how your net worth has changed from month to month or year to year. To create the graph, choose **Graphs** and **Net Worth** from the Reports menu, or select the **Net Worth** radio button from the dialog box that appears when you click the **Graphs** icon. In the Create New Worth Graph dialog box, enter the dates you want included in the graph and check the appropriate boxes if you want to limit the graph to certain accounts, categories, or classes.

A Net-Worth graph shows only a single chart, but it includes a combination of two separate types. Like the one in Figure 12.8 on the next page, your graph shows two bars for each month. The bar that extends upward from the x-axis represents the total of your assets as of the last day of that month. The bar that extends downward shows your total liabilities. It's easy to get a sense of where you stand by comparing the relative heights of the two bars; the hope, of course, is that the upper bar is larger.

FIGURE 12.8

*A sample
net-worth
graph.*

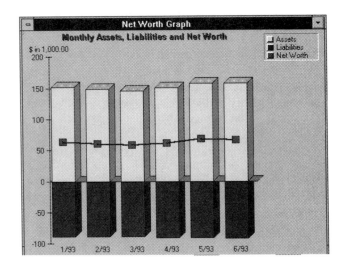

Superimposed on the bars is a line graph. This line represents your net worth: the difference between your assets and your liabilities. There's a square point along the line for each month, showing the net worth on the last day of the month. If the line is in positive territory, you own more than you owe; the trick is to get the line headed upward.

If you double-click over one of the bars, QuickZoom creates a pie chart showing the composition of your assets or liabilities (depending on which bar you clicked) by account. You can QuickZoom on any pie slice to a Transaction report showing all transactions in that account for the month in question. You can't QuickZoom on the line graph.

Tracking Your Investments Graphically

SHORTCUT

Don't forget that you can also generate graphs showing the price history of an investment while you're working with the Update Prices window. See the section on tracking investments in Chapter 9.

The final type of Quicken graph shows you the changes in your investment portfolio's value and gives you an idea of your rate of return on your entire portfolio as well as on individual investments.

To create the investment graph, choose **Graphs** and **Investments** from the Reports menu to display the Create Graphs dialog box. As Figure 12.9 shows, the buttons at the bottom of the box are different than those buttons for the other types of graphs. Since very few investment transactions include categories or classes, buttons for these aren't included.

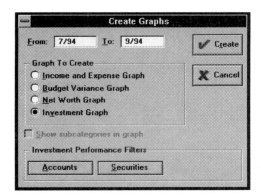

FIGURE 12.9

The Create Investment Performance Graph dialog box.

There are only two buttons labeled **Accounts** and **Securities**. After typing in a range of dates for the graph, you can choose one or both of these buttons to narrow the graph to specific accounts, securities, or both. The **Accounts** button displays the Select Accounts to Include list, but this time the only accounts listed are your investment accounts; choose among them as you did for other types of graphs.

If you choose the **Securities** button, you'll get a list of the securities in all your investment accounts. This list (see Figure 12.10) works just like the ones for accounts, categories, and classes—to include a security in the graph, it must have the notation "Include" in the final column of the list. To change the setting for a security, double-click on its name or select it and press the space bar. When you've chosen the securities you want in the graph, choose **OK**.

FIGURE 12.10

*Select the
securities you
want to include
in the graph
from this list.*

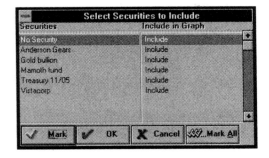

Investment graphs are slightly busier than the other types, as you can see in Figure 12.11. Ignore those buttons at the top for just a moment, and look at the top chart for now. This is a stacked-bar graph. Each bar's overall height represents the total value of your portfolio (or all of those securities you've chosen to graph) at the end of the month. When you first open the graph, the shaded blocks within each bar represent the contribution of the individual securities to the total.

FIGURE 12.11

*A sample
investment
graph.*

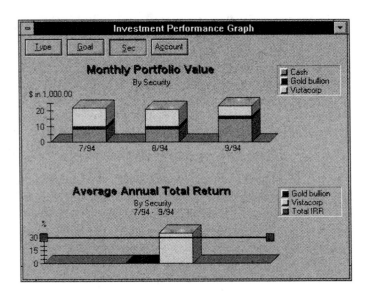

Those buttons at the top of the graph window let you change the way the bars are divided. To break down your overall portfolio value by account, security type (stocks, bonds, etc.), or investment goals (income, growth, etc.), choose the corresponding button. Quicken redraws the graph accordingly. You can go back to a breakdown by security by choosing the **Sec** button.

Using QuickZoom on any of the bars produces a pie chart offering the same sort of breakdown as the bar itself. The pie chart itself doesn't provide any new information, but it may make it easier to see the relative contributions of each item (security, account, etc.) to the portfolio total. But you do get additional numeric details in the legend: For each item, Quicken displays the percentage it contributes to the total.

The bottom portion of the Investment graph provides another of those two-graphs-in-one combinations. This part of the graph shows you how much you earned on your investments on an annualized basis during the period covered by the graph. The individual bars represent the percentage return for each kind of item selected by the buttons at the top of the graph: security, security type, account, or investment goal. The line across the graph pegs the average rate of return of all the investments in the graph (it's always perfectly horizontal, since this part of the graph doesn't give a month-by-month breakdown).

Double-click on any of the bars to QuickZoom to a transaction report covering the security or other item the bar represents.

Summary

You now know the simple steps for creating and customizing Quicken graphs to get a bird's-eye view of your financial situation. That completes your tour of Quicken's fundamental features.

It's time now to delete all the practice transactions from your records. If you haven't yet begun to enter your own real-life records, use the techniques described in the section "Modifying and Deleting Your Accounts" in Chapter 8 to delete all your accounts. Then start new accounts from your own records with the same methods you practiced in Chapters 2 and 8. If your accounts already include some of your own transactions, you'll need to find and delete the example transactions one by one using the techniques you learned in Chapter 4.

Chapter Thirteen
Financial Planning and Budgeting

Managing Your Personal Finances

Now that you've mastered all the basic Quicken skills, you're ready to tackle the challenges of financial management in your everyday life. This chapter gives you practical suggestions for putting Quicken to work on the critical tasks of realistic budgeting and overall financial planning.

Chapter 14 covers other aspects of personal financial management, such as handling your personal income taxes, monitoring assets and investments, and calculating your net worth. In Chapters 15 and 16, you'll get similar counsel on using Quicken for the fiscal chores that the small business owner or manager faces.

I'll assume that you've worked through the earlier parts of the book and are already comfortable with operations such as starting new accounts, creating or changing categories and classes, entering transactions into an account register, and producing reports. You'll find brief reminders of how to use these and other important Quicken functions here and in Chapters 14 through 16.

Tying It All Together

No matter what sort of financial management application you have in mind for Quicken, you'll need to follow the same basic game plan. Here are the basic steps you should follow:

1. Determine your financial goals, plan an overall strategy to meet them, and decide what kinds of financial records you'll need to carry out your plan.

2. Design a set of Quicken accounts to fit those needs. Decide how many accounts you'll require and of what type, and then set them up. Equally important, plan and create the categories and classes you'll need to organize your records within your accounts.

3. Use the Financial Calendar to project your income and spending patterns into the future (if you want accurate financial planning assistance at this stage, enter past records into Quicken first).

4. Create a preliminary budget.

5. Begin entering your current financial transactions into Quicken.

6. As soon as you've recorded your actual transactions for a month or more, start producing reports and graphs to keep abreast of where you stand. With them, check to see whether you're sticking to your financial plan, and whether you're progressing toward your goals. Adjust your budget if necessary to reflect the real-life patterns you detect.

With this basic sequence in mind, let's move on to explore the use of Quicken for some bread-and-butter financial chores.

Basic Financial Planning with Quicken

Quicken is loaded with features that make financial planning easier and more accurate. A variety of reports and graphs can clarify your income and spending patterns, showing you quickly where you're spending too much money and allowing you to anticipate future income needs.

NEW IN 3 New in version 3, the Financial Calendar gives you an overview of your cash flow, to give you the broad picture at a glance. And Quicken lets you set up a detailed budget, then monitor exactly how well you're meeting that budget over time.

Of course, Quicken's value as a financial planning tool depends on how much information you give it to work with. When you're first starting out with Quicken, you'll get accurate results if you enter all your actual transactions from the past year or more. Otherwise, you'll have to rely on estimates of income and spending that may or may not correspond to reality.

Planning with the Quicken Calendar and Planning Graph

NEW IN 3 Quicken 3's new financial planning graph provides the easiest way to anticipate future income and spending patterns, and to see how choices you make now—such as whether to buy a new car or take an additional part-time job—will affect your financial status over the long haul.

Because you can make changes at will, the graph lets you play "what if?" with your finances. To see how buying that new, more expensive house will affect your net worth, you just tell Quicken how much more your mortgage payment would be—your "real" records aren't affected.

NOTE
I've said that the graph is easy to use, but things get somewhat complicated if you have more than a few scheduled transactions. In that situation, it may be better to forego the graph and stick with Quicken's budgeting tools.

The planning graph is part of the Financial Calendar. To see it, display the calendar by clicking the **Calendar** icon or choosing **Financial Calendar** from the Activities menu. If the graph isn't showing in the Calendar window, choose the **Plan** (the one labelled with a chart graphic) button at the top of the window.

As you can see in Figure 13.1 on the next page, the planning graph charts the change in your bottom line over time. If you're working with a single account, the bar corresponds to the balance in that account; if you're graphing all your accounts, it represents your overall net worth.

Of course, the graph can only be accurate for the past (and then only if you've entered all your financial dealings into Quicken). For its future projections, the graph is based on two sources: your scheduled transactions (the ones you've scheduled for future payment), and a special worksheet on which you list your expected monthly income and expenses.

FIGURE 13.1

The Financial Calendar window after the Planning graph has been displayed.

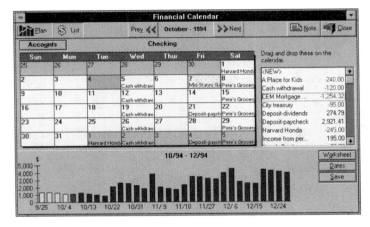

<table>
<tr><td>WARNING</td><td>Actually, Quicken includes all transactions you've recorded in your account, even the postdated ones, when creating the graph. If you've entered postdated transactions in your account, they will alter the results you'd otherwise get from your worksheet and scheduled transactions.</td></tr>
</table>

Working with the Planning Graph

The financial planning graph depicts your financial status in bar chart format over a range of dates. The height of each bar represents the overall total value of the accounts shown on the graph for that date (bars for negative values, if there are any, drop down from a line in the middle).

The date range shown begins a few days before the start of the month currently on display in the main part of the calendar. In addition to the legend below the graph, Quicken color codes the bars by date:

- Yellow bars represent the amounts in the past (prior to today's date).
- The green bar represents the date currently selected on the calendar (not today's date)—as you move the selection highlight, different bars become green.
- Blue bars show future positive values.
- Red bars show future negative values.

To graph other months, use the Arrow buttons at the top of the calendar window. You can also change the amount of time shown by choosing the **Dates** button to the right of the graph. In the small dialog box that appears, choose the radio button for the period you want to see graphed, and then choose **OK**.

Choosing Accounts to Display on the Graph

The values depicted by the Planning graph can reflect any combination of your Quicken accounts. If you want to track your overall net worth, you need to graph all your accounts. On the other hand, you can restrict the graph to a single account to see how its balance will likely change over time.

Typically, however, you'll get the most useful information by graphing your active bank, cash, and credit card accounts as a group. That way, you can see how much "liquid" available money you will have to save, to invest, or to spend, and then make plans accordingly.

To select the accounts that will appear on the graph (and the calendar), choose the **Accounts** button of the upper left of the Calendar window. A list of your accounts pops up. Double-click on each account name you want to graph, or highlight it and press the space bar; either way, the notation *Include* should appear in the far-right column. You can mark or unmark all the accounts with the **Mark All** button. When you close this window, Quicken modifies the calendar and graph to reflect the accounts you selected.

Planning with the Worksheet

When you first display the planning graph, it charts only the transactions recorded in your account and any scheduled transactions you've entered. If your past records are complete, the chart should give you a pretty good idea of the total in your accounts to date. But since you probably tend to schedule only a portion of your future transactions, the graph's projections won't be very helpful at this point.

That's where the *financial planning worksheet* comes in. You use the worksheet to tell Quicken how much you expect to earn and spend every month. Based on that information, it builds a graph projecting your net savings (or deficit) into the future.

To display the worksheet, choose the **Worksheet** button (labelled with a chart graphic) at the right of the graph. You'll see the window shown in Figure 13.2.

FIGURE 13.2

The Financial Planning Worksheet: If you haven't scheduled any transactions, you won't see the Scheduled section.

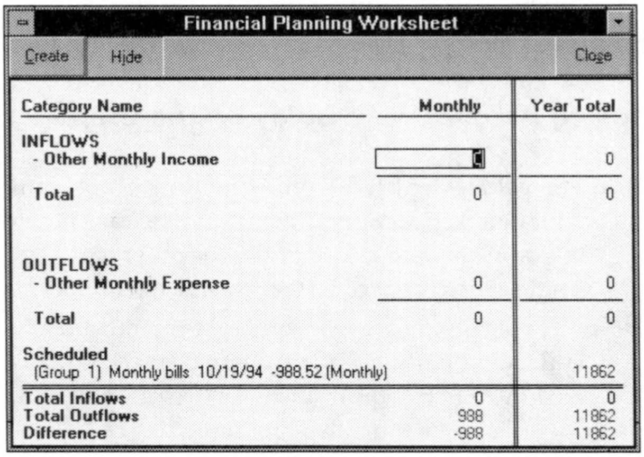

Financial Planning Worksheet		
Create Hide		Close
Category Name	**Monthly**	**Year Total**
INFLOWS		
- Other Monthly Income		0
Total	0	0
OUTFLOWS		
- Other Monthly Expense	0	0
Total	0	0
Scheduled		
(Group 1) Monthly bills 10/19/94 -988.52 (Monthly)		11862
Total Inflows	0	0
Total Outflows	988	11862
Difference	-988	11862

The worksheet always shows fields for *Other Monthly Income* and *Other Monthly Expenses*, for uncategorized amounts. But you have two options for how to display values for specific categories. The condensed worksheet view shows only those categories that contain values, whereas the full view shows all the categories in your accounts, even those with zero values in the worksheet. Choose the **Hide** button to switch between the two views.

You can enter dollar values for individual items in the *Monthly* column. (Yearly amounts and totals are calculated from your entries.) A rectangular border indicates the item you can edit. To make an entry, move to the field for that item by clicking it or with the cursor keys, just as you would in a report. Then just type in the number.

Let's say that you're just starting with Quicken and haven't entered records for previous months into your accounts. As long as you can accurately estimate your total monthly income and expenses, you can still build a useful graph by entering those amounts in the *Other Monthly Income* and *Other Monthly Expense* sections of the worksheet.

The only catch is that you must adjust your entries for any scheduled transactions that Quicken has entered for you in the worksheet. Figure 13.2 shows how the worksheet lists scheduled transactions. Your goal is to have accurate totals for income and expenses. Here's what to do to:

1. Calculate your expected total monthly income.

2. From this overall total, subtract the total amount of monthly income from all your scheduled deposits shown in the worksheet. Unfortunately, the worksheet doesn't add the scheduled transactions for you—you'll have to break out Quicken's calculator to add up the numbers.

3. Enter the result in the *Other Income* field. At the bottom of the worksheet, the amount Quicken lists for *Total Inflows* should now equal the estimate of the overall total income you made in step 1.

Repeat the same steps for the expense section of the worksheet.

After making the entries, choose **Close**. Quicken asks you whether you want to save the worksheet. When you choose **Yes**, the graph is redrawn to reflect the worksheet values.

Generating a Worksheet From Quicken Records

Obviously, the more accurate the estimates of monthly income and spending, the more useful the graph will be in predicting your future financial status. If you have a complete set of Quicken records to work with, the program can use them to complete the Planning Worksheet for you. You can then change the worksheet entries to anticipate changes in your income or expenses.

To have Quicken fill in the worksheet for you, display the worksheet and choose the **Create** button at the top left. In the little dialog box that appears (see Figure 13.3), you're offered two radio buttons: **AutoCreate from your Register** and **Read Budgets from Spreadsheet**. If you've already created a formal budget in Quicken (a process you'll learn about in the next section of this chapter), choosing the second radio button will simply copy your budget to the worksheet.

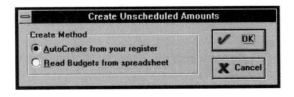

FIGURE 13.3

You will see this dialog box when you ask Quicken to create your worksheet.

However, if you haven't yet built a budget, or if want to base the graph on past trends and your budget doesn't agree with these, have Quicken calculate the worksheet for you based on your existing records. Leave the **AutoCreate** button selected. When you choose **OK**, you'll see an AutoCreate Budget window (see Figure 13.4). Here, enter the range of dates Quicken will examine in figuring your worksheet. Be sure to include only those months for which you entered all your transactions.

FIGURE 13.4

The AutoCreate Budget window.

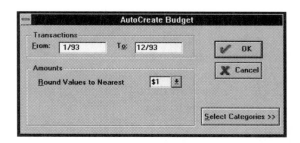

You can also change the way Quicken rounds off transaction amounts in its calculations. If you're working with big numbers, you might want to round to $10 or even $100 amounts so you won't be distracted by too much detail.

Finally, you can restrict the automatic worksheet calculations to a specific set of categories if you'd like. Perhaps you took a once-in-a-lifetime vacation to Europe last year, spending a lot of money in the process. Since you expect to spend much less on vacations for the next few years at least, you don't want Quicken to skew the worksheet by including expenses for last year's trip in the worksheet.

To pick categories, choose the **Select Categories** button. Quicken expands the AutoCreate window to include a category list, marked in the familiar way with a checkmark. To exclude one of the categories, click on it or highlight it and press the space bar so that the checkmark vanishes. In a slight departure from other Quicken lists, the usual **Mark All** button is joined by a **Clear All** button. If you want to select just a few categories, use **Clear All** to unmark all the categories first, then pick out the particular ones you'd like.

When you choose **OK**, Quicken adds up all the transactions in each category for the period you select, divides by the number of months in the period, and places this figure in the *Monthly* column of the worksheet. The *Yearly* total for the category is just the monthly amount multiplied by 12. When the process is complete, the worksheet appears with entries for all your categories.

So far so good. Here's the tricky part: You have to adjust these worksheet figures for any scheduled transactions you've set up. The problem is your worksheet probably now includes duplicate amounts for many of your scheduled transactions. Your previous records probably include transactions that you've scheduled for automatic payment, such as your monthly rent or mortgage payment.

To make your financial graph accurate, you have to modify the worksheet entry for each category to which you've assigned a scheduled transaction. If it's an Income category, subtract the amount of the scheduled transactions for that category. If it's an expense category, add the scheduled transactions. You'll probably need a piece of paper and the Quicken calculator to help you keep track of the items in the various categories.

When the worksheet is finished, choose **Close**, then **Yes** when Quicken asks if you want to save it. You'll be returned to the Planning graph, which will now reflect your worksheet entries. You can move through the calendar to see how much money you're likely to have down the road, and to see graphically how big future expenses will affect your finances.

Playing What If? with Your Financial Future

Together, the calendar, worksheet, and planning graph let you explore the repercussions on your financial future of every income or spending decision you might make. You can revise the worksheet as often as you like to see how financial decisions you're contemplating affect your net worth in the future.

One key to building hypothetical scenarios with the calendar is to schedule transactions that Quicken won't actually record in your account. When you create transactions for hypothetical planning purposes, edit the Schedule Transaction window to set the *Register Entry* field to *For Planning Only*.

Let's say you're trying to decide whether to buy a new car or stick with your old clunker for another year. You enter a one-time scheduled transaction for the downpayment and a recurring schedule transaction for the monthly payments, setting both up as For Planning Only transactions.

After studying the graph that results, you can save it to disk. Here's how: choose the **Save** button to the right of the graph. In the dialog box that appears (see Figure 13.5 on the next page) choose one of the two radio buttons labeled **Scenario** as a "parking place" for the current graph. When you choose **Save**, Quicken stores it under the name you chose.

FIGURE 13.5

*The Show
Saved
Projection
dialog box.*

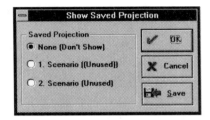

You can now revise the worksheet for an alternative set of assumptions (I didn't buy the car, but I splurged on a new wardrobe). To compare the new version of your future finances against the old, again choose the **Save** button on the main graph. This time, choose the radio button for the scenario you assigned to the old graph and choose **OK**, not **Save**. The old graph appears as a line graph "on top" of the current graph, as shown in Figure 13.6.

> **WARNING**
>
> It's important to choose the correct button when you're closing the Show Saved Projection dialog box. Choose **Save** to save the current graph to disk, **OK** to display a previously saved graph (the one stored for the scenario you've selected) with the current graph.

FIGURE 13.6

*Quicken can
overlay one
graph on
anotherto
show you the different impacts
of two sets of financial
assumptions.*

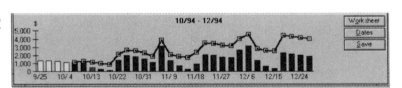

Drawing Up a Budget—and Sticking to It

Budgeting is the quintessential financial management task. Whether you consciously budget or not, you already have some method for figuring out how much you can spend, based on how much you earn. But Quicken can bring your income-and-expense picture into sharp focus, showing you clearly where your money comes from—and, more important, where it goes.

Quicken includes a built-in Budget worksheet that lets you prepare a detailed budget for all 12 months of the year. Then, after a month or more has passed, you can use Budget reports and graphs to see how well you're holding to your budget in every category.

Preparing to Budget

Before you draw up a specific budget plan, you need a clear idea of your financial goals. People budget to limit their spending on some items so they can have more money left over for others. This means cutting back on expenses now in order to have money in the future to pay off debts, save for a down payment on a home, put children through college, retire, or set aside in case of an emergency. However, despite the best intentions, day-to-day life can get in the way of longer-range financial goals.

Drawing up a formal budget can help. It implies an important psychological commitment to discipline in spending, and it also turns your vague notions about spending less on frills into clear-cut dollar limits.

SHORTCUT Since you can record mortgage and car loan payments in your checking account, these liabilities don't need separate accounts for budgeting purposes. Still, you may want to create accounts for them in order to track them more closely, and to allow you to calculate your net worth accurately.

Once you have a good sense of your budget goals, you can turn to Quicken for help with the mechanics of the budgeting process, and for reports and graphs that provide the information you'll need to budget accurately. To begin with, you need to establish accounts for each of your major assets and debts, or at least those that vary a good deal in value from month to month. If you and your spouse have separate checking accounts, you should create corresponding Quicken bank accounts, one for each of you. If you use credit cards extensively, you'll need one or more credit card accounts (ideally, one for each of your credit cards). If you receive substantial sums of cash income, or make many cash purchases, you should create a cash account. Active investors should create accounts for their stocks, bonds, and other securities.

To create each of the accounts you require, follow the steps you learned in Chapters 1 and 8. In brief, open the Account list by clicking on the **Accts** icon or by pressing **Ctrl-A**. Then choose **New** to start the account, and fill in the fields in the dialog boxes that appear to match the account you're creating.

Once you have opened the necessary accounts, you'll need to organize them for effective budgeting. Try to group similar transactions so that you'll be able to see how much you spent on food, how much on clothing, how much on entertainment, and so on. In Quicken jargon, you need to create categories and classes to which you can then assign each important transaction. But if these assignments are to be meaningful, it's vital that they be tailored to your own situation. If you followed my advice in Chapter 5 and did set up your own list of categories, you're already set. If not, go back to Chapter 5 and use the instructions there for creating a list that's custom tailored to your own needs.

When your list of categories and classes is complete, you're ready to start budgeting in earnest. I recommend that you print the Category list as a paper scratch pad for your budgeting efforts. Display the list by pressing **Ctrl-C** from the register, then click the **Print** icon or press **Ctrl-P** to print it.

Creating a Budget

Now that your accounts have been established and your categories and classes are in place, you can turn to the budgeting process itself. Setting up a budget is simple in concept: You just decide on the amount of money you want to spend on each kind of expense every month. Where budgeting gets tricky is in choosing realistic figures.

| NOTE | If your financial situation has undergone major changes recently, be sure to base your budget on the period since the change. |

As a good starting point, you need to know about how much you've been earning and how much you've been spending over the past year or so. When you first start budgeting with a new set of Quicken accounts, there are two methods you can use to determine your past income and spending patterns. If you don't mind some initial paper shuffling and pencil scratching, you can sort through your old records yourself and figure out your typical income and expenses on your own. Alternatively, if you have the time, you can enter your past records into your Quicken accounts, and have the program calculate your income and expense patterns using the Automatic Budgeting feature.

Once you have some idea of how much you've been earning and spending, you can begin to evaluate your spending habits to see where you can cut back a bit. Obviously, don't assume that just because you've spent a certain amount on a particular expense in the past, you must continue spending that much. When you've decided on a more frugal but realistic target for a given category, enter it into your budget.

Setting Up a Quicken Budget

Quicken's Budget worksheet is a great alternative to budgeting on paper. Besides, you'll need to fill it out to produce Budget reports in the future; obviously, Quicken needs your budget to calculate the difference between your budgeted income and expenses and actual figures.

In the examples here, I'll use the following sample data to illustrate the process of budgeting with Quicken. If you have them, you should use your own budget figures instead.

Category	Budget Amount
Div Income	45
Int Inc	60
Salary	1500
Auto	200
Childcare	(varies monthly)
Groceries	450
Mortgage	750

To build a Quicken budget, choose **Set Up Budgets** from the Activities menu. As shown in Figure 13.7 on the next page, you'll be presented with the Set Up Budgets window. This window is organized as a large table, similar to an accounting or computerized spreadsheet.

In the rows of the table, the window lists all the categories in your account in alphabetical order in two broad groups: *Inflows*, for income transactions, and *Outflows*, for expense transactions. The columns are for the months of the year (you can set up the screen so that the columns correspond to quarters or entire years if you like).

Notice that the Set Up Budgets window has its own button bar at the top, just below the title bar. Notice also the thin rectangle that marks the first item in the budget table. Of course, you can only make entries into one item at a time, and this rectangle tool shows you which one. The item selected by the rectangle is also highlighted—you can't miss it.

FIGURE 13.7

The Set Up Budgets window.

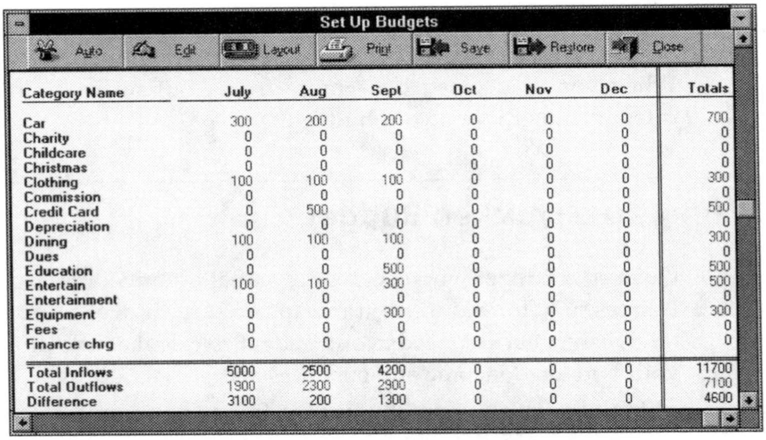

Category Name	July	Aug	Sept	Oct	Nov	Dec	Totals
Car	300	200	200	0	0	0	700
Charity	0	0	0	0	0	0	0
Childcare	0	0	0	0	0	0	0
Christmas	0	0	0	0	0	0	0
Clothing	100	100	100	0	0	0	300
Commission	0	0	0	0	0	0	0
Credit Card	0	500	0	0	0	0	500
Depreciation	0	0	0	0	0	0	0
Dining	100	100	100	0	0	0	300
Dues	0	0	0	0	0	0	0
Education	0	0	500	0	0	0	500
Entertain	100	100	300	0	0	0	500
Entertainment	0	0	0	0	0	0	0
Equipment	0	0	300	0	0	0	300
Fees	0	0	0	0	0	0	0
Finance chrg	0	0	0	0	0	0	0
Total Inflows	5000	2500	4200	0	0	0	11700
Total Outflows	1900	2300	2900	0	0	0	7100
Difference	3100	200	1300	0	0	0	4600

You can move the selection rectangle tool around the table with the cursor keys. Pressing **RightArrow** or **Tab** moves you one column (month) to the right, while **LeftArrow** or **Shift-Tab** moves one column to the left. The **UpArrow** and **DownArrow** buttons move you up and down a row in the same column, while **PgUp** and **PgDn** move you within the row an entire screen at a time. With the mouse, you can move to any one budget item by clicking on it, or use the vertical and horizontal scroll bars to display other categories or different months.

Enter the budget amounts for January into the first column for the corresponding category. To move to the next category in the window, just press the **DownArrow** key.

Once you're through with all the entries for January, you can copy them to the other months with a single command. First, be sure the highlight is still in the *January* column. Then choose the **Edit** button to display a short menu, from which you should choose **Fill Columns**. (To copy a single category to other months, use the **Fill Rows** command instead).

NOTE

In Quicken 2, there's a separate **Fill Cols** button on the button bar.

WARNING

Before using the **Fill Columns** command, always be sure that the highlight is somewhere in the column from which you want to copy the amounts. You can copy amounts from any month's column, not just January's.

Note that the amount budgeted for one of the items in the above sample budget, childcare, varies from month to month. Often, you expect your income or expense in one or more categories to change on a monthly basis.

If you buy your own health insurance, for example, you may pay in quarterly installments, so that in this category you would want to budget the installment every third month and nothing in other months. Likewise, if business booms for your roller skating rental service in the summer but dries up in the winter, you'll want your budget to reflect those seasonal changes. In our sample budget, the childcare expense is projected to vary considerably, dropping way off in the summer months (perhaps you're a teacher, so you can take care of your children yourself during vacations and holidays).

To enter different monthly budget amounts for a category, just move the highlight to that month's column in the row for childcare using the cursor keys or the mouse. When you get there, type in the right amount for that month. Here's a sample budget for the childcare category:

Month	*Amount*
Jan	120
Feb	120
Mar	120
Apr	120
May	120
Jun	65
Jul	25
Aug	25
Sep	60
Oct	120
Nov	120
Dec	100

Modifying the Layout of the Budget Window

You can change how much information the Budget worksheet displays with the **Layout** button. When you choose **Layout**, a small dialog box with several options appears (see Figure 13.8 on the next page).

NOTE   In Quicken 2, many of these **Layout** options are available as separate buttons on the button bar. For example, there are **Month**, **Quarter**, and **Year** buttons.

FIGURE 13.8

*You will see these options when you choose **Layout** from the Set Up Budgets window.*

If your budget stays the same over periods longer than a month, you can simplify the Set Up Budgets window without any loss of information. Choose the **Quarter** or **Year** radio button to limit the budget to three columns or one column for the entire year, respectively.

When you initially open the Set Up Budgets window, subcategory information is grouped according to the main categories to which it belongs. To display subcategories so that you can budget for them separately, check the **Subcats** box. Once you enter separate budget amounts for a subcategory, Quicken remembers that amount even if you turn off the subcategory display. Later, if you decide to display the subcategories again, Quicken recalls the subcategory budget amounts automatically.

Ordinarily, your Quicken budget only covers transactions assigned to **Income** and **Expense** categories. If you wish, however, you can configure the Set Up Budgets dialog box to include account names in both the Inflows and Outflows sections of the budget, allowing you to budget amounts that you transfer between accounts. To do this, check the **Transfers** box.

WARNING   If you decide later to remove the account names from the screen again, just uncheck **Show Transfers**.

Once the account names appear in your budget, you can type in amounts for each month just as you would for other budget items. If you expect to transfer $50 a month from your checking account to an investment account, for example, you'd enter that amount in the columns for the *Checking* row in the Inflows section and for the *Investments* row in the Outflows section.

You may not want to establish a budget amount for every category you've set up. To help you concentrate on the items you've budgeted, you can have Quicken remove the categories that contain a zero budget amount in all 12 months from the Set Up Budgets window. To do this, check the *Hide Zero Budget Categories* box.

Creating a Budget Automatically

If you decide to start using Quicken for budgeting after you've entered your real financial information into the program, Quicken can set up a preliminary budget for you automatically. Quicken does this by extracting the amounts you've actually spent on each category from the records in all your accounts. Of course, you're free to go in and change any of the amounts you like after the automatic budget is established.

Here are the steps for setting up a budget automatically:

1. Beginning at the Set Up Budgets window, choose the **Auto** button.
2. In the first two fields, type in the date range, in months, on which you want Quicken to base its automatic budget.
3. The *Round Values to Nearest* field lets you tell Quicken how to round off each category's monthly total: to the nearest **$1**, **$10**, or **$100**. Most of us who need to budget have to watch even small amounts, so the **$1** option is fine. If a broader-brush budget suits your situation better, pick the option you want from the drop-down list.
4. Indicate the type of budget calculation you want Quicken to make. Choose **Use Monthly Detail** if you want to transfer the actual category totals for each month to the worksheet, select the **With Monthly Detail** radio button (in this case, the date range is limited to 12 months). Choose **Use Average for Period** if you want Quicken to enter the average monthly amount for each category over the selected period.
5. To limit the automatic budgeting to specific categories, choose **Select Categories**. A list of your categories appears, on which you can mark the categories you want included with the usual methods.
6. Choose **OK** to generate the Automatic Budget.

Once Quicken fills in the budget for you, you're then free to edit these amounts as you like.

Budgeting for Biweekly Income and Expenses

Quicken budgets make special provision for income and expense items that occur every two weeks rather than monthly. Probably the most common of such items is a paycheck you get every other week. To budget accurately, you need to account for the fact that two months each year you'll get three paychecks; not two, because of the biweekly pay period.

NOTE In Quicken 2, there's a separate **2 Week** button on the button bar.

Quicken can do the work for you automatically. Select the category for the item you want to budget this way (any month will do). Now choose **Edit** from the worksheet's button bar, followed by **2-Week**, the top item in the menu. In the Set Up Two-Week Budget dialog box, type in the amount for that budget item you anticipate receiving or spending every two weeks. Then enter the date on which you want Quicken to start the biweekly cycle (e.g., the date of your first paycheck). When you choose **OK**, Quicken fills in the correct amount for each month's budget entry based on the biweekly schedule you've specified.

Editing the Budget Worksheet

The menu that appears when you choose the **Edit** button offers several choices for revamping your budget quickly. In addition to the **Fill Columns** and **Fill Rows** choices covered above, you can choose:

- **Clear Row**, to erase the values for the current category in all months
- **Clear All Budgets**, to completely erase the entire worksheet
- **Copy to Clipboard**, to copy the entire worksheet to the Windows clipboard, for sharing budget information with other programs

Also, if you ever realize you've made a major mistake when editing the budget amounts—perhaps you started in the wrong row—you can restore the budget amounts to what they were when you opened the Set Up Budgets window, before you made any changes. Just choose the **Restore** button.

The Budgeting Process

Now that you understand the nuts and bolts of budgeting in Quicken, you can go ahead and construct your actual budget. In the worksheet, enter your projected monthly income from each source in the row for that category. Then record your *fixed expenses* (the ones that you can't readily change), such as your house payment or rent, car payment, other bank loans, your taxes, and your minimum utility bills, and subtract them from your income. If you want to be disciplined about saving, you need to include in your fixed expenses a minimum contribution to your savings or retirement account that you make before you do anything else with your income.

Now comes the moment of truth. Down at the bottom of the worksheet, Quicken has subtracted the total for those fixed expenses from your total income. What's left over—the amount labeled *Difference*—is available for your remaining expenses, your "discretionary spending."

Should your figures indicate that you don't have enough money to cover these controllable expenses at their past levels, you've just identified the reason that your savings account balance has been shrinking—or worse, that you've been sinking into debt. In any case, the next and most painful step is to adjust downward the limit for each of the expenses you can control, writing the amounts on your Category list.

Keep chipping away at your discretionary expenses until your income equals or exceeds the total of all your expenses, including your savings contribution. It's at this point that you may have to make trade-offs between new clothes and nights out, between gourmet meals and an occasional vacation. Should it turn out that your projected budget is still in the red even after you've cut back to the bare necessities, you'll have to consider reducing your fixed expenses, perhaps by looking for a cheaper home or apartment, or selling your car, or raising your income to cover the discrepancy. But at least you'll know the challenge you face.

It's not necessary that you budget for every minor kind of expense that may come up, as long as your small expense items don't add up to one big budget-busting *Miscellaneous*. Instead, concentrate on setting frugal yet attainable budget limits for the "big-ticket" items. If you focus on the expenses that have the largest impact on your *bottom line*—for you, the amount of money you have left at the end of the month—a balanced budget should come together quickly.

Closing the Budget Window

You can leave the Budget window in one of two ways. The easiest method is to choose the window's **Close** button. When you do, Quicken automatically saves your changes to the budget as it closes the window. Alternatively, you can double-click on the Budget window's control box. This time, Quicken gives you the opportunity *not* to save the changes, which is handy if you realize that some of your budgetary goals were unrealistic.

Budgeting with Quicken Reports

After you've kept track of all your income and expenses in one or more Quicken accounts for several months, or if you've entered your past records into the program, Quicken reports can help you see how well you're keeping to your earning and spending plans. Reports can also help refine your budget to make it more realistic.

Two kinds of Quicken reports are most useful in budgeting: Budget reports and Itemized Transaction reports.

The steps for creating a budget report are familiar if you've worked with any Quicken reports. Choose **Home** and **Monthly Budget** from the Reports menu. In the Create Report dialog box, pick a named date range in the first field, or enter a set of months you want in the *From* and *To* fields.

Start the report by choosing **OK**. Quicken will think for a few moments, then display the finished report on your screen, which should look something like Figure 13.9.

FIGURE 13.9

A monthly Budget report on the screen.

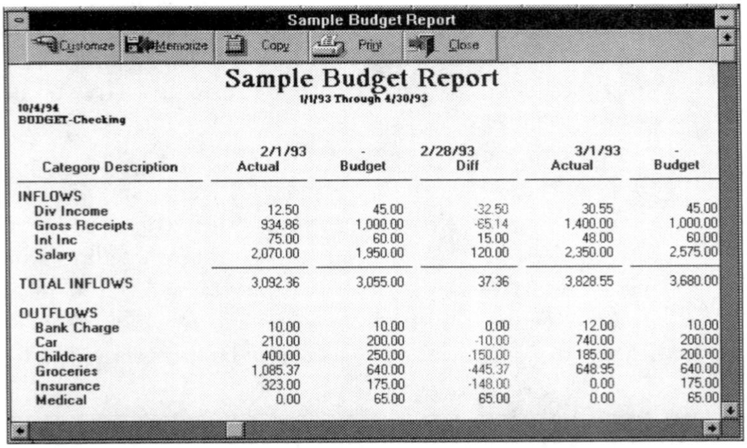

Sample Budget Report

1/1/93 Through 4/30/93

10/4/94
BUDGET-Checking

Category Description	2/1/93 Actual	- Budget	2/28/93 Diff	3/1/93 Actual	- Budget
INFLOWS					
Div Income	12.50	45.00	-32.50	30.55	45.00
Gross Receipts	934.86	1,000.00	-65.14	1,400.00	1,000.00
Int Inc	75.00	60.00	15.00	48.00	60.00
Salary	2,070.00	1,950.00	120.00	2,350.00	2,575.00
TOTAL INFLOWS	3,092.36	3,055.00	37.36	3,828.55	3,680.00
OUTFLOWS					
Bank Charge	10.00	10.00	0.00	12.00	10.00
Car	210.00	200.00	-10.00	740.00	200.00
Childcare	400.00	250.00	-150.00	185.00	200.00
Groceries	1,085.37	640.00	-445.37	648.95	640.00
Insurance	323.00	175.00	-148.00	0.00	175.00
Medical	0.00	65.00	65.00	0.00	65.00

The Budget report lists income and expense categories in rows with month-by-month subtotals for each category. For each month, the Budget report not only shows the amounts you actually received and spent, but the amounts you had budgeted and the difference between the actual and budgeted amounts. It should be fairly easy to find places where you've spent too much.

When you've seen enough of the report on the screen, you can print it by choosing the **Print** button. You'll see the same Print Report window you used to print the Cash Flow report. This report is apt to be large, so Quicken will divide the report vertically into sections that each fit within the number of columns allowed by your printer setup. When printing is complete, you can place these sections side by side to see the whole report.

Budgeting with Itemized Categories Reports

Itemized Categories reports list all the transactions in each category. They can be useful in drawing up a budget by helping you to analyze your spending in a particular category. If, say, you think your total spending for clothing over the past couple of months could have been trimmed, you can examine all your clothing expenses as recorded in the report to decide whether each purchase was really necessary or you simply splurged. To create an Itemized Categories report, choose **Home** and **Itemized Category** from the Reports menu. Fill out the window that appears and choose **OK**, and you'll have your report (see Chapter 10 for more details).

Getting the Big Picture with Budget Graphs

The quickest way to identify where you're spending too much money is to generate a Budget graph. The main graph shows you at a glance the categories in which spending has most exceeded your budget for the entire period of the graph. To see a month-by-month breakdown of your budgetary success (or failure) for a category, use QuickZoom on that part of the graph (see Chapter 12 for details on using Quicken graphs).

Sticking to Your Budget

Neat and tidy plans are nice, but by far the most important part of budgeting is to abide by your established spending limits. Although Quicken can't force you to stay within your means, it can tell you almost instantly when you've failed to do so, and by how much. All you have to do is create a Budget report. As you learned in Chapter 10, choose **Home** then **Monthly Budget** from the Reports menu. Type in the months that you want the report to cover and choose **OK**.

The resulting Budget report offers a category-by-category breakdown in three columns for each month: one for the amount you actually took in or spent, one for the corresponding budget amount, and one for the difference between the two. As usual, the most critical numbers are on the bottom line, labeled OVERALL TOTAL. There, a positive number in the *Diff* (difference) column means you stayed within your budget for the month, whereas a negative number means you spent more than you earned. Even if the total looks good, however, you should still scrutinize each category to identify any wide divergences from your budgeted amounts, and head off potential problems. For example, an unusually mild winter might have reduced your utility bills, masking your excessive spending in another category. To investigate the cause of any major budgetary lapses, use an Itemized Categories report as described previously to get a listing of all your transactions grouped by category.

Summary

You've just learned to draw on all of Quicken's resources to meet the crucial challenge of basic financial planning and budgeting. If you use these skills regularly, you should be able to put your financial house in order in no time. Of course, there's more to managing your personal finances. You'll find instructions for handling all kinds of specific financial situations in Chapter 14.

Chapter Fourteen
Managing Your Personal Finances

B eyond the basics of planning and budgeting, Quicken can aid you with any chore involving your personal financial situation. In this chapter, you'll learn how to marshall Quicken's talents to keep your tax records and help you fill out your IRS forms; to develop savings plans for retirement and your kids' college education; to keep track of your investments and other valuable assets; and to keep you informed of your net worth.

Handling Your Income Taxes

NOTE	You can transfer the information in your Quicken accounts directly into leading tax preparation programs (see the Appendix for details).

After budgeting, the next most daunting financial task most people face is dealing with income taxes. By keeping your records current in Quicken, however, you'll be able to prepare your tax returns with a minimum of effort. If you prefer to have someone else prepare your taxes, a complete set of Quicken records and reports will make getting ready a snap for you, and will make the tax specialist's job easy and accurate.

The process of using Quicken for your tax records really begins when you first start working with your accounts. As you establish the accounts you'll be using, plan your Quicken categories and classes with an eye to their role in tax return preparation. Of course, you'll want to indicate correctly whether each category you create is or is not tax related. To ensure that all transactions you enter are assigned to a category, set Quicken to the required category entry using the General Preferences dialog box as outlined in the Appendix. And above all, be sure you associate each tax-related category with the correct tax form line item as described in Chapter 5.

NOTE

If a single category can include both tax- and nontax-related items, or items that should be recorded on separate lines of your tax form, you should divide the category. There are three ways to do this:

1. You can divide the items that receive different tax treatment into separate categories.

2. You can create subcategories that distinguish between the items, assigning each subcategory to its own tax form line item.

3. You can use classes to distinguish tax- and nontax-related items. This was the only way to handle this situation in early versions of Quicken, but it's now the least efficient solution. However, it works fine if your tax situation is extremely simple, and you may prefer it if you're an experienced Quicken user.

Many people with otherwise simple tax situations find that a few special items are sometimes tax-related. At the time of this writing, for example, childcare expenses can be deducted, but only if the childcare is needed for work-related purposes. Similarly, you can deduct travel and gas expenses for moving if certain requirements are met, but never for your vacations.

In cases like these, you can use categories to distinguish between most of your tax- and nontax-related transactions, and then set up a few special subcategories for categories that can contain items that are either tax or nontax related, depending on the circumstances.

For example, if you send your kids to daycare on shopping days as well as work days, you should set up two subcategories for the **Childcare** category, assigning the one for work-related daycare to tax form 2441. If the checks you write to the daycare center cover both types of daycare, you can split these transactions and assign each portion of the split to the appropriate subcategory.

Then, when you prepare a Tax Summary report, only the tax-deductible daycare expenses will show up. You can still see how much you're spending in total on childcare with reports that aren't restricted to tax-related categories.

Here's another example. Let's say that you incur certain expenses in the performance of your job that are not reimbursed by your employer. At the time of this writing, many of these "employee business expenses" can be deducted on Form 2106. In this case, you can set up subcategories within each of the relevant categories, such as meals, entertainment, clothing, and so on, assigning them to the corresponding line of Form 2106.

Preparing Your Tax Returns

Once you've set up your categories and subcategories properly, and provided you've entered all your records for the previous year into your accounts, getting ready to pay your taxes requires only a few minutes of your time. All you have to do is prepare a Tax Schedule report by choosing **Home**, then **Tax Schedule** from the Reports menu. Enter the months you want the report to cover—for most people this will be from January to December of the tax year in question—and choose **OK**.

The report lists all transactions assigned to categories or subcategories associated with a tax form line item, calculating the subtotals for each line item for you. Since you don't need the detail of individual transactions to prepare your returns, you can remove them from the display by choosing the **Customize** button and checking the *Totals Only* box. The report should now look something like the one in Figure 14.1.

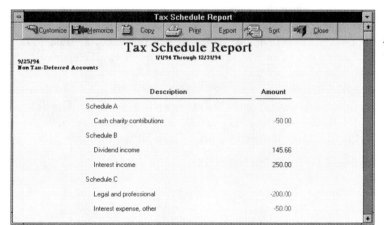

FIGURE 14.1

A Tax Schedule report with the individual transactions hidden.

It will then be easy to copy the subtotals for each line item directly to your tax forms. All you have to do now is calculate the final amounts on each form and then on your 1040—and the Quicken calculator is available to help.

Using Quicken for Tax Documentation

If the ultimate terror, the *tax audit*, should strike, and you need detailed, itemized records to present to the IRS, Quicken's tax schedule report again proves your ace in the hole. As a Transaction report, it lists every individual transaction, complete with any memo you've entered documenting its purpose. Again, they're grouped by tax schedule line item. In this case, leave the *Totals Only* box unchecked in the Customize window—you want to see the details on each transaction.

| NOTE | Of course, you'll also need to provide your auditor with receipts, check stubs, and other original documents to verify your Quicken records. |

Planning for Retirement

Eventually, you'll reach the stage of life where you no longer want to work, at least not in a regular, full-time job. With Quicken's Retirement calculator, you can easily answer the all-important retirement-planning question: How much money do I have to put aside each year for an adequate nest egg?

| WARNING | Although the Retirement calculator gives results down to the penny, don't be fooled: Its projections are only rough estimates based on a number of inevitably inaccurate assumptions you must make. Still, it's a great way to test alternative hypothetical scenarios. |

To use the Retirement calculator, choose **Financial Planners** and **Retirement** from the Activities menu. Figure 14.2 shows what you'll see. The Retirement calculator is the largest of Quicken's calculators on the screen, with a good many fields to fill out. But don't worry—it's really quite straightforward.

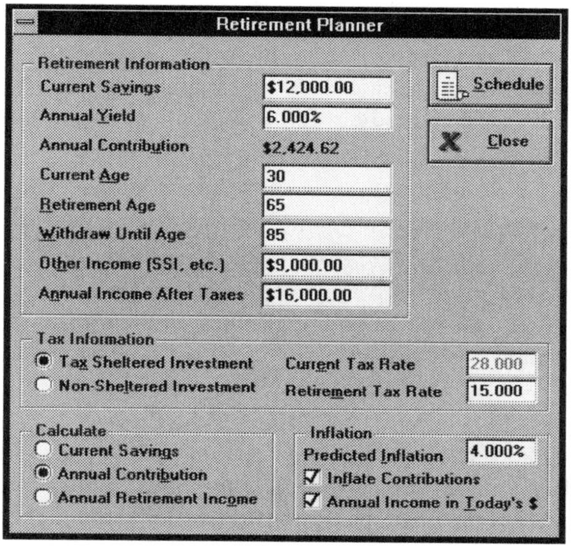

FIGURE 14.2

The Retirement calculator.

You can use the Retirement calculator to figure three kinds of results, depending on what you want to know. Select one of the radio buttons at the bottom left of the window to tell Quicken which result to calculate:

- *Current Savings* if you want to know how much money you'll have to place in your retirement account now to reach your yearly retirement income goal.

- *Annual Contribution* if you want to know how much you must add to your retirement fund each year.

- *Annual Retirement Income* if you want to know what your yearly income will be based on how much money you plan to set aside.

| NOTE | Notice that when you select a radio button, Quicken eliminates the corresponding field, placing a calculated value that you can't change in its place. |

Fill out the remaining fields with your best estimates of their correct values. The following list explains tips about the individual fields.

If you haven't asked Quicken to calculate the *Current Savings* field, enter the equivalent cash value of any investments you've earmarked for your retirement fund (not the total amount in your savings accounts). If you did ask Quicken to calculate this field, the result tells you how much "seed money" you must put into the fund when you open it, based on your other entries.

In the *Annual Yield* field, try to be conservative about estimating your yearly return on your retirement accounts and investments.

Type the amount you expect to contribute to your retirement fund each year in the *Annual Contribution* field. You'll then be able to see how much retirement income a given yearly contribution will produce. You can set Quicken to calculate this value if you want to see how much you must set aside each year to meet an income target.

You don't have to enter your actual age in the *Current Age* field. If your finances are limited at the moment, and you don't think you could put aside money for retirement yet, you can see how the age at which you start your retirement fund affects how much you must contribute, or how much retirement income you'll have.

Vary the entry in the *Retirement Age* field if you'd like to see how this affects the yearly contribution required to meet an income goal, or your expected retirement income with a given annual contribution. Since you can't predict your longevity, the *Withdraw Until Age* field has to be a complete guess, but it also influences your results in dramatic ways.

In the *Other Income* field, enter the yearly amount you expect to receive from any other sources, including social security, pensions, and so on, during your retirement.

The amount in the *Annual Income After Taxes* field is the critical determinant of your retirement standard of living. If you've asked Quicken to calculate the result, the value displayed is based on your entries in the other fields. Otherwise, type in how much income you want when you retire. Keep in mind that this field can be set to show either the actual number of dollars you can expect to receive annually, or your spending power in today's dollars, depending on whether you've checked the *Annual Income in Today's $* box.

Select the **Tax Sheltered Investment** radio button if your retirement savings won't be taxed until you withdraw them; otherwise, select **Nonsheltered Investment**. If you have a mixture of taxable and tax-sheltered retirement investments, you should prepare separate calculations for each type, and then add the totals.

Fill in the *Retirement Tax Rate* with your best guess of what your overall income tax rate will be when you retire. Unfortunately, given the vagaries of politics and tax policy, this value is impossible to predict, but it has a major impact on the calculations you make. If your retirement investments are tax sheltered, you must also enter your *Current Tax Rate*. Although your current rate should be easier to estimate, remember that the calculations you make are based on the unlikely assumption that this rate will stay constant throughout your working life. For the most accurate results, the rates you enter in both fields should be those of your overall income tax bracket, including both state and federal taxes.

Finally, handle the three inflation-related fields at the lower right of the window, as follows. Make your best estimate of the average rate of inflation in the *Predicted Inflation* field. Given the track record of many "leading economists," your own guess may be as good as anyone's—but again, your results depend very heavily on the number you enter here.

If you check the *Inflate Contributions* box, the calculator assumes you'll be increasing your contribution to the retirement fund by the percentage inflation rate you predict. This is definitely the wisest course—assuming just a 4% yearly inflation rate, in 25 years a $2,000 contribution will have the spending power of only about $500 today. If you don't increase your contribution to keep pace with inflation, you'll have to make much larger contributions from the outset to meet a given income goal.

Check the last box, *Annual Income in Today's $* if you want the results shown in the *Annual Income After Taxes* field to reflect the buying power, adjusted for inflation, of your yearly retirement income—assuming that you withdraw the equivalent amount each year. If, for example, the *Retirement Income* field displays $20,000 when this box is checked, the amount you can withdraw each year after taxes will buy goods and services now worth $20,000. To see the actual amount you'll be able to withdraw each year, uncheck the box. This figure is interesting because it can get pretty large, but you shouldn't pay any real attention to it: Since inflation rapidly erodes the value of a dollar, a figure that sounds like a lot of money may represent only modest purchasing power. Because of inflation, the amount you actually collect will increase each year, but the purchasing power remains constant.

Quicken recalculates the field you've selected each time you move the cursor from field to field. If you want to see the actual dollar amounts—unadjusted for inflation—of your yearly contributions or withdrawals, choose **Schedule** to pop up the scrollable Deposit Schedule window.

When you're done making retirement calculations, put the calculator away by choosing **Close**.

Keeping Track of Your Retirement Fund

To organize your retirement fund recordkeeping efficiently, establish a separate Quicken account for each component of your retirement investment portfolio. In a simple scenario, you might have one account for your IRAs and one for your mutual funds. With Quicken 3, use investment accounts for all tax-deferred investments (including IRAs, 401(K) plans, and tax-sheltered annuities). That way, you can designate the accounts as tax-deferred when you set them up, and Quicken will exclude their earnings from tax reports. Track retirement funds you keep in non-tax-sheltered CDs or savings accounts in Quicken bank accounts. To make these accounts easy to find, the name of each should begin with the same first few characters, as in "Ret-IRA," "Ret-Mut'l Funds," and so on.

When you make contributions to any of these accounts, transfer the money from your main bank account. Transfers to tax-deferred accounts will still appear on your tax reports, so you'll be able to deduct these amounts from your taxable income on your tax returns.

If your employer makes contributions to your IRA or 401(K) plan, enter these amounts in the same investment account you use to record your own contributions. Employer contributions require two transactions. First, account for the funds—enter **MiscInc** in the *Action* field, fill in the *Amount* field, and categorize the transaction as "EmployerIRA," "Employer401," or what have you. Then enter a **Buy** transaction for the purchased "security" (whether it's a stock or just a CD) in the same amount. The first transaction indentifies the employer contribution, while the second adjusts the value of the particular investment.

When you receive interest payments on an IRA or similar savings plan, enter them as deposit transactions directly into the corresponding account. See Chapter 9 for instructions on keeping track of changes in the values of investments such as stocks, bonds, and mutual funds and of dividends and other investment income.

You can use a Custom Account Balances report to find the current value of all your retirement-related accounts. Give the report an appropriate title, such as "Current Value of Retirement Fund." Leave the second date field set to today's date, and the **None** entry in the *Report at Intervals of* field. Then choose the **Accounts** radio button and select only your retirement accounts for inclusion in the report.

When the report appears on screen, memorize it for future use. When you memorize it, leave the radio button labeled **Named Range (as of Today)** selected in the Memorize Report window. Then, whenever you want to see the current balance of your retirement fund holdings, just recall the report.

Planning for College

Quicken's college planning calculator helps you set aside the right amount of money each year for a child's college education. Display the calculator (see Figure 14.3) by choosing **Financial Planners** and **College** from the Activities menu.

You can have Quicken calculate any one of three results: how much you should save each year, how much to start the college fund with, or the amount you can expect will be available for each year of school. Select the radio button corresponding to the calculation from those at the lower left of the window.

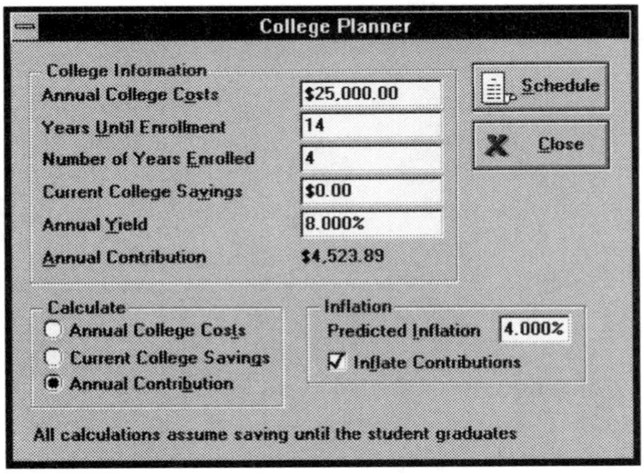

FIGURE 14.3

The College Planning calculator.

The fields in the College Planning calculator require little explanation. When you type a value into the *Annual College Costs* field, include all the costs of a year of college—room, board, books, and miscellany—not just the tuition.

Although a constant-dollar savings plan may be easier to follow, it's usually best to increase the amount of your savings each year to adjust for inflation. Check the *Inflate Contributions* box. (Of course, you must also follow through by making the increased contributions Quicken advises each year. To see a schedule of the payments required to meet your annual goal, choose **Schedule**.)

Remember that the results you get with the College Planner assume you will continue making payments to the college fund throughout the time your child is in college, not just until she enrolls. When you're finished with the calculator, press **Esc** or choose **Close** to return to your account.

Tracking Home Improvements

When it's time to sell your home, it is likely that you'll realize a profit over what you originally paid. Unfortunately, this profit is usually taxable; in fact, when you consider the effects of inflation, the tax bill can wipe out your gain. Even if you plan to defer your taxes by buying another home in the period permitted, you'll still eventually be liable for the taxes on your apparent profit.

NOTE	After age 55, you're eligible for a one-time tax deferment on the profits of a home sale. However, the IRS will eventually collect the tax from your estate upon your death.

One of the best ways to minimize your tax liability is to be sure that you add the value of all the home improvements you've made to the home's *tax basis*. When you first buy your home, the tax basis is equal to the purchase price. Each time you add an improvement, however, the basis increases by the value of the improvement. Since the IRS figures your taxable gain by subtracting the tax basis from the sale price, your tax liability decreases as the basis increases. Thus if you bought your home for $50,000 ten years ago, made $50,000 worth of improvements on it, and then sold it this year for $150,000, your taxable gain is only $50,000, not $100,000—and you'll owe the IRS many thousands of dollars less.

WARNING	Of course, you should be sure to keep the original copies of all the receipts and canceled checks you used to pay for the improvements. You'll need them to verify the information summarized in your Quicken reports.

There's one catch, however: You have to keep records of the improvements you've made. That's where Quicken comes in. With a program to provide a convenient place to keep records of all your home improvements over the years, you'll be able to document easily the additional value of your home.

To keep track of your home improvements, start a Quicken asset account as described in Chapter 9. Name the account something like "Home Sweet Home" and enter the home's purchase price as the opening balance. If you want to be able to keep track of the different kinds of home improvements you make, create separate classes such as **New Bathroom**, **Carpets**, and so on. But don't bother creating classes for every conceivable improvement you might eventually make; you can create additional classes as you go. Then, whenever you remodel your home, buy new carpets, or add an improvement of any kind, you'll record your payment as a transaction in your ordinary checking account. As you enter the payment, however, you'll transfer the funds to your "Home Sweet Home" account, since they've added to the value of your home.

To make the transfer, use QuickFill or the Category list to help you enter **Home Sweet Home** in the transaction's *Category* field. If you're keeping track of the type of improvements you're making, add the appropriate class entry.

Figure 14.4 illustrates how the register of a home improvement account might look after several improvements had been made. Note that each transaction's *Category* field indicates that the funds have been transferred from the checking account. Note also that the value of the home as represented by the account balance increases with each transaction.

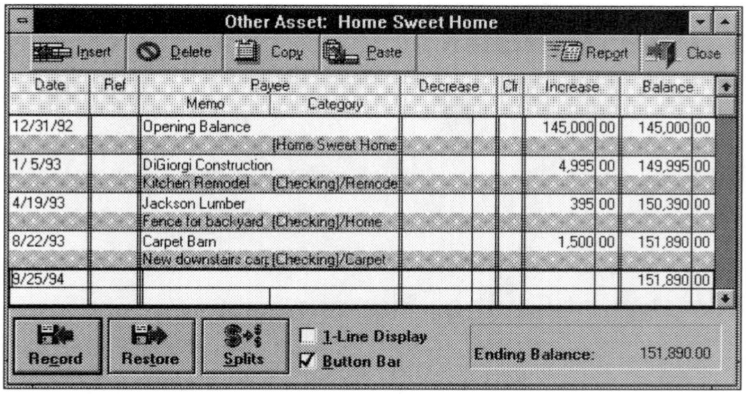

FIGURE 14.4

The register of an asset account used to record home improvements.

You should record anything that adds "permanently" to the value of your home, even additions as modest as locks and wallpaper; over the years, the cumulative total of these little improvements may considerably increase your home's tax basis. On the other hand, paint, replacement roofing, and the like are considered to come under the heading of repairs and maintenance, and can't be added to the basis. Of course, don't take my word on the specifics of what you can and can't consider a home improvement for tax purposes; consult with your tax preparer, attorney, or the IRS for details.

Tracking Mortgages and Loans

Your ordinary Quicken account will suffice to record the payments you make on large loans such as your mortgage or a car loan. Any time you want to see a record of these payments you can browse through your register to find them, or use a transcription report, filtered to the payee (your bank or finance company), to collect them for you. On the other hand, if you want to be able to look up your loan balance within Quicken at any time, or if you want to monitor your net worth accurately, you'll need to set up an account for each loan.

As you'll recall from Chapter 9, loans belong in Quicken liability accounts. Establish the account using as your opening balance the loan principal balance on the date you start the account. When you make payments on the loan from your checking account, record them as split transactions. You'll find all the instructions for starting a sample loan account and making a payment in the section "Tracking Liabilities" in Chapter 9.

Tracking Investments

Investors may need a good measure of luck, but they also need careful planning and accurate, up-to-date records to make prudent investment decisions. Once again, Quicken's recordkeeping prowess can make short work of the task.

Using the Investment Savings Planner

To assist in planning an investment strategy, Quicken 3 provides a fill-in-the-blanks calculator for savings. With this investment planning tool, you can determine easily how much money you'll have to save to reach an eventual investment goal, and what impact various hypothetical investment strategies and economic circumstances would have on your portfolio.

Call up the Investment Savings Planner by choosing **Financial Planning** and **Savings** from the Activities menu. The planner appears in a window as shown in Figure 14.5.

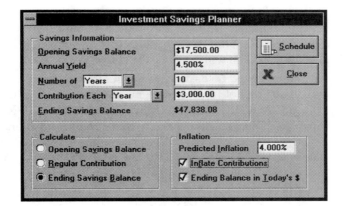

FIGURE 14.5

The Investment Savings Planner.

You can have the Savings Planner calculate one of the following three results, whether you're working with a single investment or your entire portfolio:

- The amount you should start your investment with (the *Opening Balance* field)

- The amount to save (invest) at the interval you specify (the *Regular Contribution* field)

- The ultimate value of your investment at the end of a given term (the *Ending Savings Balance* field)

Here's how to use the Investment Planner. To pick which of the three previously mentioned amounts you want Quicken to calculate, choose the corresponding radio button at the bottom left of the Planner window.

Next, get out your crystal ball and come up with a prediction for the average rate of inflation over the entire term you plan to hold the investment. Type in this number in the proper field at the lower right of the window.

Check the box labeled *Inflate Contributions* if you plan to increase the actual dollar amount of your contributions to keep pace with inflation. If you choose not to inflate your contributions, you'll have to make much larger contributions at the outset to achieve any given goal.

Now check the bottom box, assuming you want the *Ending Savings Balance* amount to show the ultimate buying power your investment will have in today's terms, based on the inflation rate you entered above. If this box is not checked, the ending balance may look large, but its inflation-adjusted buying power may well be anemic.

With all these preliminaries complete, fill out the remaining fields with the values you want to test. Each time you change a value, you must move to a different field before Quicken will calculate the new result.

There are two time-related fields, one for the number of weeks, months, quarters, or years you will hold the investment, and one for how often you plan to add to the pot. Actually, these fields always contain the same entry—when you change one, Quicken automatically changes the other to match.

NOTE	Note you should always enter the anticipated yield on an annual basis (in the *Annual Yield* field), even when you choose a shorter investment period. And by the way, be sure to enter the percentage yield you expect *after* taxes, not before—otherwise, Quicken will show your investment growing at a much faster rate than it really will.

Choose **Schedule** to see the actual dollar amount you should contribute each year (it goes up each period if you choose to adjust the contribution for inflation) and the projected cumulative balance of your investment's value for each period. You can print this schedule by choosing the **Print** button.

Planning Your Investment Accounts

I know I keep harping on this idea, but you really should have a plan for organizing your records before you start entering them in Quicken. However, given the variety of investments available, the infinite combinations you can put together, and the unique needs and temperament of each investor, there's no one ideal method that will work best for everyone. If you own more than one stock, for example, you may want to record each stock in its own account, combine all your stocks into one account, or even lump them in a single account for all your securities and other *liquid investments*, including bonds, money market funds, and so on. The choice depends on how many different investments you own, how closely you like to track each investment, and how frequently you buy or sell holdings in a given investment.

In general, the more investments you have and the more frequently you work with them, the more it makes sense to track them in separate accounts. At a minimum, it's usually a good idea to keep your liquid investments in a separate account from your "illiquid" ones. (Illiquid investments are those that you can't readily convert to cash, either because they take time to sell or because you're penalized for selling them too early—real estate, whole life insurance policies, savings bonds, IRA accounts, and so on.) Since most investors monitor their illiquid assets fairly infrequently, parking them in their own account will keep them from cluttering up the more active accounts you keep for your liquid investments.

Many investors keep a portion of their investment cash in a special account with their broker. If this is your practice and if you have more than one investment account, you'll want to set up a Quicken bank account for this brokerage account. When you sell securities and place the proceeds in the brokerage account, or when you use funds in the account to purchase an investment, you'll record these transactions just as you would if you were using your regular checking account. (You can keep track of your investment cash in an investment account instead, but that's usually wise only if you have just one investment account.)

As you learned in Chapter 10, Quicken offers several built-in reports for tracking the holdings you've recorded in investment accounts. All of these reports can provide extremely useful information about your portfolio. To see the options, choose **Investment** from the Reports menu.

Portfolio Value reports offer a snapshot look at the securities you own on a particular date. The report lists the number of shares you own, the most current price per share, their cost basis, your "paper" gain or loss, and the market value of the holding (see Figure 14.6).

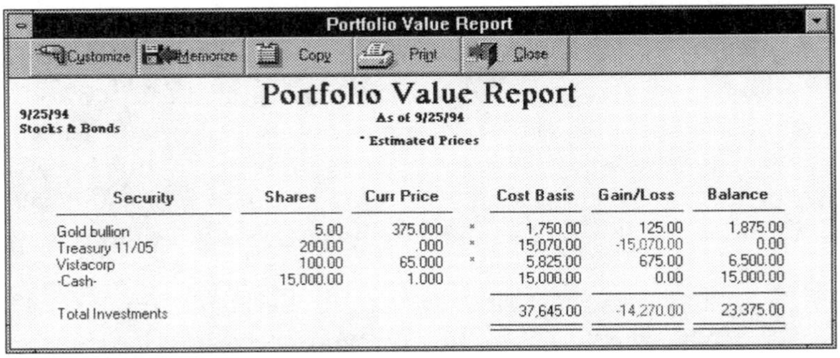

Security	Shares	Curr Price		Cost Basis	Gain/Loss	Balance
Gold bullion	5.00	375.000	*	1,750.00	125.00	1,875.00
Treasury 11/05	200.00	.000	*	15,070.00	-15,070.00	0.00
Vistacorp	100.00	65.000	*	5,825.00	675.00	6,500.00
-Cash-	15,000.00	1.000		15,000.00	0.00	15,000.00
Total Investments				37,645.00	-14,270.00	23,375.00

FIGURE 14.6

A Portfolio Value report.

Use an Investment Performance report to show the overall return from all your investments, taking into account income such as dividends and interest as well as changes in market value. The percentage shown in the right-hand column indicates the average annual rate of return on your investments, extrapolated if necessary from the time period on which you're reporting. If you want a breakdown of your results by security, security type, or investment goal, type in the appropriate number in the *Subtotal by* field when filling out the Investment Performance Report window. The result should look like the sample in Figure 14.7 on the next page.

To summarize the actual gain or loss of investment holdings you have purchased and then sold, you need a Capital Gains report. You'll be shown the number of shares you bought and sold, when you bought and sold them, how much they cost, how much you sold them for, and your dollar profit or loss.

FIGURE 14.7

An Investment Performance report subtotaled by security.

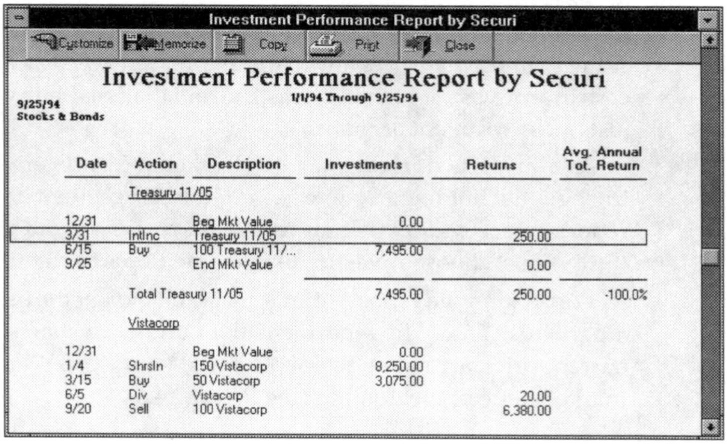

NEW IN **3**   In Quicken 3, Capital Gains reports break out separate totals for short-term and long-term gains; you can turn off this feature by customizing the report, selecting another choice in the *Subtotal by* field. The Customize Report window also lets you change the number of days the IRS defines as the short-term holding period; if you buy and sell the security within this period, the IRS treats the proceeds as a short-term gain.

NOTE   Actually, since long-term gains are taxed at lower rates, what you really want to know is how long you have to hold the issue before you can sell it at a long-term gain. That's the same figure.

An Investment Income report summarizes the income your investments have generated from all sources. Dividends, interest, realized gains or losses, and capital gains distributions are included in the total. If you like, you can also figure in the unrealized paper gain or loss due to changes in market price of investments you still own. To do so, customize the Investment Income report, choosing the **Transactions** radio button. Check the *Include Unrealized Gains* box and choose **OK** to continue with the report.

To see a complete listing of all the transactions in your investment accounts, showing their impact on your cash balance and the value of your holdings, create an Investment Transactions report. Investment Transaction reports are much like regular Transactions reports.

To study the impact your investments have made on your net worth, produce a Net Worth or Account Balances report as shown in Figure 14.8. See the section "Creating an Account Balances Report" in Chapter 11 for more information on these reports.

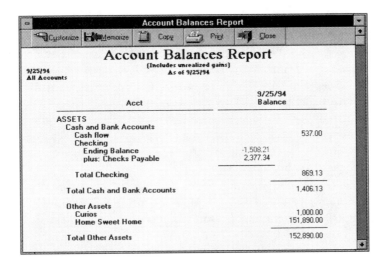

FIGURE 14.8

An Account Balances report.

Tracking Illiquid Investments

You'll need different techniques to report on investments you track in other asset accounts, since you can't use Quicken's built-in Investment reports. Your first task is to set up categories and classes for your investment transactions. You'll rely heavily on classes because many of the transactions you record will be transfers to other accounts, so you won't be able to use categories to distinguish between them. But do create two basic categories: **Inv inc** for investment income and **Inv exp** for investment expenses. Next, you'll need several basic classes no matter how you've divided the investments among your accounts:

Class	Description
InvPurch	Investment purchases
InvSale	Sales of an investment
InvComm	Amounts paid to the broker or agent when buying or selling an investment
InvAdj	Adjustments to the value of an asset

If you keep each investment in a separate account, you can stop there. On the other hand, if you've combined more than one investment in the account, you should consider the above classes as subclasses and create additional classes for each investment. For example, if you own several types of collectibles and you track them in the same account, you'll need classes such as **Furniture**, **Stamps**, and **Coins**.

Whenever you record an investment transaction, you should transfer the funds involved to or from another account, and assign the transaction to the appropriate class (and subclass and sub-subclass if you have them). Let's work through an example to see how the process goes. First, let's say you own $5,000 worth of antique furniture and you've recorded the collection along with your other collectibles in a single asset account. Now you buy another $1,000 chair. You owe your antiques broker $100 for his role in arranging the purchase, so your total payment is $1,100.

Record this transaction from the checking account that you used to pay for it, as shown in Figure 14.9. Type in **Hofnagle Antiques**, the broker, as the payee, enter **1100** as the payment, and make a note such as **Old chair** in the *Memo* field.

Now you're ready to make the transfer. Choose the **Splits** button or press **Ctrl-S** to split the transaction between the cost of the chair and the broker fee. On the first line of the Split Transaction window, enter the name of your collectibles account in brackets, using QuickFill or the Category list to assist you. Now type a slash (/) to indicate you want to enter a class. Type **Furn** as the main class and then enter **:InvPurch** as the subclass (the colon indicates a subclass entry). Now move to the *Amount* column for that line and type **1000** over the entry Quicken has made for you.

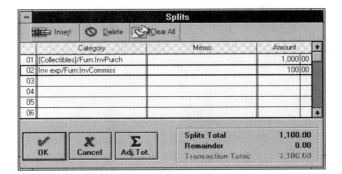

FIGURE 14.9

*Entering a
split transaction
covering a
collectible
purchase.*

Move on to the second line and enter the commission fee you paid on the purchase. Since the fee isn't a transfer, it doesn't affect the value of the chair. This time, then, you can enter a true category in the category portion of the *Category* field. Type **Inv exp**, a slash, then type **Furn**. Now type **:InvComm** as your subclass. You won't need to enter an amount on this line since Quicken has already entered the correct amount, **$100**.

When you sell assets, you should handle the transaction in almost exactly the same way, except that you begin with a deposit in the checking or brokerage account in which the proceeds from the sale end up. Again, you must split the transaction, because part of the proceeds goes to your broker as the commission.

For example, if you sold that chair for $1,250 and paid a $150 commission on the deal, you'd pocket $1,100. In your checking account, enter the transaction by typing **1100** in the *Deposit* field; next, split the transaction. Your entry in the Split Transaction window will depend on how you've organized your accounts. If you have a single account for all your collectibles, you would make these entries in the Split Transaction window.

Category	Amount
Collectibles/Furn:InvSale	$1,250
Inv exp/Furn:InvComm	-150

Quicken will calculate that $150 has to be deducted as your broker's commission as soon as you enter the $1,250 from the sale.

All sales and purchases, as well as any other investment transactions that simultaneously change the balance in both an investment account and your checking account, should be treated as transfers. On the other hand, amounts that you pay from or receive into your checking account, and that don't affect the value of your investment, should be placed only in the checking account. In this case, you record using the **Inv inc** and **Inv exp** categories. Finally, if you want to adjust the value of your holdings as recorded in your account to reflect changes in market value, you should enter such transactions in the account you use for the investment itself (see the section "Adjusting the Value of an Asset or Liability" in Chapter 9 for details).

Reporting on Illiquid Investments

Whether you'd like to monitor a particular investment or see the total value of all your investments, Quicken's reporting features will give you the information you need. Focusing on the current value of an individual investment is very easy, of course, if you've recorded the holding in an account of its own: just switch to the register of that account and take a look at the amount labeled *Ending Balance* at the lower right of the window—that's the current value of the investment.

If you've mixed two or more investments together, use a Summary report to get at the current value of the specific investment or investments in which you're interested. Switch to the register for the asset account and choose **Custom** and **Summary** from the Reports menu.

Customize the report, choosing **Class** in the *Row Headings* field and **None** in the *Column Headings* field for a simple list of class totals. If you want a month-by-month breakdown of the changes in the investments' value, choose **Month** in the *Column Headings* field instead. Choose the **Accounts** radio button, and in the list of your accounts that appears, mark only the one for your investment account. Then choose **OK** (twice, if necessary) to start the report. In the report, you'll be able to see separate totals for each investment in the appropriate class heading.

In like manner, if you want to see individual transactions that have involved a particular investment, use a Transaction report. After displaying the Customize Report window, choose **Class** in the *Subtotal by* field and select the **Current Account** radio button. The report will list all the transactions for each investment separately.

To review your investment income and expenses, switch to your checking account. Again, prepare a Summary report with classes as the row headings. This time, though, when you customize the report, set it up to include only transfers to the investment accounts and your **Inv inc** and **Inv exp** categories for investment income and expenses.

From the Customize Report window choose **Categories/Classes**. In the Category list that appears, choose **Mark All** once or twice as necessary to clear all the selections. Then select the **Inv inc** and **Inv exp** categories for inclusion in the report, as well as the investment accounts (they're at the bottom of the Category list). Choose **OK** to close the list and again to create the report. In this report, investment purchases appear as negative values since they decrease the balance in the checking account.

Again, you can use an Account Balances or Net Worth report to see how your investments have affected your overall financial status. See "Creating an Account Balances Report" in Chapter 10.

Tracking Your Personal Assets

Most people have at least a few possessions of significant value, whether it's some antique furniture, a late-model car, furs or jewelry, or even that brand-new computer system. Establishing a Quicken account to monitor personal assets such as these can be handy for several reasons. For example, a Quicken report can produce a complete listing of your belongings in seconds to document them for your insurance company. In addition, you'll need to record your assets in Quicken if you want the program to calculate your net worth with reasonable accuracy.

| NOTE | I recommend that you keep track of your most important personal asset, your home, in a separate Quicken account. See the section "Tracking Home Improvements" for details. |

Unless you own a large number of valuables, it's easiest to record them all in one account. Just set up an asset account as described in Chapter 9. In the Create New Account window, name the account something like *Personal Assets*, enter an opening balance of zero (you do have to type the 0 into the *Opening Balance* field), and then enter a long-ago date (ideally a date before you acquired any of the assets) into the *As of* field.

If you acquire assets as gifts or as an inheritance, you may want to create corresponding categories. In addition, you'll probably want an **Adjust** category for market-based adjustments to the value of your assets.

| SHORTCUT | If the value of an item has changed since you acquired it, and you want to keep an accurate record of such changes, enter the item's original value on the date on which you acquired it. Then create |

an adjustment transaction as described in the section "Adjusting the Value of an Asset or a Liability" in Chapter 9 to update the asset's value for each time it has changed or changes substantially. Next, decide whether you want to create classes for the different types of assets you own. If you have many individual items of a certain type, such as a number of pieces of valuable furniture or a large collection of fine jewelry or expensive paintings, you'll probably want to create classes for these items under appropriate names. You'll then be able to produce reports that show the current value of each type of asset separately. But if you only want to know the total value of all your assets, you needn't bother with classes.

Now draw up a list of all the assets you already own and enter each of them into the new personal assets account as a separate transaction. Figure 14.10 shows an example of how a series of entries in such an account might look. Date each transaction as of the date you acquired the item. Then enter the source of the asset in the *Payee* field, put its current value in the *Increase* column, and type in a description of the asset in the *Memo* field.

FIGURE 14.10

The register of a personal assets account.

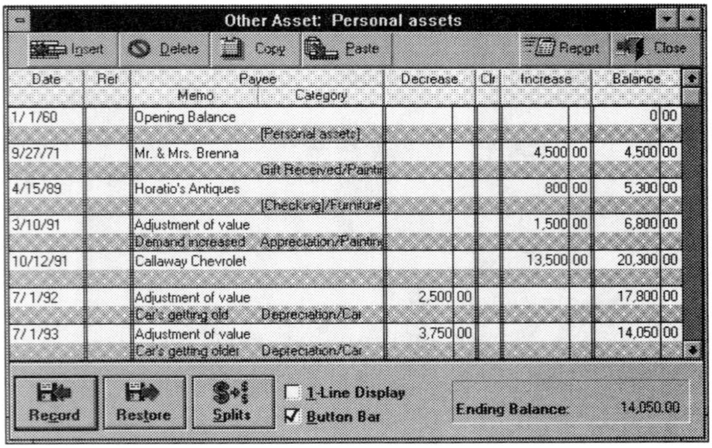

If you acquire a new asset via an inheritance or gift, simply enter a new transaction for the acquisition in your personal assets account. When you buy a new asset, the procedure is a little different. First, record the purchase as a payment transaction in your checking or cash account. As you enter the transaction there, transfer the price you paid—the asset's value—to your personal assets account by entering the name of the account in brackets in the *Category* field. As always, you can use QuickFill or the Category list to complete the entry for you. If you've set up classes for your assets, record the class name at the same time by typing / and then the class name.

NOTE	For tax purposes, *depreciation* is the process by which an asset's presumed loss of value is allocated over an extended period of time according to a predetermined formula, rather than according to its actual change in value.

Once you've recorded your assets, you'll probably need to adjust their value from time to time. For example, your car is probably losing resale value day by day, and if you list it in the account, occasionally you should probably document that painful reality. On the other hand, your collection of antiques may well be rising in value, a fact you'll probably be happy to record. In either circumstance, simply create an adjustment transaction that adds or subtracts the amount by which the asset's value has changed. You'll find the necessary instructions in Chapter 9 in the section "Adjusting the Value of an Asset or a Liability." If you sell or give away an item, enter a transaction reflecting this event by typing the value of the item in the *Decrease* column. You should then go back and mark all transactions pertaining to this item with an asterisk (*) in the *Clr* column, indicating you no longer own the asset.

Several types of Quicken reports can come in handy for monitoring your personal assets account. To get a complete listing of all your assets and their current value, for instance, create a Transaction report, as follows:

1. Switch to the account's register and then choose **Custom** and **Transaction** in the Reports menu.

2. In the last field in the Create Transaction Report window, select the **Current Account** radio button to indicate you want the report to cover only the current account.

3. To limit the report to show only the transactions you still own, choose **Filters** to display the Filter Report Transactions screen, uncheck the *Newly Cleared* box at the bottom of the window, and then choose **OK** to return to the Create Transaction Report window.

4. Choose **OK** again to produce the report.

If you use classes to distinguish between the different kinds of assets you own, you can create a Summary report, which lists the value of each class of your assets. In the Create Report window, enter a date range that encompasses all the entries in the account. Then customize the report and choose the **Class** setting in the *Row Headings* field and the **Don't Subtotal** setting in the *Column Headings* field. You'll get a simple listing of the current value of each class of assets.

To see the contribution of your assets to your net worth, produce an Account Balances report, described as follows.

Figuring Your Net Worth

Net worth is the amount of money you'd have if you sold everything you own and paid off all your debts. In accountant's terms, that's equivalent to the total value of all your liabilities subtracted from the total value of all your assets. Even though you aren't worth as much as you'd like, you're probably worth considerably more than you suspect—and Quicken can tell you just how much more with a few quick key presses.

NOTE	Of course, net worth is a theoretical value. In calculating your net worth, you assume that you would be able to realize the current market value of your noncash assets if you were to sell them.

It can be an ego boost to know your net worth, but there are practical reasons to determine it as well. By knowing what the value of your estate will be when you die, you'll be able to determine whether you'll be leaving enough to your survivors; if not, you can purchase more life insurance. In addition, you can estimate the tax bill your survivors will have to pay, and, if it appears excessive, take steps to reduce it now. The security and comfort of your own retirement will also depend heavily on your net worth, since you may need to sell some of your possessions to generate cash when you're no longer working.

Figuring your net worth in Quicken couldn't be easier, provided you set up your accounts properly in the first place. Obviously, since your net worth reflects *all* your assets and *all* your liabilities, you must record them all in Quicken. If you want to get a close approximation of your actual net worth, you have to be sure that you don't omit any assets or liabilities, even the ones you may take for granted.

Clearly, your portfolio of stocks and bonds constitutes a significant asset. But don't forget to create accounts for other assets for which you don't receive monthly statements—jewelry, works of art, valuable furniture, and so on.

Of course, if you're paying off a mortgage, your home is both an asset (the home's value) and a liability (the principal of the mortgage that remains to be paid). A new car you've purchased with a bank loan also has this dual role in your financial profile (although the value of this motorized asset tends to decline rather rapidly). You'll need to set up both an asset and a liability account for each such item.

If all your assets and liabilities are ensconced in accounts, and if the balances in all the accounts are current, calculating your net worth is simply a matter of producing a Net Worth report. Choose **Home**, then **Net Worth** in the Reports menu. If you want your most recent net worth calculation, just choose **OK** and you'll see it on your screen. If you want to calculate your net worth for another date, change the date in the Create Net Worth Report window before creating the report. And if you want to see how your net worth has changed, use the instructions in Chapter 10 to produce a Customized Account Balances report.

Keeping Other Records

With a bit of creativity, you can put Quicken to work to keep track of almost any kind of asset or investment you can imagine.

Handling Expense Accounts

If your employer reimburses you for business-related expenses, monitor them in a Quicken asset account. That way, you can print a report that details your expenses, sorting them by type. Here's what to do: Record each expense in your regular checking account as a transfer to the new account. Since you can't assign transfer transactions to categories, create classes for each general type of expense (gasoline, airfare, etc.), and use these to "categorize" the transfers. You can type specific information about each expense in the *Memo* field.

To create the expense report, use a custom Transaction report, In the Customize window, select the **Class** option in the *Sort By* field. Next, choose **Transactions**, and then, in the Status section, check only the box labelled **Blank**. Choose **OK** until the report appears on the screen, and memorize the report for future use. Then print it and hand it over with your receipts to your boss or whoever handles reimbursements.

When you get your check, record it as a deposit in your main checking account. Then switch to the asset account and type * in the *Cleared* field for each reimbursed expense transaction. That way, these transactions won't appear in the next report you prepare.

Recording Frequent Flier Miles

If you fly a fair amount, use a Quicken investment account to keep track of your frequent flier miles. After setting up the account, create a new security type named *Miles*, and create "securities" for each airline you fly. Then, after each paid flight, record the miles you earn as a transaction. Enter **ShrsIn** in the *Action* column and type the number of miles into the *Shares* column, leaving the *Price* and *Amount* columns blank. To record a trip you pay for with frequent flier miles, enter a **ShrsOut** transaction and list the number of miles you "spent."

Quicken keeps a tally of the total number of miles for each airline, but since the share price is zero, your net worth won't change. To see how many miles you've saved, just switch to Portfolio View.

Summary

In this chapter, you've put Quicken to work in the service of your real-life financial needs. You've learned how to:

- Use Quicken to plan and maintain a personal budget
- Help you keep your tax records
- Manage your investments
- Keep records of home improvements
- Calculate your net worth

Unless you're in business for yourself, these tasks may be all you need Quicken for. But even if that's the case, you may still want to consult the Appendix on using Quicken with other software. If you do plan to use Quicken for small business bookkeeping, read Chapters 15 and 16 for more practical tips.

Chapter Fifteen
Handling Basic Business Records and Reports

I f your small business is thriving, but you are overwhelmed by the paperwork, Quicken's combination of simplicity and financial stewardship makes it potentially as valuable at your shop or office as it is at home. In this chapter, you'll learn about the kinds of enterprises for which Quicken is appropriate and the skills you need to put it to work in a business setting. You'll learn how to set up business accounts and record business transactions, how to generate basic financial reports, and how to prepare business budgets. A separate section at the end of the chapter shows you how to use Quicken to manage rental real estate, one of the most popular part-time business ventures.

Quicken and Conventional Accounting

Before you proceed, however, it's time to stop and consider some important cautions about the use of Quicken in business. Quicken is prized by so many of its users because it is so simple and seems to have so little in common with the inscrutable complexities of traditional accounting systems. Instead of a profusion of unfamiliar terms, multitudes of journals and ledgers, and a confusing double-entry system, Quicken gives you a straightforward, check-book-like screen that anyone can understand.

But conventional accounting practices have evolved for a reason. All the apparent overcomplication is there to ensure that your entries are automatically double-checked, so that your financial records remain as accurate as possible. Quicken may be simple, but it lacks the safeguards that accountants hold so near and dear. Although the information in Quicken reports is similar to that in reports prepared by your accountant, the absence of accounting checks and balances in Quicken will make its reports less trustworthy to a CPA—and to the IRS. True, Quicken can record the raw information your accountant needs to prepare the verified, documented reports that you expect. Still, before you commit your record-keeping to Quicken, be sure that your accountant supports your decision and extracts the information he or she needs from your Quicken accounts.

Here are some steps that will make your work with Quicken as safe and accurate as possible:

- Keep the original records of every transaction you record in Quicken— invoices, receipts, canceled checks, and so on.

- Never delete transactions without making a record of them first. If you find an error in your account, print out a copy of the register with the error so that you and your accountant can refer to it later.

- Make backup copies of your accounts regularly, at least once a week, and print out full Transaction reports as additional insurance against accidental loss of your records.

What Kind of Business Can Use Quicken?

Quicken is appropriate for small businesses whose financial dealings are fairly simple. Although theoretically the program can keep track of thousands of transactions per account, the practical limit is far fewer. For one thing, the program has no automatic billing, and it can't calculate finance charges for you. For that reason, you'll spend too much time calculating and filling out your customers' bills if you prepare more than 25 or 30 of them per month.

Similarly, if your company has more than four or five employees, you should look for a program that can prepare your payroll and your payroll checks automatically. In fact, you can purchase a separate payroll module designed specifically to work well with Quicken from Intuit. Unaided, Quicken's payroll method is simple enough to be appropriate even when you have only a few employees.

Given these constraints, Quicken is best suited to the needs of consulting offices, service businesses, and legal or medical offices with one or two professionals. It also works well in monitoring investment real estate. While you can use Quicken effectively to keep track of most aspects of a retail or mail-order sales business, the program lacks the ability to monitor your inventory or to record sales data from your cash register.

NOTE	Quicken's publisher, Intuit, markets a separate product called QuickBooks for small business accounting. QuickBooks addresses many of Quicken's limitations, yet is easy to use and works much like Quicken itself.

Keeping Business Records with Quicken

The mechanics of record-keeping with Quicken are the same whether you use the program for personal finance management or for monitoring your business.

Planning Your Business Accounts

As always, it's vital to plan your Quicken accounts carefully to get the most from your records. Begin by deciding what kinds of accounts you'll need and how many. If you run your business from a single checkbook much as you do your personal finances, a single Quicken bank account may be adequate. In fact, as you've seen a number of times in this book, Quicken can even cope effectively with the common practice of running a sideline business from a personal checking account.

WARNING	Accountants generally frown on the practice of combining personal and business transactions in the same accounts, since there's a definite risk of getting funds from the two sources mixed up. The IRS also looks askance at the practice. If you decide to use this style of record-keeping anyway, be extremely careful about making complete and accurate entries, and keep paper copies of all your transactions.

You may need additional accounts in several situations, however:

- If you make much use of credit cards or a credit line, for example, you'll probably want a separate credit card account for each source of credit. Chapter 8 outlines how to use a Quicken credit card account.

| NOTE | Credit card accounts are intended for monitoring credit cards or any type of credit line from which you borrow regularly and on which you make payments of varying amounts. Use liability accounts to monitor long-term loans. |

- You may also want to set up an account for tracking your petty cash. See Chapter 8 for instructions on using Quicken cash accounts.

- If you bill your customers rather than taking payment at the time of the sale, you can start a Quicken asset account for your *accounts receivable*, that is, for the outstanding bills. The balance in this account should give you a good idea of how much money you'll have coming in, how soon, and perhaps, how much work you'll have to do to collect it. Details on accounts receivable bookkeeping can be found in Chapter 16.

- If you want to use Quicken for payroll, you'll need to establish a Quicken liability account for each withholding item and deduction you retain from your employees' paychecks, such as federal income tax, state income tax, FICA (social security), benefit payments made by the employees, and so on. Payroll bookkeeping is covered in Chapter 16.

- If you'd like to use Quicken to produce accurate Balance Sheet reports showing the overall worth of your business, you'll need to create additional asset and liability accounts to track the value of your business real estate, capital equipment, and loans. Again, techniques for setting up and using these accounts are outlined in Chapter 16.

- If you plan to record depreciation in Quicken, you must set up at least one asset account for the items you will be depreciating.

If you're not yet sure which of these accounts you'll need, read through the sections pertaining to each of these areas in the rest of this chapter and in Chapter 16 before you actually set up your bookkeeping system. This will give you an idea of the tasks Quicken can handle and may encourage you to turn over more of your routine bookkeeping to the program. Although you can add new accounts and modify existing ones as you work, your records will be more complete and more accurate if you start with a set of accounts that is as well-organized as possible.

WARNING   Remember that you should plan your Quicken bookkeeping system with the active participation of your accountant. While it's important that you feel comfortable with the way you'll be keeping your records, it's equally important that your accountant understand your system fully and that it fit in well with the accounting methods he or she uses.

NOTE   If you write many checks for your business, you may find it economical to print the check forms themselves (the account number and preprinted information, not just the date, payee, and amount). A company called CHEQsys (telephone number: (617) 624-7194) markets the necessary software for use with Quicken. You'll also need a laser printer, as well as a special type of toner cartridge containing magnetic "ink" that can be read by bank automated processing devices.

Organizing Your Business Accounts

Once you've decided on which accounts you'll need for your business bookkeeping, your next step should be to create the categories and classes you'll need to keep the new accounts organized. This step is critical, for without a complete and logical set of categories and classes, Quicken's reports—potentially superb—can't be as informative. Refer to Chapter 5 for complete details on using categories and classes.

Choosing Categories

For the main business checking account and for your petty cash and credit card accounts, you'll want to set up categories corresponding to each type of income and expense item you typically have. If you have a bookkeeping system that has worked well for you, you can start with its system of categorizing your income and expenses, and just create matching categories in Quicken. If you're just starting your business, or if you've been dissatisfied with the quality of your records to date, you can use Quicken's built-in list of business categories as a good starting point in developing your own Category list.

NOTE	In bookkeeping jargon, your list of categories is considered a *chart of accounts*, with each category representing an account.

No matter where you get your basic list of categories, give serious thought to expanding the list to take advantage of the automated and nearly instant reports that Quicken offers. On the income side of the balance sheet, for example, you should establish categories and subcategories that describe the goods or services you sell fairly specifically, instead of contenting yourself with Quicken's built-in **Gross Sales** category or the like.

If you provide a professional service to your customers, it shouldn't be hard to decide on an appropriate list of categories. Typically, service businesses offer only a few separate services, and most payments you receive apply to just one or two of these. For example, if you own a beauty parlor, you might have one category or subcategory for hairstyling, another for manicures, and a third for facials. In your janitorial service, window washing would rate a separate category from floor waxing if you contract with your customers for these services separately.

If you're a retailer, however, it's a judgment call as to how detailed your categories should be. Your store may sell hundreds or thousands of different items, and the typical customer may purchase a number of items of very different kinds at one time. This much complexity would overwhelm Quicken, which certainly wasn't designed to record transactions as they happen at your cash register. Obviously, therefore, it wouldn't make sense to create a separate category for each item you sell. Still, your reports will be that much more informative if they include as much detail about your transactions as you can conveniently record—particularly if your business doesn't own a modern electronic cash register to track your sales for you.

If you run a flower shop, for instance, you might set up one category for cut flowers, one for potted plants, and one for accessories. Of course, you won't be able to apportion each day's deposit precisely among the three categories. Still, your effort to do so will help you stay in better touch with the business, and your categorized records should at least help you identify broad trends.

You'll also need additional categories if you create other types of accounts or use Quicken for special purposes, such as payroll. If you do plan to keep your payroll records in Quicken, for example, you'll want categories not only for the amount you actually pay your employees but also for your contributions as an employer to employee taxes and benefits, such as social security or medical insurance. If you contract for temporary employment— the kind you report on Form 1099—you'll want an appropriate category; for example, you might call it **Contract Work** or **1099**.

If you've been using a numeric system of income and expense categories, you can continue doing so in Quicken. When you duplicate the categories in Quicken, enter each number as the category *name*, then enter the number again as the first part of the category *description*. For example, the flower shop owner might set up the following categories:

Category	Description
201	201: Cut flower income
202	202: Potted plant inc
601	601: Fertilizer expense

If you enter the descriptions this way, taking care (as in this example) to include an equal number of digits in each category number, you'll be able to produce Summary reports in which the categories are listed in order. (As you learned in Chapter 10, in Summary reports organized by category, the row titles are the category descriptions, not the shorter, generally more cryptic category names.)

If you plan to set up additional accounts to make use of Quicken's more advanced bookkeeping features, see the appropriate section in Chapter 16 for advice on creating the categories you'll need.

Choosing Classes

When you've designed a satisfactory Category list, turn your attention to classes. Classes can help you pin down which of several suppliers offers the lowest prices over the long run. They can show you your best customers, or which customers are buying which items. If your business spans several different sites or departments, or includes several different types of business activities, classes can distinguish the contribution of each site, department, or activity toward your total income and expenses in a given category.

A look at some specific businesses and professions should help you learn to design a list of classes to fit your own business situation. A retailer would want to create an **Expense** class for each supplier so that he or she could track each supplier's prices and refer to them fast in the event of a dispute. If the shop employs salespeople, the retailer would also want to set up a class for each of them to distinguish between their sales. A building contractor would want a separate class for each job, perhaps named by the location of the construction or the person or company for whom the work would be done. A psychotherapist, lawyer, or consultant with a limited number of clients would want to set up a class for each client. However, it probably wouldn't work to use a different class for each patient at a busy medical office, simply because Quicken limits the number of classes you can create.

Cash-Basis versus Accrual Accounting

Most small-business owners prefer to use the simplest possible accounting method for tracking their income and expenses. Known as *cash basis* or *cash-receipts-and-disbursement basis* accounting, this system consists of counting an income item when you receive the income in cash or the equivalent, and counting an expense item when you pay for it the same way (usually by writing a check).

> **NOTE**   Remember that in Quicken the payee is simply the name that appears in the *Payee* field of an Account register whether the transaction is a payment or a deposit. In this example, payments made to the physician would be recorded with the patient's name in the *Payee* field of the **Deposit** transaction, or in the *Description* column of the Split Transaction window for the deposit.

Quicken is suited to this logical, straightforward approach, and it's certainly the method I recommend using with the program. One advantage is that it requires no additional steps; most of the techniques you've learned so far assume you are using the cash-basis method.

Many businesses use a modified version of the cash-basis accounting system, recording income only when it is received. Most expenses are recorded when they are paid, but expenses for items with a long, useful life or that are paid for in advance are handled differently. Long-lasting items are recorded as assets. Later entries are made periodically to show the assets' gradual decline in value, a process referred to as *depreciating the assets*. Expenses for supplies, insurance, and other items that are prepaid and then used up are recorded in divided transactions over the period covered by their use, a process known as *prorating the expense*.

Quicken can cope easily with modified cash-basis accounting. To use this method to track depreciation and prorated expenses, you enter the expense for the item as a **Payment** transaction in the account from which the funds came, transferring the value of the item at the time of purchase to a Quicken asset account. From that point on, you periodically record **Adjustment** transactions for the amount you're depreciating or prorating. This process is described in more detail in Chapter 16.

If you prefer to use the *accrual* accounting method, which is widely used in larger companies, Quicken can still cope. In the accrual method, an income item is counted as of the date you issue the bill for the item, not the date you receive payment. Similarly, an expense is counted as of the date you become obligated for it, not on the date on which you make the payment.

| WARNING | In a traditional accrual accounting system, you maintain separate records for each accounting period, usually a month. In Quicken, records from each month are combined in one account, then extracted using Quicken's **Reporting** features. This departure from accepted practice is another reason Quicken is less than ideal for accrual accounting. |

The key to accrual accounting with Quicken is quite simple. All you do is set up a separate class for each accounting period. Since most businesses run on monthly accounting cycles, your Class list would probably look something like this:

01-94
02-94
03-94
...
01-95
02-95
and so on.

With a Class list like this one, you can assign each transaction to the class corresponding to the accounting period in which the item should be counted. For instance, when you write a check in March for a piece of equipment that you installed back in January, you assign it to the January class (in the previous sample, the entry in the *Category* field would be **Equip/01-94**).

This system works fairly well as far as the accrual accounting itself is concerned. With it you can produce reports showing your income and expenses by accrual accounting periods, though as you'll see in the section "Preparing Business Reports," the process is not as smooth as most Quicken operations. But the real problem is that by assigning your transactions to an accrual period class, you won't be able to use classes for other purposes, and you'll give up some of Quicken's most useful reports.

Recording Transactions

Once you've gone to the trouble to set up a set of categories and classes perfectly tailored to your business needs, you'll want to be sure to assign each transaction you enter to the appropriate category and class. This step is vital. If you don't carry it out faithfully, your accountant may desert you in frustration, your reports will be inaccurate, and you'll lose the opportunity to make well-informed business decisions.

SHORTCUT	Remember that Quicken comes set up to warn you if you try to record a transaction that lacks a category. If someone has shut off this feature, you can turn it back on using the Preferences menu, as described in the Appendix.

Assigning a transaction to a category and class is identical, whether you're working with a business or personal account. You can use any of the features in Quicken that are designed to improve the detail and the efficiency of your record-keeping. For example, to expedite transactions that occur in your business regularly, use QuickFill to memorize and recall them automatically, or memorize them yourself if you've shut off QuickFill (see Chapter 7).

If you pay several vendors at the same time each month, create a transaction group that contains memorized transactions for all the vendors. You'll then be able to record all the transactions in one quick step each month. If a transaction applies to two or more separate categories or classes, split the transaction as you enter it using the methods you've practiced since Chapter 5.

Preparing Business Reports

After you've been using Quicken for a few weeks or longer, you can start tapping its considerable reporting talents to produce accurate, up-to-date overviews of your business's financial position. Quicken reports can help you see without delay the status of your business. They are also an excellent tool for making your accountant's work faster, more efficient, and more accurate.

Many of Quicken's reports can be useful to the business owner or manager. After working through Chapters 10 and 11, you should have a good understanding of the available report types and how to use them.

SHORTCUT	Report entries listed in the **Other** category or class have not been given a category or class assignment, implying that the totals for the other categories and classes may be incomplete. Unless these amounts are very small, you should make an effort to find the transactions that lack category assignments and correct the problem.

Preparing Profit and Loss and Cash-Flow Statements

Profit and loss statements help you see how much money your business has really made or lost over a given period. Quicken's P&L Statement report lists the total income in each **Income** category, the total expenses in each **Expense** category, overall income and expense totals, and a grand total of your profit or loss for the period you specify. To generate a profit and loss statement, choose **Business** and **P&L Statement** from the Reports menu. Enter a title and the range of dates you want the report to include, and choose **OK** to generate the report.

A simple modification of the standard P&L Statement report shows separate columns for each month covered by the report. After displaying the Create Report window, or from the report itself, choose **Customize**. Enter the month range you want the report to cover and, in the *Column Headings* field, select the **Month** option. Then choose **OK** to obtain the report.

WARNING	If you use the cash-basis accounting method and create a separate account for accounts receivable as described in Chapter 16, you should not use the Quicken profit and loss statements. Since the report covers all your Quicken accounts, your income will be inflated by the balance in your receivables account, even though you haven't yet received those funds.

Itemizing Transactions

There may be times when you want to list the individual transactions from your business account in detail. Perhaps you want to study your records from an especially profitable month to see whether there is a customer worth pursuing further or some other pattern you might be able to repeat. Perhaps you need to explain some unusually high expenses for supplies to make sure that they weren't ordered in error or that you weren't overcharged. Or maybe you suspect that the reason you're finding unexpected amounts in some categories is that by mistake you assigned some transactions to the wrong category. No matter why you need transaction-by-transaction detail, it's yours for the asking.

To produce a Transaction report, choose **Other** and **Transaction** from the Reports menu. Customize the report. In the Customize Report window, type in the date range you'd like the report to include, and tell Quicken how you want to organize the report—according to time period, class, category, or account—by selecting the corresponding option in the drop-down list of the *Subtotal by* field.

Unless you have only one or two accounts, you will probably want to limit the report to one or a few accounts in which you record day-to-day business transactions. Choose the **Select Accounts** radio button to display the list of accounts, marking those you'd like to include in the report with a check. Choose **OK** to finalize your selections and again to prepare the report.

Reporting Totals by Project, Client, or Department

The reason you've assigned transactions to classes as well as categories is so that your reports can show separate figures for them. If you run a service business, for instance, and you've set up a separate class for each of your clients, you'll want a report that will show you the income you've received in each category from each of your clients. Or if you're a contractor, you'll want to be able to detail the income from each job separately, to see how much you spent on lumber, hardware, permits, and so on at each project.

There are several kinds of reports you can use to get at the information in your account according to class. The easiest way is with the *Job/Project Report* option, which summarizes the data from all the accounts in the current account group, listing categories in rows and breaking out subtotals for each category in columns. To generate a Job/Project report, choose **Business** and **Job/Project** from the Reports menu. Enter the range of dates you want the report to cover, and choose **OK** to produce the report. Figure 15.1 shows an abbreviated example of a Job/Project report prepared by a retailer who has set up classes for each salesperson's sales and commissions, and other classes for each supplier.

If you want to confine your report to a single project, client, or class, you have several options. For a report covering a single class, you can simply customize the Job/Project Report format. If you want to see month-by-month subtotals for the class in question, create a Customized Summary report from scratch. Finally, to see a listing of all transactions from a particular class arranged by category or time period, use a Customized Transaction report.

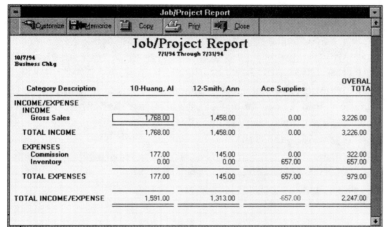

FIGURE 15.1

A sample Job/Project report for a retail shop.

To customize your Job/Project report to show a single class:

1. At the Create Job/Project Report window, choose **Customize**.
2. Choose the **Matching** radio button.
3. Move to the *Class Contains* field and enter the name of the class on which you'd like to report. For example, you could focus a report on a single salesperson by typing the class name for that person in the *Class Contains* field.
4. Choose **OK** once to close the Customize window, and again to generate the report.

To obtain a month-by-month report on a single class with a Summary report:

1. Choose **Other** and **Summary** from the Reports menu, and then choose **Customize**.
2. Leave the *Row Headings* field set to **Category**, and select the **Month** option at the *Column Headings* field for monthly subtotals.
3. Choose **Matching** to restrict the report to the desired class, as described for the previous report (enter the class name in the *Class Contains* field).
4. Produce the report by choosing **OK** twice.

When you want to list the individual transactions from a particular class, use the same filtering techniques to customize a Transaction report:

1. Display the Customize Transaction Report window by choosing **Other** and **Transaction** from the Reports menu, and then **Customize**.

2. After filling in the date range on which you want to report, choose **Category** in the *Subtotal by* field if you want the report to group and subtotal the transactions in each category, or select a time period by which you want the report organized.

3. Choose **Matching** to limit the report to the class of interest, entering the desired class name in the *Class Matches* field.

4. Choose **OK** twice to create the report.

Creating Accrual Accounting Reports

If you've chosen to use the accrual basis accounting method (see the section "Cash-Basis versus Accrual Accounting," earlier in this chapter), you can use Quicken to prepare reports that show your income and expenses for each accrual period. These reports usually turn up the information you need, but, as you'll see in a moment, there can be gaps because Quicken is not really designed for accrual-basis accounting.

To create a report listing your income and expenses by category with subtotals for each accrual accounting period:

1. Choose **Business** and **Job/Project** from the Reports menu, then **Customize**.

2. Just as you do for any report, type in the dates that you want the report to cover. But here's the catch: The dates you enter in the window must refer to the actual transaction dates. Instead of trying to guess which of your transactions you've counted in which periods, set the date range so that it covers the very first and very last transactions in your account.

3. Now customize the report so that it includes the accrual periods you'd like. Choose the **Categories/Classes** radio button to display a list of your categories. To display classes instead, choose the **Classes** radio button. Select the classes corresponding to your accounting periods by marking them with checkmarks.

4. Choose **OK** twice to start the report.

As I said earlier, then, I recommend you use Quicken for cash-basis account-ing rather than attempt to follow the accrual method. If you must practice accrual accounting, be sure to review your reports very carefully for accuracy.

Business Budgeting

Making and maintaining a budget is perhaps even more important for businesses than it is for individuals and families. In Quicken, however, the mechanics of budgeting are the same whether you're using the program to help you manage your home or business finances.

<table>
<tr><td>NOTE</td><td>The process of budgeting with Quicken is covered fully in Chapter 13.</td></tr>
</table>

In brief, you begin by establishing your financial goals, which in a business context might include the amount of money you want to put aside for emergencies, the amount you want to plow back into the business for expansion or remodeling, and the amount you intend to realize as profit. Next, you print or write out a list of all the types of income and expense you expect to have. This step is easy because the list should be simply a duplicate of the Category list from your Quicken accounts.

To budget an amount for each of these categories, use Quicken's Budget worksheet (**Set Up Budgets** in the Activities menu) to list the amounts of your projected income and your fixed expenses on a monthly basis. In the worksheet, if the budgeted amount for a category is the same for each month, choose **Fill Row** in the Edit menu to copy the amount to all months in the budget.

Next, subtract the total of all your fixed expenses from your total projected income. The hard part is to provide each of the remaining expense categories on your Budget list with adequate funds each month while reserving enough money to meet your financial goals.

When you've finished entering budget amounts, choose **Close** to return to the register. Later, after you've kept your records with Quicken for a while, you can prepare a Budget report to see how well you've adhered to your budget. Choose **Home** and **Budget** from the Reports menu (the Home Budget report works just as well for business use).

In the Create Budget Report window, enter the dates you'd like the Budget report to cover. When you choose **OK**, the resulting report will show you the amount you actually spent in each category versus the budgeted amount and will calculate the difference for you.

Managing Rental Real Estate

If you own or manage rental real estate, Quicken makes a helpful partner, since it reduces considerably the drudgery and complications of record-keeping.

NOTE	If you record your ordinary expenses in your checking account as you pay them and maintain a separate Quicken asset account for tracking the value of your properties, you're practicing an accounting method known as *modified cash-basis accounting*. This method is described in the section "Cash Basis versus Accrual Accounting," earlier in this chapter.

When you use Quicken for property management, the basic idea is easy to remember and understand: set up a class for each property. Your first step is to set up Quicken accounts for your properties. If you pay the expenses on your rentals from your personal checking account, you'll be recording them in your main Quicken bank account. If you devote a separate checking account to your rentals, however, establish a corresponding second Quicken bank account using the same methods you learned in Chapter 1. A separate account makes figuring your rental-related income and expenses easier, but it complicates your overall record-keeping a little since you have to carry around two checkbooks and switch between two Quicken accounts.

Regardless of which arrangement you use, you'll need an additional Quicken asset account for each property. In this account, you'll record changes to the value of the property for tax purposes, such as improvements and depreciation, as outlined in the section "Monitoring the Value of your Properties," at the end of this chapter.

Once your accounts are in place, you'll need to set up the categories and classes you'll be using to organize your income and expense records. Create categories for each type of income and expense with the techniques you learned in Chapter 5. A brief study of your past records should show you which categories you'll need. Your list of income categories will probably include entries for security and cleaning deposits, rent, late fees, and tenant utility payments. Expense categories probably will cover advertising, maintenance and repairs, the various types of licenses and taxes you pay, legal fees, insurance, and utilities.

Designing a Class list for rental properties is simple: just create a separate class for each property you own. For the class names, the street locations of the properties will probably suffice; the class for your town house on Broadway would simply be **Broadway**, the class for your bungalow on Baltic Avenue would be **Baltic Ave**. Alternatively, you can employ a numbering system of your own. You may also want to create an additional **Rentals** class for miscellaneous expenses that you can't divide easily into separate amounts by property.

NOTE	If you own only one rental, and if you maintain a separate checking account devoted to that property, you won't need to create classes at all.

If you plan to rely heavily on Quicken for tax record-keeping, be sure to assign the categories you use to the appropriate tax schedule form and line as described in Chapter 5 (rental property income and expenses are reported on Schedule E of your federal income tax return). If you record your rental income and expenses in your personal checkbook, you can use a tax schedule report filtered to exclude all nonbusiness classes to get the totals you need for your tax forms.

Recording Rental Transactions

Whenever you receive a rent check or pay a bill for a particular piece of property, record the transaction in the checking account you use for your rentals, filling in the *Category* field with the correct category and class assignment. For example, to record a rent payment on your Broadway town house, you should enter **Rent/Broadway** in the *Category* field. Likewise, if the transaction is a payment for maintenance expenses on the Baltic Avenue bungalow, the entry would be **Maint/Baltic Ave**.

When a single payment covers expenses for two or more properties, all you have to do is split the transaction. For example, if you bought plumbing supplies for the Broadway town house and some wallpaper for the Baltic Avenue bungalow on the same trip to the hardware store, you would type the total amount of the purchase in the *Payment* column of the register or the *$* field on the Quicken check. You'd then choose **Splits** or press **Ctrl-S** to split the transaction.

On the first line of the Splits window, your entry in the *Category* column would be **Supplies/Broadway**. On the second line, it would be **Supplies/Baltic Ave**. Of course, you'd also enter the amount of the total purchase that went to plumbing supplies on the first line. Quicken would place the remainder on the second line for you. If you wanted to record the sales tax separately, you'd have a third line entry, **Sales tax/Rentals**. The completed Splits window would then look like the one in Figure 15.2.

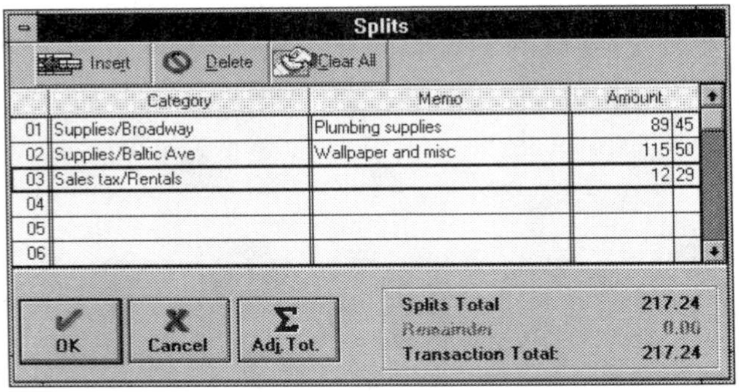

FIGURE 15.2

Splitting an expense transaction for rental property supplies.

Handling Security Deposits and Advance Payments of the Final Month's Rent

When you take a deposit from a tenant for cleaning or security, or receive a last-month's rent payment, you should record the transaction in your Quicken Bank Account register, listing the money you receive in the *Deposit* column and assigning it to an appropriate category, such as **Sec dep** (for **security deposit**). If you want to keep track of the amount that you may eventually have to return, you should at the same time enter a second transaction of equal amount in the column assigned to a category such as **Sec dep repay**.

WARNING Remember that upon return of a deposit, in some states, you must pay your tenant interest on that deposit for the period in which you held it.

Figure 15.3 shows both kinds of transactions as they would look in your register. Notice that Quicken adjusts the *Ending Balance* amount (visible in the lower-right corner of the register and Write Checks window) back to what it was before you entered the deposit, so you won't be fooled into thinking you have more money than you actually have. However, the amount of the deposit is reflected in the *Current Balance* amount shown just above the *Ending Balance*. In addition, you'll be able to create a Customized Summary or

Transaction report filtered to **Sec dep repay** anytime you want to see how much you're holding in tenant deposits.

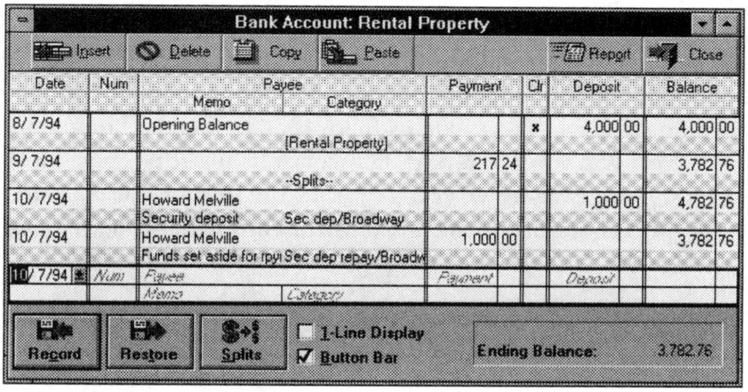

Date	Num	Payee		Payment	Clr	Deposit	Balance
		Memo	Category				
8/ 7/94		Opening Balance	[Rental Property]		x	4,000 00	4,000 00
9/ 7/94			--Splits--	217 24			3,782 76
10/ 7/94		Howard Melville				1,000 00	4,782 76
		Security deposit	Sec dep/Broadway				
10/ 7/94		Howard Melville		1,000 00			3,782 76
		Funds set aside for rpy Sec dep repay/Broadw					
10/ 7/94	Num	Payee		Payment		Deposit	
		Memo	Category				

Record Restore Splits   1-Line Display ☑ Button Bar   **Ending Balance:**   3,782.76

FIGURE 15.3

A security deposit and the expected repayment of the deposit.

SHORTCUT
If you don't mind a bit more work, you can set up a separate liability account to handle your security deposits as accounts payable. Chapter 16 covers techniques for working with accounts payable. In this case, you'd enter each security deposit in your checking account as a transfer to the liability account, typing the amount into the *Deposit* field and assigning the liability account's name, in brackets, to the *Category* field.

Preparing Real Estate Reports

As long as you enter all the rental-related transactions with the right category and class assignments, it will be a snap to produce reports that break down your income and spending for each property. The easiest route to this goal is via a quick modification of the built-in Job/Project report, as follows:

1. Starting from the register of the account you use for your rental property records, choose **Business** and **Job/Project Report** from the Reports menu, followed by **Customize**.

2. Enter the date range you'd like the report to cover, and add a title if you'd like.

3. Choose the **Selected Accounts** radio button. On the list of accounts that appears, be sure that only the account you're working on is checked.

4. Choose **OK** twice to produce the report.

You'll get a report showing the income and expense for each of your properties, with overall totals in each category in the far-right column. It should look generally like the one shown in Figure 15.4.

If you want to see the figures for only one property, all you have to do is customize the Job/Project report. After Step 3 in the previous instructions, choose **Matching**. In the *Class Contains* field, type in the class name of the property on which you want to report. For example, to see a report focused on your Baltic Avenue bungalow, you'd type **Baltic Ave** in the *Class Contains* field. Choose **OK** once to close the Customize window, and then again to generate the report.

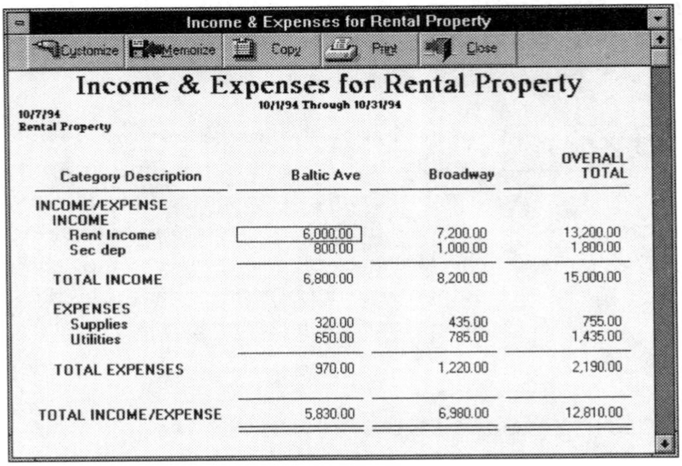

Income & Expenses for Rental Property

10/1/94 Through 10/31/94

10/7/94

Rental Property

Category Description	Baltic Ave	Broadway	OVERALL TOTAL
INCOME/EXPENSE			
INCOME			
Rent Income	6,000.00	7,200.00	13,200.00
Sec dep	800.00	1,000.00	1,800.00
TOTAL INCOME	6,800.00	8,200.00	15,000.00
EXPENSES			
Supplies	320.00	435.00	755.00
Utilities	650.00	785.00	1,435.00
TOTAL EXPENSES	970.00	1,220.00	2,190.00
TOTAL INCOME/EXPENSE	5,830.00	6,980.00	12,810.00

FIGURE 15.4

A Job/Project report covering rental property income and expenses.

If you need a month-by-month breakdown of your income and expenses related to a particular property, use a customized summary report. Just follow these steps:

1. Choose **Other** and **Summary** from the Reports menu, and then **Customize**.
2. Select **Category** in the *Row Headings* field and **Month** in the *Column Headings* field to organize the report so that the categories are in the rows and the monthly subtotals for each category are in the columns.
3. Choose the **Selected Accounts** radio button. In the list that appears, mark only the rental property account with a check.

4. Choose **Matching**. Restrict the report to the property in which you're interested by typing the property's class name in the *Class Contains* field.

5. Choose **OK** once to confirm your entry, and again to generate the report.

If you need an itemized report showing details of each transaction involving your rental properties, you can customize a Transaction report using techniques similar to those just described.

Monitoring the Value of your Properties

In addition to keeping records of the day-to-day transactions that pertain to your rentals, it's vital to keep track of changes in the value of the properties themselves over time. This is especially important for tax purposes, as you'll see in a moment. To enlist Quicken's help, set up a Quicken asset account as described in Chapter 9 or in the section "Tracking Home Improvements" in Chapter 12. Record the purchase value of each property in the account as an initial transaction.

When you own rental or commercial property, you can deduct its depreciation from your income. The specifics of how much depreciation you can claim for each type of property are beyond the scope of this book, but you can obtain these details from the IRS or from any reputable tax accountant or tax guide. To record depreciation at the end of each accounting period, enter the amount of depreciation you claimed during that period as an **Adjustment** transaction in the *Decrease* column of the asset account for the property.

NOTE	Only the value of the structure, not the land on which it is built, is depreciable. For more information on depreciation, see the section "Tracking Depreciation" in Chapter 16.

While depreciation reduces your income tax in the present, it also reduces the property's basis (its value according to the IRS) by the depreciated amount. This means that when you sell the property, your taxable gain—that is, the difference between your sale price and the basis—will be greater. It follows that, at least under the tax rate for capital gains in effect at the time of this writing, depreciation essentially just delays your tax liability into the future.

You should also record any major improvements you make in your properties (the type the IRS considers as permanent additions) in your asset account. These improvements raise the basis of the property by the amount of the improvement, reducing the taxable gain for which you'll be liable when the property is sold. To record a transaction for an improvement, enter its amount in the *Increase* field of the account. You must then begin depreciating the additional value of the improvement along with the rest of the property. When you sell your property, you can figure your taxable capital gain by adding the cumulative depreciation you've claimed to the sale price and subtracting the following from this figure:

- The total of the original cost, or basis, of the property.
- The total of all the improvements you've made.
- The costs of selling the property, such as real estate fees and recent repairs.

Summary

If you run a small business, the skills you've learned in this chapter will help you keep orderly, informative business records with a minimum of effort. You now know how to use Quicken to define business accounts and set up categories and classes for business use; to prepare common types of business reports; and to handle business budgeting. You've also learned the basic techniques required for managing rental real estate with Quicken. Once you and your accountant have implemented a plan for keeping your business records, you'll want to add Quicken's still more powerful tools for managing your business finances, covered in Chapter 16.

Chapter Sixteen

Business Bookkeeping and Payroll

Information and time are two of the most prized commodities in today's highly competitive business environment. As the key to making informed business decisions and to keeping you on happy terms with the IRS, your business records must be complete and accurate; despite this, you can't afford to waste any time entering and organizing them. The need to streamline your business bookkeeping will only increase as your business prospers and grows, and as the number and variety of transactions steadily multiplies. The more bookkeeping tasks you can speed up with Quicken, the more time you'll have for planning and implementing your business strategies.

With this chapter and a little additional work, you'll advance well beyond simply recording your purchases and deposits, thereby harnessing Quicken to help you manage your accounts payable and receivable, your cash flow forecasting, your payroll, your capital equipment records, and your balance sheets. The techniques covered here are somewhat more complex than those you learned in Chapter 15, but the extra effort required to master them will pay off fast by helping you cope with the mountains of paperwork that confront any thriving business, as well as to make better business decisions.

Handling Accounts Payable

Accounts payable are the debts you still owe to suppliers and other creditors. Knowing how much you owe and when you're going to have to pay are crucial pieces of the juggling act you have to perform when running a profitable business. Fortunately, Quicken provides a simple way to track these amounts. All you have to do is record all the bills and invoices you receive as payments in your checking account. The only trick is to enter the transaction as a postdated check using the date on which you think you'll actually be paying.

Recording Other Future Payments

If you want to be able to predict your future expenses and cash needs as accurately as possible, you should enter postdated transactions for all payments you expect to make later, not just the bills you've received. You'll then be able to use the reporting methods described in "Preparing Accounts Payable Reports" to see how much money you'll need.

Paying Your Bills On Time

As long as you use Quicken regularly, you'll never mistakenly miss a payment on a bill. Each time you start the program, if your account contains unprinted checks dated today or earlier, you'll see a reminder message in a small window on top of all the others. Quicken only gives you this reminder for unprinted checks you wrote from the Write Checks window. However, it's easy to find and review future payment transactions you've entered in the register. They're the ones below the heavy line in your register that indicates entries dated after today.

The Billminder program will remind you of payments that are due even if you don't start Quicken. You can set up Billminder so you get your messages when you turn on your computer or when you start Windows. See the Appendix for details.

Preparing Accounts Payable Reports

If you pay your bills by writing Quicken checks, the total of all your postdated checks is your accounts payable balance. The easiest way to see this total is to switch to the Write Checks window (press **Ctrl-W** or click on the **Check** icon), where the amount is labelled *Checks to Print* in the lower right of the window. If you enter accounts payable and other future payments as register payment transactions, you can calculate the balance by subtracting the account's *Ending Balance* from its *Current Balance*. Both figures are also shown at the bottom right of the register and Write Checks window.

If you want to look over individual **Accounts Payable** transactions, the quickest method is simply to examine the register entries that fall below the double line. To print out a list of this part of your register, click the **Print** icon or press **Ctrl-P**, then enter tomorrow's date as the "from" date and a date far in the future as the "to" date in the Print Register window. Of course, this assumes you haven't fallen behind in printing your checks. Once their dates have passed, overdue but still unprinted checks won't appear below the double line or on a transaction printout dated from today on.

To get a reliably accurate list of individual **Accounts Payable** transactions, use a Customized Transaction report:

1. Choose **Other** followed by **Transaction** from the Reports menu, and then choose **Customize**.
2. Type in a date range far enough backward and forward in time to ensure that all your unprinted checks are included.
3. In the *Subtotal by* field, select **Payee** if you want the transactions in the report sorted by payee; select an appropriate time period if you want to see how large the drain on your cash flow is going to be during the upcoming weeks or months.
4. Choose the **Transactions** radio button, then limit the report to unprinted checks by selecting **Unprinted Checks** in the *Transaction Types* field.
5. Choose **OK** twice to generate the report.

For a summary of your outstanding accounts payable, prepare a report with the built-in A/P by Vendor format. This report will show the total amounts of all unprinted checks you've written to each vendor, broken down into subtotals for each month. To prepare the report, choose **Business**, then **A/P by Vendor** from the Reports menu. Fill in the date range for the report and choose **OK** to see it on the screen.

Handling Accounts Receivable

Accounts receivable are the payments you're expecting from your customers. Keeping track of accounts receivable in Quicken will enable you to gauge how much money you'll be receiving and will help with bill collection.

Preparing Your Accounts

You'll need a separate Quicken asset account to handle your accounts receivable records. Set up the account using the methods you learned in Chapter 9, naming it AR or something else appropriate, and entering a zero opening balance. Next, create categories for all the types of accounts receivable you expect to receive—sales, consulting fees, royalty payments, and so on. Use different category names from the ones you use to record actual payments in your regular business checking account; otherwise, reports based on all your accounts will commingle the accounts payable amounts, which aren't actually in your possession yet, with the assets that are.

WARNING   Accounts receivable do not belong in your business checking account, where they would cause your balance to look higher than it actually is.

You may also wish to assign transactions in this account to classes according to customer. That way, you can produce reports showing the amounts each customer owes by subtotalling on class. You can create these classes as you enter transactions, either using the customer's name or a number for the class name.

WARNING   Reporting by payee instead of class will give you the same information, but only if you enter the payee's name in exactly the same form each time. With classes, you' must use the same spelling for each transaction.

Recording Accounts Receivable

Each time you bill a customer, switch to the accounts receivable account and enter the bill as a transaction. Be sure to type the due date of the bill, not the date you issue it, as the transaction date. You can use the *Ref* column for the invoice number. The customer's name goes in the *Payee* field, of course, and the amount of the bill goes in the *Increase* field since it represents an asset. Put the date you issue the bill under *Memo*, and fill out the appropriate category and class under *Category*.

Recording Payments

Quicken provides two methods for recording customer payments. Which of them is best for you depends on how most of your payments are made. If the majority apply to a particular bill, you'll use the *open item receivables method*. But if you provide credit accounts for your customers, so that a payment reduces the overall outstanding balance rather than going toward a specific bill, use the *balance forwarding method*. Whatever you do, stick with the method you decide on.

Using the Open Item Receivables Method

When customer payments cover specific bills, use the open item receivables method to record the payments. The key to this approach is that you record each payment in the same transaction you originally created for the receivable, using a Split transaction to transfer the payment funds to your main business checking account.

For example, let's say that you billed customer Smith $100 for a lawn mower last month. She sends you a check for $75 this month, promising to remit the rest after her next payday. You would record this payment by switching to your Quicken account for accounts receivable. Locate and highlight the original transaction you entered for customer Smith's $100 bill. If you recorded an invoice number as part of the transaction, all you have to do is pop up the Find window, enter the invoice number in the *Find* field, select **Check Number** in the *Search* field, and have Quicken go directly to the transaction in question.

With the **Invoice** transaction highlighted, split it as shown in Figure 16.1. Move to the first open line in the Split Transaction window, and enter the payment as a transfer to your regular checking account by entering the checking account name in the *Category* field. If you're using classes to identify customers, type a slash and enter the class for this customer. Type the date of the payment in the *Memo* field and the $75 amount of customer Smith's payment as a negative number in the *Amount* field. Before you leave *Amount*, choose **Adj. Tot.** to have Quicken recalculate the total for the entire transaction, $25, then choose **OK** to close the Split Transaction window.

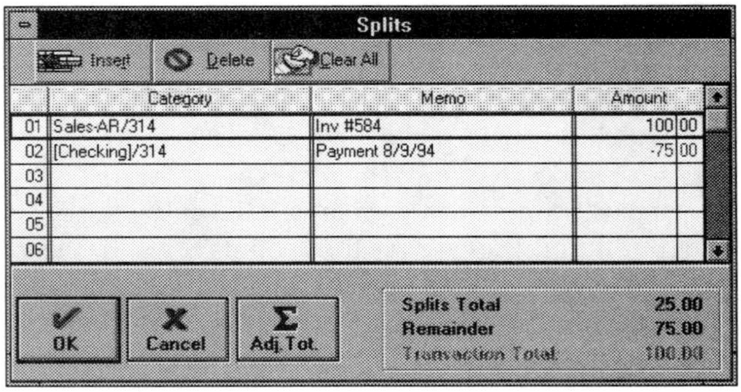

FIGURE 16.1

*This **Split** transaction records a customer payment covering a bill previously recorded in an accounts receivable account.*

When you return to the register, the $25 you're still owed will be showing in the *Increase* field for this transaction. If the customer has overpaid the bill, the *Increase* field will be empty and the amount of the overpayment will show in the *Decrease* column; simultaneously, the payment will automatically be recorded as a deposit in your checking account.

Whenever a bill is paid in full, type * in the *Clr* column to indicate that the item is cleared. Then re-record the adjusted transaction.

Using the Balance-Forwarding Method

You should use the balance-forwarding method of recording accounts receivable payments if the payments don't apply to specific bills, but rather to a general account for each customer. In this case, you enter each payment as a separate transaction. Since payments aren't tied to specific transaction dates, you won't be able to report specifically on overdue payments.

Let's see how this works out. Say that you're a psychotherapist and you see client Jones regularly. He pays you by simply making periodic payments against his credit balance. To record a $100 payment using the balance-forwarding method, switch to the accounts receivable account and enter the payment as a new transaction. Enter the date the payment came in as the transaction date, put the client's name, Jones, in the *Payee* field, and enter the **$100** amount of the payment in the *Decrease* field, as shown in Figure 16.2.

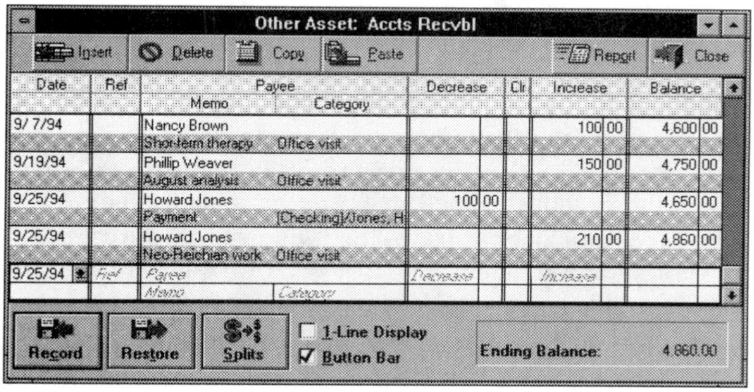

FIGURE 16.2

The selected payment has been recorded in accounts receivable and forwarded automatically to the checking account.

In the *Category* field, transfer the payment to your checking account by entering the checking account name. Follow this with the class you've created for this customer. When you record the transaction, the overall balance of your accounts receivable account will be reduced by the amount of the payment, and the funds will be recorded automatically as a deposit in your checking account.

Preparing Accounts Receivable Reports

You can use a variety of Quicken reports to get information about your accounts receivable. In all such reports, items listed in the Inflows section are amounts owed you by your customers, whereas items listed in the Outflows section are customer payments.

If you'd like to see a listing of individual invoices organized by week, month, or some other time period, prepare a Customized Transaction report. Starting from the register of your receivables account:

1. Choose **Other** followed by **Transaction** from the Reports menu, and then **Customize**.

2. Set the date range to cover all of your receivables transactions.

3. Subtotal the report by the time period for which you organized the report.

4. Choose the **Accounts** radio button, then check only the receivables account.

5. If you want the report to show only the invoices that haven't yet been paid, choose the **Transactions** radio button, then uncheck the *Newly Cleared* and *Reconciled* boxes at the right side of the window, leaving the *Blank* box checked.

6. Display the report by choosing **OK** twice.

For a listing of your **Receivables** transactions organized by customer instead of time period, use a Transaction report again, but this time subtotal by payee. Since you've been recording the date on which each payment is received in the *Description* column of the Split Transaction window, you can compare the date in the *Memo* column of the report with the date the payment was due. In that way, you'll be able to see whether you were paid on time.

If you want to see the total amount each customer owes you, your approach will depend on which method you're using to record customer payments. If you use the open item method, in which you record each payment as a split item in the invoice to which it applies, use an A/R by Customer report, one of Quicken's standard business reports. This report totals the uncleared transactions for each payee by row, with monthly subtotals. To report on overdue payments only, select the **Earliest to Date** choice in the *Date* field, and customize the report so that it only includes the accounts receivable account.

If you use the balance-forwarding method, you'll need a Customized Summary report to see the amounts you've billed each customer and the payments you've received for each week, month, or other time period. Set up the report with payees in the rows and the time period you prefer for subtotals in the columns. Then select the *Accounts* radio button field to confine the report to the receivables account. In the report, the amount under OVERALL TOTAL for each payee is the final debit balance for the period covered in the report (a negative amount indicates a credit balance).

NOTE	Since you don't clear transactions with the balance forward method, you can't report directly on overdue payments. However, you can scan the Summary report to look for zero entries.

Use QuickZoom to see the individual transactions that make up any total on the report.

A Caution on Other Business Reports

Most Quicken users adopt the cash-basis accounting method, in which you count each income item on the date you receive payment, not the date you issue the invoice. The problem with this approach when you use Quicken for accounts receivable is this: The receivables balance represents what you think you'll be getting, not the payments that you've already received; but Quicken doesn't know this. So, if you create reports that include your accounts receivable account with other accounts, the overall income shown will be higher than it actually is.

For this reason, you should customize reports that show your overall income and expenses so that they exclude the accounts receivable account. Alternatively, you can rely on the **Cash Flow** choice on the Business Reports menu, since the Cash Flow report is automatically limited to bank, credit card, and cash accounts.

Billing for Professional Services

If you're a consultant, a lawyer, or a plumber—or any type of professional who bills for time—you can use Quicken to keep track of your billable hours. The best way to handle this situation is to set up an asset account called **Billings**, in which you'll treat the amounts you expect to receive as your accounts receivable—see the previous section for details on accounts receivable bookkeeping.

If you can muster a little extra effort, you can get Quicken to keep a running tally of the hours you bill, not just the money you're owed. Set up a separate investment account named **Time Billed**. Here, record each service you provide as a separate **SellX** transaction (enter **SellX** in the *Action* field). Your hourly rate goes in the *Price* field, while the number of hours you billed go in the *Shares* field. Transfer the transaction to the Billings asset account in the *Xfer Acct* field.

You can identify the client either by entering the name in the *Security* field or as a class in the *Xfer Acct* field. The advantage of listing clients in the *Security* field is that you can analyze the Billings asset account with a standard A/R by Customer report, showing you how much each client owes you.

On the other hand, if you enter clients as classes, you can then use the *Security* field for the type of billable service you performed (you'll be setting up a security for each service). Quicken will then total the number of hours you've billed for each service in the Portfolio View window, instead of showing you a long list of individual clients. You can still see the hours for each client with a report limited to the client's class. You can still get a client-by-client breakdown of your receivables, but you must customize the A/R report: Choose **Class** in the *Row Headings* field instead of Payee.

Business Forecasting

Your Quicken records can give you a critical advantage when it comes to business financial management: knowing in advance how much cash you'll need and how much you'll have. A forecast of your cash flow can tell you when it's safe to spend that windfall profit you took in, and when you should hold the excess for future expenses. If you can safely anticipate a rising cash flow before it happens, you'll be able to cut back on borrowing, plan business improvements, or look for a longer-term and potentially more profitable investment than you could find if you found yourself with extra cash unexpectedly. On the other hand, if it appears your net cash flow will decline, you can head off the damage by cutting back on your inventory or shopping for an inexpensive loan.

WARNING	Like accounts receivable, anticipated future deposits must not be entered in your business checking account.

Developing a complete business forecasting system with Quicken involves several steps. To prepare for forecasting your cash needs you must enter your accounts payable with all future payments you can predict as postdated Payment transactions (put them in your checking account—see "Handling Accounts Payable" earlier in this chapter). You can use the Quicken calendar to make it easier to schedule these future transactions. To play what-if? with your future cash flow, enter hypothetical future transactions: edit the scheduled transactions and select the **For Planning Only** option in the *Register Entry* field. (See Chapter 7 for details on the Quicken calendar).

To record your anticipated future deposits, you should start an account for accounts receivable as already described. If you expect to make additional deposits that aren't included in your accounts receivable, create a separate asset account called Predicted Deposits or the like, begin with a zero balance, then enter all the deposits you can predict as **Increase** transactions in the account. Again, the Quicken calendar makes this easy.

Although, the cash-flow forecasts you create based on this information will be approximate, they can still be extremely useful. Obviously, however, their validity will depend on the accuracy of your assumptions about future deposits and on how completely you enter your accounts payable (plus other future expenses), and your accounts receivable (plus other future deposits). For optimally accurate forecasts, you'll need to keep up-to-date records of accounts receivable and accounts payable. You'll also need to review the postdated future payments regularly in your checking account and the entries in your Predicted Deposits account, altering, adding, or deleting transactions as necessary to keep them as accurate as possible.

Once you've entered all future transactions, the Planning graph on the Quicken calendar can give you a quick idea of how your business will be doing in the future. Use the **Accounts** button on the calendar to limit the graph to your business checking account, your accounts receivable account, and your Predicted Deposit account. Chapter 13 covers forecasting with the Planning graph.

You can also use several types of Quicken reports to draw up your cash-flow forecasts. For transaction-by-transaction detail on how your cash status will change from week to week or month to month, use a Transaction report. In the Create Transaction Report window, set the date to start with tomorrow and extend as far into the future as you'd like. Next, set up the report so that it is subtotalled by the time period you'd like—every week, every two weeks, or every quarter, for instance. Finally, choose the **Accounts** radio button to restrict the report to your business checking account, your accounts receivable account, and your Predicted Deposit account. The resulting report will start with today's balance and then show you all the income and expense items you've predicted, grouped by time period, along with a running balance for each period.

Use Customized Summary reports instead of Transaction reports to show you the broader patterns in your cash flow when you forecast it. You can organize the report rows by category if you want to see how much you'll be receiving and spending for each type of income or expense. To see where the money will come from and where it will go, organize the rows by payee. Either way, you can choose a time period for the columns to see how your overall cash status will vary during the upcoming weeks and months.

Handling Payroll

Taking on even a single employee increases your paperwork alarmingly, but Quicken can lighten the burden. Quicken makes short work of writing your payroll checks, recording payroll deductions, and calculating your payroll taxes; for a few employees, you won't have to learn or invest in a more complicated system. You'll learn all the techniques you'll need in this section.

However, you must move beyond Quicken if you have more than about five employees. The program wasn't designed specifically for payroll tasks, and it does have some limitations. For example, Quicken can't automatically calculate how much gross pay you owe an employee based on an hourly wage. You'll have to do the multiplication yourself. Nor will Quicken calculate the amount you should withhold from each employee's gross pay; you'll still have to look up the withholding tax in the pamphlets supplied by the federal and state governments, and figure out the amounts of benefit deductions and other withholding items.

If you have a larger number of employees, then, or simply want more help with your payroll than Quicken alone can offer, you should purchase a separate payroll software package. While you have many good options, you should certainly consider *QuickPay*, an easy-to-use payroll package specifically designed to work in concert with Quicken. QuickPay is marketed by Quicken's publisher, Intuit. Even if you use a separate payroll program such as QuickPay, you'll still want to record the payroll checks you write in Quicken.

Setting Up a Payroll System

NOTE Use the techniques described here to set up Quicken for recording **Payroll** transactions even if you'll be using QuickPay to actually calculate and write your payroll checks. Just be sure to name the accounts and categories you create yourself so that they'll work properly with QuickPay see your QuickPay manual for details.

To use Quicken for payroll accounting, begin by creating the accounts and categories you'll need to track your payroll expenses. In all likelihood, you'll be writing your payroll checks against your regular business checking account, so you don't have to open a new Quicken account for this purpose. However, you will need to start one liability account to record each separate type of deduction withheld from your employees' checks.

In the United States, at a minimum, you'll need accounts for federal withholding, state withholding, social security (FICA), Medicare, unemployment insurance, and disability insurance. If you deduct other taxes, retirement or pension contributions, health insurance payments, or any other items, you'll have to create an additional account for each such deduction. On the other hand, you don't need any new accounts for the contributions your company pays, such as the company's portion of the FICA tax. Name all these accounts systematically. A good strategy is to begin each account's name with the word *Payroll*, followed by an identifying abbreviation such as *FWH* (for federal withholding) or *SDI* (for state disability insurance, not strategic defense initiative).

When you're through creating the accounts, it's time to set up your payroll-related categories and classes. Switch to the register of any account, and press **Ctrl-C** to display the Category & Transfer list.

The **Payroll** category encompasses all payroll expenses your company incurs; you'll need subcategories to break down your payroll expenses by type, including the employees' gross pay, your company's FICA contribution (**Comp FICA**), the company's unemployment insurance contribution (**Comp FUTA**), and so on. You'll need a **Comp Pension** subcategory if your firm makes matching contributions toward a pension plan and a **Comp HMO** for your part of the employees' HMO subscription fee. Figure 16.3 shows the Category list with some payroll-related subcategories in place.

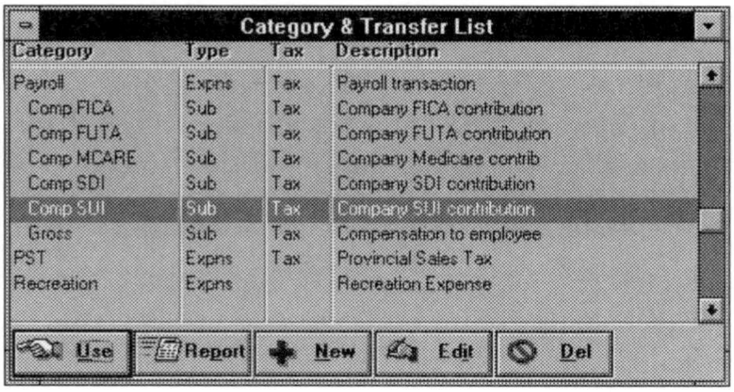

FIGURE 16.3

The Category & Transfer list showing some payroll-related subcategories.

You don't need subcategories for the items deducted from the employee's gross pay; these are taken care of by your payroll liability accounts. To make things consistent, name the subcategories with the same abbreviations you used in your liability account names.

Finally, create your classes. If you have employees doing different kinds of work, you may want to use class names or numbers that indicate the type of work they do. You might have a class for cashiers, one for stock workers, a third for salespeople, and so on. Since space in the *Category* field is limited, try to choose class names no more than two or three characters long.

As an alternative you can create a class for each employee. This isn't necessary for reporting on each employee individually, since you can always prepare a Summary report totalled by payee. Still, by setting up employee classes you'll be able to use the built-in Job/Project report to see employee subtotals at the same time you report on other kinds of income and expense items by category. For class names you can use employee names or numbers at your discretion, but be sure to type in the full name of the employee as the description of the class.

Finally, you need a single subclass to identify contributions you've made to employee benefits and taxes such as FICA, health insurance, and pension plans. This may sound redundant, since you already have subcategories for this purpose, but you'll see the point in a bit. At any rate, create another class for company contributions. For clarity, I'll use **Comp cont** in the examples, but you should choose a shorter name so you'll have room for other items in the *Category* field. As you'll recall, a class becomes a subclass when you use it after another class in the *Category* field.

Memorizing Payroll Checks

Ideally, you should prepare for your first payday in advance by writing a check for each employee and having Quicken memorize it. At this point, of course, you'll leave the amount of each check blank. You'll then create a transaction group containing the paychecks for all your employees. That way, you'll be able to have Quicken recall and write all the memorized payroll checks in a single step.

| NOTE | Instructions for memorizing transactions and using transaction groups are given in detail in Chapter 7. |

To set up your payroll checks, begin by gathering your records pertaining to each employee. For each one, you'll need a list of all the payroll deductions and all the contributions you make in that employee's behalf. With this information at hand, switch to the Write Checks window and start a new check for the first employee on your payroll. Fill in the employee's name, and, if you mail the check, an address, but don't type a dollar amount. Then comes the key step that will save you lots of time later: splitting the transaction. You do this by choosing **Splits** or pressing **Ctrl-S**. In the Splits window, record the various components of the check, including the employee's gross pay and all the deductions and withholding items as shown in Figures 16.4. Referring back to the illustration from time to time should help you follow the remaining instructions.

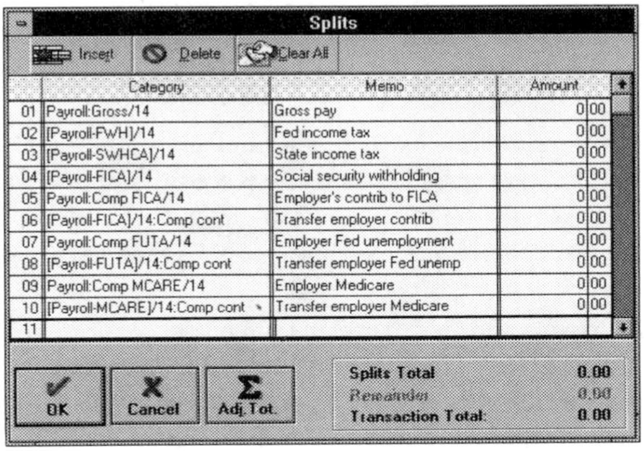

FIGURE 16.4

Preparing a payroll check to be memorized. You must resize the Splits window to see all ten lines at once, as shown here.

Devote the first line of the Splits window to gross compensation. You'll enter **Payroll:Gross** in the *Category* column. Then type / and enter the class for this employee (job description or employee number).

When the first *Category* column is complete, press **Down Arrow** (not **Tab**) to move to the next line. This one will probably be for federal tax withholding. You'll use a Quicken transfer to designate any withholding item or other deduction. At the bottom of the drop-down list or the main Category List window, locate the name of your payroll liability account in which you track this deduction. For federal tax withholding, you'll be looking for the account you've named Payroll-FWH. Choose the account to have Quicken enter its name in brackets in the *Category* column on the second line of the Split Transaction window. You don't need a subcategory here, but type / and then copy the class from the previous line. Repeat this process for all the deductions you make from the employee's gross wages.

Next come the payroll-related contributions you make for unemployment insurance, FICA, health insurance, and so on—expenses that come out of your pocket, not from your employee's wages. This part of the process is just a little trickier. For each of these contributions, you'll need to enter two items in the Split Transaction window (this is the same check and the same split window you've been using). The first of this pair of lines refers to the expense that comes out of your checking account to pay for the contribution. Use the Category list to enter the category and subcategory that pertain: **Payroll:Comp FICA** or **Payroll:Comp SDI**, for example. Add the same class name you used before. The completed entry in the *Category* column for an employer FICA contribution will then look something like this: **Payroll:Comp FICA/**. Type in a memo if you like, but leave the *Amount* column blank.

You'll see why you need two entries for each company contribution in the next section "Writing Payroll Checks."

Move down to the second line of the pair and create a transfer to the corresponding liability account by entering the account's name in brackets in the *Category* column. Add the same class as you did on the previous line. This time, however, add a subclass too: type **Comp cont**. Again, make no entry in the *Amount* column.

Repeat the process by adding a similar pair of entries for each of your contribution items. Figure 16.4 shows the way the Split Transaction window will look with employer contributions for FICA, unemployment, and Medicare.

When you've finished entering all the payroll items, check the window for accuracy. Be sure there are three lines for each benefit or tax program to which both you and the employee make contributions. Then close the window by choosing **OK**. Memorize the partially completed check by pressing **Ctrl-M** or choosing **Memorize Transaction** from the Edit menu.

Memorizing checks for the rest of your employees should be much easier, since you'll probably have to change only the employee's name and address. After you've memorized the first check it will still be on your screen. Type the next employee's name and address over the old one. Referring back to your written payroll records, compare this employee's withholding items and deductions with those listed on the previous employee's check. If they're the same, you're already set to memorize the new check. If you do need to add or delete a deduction, just display the Splits window again and make the necessary changes. When you do memorize the new check, you'll be asked whether you want to replace the original one or add a new transaction to the list. Be sure to choose the latter option.

This process should be repeated for all of your employees. When you've finished memorizing checks, and assuming you pay all your employees on the same day, create a transaction group for the entire payroll. If you need help with the details of setting up transaction groups, see Chapter 7.

Writing Payroll Checks

If you set up your payroll as previously described, the rest is easy. When payday rolls around, Quicken automatically places the payroll checks into your account. Actually, Quicken will inform you first if you set this up as a "Prompt before entry" group. You can change the date of all the checks, or cancel the automatic check-writing process altogether if need be. When you choose **OK**, Quicken will recall and write out checks for all your employees.

At this point, of course, the amounts of the checks are still blank. You'll complete each check in turn by splitting the transaction (press **Ctrl-S**). Figure 16.5 shows an example of how the completed Splits window will look. On the first line, type in the employee's gross pay in the *Amount* column as a positive amount. On the next lines, which are for employee deductions, enter the amount of each deduction as a negative number, since these amounts will be subtracted from the actual check total.

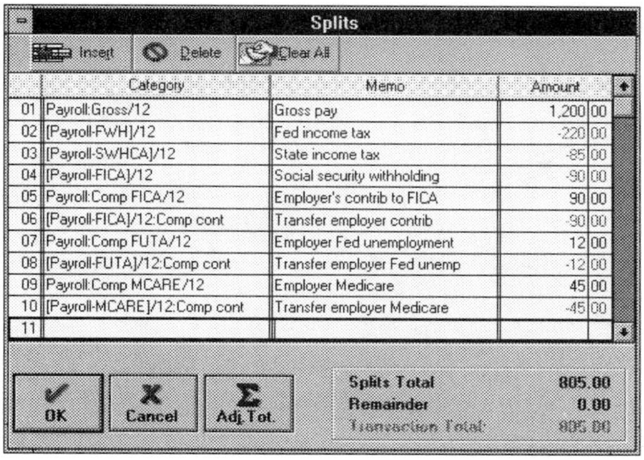

FIGURE 16.5

The Splits window after you recall a memorized payroll check and fill in the missing amounts. Again, the window has been resized to show all the split items.

SHORTCUT   To figure each employee's gross compensation based on hours worked with the Quicken calculator, make the computation before you open the Splits window. Click the **Calc** icon or choose **Use Calculator** from the Activities menu, do the math, and switch back to your account and choose **Splits**. When you reach the *Amount* column of the first line, press **Shift-Ins** to past the result.

The last section of the split is devoted to your company's contributions, the ones that aren't deductions from wages. Recall that each employer contribution is represented as a pair of lines in the Splits window—the first line for your payment from your checking account, the second line for a transfer to the other liability account. The key to filling out each pair of lines is simple: just enter the amount of your contribution as a positive number on the first line, and enter the same amount as a negative number on the second line. The result for each of these paired items is that the contribution does not affect the check total, but will show up as a liability you must pay in the corresponding other liability account.

When the amounts have been entered, close the Splits window by choosing **OK**. Quicken will total the overall amount of the check for you. Record the check and print it, then fill out, record, and print each additional employee's check in turn. If an employee hasn't worked during the current pay period, you have two options. Your safest alternative for avoiding tax complications is to go ahead and fill in a zero amount for the check, and keep it in your records permanently. You don't have to print the check, of course. The other way to handle this situation is to delete the check from your records, but make a notation of the employee's absence in a separate paper record book you keep for tax purposes.

If you have a payroll check for a zero amount that you don't want to print, you'll want to remove the check from the list of unprinted checks so that Quicken doesn't keep telling you to print it. Switch to the register and highlight the check transaction. Move the cursor to the *Num* column and replace the notation "Print" there with a dummy check number you set aside for this purpose, such as 0000. After you record the transaction, Quicken will think that the check has been printed.

Paying Payroll Taxes and Insurance Premiums

Every time you write a payroll check, the amounts you enter in the Split Transaction window for withholding, deductions, and employer contributions are transferred to the appropriate other liability accounts. These accounts thus keep a running balance of how much you owe the IRS for withheld federal income tax, the state government for state income tax, your business's insurance company for your employees' health insurance premiums, and so on.

When you make a payment against any of these debts, just be sure that you record it as a transfer to the correct other liability account in the *Category* field. When you do, the balance you owe on that liability will be decreased automatically by the amount of your payment.

Preparing W-2 Forms

At year end, your Quicken payroll records will make filling out your W-2 forms almost instantaneous. Simply prepare a Summary report as follows:

1. Choose **Other** followed by **Summary** from the Reports menu, and then choose **Customize**.

2. In the *Date* fields, choose **Last Year** (or type in the first and last days of the year for which you're preparing the form).

3. So that the report lists amounts for each employee separately, select **Class** in the *Row Headings* field if you've set up classes for your employees, or **Payee** if you haven't.

4. Select **Category** in the *Column Headings* field to obtain subtotals for individual categories for each class or payee.

5. Choose the **Accounts** radio button, and then mark only the checking account you use to write your payroll checks for inclusion in the report.

6. Choose **Matching** and enter **Payr..** in the *Category matches* field.

7. Choose **OK** to close the Customize window, and again to start the report.

The results should look similar to Figure 16.6.

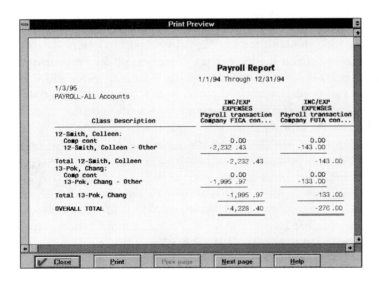

FIGURE 16.6

A sample Payroll report used to calculate yearly totals for W-2 forms.

From the screen report or a printout, you'll be able to copy the gross pay and, from the *Transfer* columns on the lines listed as "Other" subclasses, the amounts you've withheld for each type of tax for the entire year. Before you copy the gross pay amount from the Payroll report to the "Social security wages" blank on the W-2, check to make sure that the amount doesn't exceed the maximum wages to which social security taxes are applied. If it does, enter the social security maximum in this blank instead of the gross pay.

If you have set up a 401(K) or other retirement plan for your employees that reduces the amount of their taxable income, the amount in the *Gross Pay* column of the Payroll report should not be copied to the "Wages, tips, other compensation" blank on the W-2. Instead, you'll need to calculate manually the correct W-2 entry by subtracting the employee's contributions to the plan from the gross pay figure.

Preparing Payroll Tax Returns

You can handle other payroll tax forms just as easily. The same Summary report used to prepare the individual W-2 forms will give you the overall totals for wages and for income and social security taxes withheld that you need in order to fill out your W-3. Again, before you enter the social security wages and taxes, be sure to check the total wage for each payee against the social security maximum.

To report your quarterly employer's federal tax payments on Form 941, begin by creating the same type of Summary report to determine the total wages you've paid and the income tax you've withheld. Of course, you'll need to change the report's date range to match the quarter for which you're filing. After you've checked each employee's wages against the social security maximum and made any corresponding adjustments to the tax owed, copy the amounts in the report to the form.

You'll also need to prepare a second Summary report to calculate the totals you owe for each payroll period. Define the report with accounts, not payees, as the row headings and the time interval between paydays (weekly, bi-weekly, or monthly) as the column headings. This time, include in the report only the liability accounts you use to record withheld federal income tax, FICA, and Medicare payments (in the Customize window, choose **Accounts** and mark those accounts in the list).

As shown in Figure 16.7, the final report will list the amounts transferred to each of the accounts each pay period in a column with a total for that period at the bottom of the column. Transfer that total to the corresponding *Tax Liability* column on Form 941.

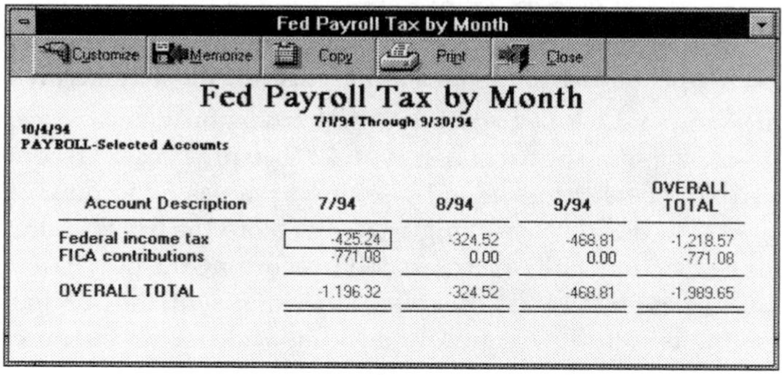
Fed Payroll Tax by Month

Customize Memorize Copy Print Close

Fed Payroll Tax by Month

7/1/94 Through 9/30/94

10/4/94

PAYROLL-Selected Accounts

Account Description	7/94	8/94	9/94	OVERALL TOTAL
Federal income tax	-425.24	-324.52	-468.81	-1,218.57
FICA contributions	-771.08	0.00	0.00	-771.08
OVERALL TOTAL	-1,196.32	-324.52	-468.81	-1,989.65

FIGURE 16.7

A sample report used to determine federal quarterly payroll tax liability by monthly pay period.

Tracking Depreciation

Quicken can help you track the tax-related value of your capital assets, such as cars and trucks, buildings, manufacturing equipment, and furniture and fixtures. As you depreciate each of your assets, you can record the depreciation in a Quicken account to keep your financial profile up-to-date and for use when you prepare your tax returns.

The best way to handle depreciable assets is to set up a separate Quicken asset account for each one. That way, if you keep the account current, its balance will always be equal to the depreciated value of the asset. You'll need that figure when you sell the asset. If your business owns many different assets, however, you may run into Quicken's limit of 255 accounts in a single account file. In that case, you'll have to combine groups of related assets into single accounts, define a class for each asset, and then do a little extra work on the Summary report to calculate the depreciated value of each asset separately. In either case, be sure to create a **Depreciation** category for depreciation transactions.

For assets you purchased before you began keeping records with Quicken, start each asset account with a zero balance, and then enter a transaction in the Account register showing the purchase value of each asset in the *Increase* column. Set up the accounts for assets you buy later with a zero balance as well, but immediately record the purchase of each of these items as a transaction in your checking account. In the process, transfer the purchase price to the other asset account by assigning it to that account in the *Category* field.

From this point, you'll treat both groups of assets the same. To record depreciation of an asset, enter a transaction in the corresponding other asset account, showing the amount of the depreciation in the *Decrease* column and listing the category you've created for depreciation in the *Category* field. If you've mixed two or more assets in an account, be sure to assign both the purchase and depreciation transactions to the class for the item involved.

Here's an example. Let's say you buy a new truck for your landscaping business on November 1. The truck costs you $20,000 plus tax. To record the transaction and the new asset, begin by setting up an asset account called Truck. Then, in your business checking account, record the truck's purchase as a payment transaction. Split the transaction, recording the purchase price of the truck, the sales tax, and any other fees associated with the purchase on separate lines of the split. On the line in the Splits window for the purchase price, transfer the value of the truck to the new truck account by entering the account's name in the *Category* column in brackets. The completed Splits window will then look like Figure 16.8.

FIGURE 16.8

Splitting a transaction to record the purchase of a truck as a transfer to an asset account.

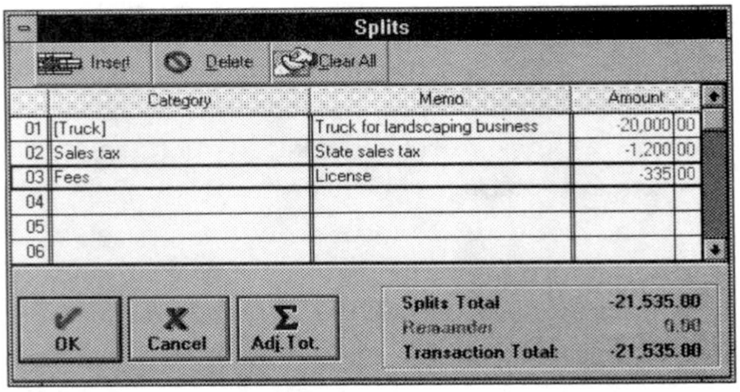

According to IRS rules, light trucks are to be depreciated over a five-year period. If you use the straight-line method, in which the depreciation is divided evenly over the depreciation period, you would claim $2,000 in depreciation the first year. ($20,000 divided by 5 is $4,000, but the IRS requires you to consider depreciable items as placed into service for half a year no matter when you actually purchased them).

To record the first year's $2,000 depreciation in Quicken, you would switch to the other asset account named Truck and enter a transaction dated December 31 of the year you purchased the truck. You'd type **2000** into the *Decrease* column, and assign the transaction to the **Depreciation** category. The final transaction would then look something like Figure 16.9.

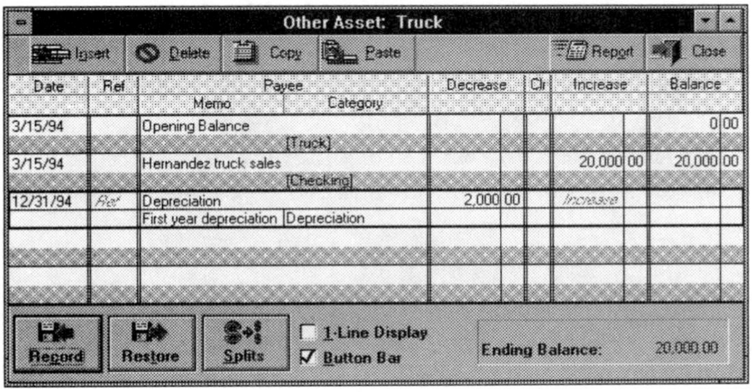

FIGURE 16.9

A transaction recording a year's depreciation of a truck purchased for business use in an asset account.

To obtain depreciation totals, prepare a Summary report restricted to the accounts for the assets you're interested in. If all the accounts contain only one asset, select accounts as your row headings; if some of the accounts contain more than one asset, select classes instead. For column headings, use the time period (probably months) by which you want to subtotal the depreciation amounts. Restrict the report to selected accounts and include only those accounts pertaining to the depreciated assets.

To find the current depreciated value of each asset in an account containing two or more assets, prepare a Summary report as before, but this time set the date range to cover the date the account was opened through the date of the last transaction recorded in the account. Choose classes as your row headings and then select **Don't Subtotal** in the *Column Headings* field. Your report will have one column showing the final amount for each asset.

Drawing Up a Balance Sheet

If you'd like to use Quicken to give you an overall summation of your business's worth, you'll need to create accounts for all your assets and liabilities—including accounts receivable, capital equipment, loans, and mortgages—and keep these accounts current. Once a complete set of accounts is in place, figuring the worth of your business is a snap. Just create a Balance Sheet report, one of the choices on the Business Reports menu. When the Balance Sheet Report window appears, all you have to do is enter the date for which you want the balance sheet calculated.

The standard Balance Sheet report includes all your accounts and calculates the overall balance, but for one date only. If you want to see account balances for a limited number of your business accounts, or if you want to report on your business's worth at two or more different points in time, customize the Balance Sheet report. Enter the dates over which you want to report balances and, in the *Interval* field, list the time interval for which you want balances to be listed. If you want to include only certain accounts in the report, choose the **Accounts** radio button and mark those accounts on the list.

Summary

In this chapter, you've learned to apply Quicken to some of the major challenges of business bookkeeping: accounts payable and receivable, payroll, business forecasting, depreciation of capital equipment, and preparation of a balance sheet. With your mastery of these record-keeping and reporting techniques, you'll be able to rely on a rich information base to guide you in making the decisions that keep your venture in the financial fast lane.

Chapter 16 completes your tour of Quicken's own financial management features. In Chapter 17, you'll learn how to pay your bills electronically with CheckFree to increase your efficiency still further.

Chapter Seventeen

Paying Your Bills Electronically with CheckFree

I n this age of fax machines and supermarket bank card paypoints, writing checks on paper and sending them through the mail begins to seem an antiquated and inefficient practice. With Quicken and the CheckFree service you can bring the speed and convenience of telecommunications to bear on all your bill-paying chores while maintaining highly accurate, up-to-date financial records.

| NOTE | To obtain information on CheckFree, call (800) 882-5280. You must obtain a separate CheckFree account for each Quicken account you'll be using for electronic payments. |

CheckFree is a computer-based checking service with which you can make payments to any person or business via your PC and a modem. When CheckFree receives your check information—the payee and the amount of the check—it either transfers your funds directly to the payee by electronic means or prints out a paper check for you and mails it to to the payee.

| WARNING | If you are accustomed to sending in payments just before they're due, it's best to schedule your CheckFree paper check payments to be sent a few days earlier than you now mail them. Intuit |

recommends that you schedule each payment at least five business days before it is due—enough time for the check to arrive in the mail from CheckFree's office in Ohio, and for any special handling required by the recipient.

CheckFree has many advantages over traditional checking practices; chief among them is convenience. Instead of having to fiddle with paper checks, stamps, and envelopes, all you have to do is type in the information on your computer screen and connect to the CheckFree service with your modem.

Because CheckFree allows you to schedule automatic payments on your monthly bills, you don't have to worry about missing those due dates. With no further action on your part, CheckFree will make the monthly payments on a home mortgage or car loan, or on any fixed-amount bill that you pay regularly, for the length you specify. Quicken automatically records each payment in your register at the proper time.

CheckFree also allows you to earn the maximum possible interest on your money. Many merchants accept electronic payments directly. This means you can schedule automatic payments on these bills for the actual due dates and continue to earn interest on your money until the day the funds are transferred to the payee. Even if the payee is not set up to receive electronic payments, you can still schedule your CheckFree checks to be sent near their due dates to maximize your interest earnings.

Using Quicken with CheckFree

Quicken and CheckFree are a terrific combination. Quicken is designed to pay all your bills electronically within Quicken itself. You can even initiate stop payment orders, submit payment inquiries, and send messages to the CheckFree customer service via electronic mail without ever leaving Quicken.

Getting Ready to Use CheckFree

Before you can use Quicken with CheckFree, you must sign up with the CheckFree service and equip your computer with a Hayes-compatible modem. Be sure to make note of the computer port (serial port) to which your modem is connected.

If you don't currently have a CheckFree account, the best way to sign up with CheckFree is via the CheckFree Service form provided with your copy of Quicken. Fill in the form, sign it, and send it to Intuit with a voided check from the account you'll be using to make electronic payments. Once the CheckFree service has set up your account, you'll be sent a confirmation letter containing your Personal Identification Number and the telephone number to use for transmitting payments to the service. When you receive this letter, you're ready to go. Follow the instructions in "Setting Up Quicken for CheckFree."

If you already have a CheckFree account and have been using the CheckFree software to write your checks, and if you now want to use Quicken instead for this purpose, you'll need to make some changes in your account. After setting up Quicken as detailed in the next section, you must also follow the steps laid out in "Switching to Quicken From CheckFree Software," later in this chapter.

Setting Up Quicken for CheckFree

Before you can use Quicken with CheckFree you must set up the program for electronic payments. To do this, you'll need several pieces of information:

- The serial port to which your modem is connected (COM1, COM2, etc.).
- Your modem's speed (300, 1200, 2400, or 9600 baud).
- Whether or not your telephone line permits touch-tone (push button) dialing.
- The telephone number of the CheckFree service in your area. (You received this number in the package of information sent you when you opened your CheckFree account).
- The names of the Quicken account or accounts from which you'll be making electronic payments.
- The CheckFree account number for each account—this will be your social security number unless you have opened more than one CheckFree account.
- Your CheckFree personal identification number.

NOTE　　In Quicken 2, choose **Modem** from the Preferences menu to display the Modem Preferences dialog box.

With this information, you're ready to set up Quicken to work with CheckFree. Start by telling Quicken how your modem is set up. Choose **Preferences** from the Edit menu to pop up the Preferences window, and then choose the **Modem** button. You'll see the Modem Preferences dialog box, shown in Figure 17.1.

FIGURE 17.1

The Modem Preferences dialog box.

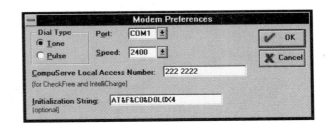

1. Make any necessary changes to the existing entries in the first three fields for dialing method, serial port, and modem speed.

WARNING   If you have call waiting or any other service that might interrupt your telephone calls, it's best to turn off such features whenever you use your modem. You can have Quicken do this for you automatically by entering the dialing sequence necessary to turn off the feature at the beginning of the field for the telephone number.

2. Type in the telephone number you dial to connect to CheckFree in the fourth field just as you would dial it by hand, including any long-distance access codes, area code, or other special dialing codes. To make the modem pause between numbers—while waiting to connect to an outside line or long-distance service, for example—type one or more commas in the dialing sequence. With most modems, each comma creates a pause of about two seconds. Thus, if you have to dial 9 and then wait four seconds before you can use an outside line, your entry in this field would look something like this: **9,,404-555-1212**.

3. If your modem requires special commands to function properly, type them into the *Initialization String* field, but don't make any changes unless you know exactly what you're doing.

4. Choose **OK** to confirm your entries and close the dialog box.

Your next job is to select and set up the Quicken account or accounts from which you'll be making electronic payments via CheckFree. Note that you need to apply for a separate CheckFree account for each Quicken account from which you want to make payments via CheckFree. You'll receive a separate account number and Personal Identification Number for each account, and you must pay a separate monthly service fee for each one.

SHORTCUT	To deactivate the Electronic Payment function on an account, highlight the account name in the Electronic Payment Setup window and choose **Setup**. Then uncheck the box for the first field, *Enable Electronic Payments for Account* and choose **OK**. In the Electronic Payment Setup window, the *Electronic Pmts* column for that account should now be empty.

1. Choose **CheckFree**, then **Setup** from the Activities menu to display the Electronic Payment Setup window (see Figure 17.2). The window lists all your bank accounts in the current account file and tells whether electronic payments have been enabled for each account.

FIGURE 17.2

The Electronic Payment Setup window.

2. Select the account you'll be using with CheckFree and choose **Setup**. The Electronic Payment Account Settings window appears (see Figure 17.3).

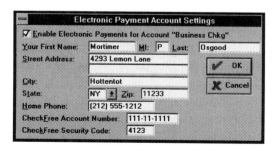

FIGURE 17.3

The Electronic Payment Account Settings dialog box.

3. Be sure the box labelled **Enable Electronic Payments** is checked.

4. Enter your name, address, and home phone number.

5. Type in your CheckFree account number (usually your social security number).

6. In the final field, type your CheckFree Personal Identification Number. Then choose **OK** to close the Window and return to the list of bank accounts. You'll see the notation *Enabled* followed by a tiny lightning bolt in the column labelled *Electronic Pmts*.

7. Repeat Steps 2 through 5 for each account you'd like to set up for electronic payment.

8. Press **Esc** to close the list of bank accounts.

Switching to Quicken from CheckFree Software

If you've already been using the CheckFree software to send checks electronically, you must complete a transition process before you can use Quicken for that purpose. You'll be making a complete switch from the CheckFree software to Quicken—once you've used Quicken to make your first CheckFree payment, you won't be able to access the service for payments with your CheckFree software any longer.

| NOTE | You can only import CheckFree data from version 3.0 or greater of the CheckFree software—if you've been using an earlier version, contact CheckFree for an update. |

To switch from CheckFree software to Quicken, all you really have to do is start using Quicken. But you'll probably want to import your earlier CheckFree transactions into Quicken so that you'll have complete financial records. You should definitely import the CheckFree data if you've been making automatic payments on a regular schedule (fixed transactions) with CheckFree.

In the latter case, you should start the CheckFree software immediately before you begin the import process. You don't need to do anything with the CheckFree software; just run the program, then quit (since CheckFree is not a Windows program, you must run it in a DOS window or do so prior to starting Windows). This ensures that any fixed payments are in the CheckFree register where Quicken can retrieve them.

Now you're ready to import the CheckFree information. Follow these steps:

WARNING	Since you'll be temporarily cancelling your CheckFree payment schedule, you should plan to complete all of these steps at one sitting, to avoid missing or delaying any payments.

Start your CheckFree software and print a list of all of the payees or merchants for whom you've set up entries with the CheckFree service.

Delete all the merchants from your CheckFree account (be sure to send the order to delete them to CheckFree via your modem). Deleting your current Merchant list is critical for smooth operation when you switch to Quicken for communications with CheckFree.

WARNING	Deleting the Merchant list automatically deletes any future payments you have scheduled, so be sure to reschedule these payments from Quicken. However, you can't delete payments scheduled for today's date.

If you've been using the CheckFree software to make payments but haven't previously recorded those payments in Quicken, or if your Quicken records aren't up to date, import your CheckFree information into Quicken. Begin by starting Quicken and switching to the register of the account you'll be using with CheckFree.

Choose **Import** from the Edit menu or press **Ctrl-I**. You'll see the window shown in Figure 17.4 on the next page. Uncheck the *Special Handling for Transfers* field at the bottom of the window. This sets up Quicken to import the CheckFree file properly.

To enter the name of the file you're importing, choose the **Browse** button. This displays the familiar Windows dialog box used to pick files. Navigate using the various list fields to the path (disk drive and directory) where your CheckFree data is stored. Then, in the *File Name* field, type the full name of the file, **REG.DAT**. Choose **OK** to return to the main Import window.

FIGURE 17.4

You'll see this window when you begin the Import process.

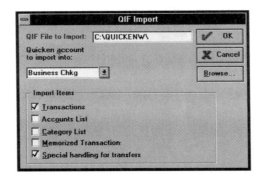

> **NOTE**   Quicken 2 lets you limit the transactions you import to those before or after a particular date.

Choose **OK** to begin the import. Quicken displays each transaction briefly as it's imported. Quicken matches the category of each CheckFree transaction to those in your Quicken account.

When the import is complete, Quicken tells you how many transactions you imported successfully. If you skipped over categories that didn't exist in Quicken, the message tells you how many such categories you "ignored." Note this last figure, and choose **OK**.

That completes the Import process proper, but you may want to go through the imported transactions to find and correct those that weren't assigned to categories. You can aid your hunt by printing out the CheckFree Category list and comparing it to your Quicken categories as you hunt down the uncategorized transactions.

Setting Up CheckFree Payees

Before you can send a payment to any payee via CheckFree, you must first set up your CheckFree account for that payee. All you have to do is supply Quicken with the payee's name, address, and phone number, and the account number you have with the payee. The first time you use CheckFree to transmit a payment to that payee, Quicken automatically sends the payee setup information to CheckFree electronically.

Setting Up a New CheckFree Payee

It's best to set up all the payees to whom you expect to be sending payments before you start making CheckFree payments with Quicken. You can add new payees at any time, even while you're filling out checks.

<table>
<tr><td>

NOTE

</td><td>

If **Electronic Payee list** appears in gray type on the CheckFree menu, meaning that it's an inactive choice, you haven't set up your file for electronic payments. Go back to the instructions at the beginning of the chapter.

</td></tr>
</table>

Choose **CheckFree** and **Electronic Payee list** from the Activities menu. You'll see the Electronic Payee list shown in Figure 17.5 (the first time you use this window it will be empty, of course). Repeat the steps covered below for each new payee you'd like to set up. When you're through, press **Esc** to close the Electronic Payee list.

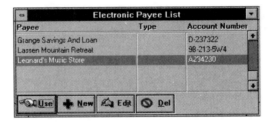

FIGURE 17.5

The Electronic Payee list.

To set up a new electronic payee, choose the **New** button. Quicken first displays a one-field dialog box asking you to choose the "type" for this electronic payee, normal or fixed. If you want CheckFree to make an automatic fixed-amount payment to this payee on a regular schedule, select the **Fixed, Recurring Payee** radio button. Otherwise, select **Normal Payee**.

The next dialog box you see depends on whether you're setting up a normal or fixed payee. The two dialog boxes are shown in Figure 17.6 on the next page. They have identical fields for information about the payee, but the Fixed Payment dialog box includes additional fields for defining the regular payment. Figure 17.6a is for setting up a "normal" payee, Figure 17.6b is for a fixed payee.

FIGURES 17.6

You'll use one of these two dialog boxes to set up a new electronic payee.

A

B

No matter which type of payee you're setting up, fill out the payee *Information* fields with the information requested (the payee's name, address, and phone, and your account number with the payee. Be sure to double-check all your entries for accuracy—they're crucial in getting your payment to the right payee as well as ensuring that you get credit for the payment. It is vital you type your payee account number accurately. The number you need will appear on your bills from the payee as your account number, customer number, policy number, or something similar. But if you don't have an account number from the payee or don't know it, just enter your last name.

If you're setting up a normal payee, that completes your entries. Choose **OK** to confirm them and return to the Electronic Payee list.

Setting Up a Fixed Payee

If you're setting up a fixed payee, continue with the fields on the right side of the window pertaining to the fixed payment you'll be making.

At the top right of the window, the dialog box lists the account you'll be using to make the regular payment—unless, that is, you have more than two accounts set up for CheckFree. In that case, you'll see a *Bank Account* field. Here, enter the name of the right account.

In the next three fields, enter:

- The amount of the payment.
- The frequency of payments (in the *Frequency* field, select the appropriate time interval from the drop-down list).
- The date of the first payment in the series.

Next, in the group of fields labelled *Duration of Payments*, tell Quicken how many of these fixed payments to make. If you want payments to continue indefinitely, select the **Unlimited** radio button; otherwise, select **Stop After** and type in the total number of payments that CheckFree should make.

Finally, assign the category, class, and memo assignments you want for these Fixed Payment transactions. Start by choosing the **Categories** button.

In the new dialog box that appears (see Figure 17.7), the first field lets you change the amount of the fixed payment. Then come fields for the **Category** and **Memo** entries. QuickFill works in the *Category* field, of course, but you can't pop up the Category list from within this dialog box.

FIGURE 17.7

Setting up a fixed CheckFree payment.

You can split the fixed payment just like any other Quicken transaction. Choose **Splits** to display the Split Transaction window.

NOTE   Of course, a fixed-payment schedule won't work for an adjustable-rate loan, so don't amortize such a loan here. You can still pay your bill semiautomatically by memorizing a payment transaction in your checking account and amortizing it according to the instructions in Chapter 8, then recalling it at the proper interval in a memorized transaction group.

If this is a payment on a fixed-rate loan, you can have Quicken amortize the loan, apportioning each payment to principal and interest according to the amortization schedule. You use the same method you learned in Chapter 8, but you don't go through the memorized Transaction list. After splitting the payment, amortize it by choosing **Amortize** on the window shown in Figure 17.7.

Now complete the Set Amortization Information window (see Figure 8.45) as presented in Chapter 9. When you finish, choose **OK** to close the window. Choose **OK** in the Category and Payee Setup windows as well to return to the Electronic Payee list.

Creating Duplicate Setups for One Payee

There may be times when you need two or more separate setups for the same payee. For example, if you own rental real estate, you might have two separate accounts with the local Big Barn Home and Garden Center: one account for lumber and hardware, the other for landscape items such as plants, fertilizers, and sprinkler equipment.

Quicken provides for such situations by allowing you to type in additional characters after the payee's name when you set up each payee. This helps you keep the two accounts straight when choosing payees from the Electronic Payee list. You enter the extra characters inside curly braces ({ }). In the previous example, you might list the payee for the first account as **Big Barn {Hardware}**, entering your account number for hardware purchases on that setup. You could then enter **Big Barn {Landscape}** as the payee for the second account.

The two accounts would then appear in the Electronic Payee list, as shown in Figure 17.8. The notation inside the braces is there simply to remind you which account to use for which payments. Quicken omits the braces and the characters between them when it transmits your payee setups and payment information to CheckFree.

FIGURE 17.8

The Electronic Payee list, showing two separate setups for the same payee.

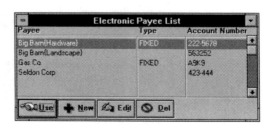

Changing Payee Setups

Editing an existing CheckFree payee setup is as simple as creating the setup the first time. Bring up the Electronic Payee list and select the payee setup you wish to modify. Choose **Edit** or press **Ctrl-E** to display the Edit Electronic Payee window, which is identical to the window you used previously to enter the payee information the first time.

NOTE   There are two changes you *can't* make to existing payee setups, however: You can't convert a fixed-payment payee to a normal one, and you can't change the account from which a fixed payment is made. Instead, you must delete the existing payee setup and create a new one reflecting the changes you want. These restrictions ensure that all your fixed payments will be handled properly, with no extra or missed payments. After making your changes in the Edit Electronic Payee window, choose **OK** to return to the Payee list.

You can also delete any setups for payees you're no longer sending payments to. Just select the payee in the Electronic Payee list and choose **Del** or press **Ctrl-D**. If the **Require Confirmation** box is checked in the General Preferences dialog box (see the Appendix), you'll be given a chance to change your mind.

Quicken sends your changes and deletions to CheckFree the next time you transmit any transactions (see "Transmitting Transactions to CheckFree"). However, Quicken will wait to delete a payee until all the checks you've written to that payee have been transmitted and processed.

Writing CheckFree Checks

Once you've signed up with the CheckFree service, set up Quicken to match, and created your Payee list, you're ready to make electronic payments from your Quicken account. This part's a snap—essentially, you simply write Quicken checks as you would normally. However, two parts of the process work just a bit differently than when you fill out a check that you'll be printing yourself: With electronic payments, Quicken automatically postdates the check for you, and you don't have to type in the payee's address.

WARNING   Simply writing a check doesn't send its information to CheckFree. Instead, you must transmit checks to CheckFree in a separate step covered in the section "Transmitting Transactions to CheckFree."

The following list shows the correct method for writing checks for electronic payment:

1. Move to the Write Checks window of the account you've set up for CheckFree. The screen check looks a little different—in place of the *Address* field, there are two big orange lightning bolts. In addition, below the check there's a new checkbox labelled **Electronic Payment**. (If you uncheck this box, the check reverts to its conventional look so you can write and print ordinary Quicken checks).

2. Note that Quicken has already postdated the check five working days from today's date in the *Payment Date* field. Assuming you transmit the payment today, that's usually about right for payments that CheckFree will send through the mail to your payee. However, you may wish to schedule the payment for another date. For example, if you're writing out the check in advance of when it should actually be paid, you may want to enter a later date. On the other hand, if you know the payee accepts electronic payments, an earlier date might be better.

<table>
<tr><td>SHORTCUT</td><td>If you don't want to type anything at all, display the Electronic Payee list to select your payee from the list.</td></tr>
</table>

3. Type in the payee's name in the *Pay to the Order of* field and press **Tab**. If QuickFill is turned on, it will try to find a match for what you type from all your previously memorized checks (not just electronic payments), so you may need to type out the payee name in full to correct an incorrect entry made by QuickFill.

4. Move to the $ field and enter the payment amount.

5. Complete the rest of the check as you would normally, typing in a memo and category/class information as appropriate.

6. Record the check. A new, empty check appears on the screen. The amount of the check you just wrote is added to the value *Checks to Xmit* displayed at the lower-right corner of the window. (Whenever the **Electronic Payments** box is checked, you'll see *Checks to Xmit* instead of *Checks to Print* if you have written but not yet transmitted one or more checks to CheckFree.

Making CheckFree Payments with Memorized Transactions

You can memorize electronic payments for reuse later just as you can ordinary checks: automatically, with QuickFill, or manually, by pressing **Ctrl-M** or choosing **Memorize Transaction** from the Edit menu. And you can recall memorized transactions the same way, too, using QuickFill and the drop-down list in the *Pay to the Order of* field.

If the check you're memorizing is an Electronic Payment, it will be memorized as such automatically. Likewise, checks memorized as electronic payment transactions are recalled automatically as electronic payments. Quicken adds five business days to today's date and enters the result in the *Date* field.

Making CheckFree Payments with the Register

Electronic payments are listed in the registers just like the other types of transactions you're used to. The only thing that distinguishes them from other transactions is a notation in the *Num* column: XMIT for payments that have not yet been transmitted to CheckFree, or EFT (electronic funds transfer), indicating payments that have already been transmitted.

You can enter new CheckFree payments into your Account register rather than by writing checks on the Write Checks window if you prefer. Here's how:

1. Move to the bottom of the Register list, to the first empty item.
2. Enter the date on which you want to make the payment.
3. Identify this as an electronic payment that you'd like to transmit later: type **XMIT** in the *Num* field. Quicken also checks the date you entered; if the date isn't already at least five business days ahead of today's date, Quicken makes the necessary change.
4. Now enter the payee's name using QuickFill or by selecting it from the Electronic Payment list.

5. Type in the payment amount.

6. Enter an Expense category. Remember that if you don't enter an Expense category, the payment will be automatically charged to *Expenses-Other*.

7. Record the transaction.

How Automatic Payments Work

As soon as you set up a fixed, regularly scheduled CheckFree payment, Quicken enters the first transaction in the series into your register for you, scheduling it as a payment to be transmitted by typing **XMIT** in the *Num* field. Following the date that CheckFree actually makes the payment, Quicken changes the *Num* entry to **EFT** and adds the next payment in the series to your account, typing **XMIT** in the new transaction's *Num* field.

Transmitting Transactions to CheckFree

After you've written one or more electronic payment checks in Quicken, you must complete the process by transmitting them to CheckFree.

1. Turn on your modem and make sure that it is connected properly to your computer.

2. Choose **CheckFree** and **Transmit** from the Activities menu. You'll see a window indicating how many payments are ready to be transmitted (see Figure 17.9).

FIGURE 17.9

This window tells you how many electronic payments are scheduled to be transmitted to CheckFree.

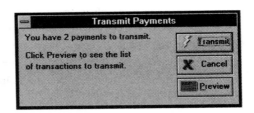

3. To see details on the individual payments before you transmit them, choose **Preview**. The **Preview Transmission to CheckFree** window, shown in Figure 17.10, displays a list of all the checks you've written but

not yet transmitted. You'll also see any additions, changes, or deletions to your payee setups that remain to be sent below the list of payments.

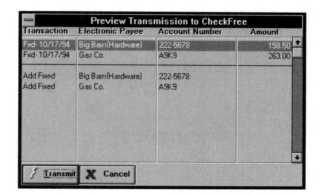

FIGURE 17.10

The Preview Transmission to CheckFree window.

4. To transmit your transactions to CheckFree—whether or not you preview them—choose **Transmit**. Using your modem, Quicken will dial CheckFree and send in the transactions. During the process you'll see brief messages telling you how the procedure is going. If you get a message telling you something went wrong, you can press **F1** for help on ways to correct the problem.

CheckFree provides a unique confirmation number for each transaction you transmit. You don't have to worry about recording this number—Quicken does it for you automatically. If you ever need to send a stop payment request or an inquiry about a payment, Quicken will retrieve the correct number and send it to CheckFree with your communication. If you need the confirmation number for some other reason, you can obtain it as described in "Sending Payment Inquiries."

Sending Stop Payment Requests

With Quicken, you can stop payment on any check transmitted to CheckFree that has not yet been sent to the payee. There's no charge for this service. Quicken will figure out whether you've made your stop payment request early enough for this method to work, and will let you know if you're too late. After CheckFree processes a stop payment order received from Quicken you'll receive a report of the action taken by mail.

| NOTE | If CheckFree has already sent your payment to the payee, you may be able to place a stop payment order on the check. In this case, however, you'll have to call CheckFree yourself, and you'll be charged a service fee. |

To send a stop payment order, begin by turning on your modem if necessary. Display the register and select the transaction in question, then choose **CheckFree** and **Stop Payment** from the Activities menu. You will see a message indicating the scheduled date of the payment and informing you whether you can still issue a successful electronic stop order. If so, you'll be asked whether you want to proceed. Choose **Yes**.

Quicken calls CheckFree, transmitting the stop payment order for you. Assuming everything goes without a hitch, the transaction will be marked as VOID in the register, and the confirmation number for the stop payment order will be placed in the *Memo* field.

Cancelling a Fixed Payment

If you stop a Fixed Payment transaction using the **Stop Payment** command just described, Quicken terminates the entire fixed payment schedule—no more payments in the series will be transmitted. However, all the other information you previously entered for this payee remains intact, and you can go back and change it—and even restart the fixed payment series—by editing the payee from the Electronic Payee list.

| NOTE | The entry in the *Type* column will also be "Inactive" after the fixed payment schedule for a payee has been completed. Keeping information about inactive payees on hand is a good idea if you think there's any chance you'll need to set up a new fixed payment schedule, contact the payee again for other reasons, or document your payment history. |

On the other hand, editing the payee information is another way to cancel upcoming fixed payments. From the Electronic Payee list, select the payee name and choose **Edit** or press **Ctrl-E**. Then in the *Duration of Payments* section of the Edit Payee window, select the **Stop After** radio button and type in **0** in the following field. When you choose **OK**, Quicken places the notation *Inactive* in the *Type* column of the Electronic Payee list. The payee information is still there, though, and you can edit it again to restore the fixed payment schedule, or start a new one.

Alternatively, you can delete an existing fixed payee entirely. With this approach, you cancel all remaining payments in the fixed payment schedule, and you also delete permanently all the payee information. To complete out this drastic step, select the payee name in the Electronic Payee list and choose **Del** or press **Ctrl-D**.

Sending Payment Inquiries

From time to time you may need to ask the CheckFree service about a payment you previously transmitted. For example, say you get an overdue notice on a bill that you paid via CheckFree. You'll probably want to ask CheckFree for confirmation that the payment was actually sent. Quicken provides an automated method for doing just that, or for asking any other questions about a particular payment.

NOTE	Obviously, you can't ask CheckFree for any information about a payment until after you've transmitted the payment order.

To send a payment inquiry, start from the register, turning on your modem if necessary. Select the transaction you want to inquire about, then choose **CheckFree** and **Inquiry** and the Activities menu. You'll see a small window with the details Quicken has recorded about this transaction: your payee account number, the date the payment was scheduled for, the date you actually transmitted the payment to CheckFree, and CheckFree's confirmation number for the transaction.

If you want to proceed to send a message to CheckFree about the payment, choose **OK**. Quicken displays a "form letter" to CheckFree with the date, payee information, and even the salutation and signature already filled in for you. You get three empty lines for your message; after typing it in, choose **Transmit** to send the payment inquiry. You'll get your answer back via electronic mail or by telephone.

Sending and Receiving CheckFree Electronic Mail

Use Quicken's electronic mail capability when you need to send messages to CheckFree pertaining to your account in general, not to a particular payment.

You can use electronic mail to receive responses from CheckFree to your payment inquiries and other electronic mail messages.

For faster response, call CheckFree customer service at (614) 899-7500.

Here's how to use CheckFree electronic mail. To begin, check to make sure your modem is on, if it's an external model. Then choose CheckFree and E-Mail from the Activities menu. You'll see the window, as shown in Figure 17.11.

FIGURE 17.11

Use this window to send or receive CheckFree electronic mail.

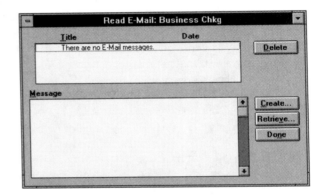

At this point, the window is empty, since you haven't received any messages. To get your "mail" from CheckFree, choose the **Retrieve** button. Quicken dials CheckFree and picks up your messages, displaying information about each one in a list ordered by date in the top part of the window. To read a message, double-click on it in the list or use the cursor keys to select it with the outline highlight and press **Enter**. The message appears in the lower part of the window. If the whole thing doesn't fit in the window, you can scroll through it with the cursor keys or the scroll bar.

Once you've received a message from CheckFree, it's stored on your hard disk and stays in the list of messages until you delete it. To delete an electronic mail message, highlight the message in the list at the top of the window and choose **Delete**.

To send an electronic mail message to CheckFree, choose the Create button at the right of the window. A secondary window appears, with a salutation (*Dear CheckFree Corporation*) and a closing with your "signature" already in place. In the large empty area, type in your message to CheckFree. The standard Windows **Cut, Copy,** and **Paste** keys are active in this *Text* field. When you're through typing, choose the **Transmit** button to send the message to CheckFree.

Allow a day or two after sending your inquiry or message. Then use the steps previously outlined to retrieve your message.

Recording the CheckFree Service Charge

You'll need to account for the monthly fee charged to your real bank account for the CheckFree service. The fee will appear on your bank statement each month.

You have two options for accounting for this service charge. One method is to record it when you reconcile your Quicken account to your bank statement each month. Add your CheckFree "dues" to any other fees charged by your bank and enter the total in the *Service Charge* field in the initial Reconciliation window. Your other choice is to enter the fee as a payment item in the register each month. To automate this process, you can memorize the transaction and add it to a transaction group that you execute each month (see Chapter 7).

Summary

With Quicken and the techniques you've learned in this chapter, you'll now be able to take full advantage of the efficiencies of electronic banking using the CheckFree service. You've learned how to set up Quicken for use with CheckFree, how to write checks for CheckFree payments, and how to transmit them electronically to CheckFree. You've also become familiar with some essential skills for maintaining your CheckFree account, including how to issue stop payment orders, make inquiries about specific payments, and send other electronic messages to CheckFree.

Appendix

Installing Quicken, Setting Options, and Exchanging Data

T his Appendix contains a collection of useful tips on the fine points of operating Quicken. If you haven't yet installed the program, you'll find the necessary instructions for a "quick start" here. You'll also learn how to customize the program to suit your personal preferences and the equipment in your system. The final section discusses techniques for exchanging financial information between Quicken and other programs.

Installing Quicken

If you haven't already installed Quicken, the instructions here will get you started. The process is extremely simple and should take only 10 minutes or so.

1. Before you install the program, make backup copies of your program disks and put them away in a safe place.

2. Start Windows if you haven't already done so.

3. Put the first Quicken disk into a floppy drive.

4. Use the **Run** command from the Program Manager's File menu or use File Manager to start the program SETUP.EXE on the floppy disk.

5. Setup noses around in your system to determine whether you have enough hard disk space for the Quicken files. You'll soon see a screen that suggests the drive and directory where you should install the program. Make any changes you'd like, and then choose **OK** to go ahead with the installation.

6. Setup copies the Quicken files to your hard disk. You'll be notified if and when you need to insert additional disks.

7. When the installation process is complete, store the original Quicken master disks in a safe place.

Controlling Quicken Features

Quicken is a very flexible program. You can easily control the way many of its features work to suit your personal taste and your bookkeeping needs. For instance, you can specify a set arrangement of windows that will appear on the screen whenever you start the program, and you can control the appearance of your checks, reports, and graphs to a certain extent. Other options let you determine how much help you get (in the form of Qcards) and whether you'll be warned by messages on the screen under certain conditions (e.g., if you record an uncategorized transaction). You can also assign passwords to your files and transactions to prevent unauthorized access to them.

In Quicken 3, you access most of these controls via a special Preferences window, shown in Figure A.1. The commands for setting and changing passwords are located on the File menu.

FIGURE A.1

The Preferences window.

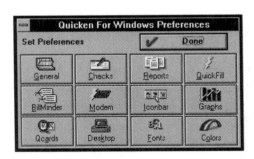

To display the Preferences window, click the **Prefs** icon or choose **Preferences** from the Edit menu. The window consists of a set of buttons, each with its own icon.

Setting Miscellaneous Options

Quicken lets you control a variety of miscellaneous settings that don't fall into any specific category from a General Preferences dialog box, shown in Figure A.2. To access this dialog box, choose the **General** button on the Preferences window. The options available in the window are described in order as follows.

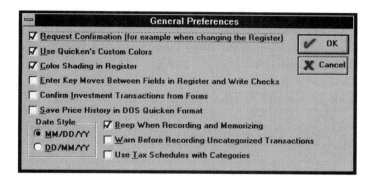

FIGURE A.2

The General Preferences dialog box.

Requiring Confirmation When You Record Transactions

Quicken can be set up so that it pauses to ask for confirmation before recording any changes to an existing transaction. When this setting is on, if you make changes in a transaction and then try to move to another transaction before recording the changes, Quicken displays the message "Leaving Transaction. Record Changes?"

Responding to this confirmation request slows you down a little, but it gives you an extra measure of protection against mistakes. If you were actually just trying to move to another field, or if you realize you made an error in the transaction, you now have a chance to back out of recording and stay in the original transaction by choosing **Cancel**. Alternatively, you can go ahead and move to the new transaction. In the process, you can record your changes by choosing **Yes** or restore the transaction to its original form by choosing **No**.

To turn the confirmation feature on, check the first box in the General Preferences dialog box, the one labelled **Request Confirmation**. If you don't want Quicken to ask you for confirmation, uncheck this box.

Changing Screen Colors

For many parts of the Quicken display, the color you see on your monitor is determined by the color settings for Windows in general. To change the colors of the title bar, the menu bar, or the background workspace, you must use the Windows Control Panel program, as described in your Windows manual. Independently of Windows, however, Quicken uses a "custom" gray shading for other elements such as its own dialog boxes, lists (of categories and accounts), and the lower portions of registers and the Write Checks windows.

If you want to turn off this gray shading, just uncheck the box labelled **Use Quicken's Custom Colors** in the General Preferences dialog box. In this case, all the screen elements under Quicken's control will appear in plain black and white.

After you've changed the color scheme setting in the dialog box, Quicken doesn't actually start using the new colors until the next time you start the program. You'll see a message describing this situation when you choose **OK** to leave the General Preferences dialog box.

Controlling Register Color

Ordinarily, Quicken shades the second line of each register transaction in a color—yellow for bank accounts, light blue for credit card accounts, and green for the remaining types. If you don't like the effect, turn off the colors by unchecking the **Color Shading in Register** box in the General Preferences dialog box.

Requiring a Category Assignment

If you want to ensure that the information in your reports is categorized accurately, you must assign every transaction in your accounts to the correct category. To help you do this, Quicken can be set to warn you if the *Category* field is blank when you go to record the transaction. By the way, Quicken isn't satisfied by a class assignment; you'll see the warning message unless you assign the transaction to a category.

A small window appears asking you how you want to deal with the situation. You have three alternatives, each one with a button you can choose: **Select**, to select an existing category from the list; **Skip**, to tell Quicken to record the transaction without a category; and **Cancel**, to return to the transaction for further editing.

To have Quicken require category entries, check the box labelled **Warn Before Recording Uncategorized Transactions**, the next-to-last field in the General Preferences dialog box. To turn off the warning so that you can freely record uncategorized transactions, uncheck this box.

Controlling the Function of the Enter Key

Quicken for Windows comes set up so that the **Enter** key works as it does in most Windows programs to activate the function of whatever button is currently active in the window in which you're working. In practical terms, that means you can OK a dialog box, record a transaction or check, or pick an item from a list simply by pressing **Enter**—unless you've specifically activated another button first.

However, if you've previously used Quicken for DOS, you're not used to working this way. In Quicken for DOS, the **Enter** key works much like **Tab**, advancing the cursor from field to field. Since many users are switching from the DOS version, Quicken for Windows lets you set the program so that the **Enter** key works in the familiar way—but only part of the time, when entering checks and **Register** transactions.

To control how the **Enter** key works, use the box labelled **Enter Key Moves Between Fields in Register and Write Checks** in the General Preferences dialog box. Check the box if you want the **Enter** key to move the cursor from one field to the next instead of recording transactions. As in the DOS version of Quicken, pressing **Enter** once you get to the last field, *Category*, then records the transaction (unlike **Tab**, which moves to the buttons at the bottom of the window, then to the top field). In dialog boxes and lists, it doesn't matter whether you check the box in the General Preferences window—the **Enter** key always works the same way.

Controlling the Investment Transaction Entry

Quicken 3 lets you enter transactions in your investment accounts in two ways: by entering them directly into the register, or by filling out a special dialog box (a "form") for each transaction, with fields corresponding to the columns in the register. Check the box labelled **Confirm Investment Transactions from Forms** if you want Quicken to ask for confirmation before it records an **Investment** transaction you enter via one of these forms. If you uncheck the box, Quicken records the transaction as soon as you choose **OK** in the form.

Controlling the File Format of Investment Prices

Quicken 3's standard system for recording the price history of investments on disk is different from the system used by Quicken for DOS. However, you can set up Quicken 3 to use the DOS version's system instead, allowing you to share files that include investment data between the two versions. Check the box if you want this modification.

Choosing the Date Format

The *Date Style* field of the General Preferences dialog box determines the format Quicken uses to display dates. When the program is first installed, it uses the month/day/year format standard in the U.S., and the **MM/DD/YY** is selected. If you'd like to use the "European" day/month/year format instead, select the **DD/MM/YY** radio button.

Turning Quicken's Beep On or Off

Normally, Quicken beeps musically when you record or memorize a transaction. If you find this sound distracting, turn it off by unchecking the box labelled **Beep When Recording and Memorizing** in the General Preferences dialog box. If you've turned off the beep, you can turn it back on by checking the box.

Associating Categories with Tax Schedules

One of Quicken's most useful features is its ability to keep track of your transactions according to the standard IRS tax forms. You can assign each of your Quicken categories to a specific line on a specific tax form; at tax time, you just ask for a Tax Schedule report, and you'll instantly have the numbers you need to fill out all your tax forms. (Chapter 5 tells you how to assign categories to tax forms, and Chapters 10 and 14 cover using Quicken for income tax preparation).

The only tricky part is that you first have to tell Quicken that you want the Tax Form feature turned on—otherwise, when you set up or edit a category, you won't see the field for assigning a tax form to the category. In the General Preferences dialog box, check the box labelled **Use Tax Schedules with Categories**. If you're sure you don't want to use Quicken in this way, you can leave this box unchecked so you'll have one less field to deal with when you're defining categories.

Setting Options for Checks

You can control the way Quicken handles the checks you write on the Write Checks window and in print with the Check Preferences dialog box, shown in Figure A.3. Choose the **Checks** button on the Preferences window to display this dialog box.

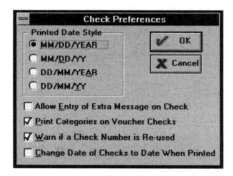

Choosing a Date Format for Printed Checks

Quicken lets you pick from several options governing the way dates print on your checks. You can pick either the American month/day/year style or the European day/month/year format, and for each of these you can decide whether to print the year in full, or just the year's last two digits. Among the set of radio buttons labelled **Printed Date Style** in the Check Preferences dialog box, select the radio button for the date style you'd like.

Printing Additional Messages on Checks

If the space available in the *Memo* field isn't enough, Quicken will let you print an additional line of text to the right of each check's address. Unlike your memo, this extra message isn't recorded in the Check register. As soon as the check is printed, the message is erased from your records. On the other hand, the message is stored along with all the other information when you memorize a check.

To turn on the extra line, check the **Allow Entry of Extra Message Line on Check** box on the Check Preferences dialog box. Uncheck the box when you want to turn off the message line again.

Printing Categories On Voucher Checks

Quicken always prints the entries in the *Description* column of the Split Transaction window on the lower portion of voucher checks. As the program is normally set up, it also prints the entries in the *Category* column as well. If you want to print descriptions only, uncheck the **Print Categories on Voucher Checks** box in the Check Preferences dialog box. To print **Category** entries, the box should be checked.

Guarding Against Duplicate Check Numbers

Quicken allows you to record checks with duplicate numbers in a single account. However, you can have the program warn you when you're about to duplicate an existing check number at the time you print. To turn on this warning feature, check the **Warn if a Check Number is Reused** box in the Check Preferences dialog box.

When you print checks, Quicken numbers all the new checks consecutively, starting with the number you enter in the *First Check Number* field. With this setting on, if any of the new checks would have the same number as a check already printed, Quicken warns you with the message "Duplicate check number. Are you sure?." If you want to go ahead and print the checks with the duplicate numbers, choose **OK**. Otherwise, choose **Cancel** to go back and correct the *First Check Number* field.

Redating Checks Automatically

Ordinarily, Quicken prints each check with the date you entered originally on the Write Checks window. If you want to have the program automatically print all checks with today's date instead, check the box labelled **Change Date of Checks to Date When Printed**. The box should be unchecked if you don't want Quicken to change the date.

Controlling Report Options

Choose the **Reports** button in the Preferences window to set options related to reports. You can tell Quicken how much information to print about categories and accounts on reports, whether to use colored text in titles and headings, and whether to generate the report without pausing to accept modifications in the report design. You can also choose the date range that Quicken automatically bases reports on (you're still free to change the dates for each report). The Report Preferences dialog box is shown in Figure A.4.

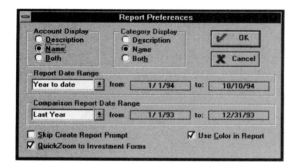

FIGURE A.4

The Report Preferences dialog box.

Using Category/Class and Account Names in Reports

In reports, Quicken normally substitutes category and class descriptions for the brief names you enter in the *Category* field on your checks and **Register** transactions (if you haven't entered a description, the category or class name appears in the report instead). In the same way, printed reports show account descriptions rather than the shorter account names.

If you'd rather see the actual category/class or account names in your reports—perhaps to leave more room for the report itself—the Report Preferences dialog box lets you make this change. In fact, you can set up Quicken so that it prints both the names and descriptions. At the top of the dialog box are two sets of radio buttons, one for categories and classes, the other for accounts. In each set, select the radio button for the type of information you want to display.

Setting the Report Date Range

The Report Preferences dialog box has two areas for presetting the dates for your reports, each with three fields just like those in the Create Reports window (see Chapter 10). The first of these two sets of fields applies to all your reports; the second set is only for Comparison reports. Just as in the Create Reports window, you can set up the date range in two ways:

- By selecting a named date range in the first field
- By typing in a custom date range in the *from* and *to* fields (you must first select the choice **Custom Date** in the first of the date fields)

Of course, you change the date range at the time you create any report (unless the box labelled **Skip Create Report Prompt** is checked).

The available named date ranges are listed as follows:

Date Option

Include all dates
Current Month
Current Quarter
Current Year
Month to date
Quarter to date
Year to date
Earliest to date
Last Month
Last Qtr
Last Year
Custom Date

Creating One-Step Reports

If you're certain the standard settings for reports fully meet your needs, you can have Quicken generate reports immediately when you choose the report type, without pausing to see if you want to change any options. Normally, Quicken displays a window that lets you change the date range it covers when you're creating one of the standard Home, Business, or Investment reports, and gives you a chance to customize the report before it appears on the screen.

NEW IN 3 If you check the box labelled Skip Create Report Prompt (Bypass Initial Report Dialog box in Quicken 2) in the Report

Preferences dialog box, Quicken no longer asks for new instructions. Instead, it uses the settings already in effect and immediately displays the report.

Since this setting applies to all types of reports, you'll probably find it useful only if you regularly generate just one or two report types and almost never customize your reports.

Controlling QuickZoom in Investment Reports

NOTE

Quicken 2 lacks this control, since it doesn't have the forms for investment transactions.

You can set up QuickZoom to work in two different ways in Investment reports that list transactions individually. This setting is controlled by the **QuickZoom to Investment Forms** box in the Report Preferences dialog box. If you check the box, using QuickZoom takes you to the dialog box (the "form") that lists all the entries for that transaction. If the box is unchecked, QuickZoom takes you to the register transaction instead.

Using Color in Reports

Normally, Quicken displays report titles and row and column headings in blue and negative dollar amounts in red. If you want to display the report all in black, uncheck the **Use Color in Reports** box in the Report Preferences dialog box. You might want to do this if the report title and headings don't show up well on your laptop's screen. Changes in this setting apply immediately, even to reports that are already on the screen.

Customizing QuickFill

The QuickFill feature makes entering recurring transactions extremely easy, but it can sometimes get in the way, particularly if you record many transactions with unique payees. Fortunately, Quicken lets you customize the way QuickFill works and shut it off altogether if you prefer.

To make changes to QuickFill, you'll use the dialog box shown in Figure A.5 on the next page. To display this dialog box, choose the QuickFill button on the Preferences window.

The checkbox labelled **Automatic Memorization of New Transactions** determines whether or not QuickFill memorizes each check or **Registration** transaction you add to your account when you record it. If you don't want your Memorized Transaction list cluttered up with many transactions you'll probably never use again, uncheck this box.

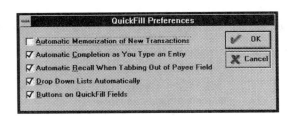

The box labelled **Automatic Completion as You Type an Entry** turns on or off QuickFill's primary feature, its ability to finish filling out transactions for you. Uncheck this box if you no longer want QuickFill to complete your entries as you start typing. You'll then have to type out all your entries in full.

If the **Automatic Recall When Tabbing Out of Payee Field** box is checked, QuickFill not only completes your payee entry, it copies the rest of the information from the corresponding memorized transaction into the remaining fields as soon as you press **Tab** to move to the next field. If you don't want this much help, you can uncheck this box. QuickFill will still complete the payee for you (assuming the **Automatic Completion** box is checked), but it won't copy the rest of the transaction data when you press **Tab**. (Actually, even with the **Automatic Recall** box checked, you can avoid copying memorized transaction data by using the mouse rather than the **Tab** key to move to another field).

Checking the **Drop-Down Lists Automatically** box causes Quicken to open the appropriate drop-down list of options when you first enter the *Num, Payee,* and *Category* fields. If you uncheck this box but the **Buttons on QuickFill Fields** box remains checked, you can still drop-down the lists yourself by clicking on the buttons.

When checked, the **Buttons on QuickFill Fields** option tells Quicken to place drop-down list buttons in the *Num, Payee,* and *Category* fields. If you uncheck this box, the buttons disappear.

If the **Drop-Down Lists Automatically** box is also unchecked, you won't be able to access the drop-down lists at all (though QuickFill will still complete entries for you, assuming the **Automatic Completion** box is checked). Even if the **Drop-Down Lists Automatically** box is checked, you'll only see the drop-down lists when you first enter one of these field—if you close the list, you can't display it again without leaving the field and then returning.

Setting **Automatic Reminder** Options

To be sure you pay your bills on schedule, you can specify how far in advance Quicken begins reminding you about upcoming transaction groups and postdated checks. When you install Quicken, the program is set to remind you three days before you're due to print a postdated check or execute a transaction group. When appropriate, you'll see this reminder in a small window each time you start Quicken.

Quicken also comes with a separate program called Billminder that can remind you when it's time to print checks or pay bills when you start Windows (before you ever run Quicken). Billminder displays its messages in a simple window like the one shown in Figure A.6.

FIGURE A.6

You'll see a message like this one when you first start Windows if Billminder is installed.

The only time you can install Billminder and indicate your preference about when it should display its messages (when you start your computer or start Windows) is when you install Quicken; if you want to make changes in the basic Billminder setup, you'll have to reinstall Quicken.

However, you can turn Billminder on or off and change the number of days of advance warning you get from within Quicken. To do this, choose the **Billminder** button from the Preferences window. You'll see the dialog box shown in Figure A.7 on the next page.

Check the **Turn on Billminder** box if you want Billminder messages. To disable Billminder, uncheck this box.

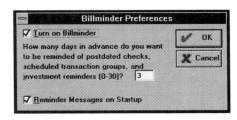

The three-day warning is fine if you use Quicken every day. If you only work with the program once a week, however, you may not see the reminder until after the payment date has passed. In this case, you should change the setting in the next field to one that corresponds to how often you use the program.

Take weekends into account in deciding how many days of advance warning you'd like. Thus, if you use the program every other day and you set it to remind you one day in advance, you won't get a reminder on Friday for the checks you're supposed to print the following Monday. On the other hand, if you've postdated a check or scheduled a transaction group for a Saturday or Sunday, Quicken will assume you don't work weekends and will remind you as if the scheduled date were the Friday before.

The final checkbox, labelled **Reminder Messages on Startup**, determines whether you see the small reminder windows within Quicken itself when you first start the program. Uncheck the box if you don't want those reminders cluttering up your screen.

Setting Up Your Modem

If you use Quicken for electronic bill paying via CheckFree, or if you receive IntelliCharge statements via the phone lines, you need a modem—and you must set up Quicken correctly for your modem. Configure Quicken for the modem by opening the Preferences window and choosing the **Modem** button. The dialog box you'll see is shown in Figure A.8.

FIGURE A.8

*The Modem
Preferences
dialog box.*

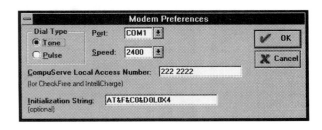

The two Radio buttons at the upper left let you tell Quicken whether to use tone (push button) or pulse (rotary-phone type) dialing. Since almost all modems are capable of tone dialing, the only reason to use the pulse method is if tone dialing won't work on your phone line—in this day and age, that's rare.

In the *Port* field, use the drop-down list to tell Quicken which serial port your modem is connected to (Com1, Com2, etc.). If you have an internal modem, the type that comes on an add-in card that you install inside your computer, the serial port is determined by settings on the modem itself. You should be able to figure out which port the modem is set for with the help of the modem's manual. For external modems, the kind that sit on your desk and connect via a cable to a jack on the back of the computer, look for a label near the jack indicating which serial port it is. If the jack isn't labelled, and if your computer's manual doesn't help, you'll have to experiment with the settings in the *Port* field.

Ideally, you should set the *Speed* field to correspond to your modem's top speed. However, if you experience problems running that fast, try the next slowest speed. This may be necessary if the phone lines are poor or the modem at the other end of the connection can't keep up with your modem.

In the *CompuServe Local Access Number* field, type in the telephone number your modem should dial to connect to CompuServe (electronic communications for both CheckFree and IntelliCharge are handled by CompuServe). To get this number, get pen and paper ready, then dial (800) 848-8980 with a touchtone phone. When you hear the recorded message, press 2 on your phone. You'll be asked to type in the phone number you'll be calling from and the speed of your modem. Based on this information, the system gives you an access number.

Don't change the entry in the *Initialization String* field unless you have trouble with your electronic communications. The entry here is a command that Quicken sends to your modem prior to dialing the access number. If Quicken doesn't dial the modem or can't connect to CompuServe, you may need to change the entry. Start by writing down the current entry. Then, the first change to try is simply to delete the entire entry. If that doesn't work, try entering **ATZ**. If you still have problems, consult your modem's manual or your dealer.

Customizing the Iconbar

Even in its standard configuration, the Iconbar makes Quicken for Windows extremely convenient for mouse users. However, you can increase your efficiency still further by customizing the Iconbar to fit the way you work with Quicken.

It's easy to add new buttons to the Iconbar, change the functions or the icons of existing buttons, and delete buttons you're no longer using. You can even assign keyboard shortcuts that duplicate the actions of the **Iconbar** buttons.

You can display the Customize Iconbar dialog box (see Figure A.9) opening the Preferences window and choosing the **Iconbar** button.

FIGURE A.9

The Customize Iconbar dialog box.

When you first run Quicken, each button on the Iconbar has both an icon and a short title explaining its function. If you prefer to see only icons or only text, all you have to do is uncheck the appropriate box in the lower portion of the Customize Iconbar dialog box. To shut off the Iconbar altogether, uncheck both boxes. This is an excellent idea if you're working with Quicken without a mouse, since you can't use the Iconbar from the keyboard.

Assuming you do want the Iconbar on the screen, you can customize the function and the look of each button on the bar, and you can add or remove buttons as you like. As you've probably seen, the main part of the Customize Iconbar dialog box displays a scrolling representation of the Iconbar itself. To change an existing button, scroll to it using the scroll bar or the **LeftArrow** and **RightArrow** keys, so that the button appears to be pressed and has a bolder outline. Now choose the **Delete** button, if you want to remove the button from the Iconbar, or the **Edit** button if you want to change the way the button works.

When you choose **Edit**, you'll see a new dialog box titled Edit Action on Iconbar (see Figure A.10). Here, choose the action you want the button to perform when you click on it in Quicken (display the security list, transmit electronic payments, etc.). As you scroll through the list, you'll notice that Quicken automatically assigns a new icon for each action. The message in the *Description* field tells you what the selected action accomplishes; you can't edit the entry here.

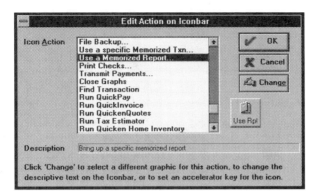

FIGURE A.10

*The Edit Action
on Iconbar
dialog box.*

Although most of the icons are fairly suggestive of the corresponding actions, you can select a different icon for any action if you'd like. Here's how: With the action you want for the current button selected in the list, choose the **Change** button. You'll see another small dialog box labelled Change Iconbar Item (see Figure A.11). Here, pick out the icon you want from those shown, using the scroll bar or the **Up Arrow** and **Down Arrow** keys to find the one you want. Again, the selected icon looks like it's pressed, and it has a darker outline.

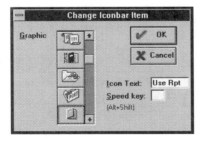

FIGURE A.11

*The Change
Iconbar Item
dialog box.*

Then, if you'd like, type in a new title for the button in the *Icon Text* field—keep it brief, since you can only use six characters. If you want to be able to perform the button's function via the keyboard, enter a letter in the *Speed Key* field. When you're back in Quicken proper, simultaneously pressing **Alt**, **Shift**, and the speed key letter will do the same job as clicking the button would. In fact, the Speed key will work even if you've completely turned off the Iconbar display as described earlier in this section.

When you're through, choose **OK** to go back to the Edit Action on Iconbar dialog box. To confirm your changes to the **Iconbar** button, choose **OK** again.

You'll be back at the Customize Iconbar dialog box, where you can make similar changes to any of the other buttons shown.

To add a new button to the Iconbar, choose **New** from the Customize Iconbar dialog box. You'll be taken to the Add Action to Iconbar dialog box. Except for its title, this window looks and works exactly the same as the Edit Action on Iconbar dialog box (shown in Figure A.10).

The actions available for assignment to the Iconbar on the Edit Action and Add Action windows cover a wide range of Quicken functions. You can have a button that backs up the current file, one that sets up a budget, and even one that closes all the graph windows on your screen when things get too untidy.

Several of the actions let you assign specific items to a button. As you've already seen, the standard Iconbar includes a button for calling up a specific account and one for recalling a specific memorized transaction. Other similar Iconbar actions let you use a particular transaction group, generate a given memorized report, or print checks for a specific account.

When you select one of these actions and then choose **OK**, Quicken asks you to choose the item you want to associate with the button, be it a memorized transaction, or an account, and so on. Figure A.12 shows the window you'll see when you're assigning an account to a button. In this case, you select the account you want the button to open from the drop-down list, and then choose from the available radio button options to specify how you want the account to open.

FIGURE A.12

The Assign Account to Icon dialog box.

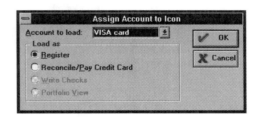

> **NOTE**　You can add to the Iconbar multiple buttons of the same type, each assigned to a different specific item (account, transaction, etc.).

Choosing Graph Preferences

Quicken gives you several options for controlling how it displays graphs on your screen and in print. To modify the look of your graphs, start by choosing the **Graphs** button on the Preferences window to display the Graph Preferences dialog box, shown in Figure A.13.

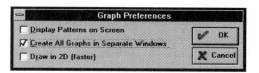

Normally, Quicken displays graphs in full color. If you have a monochrome screen, however, you may find it hard to distinguish one color from another. By unchecking the box labelled **Display Patterns on Screen**, you can have Quicken prepare its graphs in black and white, using various patterns of shading and hatch marks to ensure contrast between nearby parts of a graph.

Quicken generates two separate graphs for each of the main graph commands (**Income and Expense**, **Budget Variance**, **Net Worth**, and **Investments**). The box labelled **Create All Graphs in Separate Windows** determines whether these two graphs appear together in one large window or separately, each in its own window. Check the box if you'd like the latter format.

Quicken's standard graph style endows the graphs with an imitation three-dimensional look. Check the **Draw in 2D** box if you prefer graphs with no "depth."

NOTE	The **Print in Color** box corresponds to the box **Print reports and graphs in color** in Quicken 3's Report/Graph Printer Setup dialog box—see the "Printing Graphs" section in Chapter 12.

Customizing Qcards

When you're first getting started with Quicken, or if you use the program only occasionally, you'll appreciate the pointers on basic Quicken skills you get from the Qcard feature (described in Chapter 1). But since the Qcards take up a fair amount of space on the screen, you probably won't want to see them after you've become thoroughly familiar with Quicken.

NOTE	You can shut off Qcards for a particular part of Quicken by choosing the button labelled **Close Qcards** on the Qcard itself. This button doesn't always appear, but when it does, choosing the button is just as effective as unchecking the corresponding box in the Qcard Preferences dialog box.

When you reach that point, you can shut off the Qcards by opening the Preferences dialog box and choosing the Qcards button. In the dialog box that appears (see Figure A.14), uncheck the boxes of any Quicken components with which you don't want to use the Qcards. As the labels for the checkboxes suggest, you can activate or disable Qcards independently for a number of separate Quicken functions, including creating new accounts, using the register of any bank or investment account, reconciling bank accounts, or working with graphs.

FIGURE A.14

The Qcard Preferences dialog box.

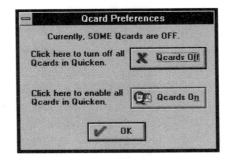

Controlling the Layout of Quicken's Windows

Quicken offers several menu commands for manipulating its own windows. After you've opened and worked with a number of windows, they're apt to become a confusing jumble on the screen. To tidy up, choose **Cascade** from the Windows menu. Quicken arranges all the Windows in an orderly, overlapping "stack." The windows are offset slightly so that you can see the title bar of each window.

When you've minimized a window so that you see only its icon, you can move the icon around to any convenient location on the screen. If you lose track of one or more icons by covering them with other windows, you can choose **Arrange Icons** from the Windows menu to move all the icons to a neat row at the bottom of the main Quicken window.

NEW IN 3 Quicken for Windows lets you decide how the Quicken screen (the "desktop") will look each time you start the program. In Quicken 3, access this control by choosing the **Desktop** button on the Preferences window. You'll see the little dialog box shown in Figure A.15.

FIGURE A.15

The Save Desktop dialog box.

Whenever you start Quicken, the program uses a file stored on your disk to tell it how to arrange windows on the screen. The two choices in the dialog box determine when Quicken generates that screen file. If you check the **Save Desktop on Exit** box, Quicken records the screen file at the time you close the program. That way, the next time you start Quicken, all your windows will appear just as they were when you last left the program.

If you'd rather have Quicken arrange its windows the same way every time, regardless of how things looked when you last exited the program, uncheck the **Save Desktop on Exit** option. Then, to save a specific window arrangement, choose the **Save Current** button. Each time you do, Quicken stores the current desktop in the disk file, erasing the previous desktop file.

Selecting the Register Font

NEW IN 3   Font selection is new in Quicken 3. This feature lets you choose the font for text displayed in the register and items in lists. In registers, Quicken displays column headings and your transaction information using the selected font, but some buttons retain the standard font. Figure A.16 on the next page shows the register displayed with 13-point Dom Casual.

To select a new font, choose the **Fonts** button from the Preferences window. The new window that appears lists all the available fonts. Scroll to the font you want and highlight it in the list by clicking on it with the mouse, or by moving the highlight with the cursor keys. Choose the font size you want in the *Size* list. You can type in the size if you want, but Quicken only accepts entries from 9 to 13 points, the same sizes shown in the list. If you want to return to the standard font, choose the **Default** button.

FIGURE A.16

This Asset
Account register
uses the Dom
Casual font to
display text.

Date	Ref	Payee		Decrease	Ch	Increase	Balance	
		Memo	Category					
10/12/91		Callaway Chevrolet	/Car			13,500 00	20,300 00	
6/ 1/92		Adjustment of value	Car's getting :Depree/Car	2,500 00			17,800 00	
6/ 1/93		Adjustment of value	Car's getting :Depree/Car	3,750 00			14,050 00	
8/ 1/94	Ref	Payee		Decrease		Increase		
		Memo	Category					

Record Restore Splits ☐ 1-Line Display ☑ Button Bar   Ending Balance   14,050.00

Choosing Register Colors

NEW IN 3 You can't change register colors in Quicken 2. In Quicken 3, however, you can change the colors that Quicken displays in the main part of the register, the area where your transactions are displayed. To make a color change, open the Preferences dialog box and choose **Colors**. In the little dialog box that appears (see Figure A.17), begin by choosing the type of account you want to change (Bank, Cash, etc.), then pick the color from the scrollable list of color bars. You can return to the original color by choosing the **Default** button.

FIGURE A.17

The Choose
Register Colors
dialog box.

Protecting Your Records with Passwords

If you use Quicken in a business or office, or in any location where others might have access to your computer, your records are vulnerable to unauthorized inspection or alteration. To help counter that threat, Quicken allows you to assign a password to each of your files in its entirety, and lets you create a *separate transaction password* that prevents unauthorized changes to records prior to a particular date.

A Quicken password applies only to the file that is active at the time you define the password. If you have more than one file, be certain that you've switched to the file that you want to protect with the password. You can use the same password for other files if you'd like, but you have to define it anew for each file in turn.

Defining the File Password

The file password limits any type of access to the account file. Once you've defined this password, no one can use Quicken to see or change previously recorded transactions in the file, or enter new ones, unless they type in the password correctly. Of course, this applies to you as well as to potential spies and thieves; if you forget the password, you'll be able to start Quicken, but you won't be able to access the file.

To create the file password, choose **Passwords** and then choose **File** in the File menu. In the Set Up Password dialog box, type in your password, which can be up to 16 characters long and can contain spaces and punctuation marks. Quicken does not distinguish between upper- and lowercase letters in the password. As you type, you'll see a series of asterisks, not the actual characters you enter. Choose **OK** when the password is complete.

Quicken asks you to retype the password to ensure that you spelled it correctly the first time. That done, choose **OK** again to finalize your entry (if the two entries don't agree, you'll have to start again). Once the password is accepted, Quicken will require anyone who attempts to use the file to enter the password correctly before being allowed access to the data.

Defining the Transaction Password

The transaction password adds "look-but-don't-touch" protection to your file. When a transaction password is in effect, a user without it can view previously recorded transactions but can't change or add entries dated prior to the date you specify. This is handy if you have your employees entering new transactions and don't want them to alter earlier records inadvertently.

If it's ever necessary to change an older transaction, just start editing the entry. Quicken will ask you to enter the transaction password when you try to record the changes; once you do, the program accepts the modified transaction into the file.

To create a transaction password for the current file, choose **Passwords** and then **Transaction** from the File menu. In the Password to Modify Existing Transactions dialog box, illustrated in Figure A.18, type in your transaction password. It can be up to 16 characters long and can include spaces and punctuation marks. Quicken does not distinguish between upper- and lowercase letters. Your entry appears as a row of asterisks in the *Password* field.

FIGURE A.18

Use this dialog box to enter a transaction password.

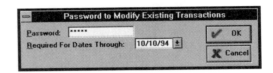

When you've finished typing the password, move to the *Required For Dates Through* field. Quicken will let anyone access transactions recorded after the date you enter here. But you'll have to enter the password correctly to access all transactions recorded on or before this date. Choose **OK**. Quicken will ask you to retype the password to protect you against spelling mistakes. Do so, then choose **OK** again to finalize the entry.

Changing a Password

To change or remove a password, choose **Passwords** from the File menu, and then choose the menu item for the type of password you want to change, file or transaction. As shown in Figure A.19, the window that appears has a file labelled *Old Password*, where you type in the current password, and a field labelled **New Password**, where you type in the password to which you want to change. If you want to clear the password, simply leave the *New Password* field empty. If you're changing the transaction password, the window also has a field for the date before which the new password will be required.

FIGURE A.19

The Change Transaction Password dialog box.

Sharing Quicken Data with Other Programs

Quicken is just one of many Windows and DOS programs that you can use for recording, manipulating, reviewing, and reporting on financial data. If you do use another program to complement Quicken's features, you will often be able to move information back and forth between that program and Quicken.

If you use tax preparation software, for example, you'll surely want a way to move all the figures on your tax-related income and expenses out of Quicken and into the tax software. As we've seen, Quicken's own reporting features are quite capable, but there still may be times when you'll want to analyze your accounts with a more powerful program, such as a spreadsheet or database. And if you've decided to switch from a spreadsheet or database to Quicken for your day-to-day financial record-keeping chores, you'll want to be able to move your old records into Quicken. Whatever the scenario, when you want to exchange information between Quicken and another program, the techniques you'll learn in this section provide the means.

You can exchange two kinds of Quicken information with other programs:

- Data in your accounts, including register transactions, and the list of categories and classes.
- The information in a Quicken report.

The techniques you use to share information depend on which of these types of data you're working with.

Sharing Account Information

Quicken normally stores all your account data in special files that only Quicken itself can understand. In order to transfer data between Quicken and another program, you must place the information in files that both programs can work with. The process of preparing a file destined for another program is called *exporting*, while the process of reading in a file prepared by another program is called *importing*.

Via the **Import** command on the File menu, Quicken can import transaction data from two sources: special Quicken Import Format (QIF) files, and CheckFree files. When you want to go the other direction, you can use the Export command to generate QIF files from your accounts.

As detailed in Chapter 9, you can also import price history information on investment securities using ASCII files.

Exporting QIF Files

In addition to the transactions themselves, QIF files can hold three other types of information drawn from the Quicken file from which the data came: category and class details, the list of accounts, and the Memorized Transaction list. The main value of QIF files is for transferring data between Quicken accounts, even accounts in separate files. I'll discuss the reasons you might want to move data between your accounts or files in "Transferring Data between Accounts." A few other programs can generate QIF files that you can then import into Quicken, but I'm unaware of any programs that can accept QIF files you create.

Quicken's **Export** command lets you export transactions from a single account to a QIF file. You can export all of the account's transactions or limit the export to a given date range.

To export information from a Quicken account, switch to the Register window for that account. If you're planning to export only some of the transactions in the account, make note of the dates of the first and last transactions in the range you'd like to export. Even if you'll be exporting all the information in the account, it's a good idea to check the dates of the first and last transactions listed in the register. When you're ready to begin, choose **Export** from the File menu. The QIF Export dialog box will appear, as shown in Figure A.20.

FIGURE A.20

The QIF Export dialog box.

QIF Export
QIF File to Export: `C:\QUICKENW\`   ✓ OK
Quicken account to export from: ✗ Cancel
Checking ▼   Browse...
Transactions Starting: `1/ 1/ 1` ▼ to: `12/31/99` ▼
Export Items
☑ Transactions
☐ Accounts List
☐ Category List
☐ Memorized Transaction

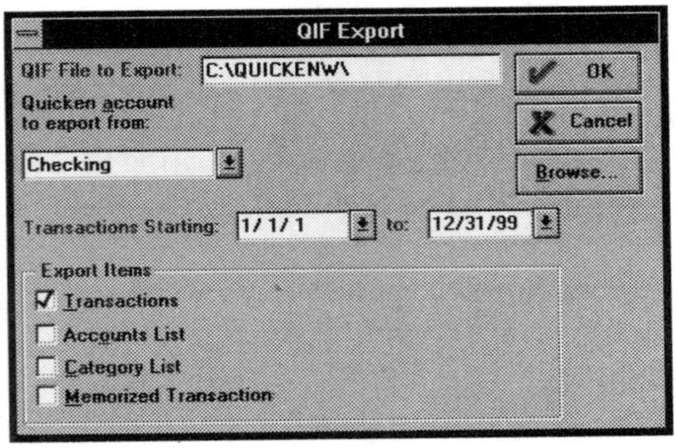

In the top field, type in the name of the QIF file you want to create. If you need to switch first to a different disk or directory, choose the **Browse** button to select the location where you want to store the file. The file name must be a standard DOS name consisting of up to eight characters; no spaces are allowed, and certain punctuation marks aren't permitted. Quicken supplies the period and the QIF extension. (See your DOS manual for details on DOS path and file names).

The next field in the QIF Export window is where you tell Quicken the account from which to export data. Pick the account name from the drop-down list. You can export from an entire file by picking **All Accounts**, the first choice on the list. Make any necessary changes in the date range indicated by the *Transactions Starting* and *To* fields, so that the dates listed cover the transactions you'd like to export.

You can also decide what type of information to export with the checkboxes at the bottom of the window. Aside from the transactions themselves, you can also export the current Quicken file's list of accounts, Category list, and memorized transactions. Choose **OK** to start the export process. When the QIF file has been successfully created, you'll be returned to the Account register.

Importing QIF Files

Quicken's **Import** command can import files of two types: those in the QIF format, and CheckFree files. In this section, you'll learn how to import QIF files; importing CheckFree files is a similar process, but is described separately in Chapter 17.

There are at least three ways to get the data you want to import into the correct QIF format. One way, obviously, is to export data from Quicken itself, as previously described. You'll use this method whenever you want to move information from one account to another, a process we'll cover in the next section. Certain other software programs such as Prodigy can also generate QIF files. Finally, if you're technically minded, you can write a program to convert output from a spreadsheet or database into the QIF format.

Once you have the information you want to import in a properly formatted QIF file, the rest of the import process is simple. Open the register of the account into which you want to import the data. Now choose **Import** from the File menu, or press **Ctrl-I**, and you'll see the QIF Import dialog box.

If you know the name of the file you want to import, you can type it into the top field. It's usually easier to choose **Browse**, bringing up a second dialog box. Here, navigate to the drive and directory where the file you want to import is stored, then choose its name in the list below the *File Name* field. Choose **OK** to return to the QIF Import dialog box.

The field labelled *Quicken Account to Import into* determines the account in the current file to which the import data will be added. Quicken has already entered the name of the account that you used last prior to starting the import process. If you want to import into a different account, choose the correct one from the drop-down list.

The first four checkboxes at the bottom of the dialog box let you decide which types of information to import from the QIF file: the transactions themselves and the lists of accounts, categories, and memorized transactions. You can select them in any combination by checking the relevant boxes. When you import the file, only the types of information you specify will actually reach your account, regardless of how much information the QIF file contains.

The last checkbox, labelled **Special Handling for Transfers**, applies when the file you're importing contains data from multiple Quicken accounts. This might be the case if it were created with the DOS version of Quicken. In this situation, you should check this box if the data includes transactions that are transfers between the accounts, to instruct Quicken <u>not</u> to import transfers that don't add to your net worth. This helps prevent the importation of duplicate pairs of transfer transactions.

When you've completed all the fields, choose **OK** to import the QIF file. Quicken will read each transaction in the import file, comparing its category and class assignments to the Category and Class lists in your active Quicken file. If the transaction is assigned to a category or class you don't already have, Quicken will display a window containing a brief summary of the transaction with its category or class assignment. Choose **Set Up** to create the category or class from scratch, **Select** to select a new category or class for the transaction from the appropriate list, or **Cancel** to omit this transaction from your account.

As soon as Quicken has completed the importation, you'll see a message telling you how many transactions were successfully imported. After choosing **OK**, you'll be returned to the register with the imported transactions added to your account.

Transferring Data between Accounts

There are several reasons you might want to move transactions from one Quicken account to another. For instance, after keeping track of your assets in a single account for a while, you may decide that you'd prefer to have separate accounts for each asset. Or you may want to consolidate a number of separate accounts into one. And there's always the chance that you'll enter a set of transactions into the wrong account by mistake. Instead of retyping them from scratch, you can move them to the right account and then just delete the mistaken entries.

In situations like these, the only way to move or copy entire transactions from one account to another in Quicken is by exporting them to a file from the first account and then importing that file into the second account. Using this method, you can copy transactions from your account to another account within the same Quicken file, or move an entire account or any part of it to a different Quicken file.

Since Quicken handles both the export and import steps, there's little chance for error. Start in the account from which you'd like to transfer the information and export it to a file as just described. You can narrow the date range to limit the export to transactions for a particular month or year, or even a single day.

| WARNING | If you're importing a file exported from a Quicken account that's protected by a password, you'll be required to enter the password before Quicken will import the transaction. |

Then switch to the second account and import the same file. Since you're importing a file previously exported by Quicken, you'll need to be concerned about your entry in the Import window's **Special Handling for Transfers** checkbox. The setting here pertains to transactions which were one of a pair of transfer transactions in their original Quicken account. Check the box if the QIF file you are importing contains data from multiple Quicken accounts. Otherwise, if the data contains transfer transactions, you're likely to end up with duplicate pairs of transfer transactions once the import process is complete.

Transferring Data to Spreadsheets, Databases, and Word Processors

Quicken makes it easy to transfer information to other programs such as spreadsheet, database, word processing, and tax preparation programs. The only trick to remember: use **Reports**, not the **Export** command to do the job.

Transferring Information via the Windows Clipboard

NEW IN 3 For the first time, Quicken 3 lets you copy report data to the Windows clipboard. That makes it a snap to move information in a report to another program.

Once you've prepared a report and it's on your screen, start the process by choosing the **Copy** button on the report's button bar. To complete the transfer, switch to the destination program, position the cursor where you'd like the Quicken data to go, and choose **Paste**. It's that simple. Since Quicken places the data on the clipboard in tabular form, a receiving spreadsheet or database should be able to place each item in its own cell or field.

You can't import data from other programs using the clipboard.

Transferring Information by Printing Quicken Reports

If you don't own the program you're exporting to (or if you have Quicken 2), you can accomplish the same end result by "printing" reports to disk files. If you want to export all the transactions in your account, choose a Customized Transaction report with the *Subtotal by* field set to **None**, giving you a simple listing of transactions by date. You can export any other type of report as well. Chapters 10, 11, and 13 through 16 have all the details you'll need on how to create the proper report.

NOTE In a **.PRN** file, the characters in each column of the report are surrounded by double quotation marks, a comma appears between each column's data, and each row is separated by a carriage return and line feed. Tab-delimited files have tabs between each column, with rows separated by carriage return and line feed.

For transfer to spreadsheets or databases, "print" the information to a disk file formatted as a Lotus 1-2-3 print (.PRN) file or as a tab-delimited file. The receiving software may handle one of these two formats better than the other, though most spreadsheet and database programs can read either one; check the manuals of the other software under "Importing" for details.

To transfer a report to a word processor, print the report either as an ASCII file (with spaces between columns) or a tab-delimited file. Tab-delimited files are the better choice if you'll be displaying or printing the information in a proportional font (whose characters aren't all the same width).

Here's how to create the file: Once the report is on your screen, click on the **Print** button or press **Ctrl-P** to display the Print Report window. As shown in Figure A.21, choose the radio button labelled **123 (.PRN) Disk File** or the one labelled **Tab-Delimited Disk File**. When you choose **OK**, you'll be asked to type in the DOS path and file name you want Quicken to use.

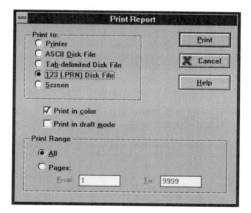

FIGURE A.21

The Print Report window set to print a Lotus 1-2-3 file.

You can now import the file into any program that reads Lotus 1-2-3 **.PRN** files or "comma-delimited" ASCII files. In DOS versions of 1-2-3, type **/FIN** to import the file. If any column in the worksheet is too wide or too narrow for the imported data, move the highlight to the column, type **/WCS** to select the **Set Width** command, and enter the new width for that column.

Using Quicken with Tax Preparation Software

Several tax preparation software products can import data from Quicken reports. With this capability, you can prepare your tax returns without having to reenter any of the information you've stored in Quicken over the past tax year.

ChipSoft's TurboTax is the most popular tax preparation software for PC's and compatibles. In the latest version of TurboTax for Windows, the process of converting your Quicken data into tax returns is nearly automatic.

When you install TurboTax, the installation program creates a new Program Manager group called ChipSoft Applications. In this group's window you'll find the icon for TurboTax itself (an Uncle Sam top hat), but there should also be an icon for importing Quicken data (a Quicken dollar sign).

Assuming the Quicken file you most recently worked contains the records you want to import, all you have to do is double-click on this icon. TurboTax will locate Quicken, extract all the tax-related transactions, and bring them into TurboTax for final tax form calculations. If you used a different file the last time you ran Quicken, you'll have to start Quicken first, open the correct file, and then activate the TurboTax import procedure.

You can also import your Quicken tax information from within TurboTax. Choose **Import** from the File menu, and in the dialog box that appears, select the Quicken 2 for Windows radio button and choose **OK**.

If you're using another tax program, the steps are only a little more complicated. Begin in Quicken by creating a report summarizing all your tax-related transactions for the period covered by your tax return: Choose **Home** and **Tax Schedule** from the Reports menu. In the Create Tax Schedule Report window, be sure to enter the correct date range for the report. When you choose **OK**, you'll see the report on your screen.

SHORTCUT   In Quicken 2, click the **Print** button on the Iconbar or press **Ctrl-P** in the Print Report window. Then select the **Disk (Tax Export)** radio button to "print" the report to a disk file.

Now choose the **Export** button on the report's button bar (this button appears only when you've prepared a tax schedule or capital gains report). In the next window, select the disk and directory where you want to store the file, and type in its name. Choose **OK** to send it to disk.

NOTE   To export only tax-related investment information to the tax program, use a Capital Gains report instead.

After you've saved the file, switch to your tax program and import the report using that program's facilities.

Using the Quicken Companions

The Quicken Companions are a set of three useful programs that help out with common financial chores: compiling a household inventory for insurance purposes, estimating your income taxes, and obtaining stock quotes electronically. The Companions are included on the CD-ROM version of Quicken 3, but you can also buy them separately from Intuit, Quicken's publisher.

Running the Quicken Companions

Although you don't actually need Quicken to run any of the Companions, they integrate nicely with Quicken. When you install the Companions, their icons are automatically added to Quicken's Iconbar, so you can start any of them with one quick click. They also appear at the bottom of Quicken's Activities menu. If you're not working with Quicken at the moment, you can start any of the Companions by clicking on the proper icon in Program Manager.

Recording a Home Inventory

Quicken Home Inventory helps you assemble a complete inventory of all of your possessions. With an accurate inventory, you'll know just how much insurance you need. And should disaster strike, you'll have a full written record with which to document your insurance claims.

The core of the Home Inventory program is simply a table that itemizes your belongings; at any one time, you see the items for one room in your home (see Figure A.22 on the next page). To add an item to the inventory, you enter a brief description and assign it to a category (such as Furniture, Appliances or Jewelry). Then you list its replacement cost (how much you'd have to pay for the same item) and resale value (how much you'd likely get if you sold the item). Quicken keeps running totals of these amounts near the bottom of the screen.

The easiest way to enter new items is to pick them from the Suggested Items list to the right of the main work area. The list shows common items in the currently selected category. You just double-click on an item in the list to transfer it to your inventory. In addition to the generic item description (such as "refrigerator"), the program fills in the Replacement Cost and Resale Value columns with its estimate of what the item is worth. You can edit any of these entries just as you would a field in the Quicken register.

FIGURE A.22

The main Quicken Home Inventory window.

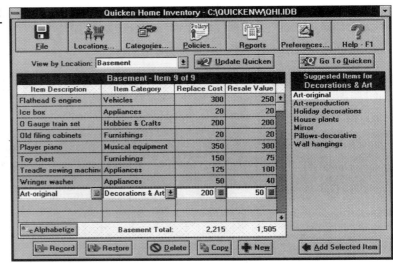

If you want to add more detail, you can switch to a "detail view" window that displays information for one inventory item at a time. To see the window, click the little icon in the Item Description column for the active item. Here, you can:

- Enter the price you actually paid for the item and the date you bought it.
- Fill out fields for the make, model and serial number.
- Identify the particular insurance policy that covers the item.
- Add miscellaneous notes.

Preparing Inventory Reports

Quicken Home Inventory can produce four standardized reports:

1. *Inventory Value report:* This summary report gives you much the same information as the main display, showing each item and its replacement

cost and resale value, adding also the purchase date and original price. You can group items in the report either by location or by category.

2. *Inventory Detail report:* This report presents all the details you've entered for every individual item, one at a time.

3. *Insurance Coverage report:* This report is organized exactly like the Inventory Value report. The difference is that it is restricted to the items covered by a single insurance policy, and compares the total value of the items shown to the coverage provided by that policy.

4. *Insurance Claim report:* This report gives the same information as the Inventory Detail report, limited to a particular insurance policy, for use in filing a claim. If you suffer only a partial loss, you can restrict the report to show the specific items for which you're filing your claim.

To produce a report, you just choose the Reports button at the top of the screen. After the report appears on your screen, choose the Print button if you want to print it out on paper. Quicken Home Inventory can only print using the default Windows printer, so to use a different printer, you must change the default using the Windows Control Panel.

Exchanging Inventory Data with Quicken

You can send the information you assemble in Quicken Home Inventory to Quicken proper, so that your Quicken accounts more accurately reflect your net worth. Start by switching to Quicken with the Go to Quicken button. There, make sure that the Quicken file you want to use for your inventory data is open. Go back to the Home Inventory program and choose Update Quicken. Inventory items are placed in a Quicken asset account called Home Inventory. To prevent accidental duplications or deletions, the entire account is replaced each time you update it.

Whenever you use Quicken to record a purchase of something of value, you can have Quicken send the transaction to the Home Inventory program. After you enter the transaction, select it in the register, then choose Quicken Home Inventory from the Activities menu, or click the Iconbar's Inventry icon. You'll be taken to the window for inventory item details, where you can add information such as purchase date and the make and model.

Getting Stock Quotes Electronically

Quicken Quotes lets you pull in current prices for your stocks and other securities via your modem. You can have Quicken Quotes pass the information directly to your Quicken investment account. Figure A.23 shows the Quicken Quotes screen.

FIGURE A.23

*The main
Quicken
Quotes
window.*

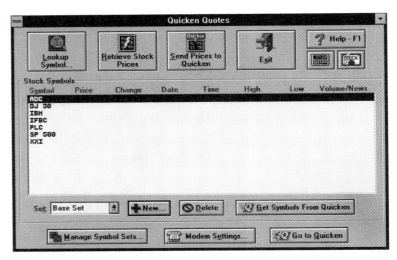

Setting up Quicken Quotes

Before you actually retrieve any stock quotes, you must set up Quicken Quotes for your modem and for the electronic information service you'll be accessing (you can get price quotes through CompuServe or from a special 900-number service called Quicken Quotes Hotline). Choose Modem Settings at the bottom of the window and select the correct speed for your modem and the serial (COM) port it's configured for. Initially, the Phone field contains the Hotline number; if you're planning to use CompuServe—you should, it's cheaper—fill in your CompuServe access number, and type in your CompuServe ID number and password in the appropriate fields.

You must also set up Quicken Quotes with the right symbol for each security, that is, the standard abbreviation used by brokerages and the press to identify the security. Choose the New button to enter symbols (your stockbroker can give you the correct ones). Alternatively, you can choose the Lookup Symbol button. Quicken Quotes will dial your electronic service and help you find the correct symbols from the on-line securities list. (You should also check your Quicken accounts to make sure the symbols match.)

Once you've entered the symbols, Quicken Quotes lets you group them into sets. That way, you can dial in to pick up the quotes for the specific securities you want information about. Use the Manage Symbol Sets button for this purpose.

Using Quicken Quotes

Obtaining quotes is as simple as selecting the symbol set you want information on in the Set field and then choosing the Retrieve Stock Prices button. As the current prices come in, you'll see them in the main display area.

To transfer the prices to Quicken, choose the button labelled Send Prices to Quicken. You can then choose Go To Quicken and open the Portfolio View window to see how the value of your holdings have changed, study price histories, and so on.

Estimating Your Income Taxes

The Quicken Tax Estimator calculates an estimate of your federal income taxes, helping you to decide how much to pay in withholding and estimated tax payments. You can transfer Quicken records into the Estimator to make the process accurate and efficient. The Estimator comes set up to make calculations based on 1993 and 1994 tax laws, but you can redefine the tax brackets and their rates for future years.

In the main Estimator window (Figure A.24 on the next page), most of the space is devoted to fields for entering basic tax data: your income, deductions, exemptions, credits, and so on. You can enter your best guesses for these items manually, or access tax-related information from your Quicken accounts.

To import Quicken data, you should first get Quicken running with the file containing your tax records. After switching back to the Estimator (choose Quicken Tax Estimator from the Activities menu) choose the Quicken Import button. You'll see a list of Quicken transactions from the beginning of the current year to the end of the last month. Only transactions whose categories are assigned to tax schedules are included.

If the imported data covers less than a full year the Estimator will assume you want to annualize the amounts for each category, projecting what they would be over 12 months. Your job is to look through the list and locate any one-time-only or once-a-year items that would throw off the annualizing calculations. If you find some, double-click them so that the word No appears in the Annualize? column. Then choose OK to proceed with automatic fill-out of the main Estimator screen. You can then edit any items that are incorrect.

When you're satisfied with all the entries, look at the bottom right of the main window, where Estimator shows you how much tax you have to pay (or calculates your refund). Based on this information, you can decide whether to change the withholding amount or how much to pay in quarterly estimated taxes.

FIGURE A.24

The Quicken Tax Estimator window.

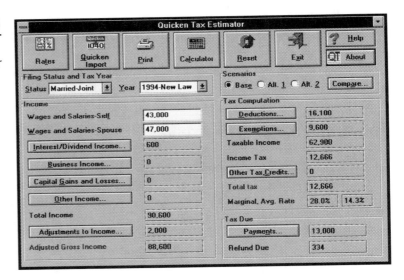

Index

Symbols

', 130
*, 93, 99, 144
/, 125
:, 125

A

Account Balances report, 403
Account files, 221-227
Accounting
    accrual basis, 420, 421
        reports, 426
    cash basis, 420
        modified, 428
        using in Quicken, 443
    conventional practices and
Quicken software, 413-414, 421
    double-entry, 3
Accounting programs compared to
Quicken, 3
Account List window, switching,
137
Account names, 22
    using in reports, 489
Accounts
    asset, 220
    balance reports, 319, 344-346
    bank, 20
    business, 415-419
    cash, 194-204
    combining, 220
    credit card, 206-213
    date of, 24
    description, 24
    investment, 229-269, 400-403
    modifying, 219-220
    naming, 22
    organizing, 109-115
    personal asset, 407-410
    selecting to include, 324, 369
    starting one for the first time,
13-24
    switching between, 197
    types of, 38, 189, 415-416
Accounts payable, 189, 436-438
    outstanding, 437-438
    reports, 295, 311-312, 437
Accounts receivable, 189, 416,
438-443
    balance forwarding, 440, 442
    reports, 295, 312, 441
Accrual accounting, 421
    reports, 426
    vs. cash basis accounting,
420-421
Action list, 236-237
Adding
    Category and Class lists, 124
    shares of stock, 236
    transactions, 95-96
        to checking account
register, 143-144
Address, 43, 48
Adjustable-rate loans, 285
    fixed payment schedule for, 469
Adjusting
    cash account balance, 203
    credit card account balance, 212
    final balance, 155
    investment balances, 247
    opening balance, 146, 154-155
    transactions 150-151, 153,
154-155
    value of asset/liability, 273-274
Airline mileage accounts, 412
Alignment of checks in printer,
77-78, 84
Amortization, 170, 270, 279-287
A/P by Vendor report, 311-312
A/R by Customer report, 312
Archives, 226
Arrow keys, 22
ASCII files, 268, 506, 511
Asset accounts, 38, 220, 230,
270-275
    for accounts receivable, 438
    for depreciation, 416
    for home improvements, 397
Assets, 189, 229, 238
    accounts receivable, 312

depreciation of, 420, 455-457
personal, 407-410
related to net worth, 410
selling, 409
summarizing, 308
tracking, 269-279
ATM withdrawal, 98
Automatic
    bill payment, 165-173, 182-
188. See also Billminder.
        credit card, 212-213
        mortgage, 279
        using CheckFree, 474
    budgeting, 381
    reminders, 493-494

B

Backspace, 22
Backups, 101-103
    of files, 225-226
    shortcut commands, 102
Balance
    calculating, 319
    current, 61
    ending, 61
    opening, 136, 138, 145-148
    reports, custom , 319
    starting, 24
Balance forwarding, 440, 442
Balance sheet report, 295, 313,
416, 457-458
Balancing, 99
    account does not balance,
148-150
    cash account, 203
    checking account, 135-148
    credit card account, 210-213
    difference, 145, 148
    interruption of process, 142-
143
    investment accounts, 247
    resolving discrepancies, 150,
154
Bank accounts, 38

519